VICTORIOUS IN A DARK WORLD

TIM MORGAN

LUCIDBOOKS

Victorious in a Dark World

Published by Lucid Books in Houston, TX
www.LucidBooks.com

Edited by Carol Helland, with special help from Betty Stende

ISBN: 979-8-90344-000-9
eISBN: 979-8-90344-001-6

Special Sales: Most Lucid Books titles are available in special quantity discounts. Custom imprinting or excerpting can also be done to fit special needs. Contact Lucid Books at Info@LucidBooks.com

Dedicated to Pastor Leonard Radtke, his wife Donna and their family, and to the family of believers, the church, he taught who gave so many others an understanding of God's Word. Week after week, year after year, he preached and taught the Word, book by book, chapter by chapter, verse by verse, in one of the "uttermost parts of the earth," the "wilderness" of a small town in northern Minnesota. Who would have thought that an obscure village could reflect light and bring blessing to people in many other parts of the nation? Those few early listeners expanded to a large and still expanding number of people whose lives were deeply touched and changed for the good, people who understood God's Word and passed that understanding on to an unknowable number of others. That very teaching lives on, guided by later pastors who in this dark world continue to teach, week after week, from those same scriptures.

SPECIAL THANKS

Special thanks go to Carol Helland and Betty Stende. I thank my friend and editor, Carol Helland, for her insightful coaching about putting this story together. She dared tell me when things needed fixing and had the skill to know how to fix them. Her encouragement gave me the confidence to keep going and finish the work. Betty helped with painstakingly checking for errors and giving her "unvarnished" opinion about things that could be worded better, needed more explanation (or less), should be left out altogether, or maybe something that would be helpful to add. I think she was right in every comment she made.

TABLE OF CONTENTS

FROM THE AUTHOR

Does one of the oldest books in the world still speak to us today, a book that foretold with surprising detail the rise and character of many of its later kingdoms and also shed light into the innermost depths of the human heart? Is it wise to ignore and count as nothing its words and the durability of its message? Are we so advanced today beyond the people of the past and the perceptions they recorded that we are wise to ignore them?

The Bible was written by some forty human authors over roughly fifteen hundred years. It makes the claim that these writers were inspired by God, the Creator of earth and all things, including man. Its thoughts bear a design and a consistent message to all who study and take them seriously. Those who never bother to pay attention see only contradictions and supposed exaggerations. Those who listen hear something else.

Just relax and read the story. Hear it like children hear stories. Take the words in. Think about them later.

INTRODUCTION

The late pastor and Bible teacher, Dr. Charles Stanley, posed a question on his radio program: "What would God have to do to prove Himself to you?" What would it take beyond His simply saying that He is our Creator? that His assessment of us is correct? that we fall far short of His holiness? that Jesus is His Son whom He sent to rescue us from our predicament? What would He have to do to prove that what He says is true and that He inspired the words we call scripture to be written and preserved for all mankind?

"Come on a thought with me . . ."

Jesus said of John the Baptist, "Among those that are born of women there is not a greater prophet than John the Baptist . . ." (Luke 7:28). Quite an endorsement, coming from the Son of God. John's short ministry was a call to the nation of Israel, and through them to all the world, to prepare for the coming of their long awaited Messiah. On a certain day a man named Jesus walked down Jordan's riverbank to John as he was baptizing. The Lord caused John to see that this man approaching, who looked so human, was the One, the Messiah. In awe he announced to the crowd, "Behold the Lamb of God that takes away the sin of the world." He baptized Him and while doing so saw the Spirit of God descend and land on Him like a dove. At the same time a voice spoke from heaven, "This is my beloved Son, in whom I am well pleased." A Father who spoke, a Son who came, a Spirit who alighted—three personages of the Godhead confronted man in that moment (Matthew 3:13-17). Few people of the world's population were present that day, yet this scene was recorded for all to witness far into the future. Sometime later, though, John was puzzled, for now instead of a glorious kingdom arriving as expected, John had been thrown in jail, probably to be executed—and no kingdom had arrived. Had he been mistaken?

From prison he sent a question to Jesus: "Are you he that should come or do we look for another?" Jesus showed no offense at the question and sent the following answer:

> Go your way and tell John what things you have seen and heard, how that the blind see, the lame walk, the lepers are cleansed, the deaf hear, the dead are raised, to the poor the gospel is preached. (Matthew 11: 2-5)

John knew the scriptures. What Jesus told him was written by the prophet Isaiah some seven hundred years before Jesus appeared on earth, worked His miracles and spoke those words. John died knowing he had been right about Jesus.

CHAPTER 1

ONE JOURNEY ENDS—ANOTHER BEGINS

The long awaited moment had come. Five hundred years earlier God had promised an elderly childless couple, Abram and Sarai, that if they left the land of their upbringing and followed Him, He would lead them to a land He would give them, a land carved out of a world He had given to man so many generations earlier. They would bear a son whose descendants would multiply into a nation through which He would bless the entire troubled world. Now these improbable descendants, the fledgling nation called Israel, slightly over two million strong, stood on a low hill overlooking the Jordan river. In view on the other side lay the Promised Land, about which He had spoken so long ago, and to which He today had led them. The Israelites had traveled recently for forty years through a barren wilderness, and prior to that, had been miraculously delivered from hundreds of years of slavery in Egypt. They stood silently, outwardly calm, a slight breeze at their backs seeming to encourage them on, and drew deep, quiet breaths, thoughts racing through their minds. The slavery endured by this nation was hard to understand. It did not seem to fit with God's proclamation that all the families of the world would be blessed through Abram's descendants. But God had said this nation would serve a "strange nation for four hundred years and afterward come out with great substance." But why? What did it all mean? It was difficult to comprehend the true import of it all. And today, blue sky and faithful sunshine introduced the beginning of a brand new chapter in their lives under the leadership of God Himself. In the rest of the world the gods did not work long term with people—nor even care about them. They did not reveal plans centuries before they came to pass. They did not promise to dwell among the people to guide them and take care of them. They did not because they were not—they sprang from wayward man's imagination. The true God, the Creator of heaven and earth, who had spoken to their ancestor Abram, did exist. The words He had spoken so long ago seemed, like a seed buried and out of sight, lost in the dark earth. Yet they, more real than man's imaginary gods, and containing life itself, had begun to sprout, unrelentingly but silently, in the last several years. The invisible life hidden within continued to break forth, day after day, into a world marred by man's doings yet now yielding to the power of life, new life, growing, rising with ever more visible power, from dark earth and death. God Himself was conquering the chaos and its accompanying misery that the first human beings had unwittingly invited into the world. He had set the plan in motion the very day Adam and Eve fell into trouble in Eden, and now He continued to move it to its completion. This arrival at the Promised Land was a further step in God's plan, larger than Israel realized, toward rescuing the human race from the misery pervading the world and would capture its attention. It would be remembered for the next thirty-five hundred years . . . and on into eternity.

Matthias and his lovely wife, Jerusha, the wife of his youth, stood hand in hand among them. He looked into her eyes and knew her thoughts. *God brought us here* was the silent message between them.

They had been through so much together, and now a whole new adventure was about to begin. Born slaves in Egypt, they had met and walked together as teenagers in God's deliverance through the Red Sea. Today were ending forty years of waiting, wandering in a parched wilderness. They had been preserved alive in that difficult land and led to the shore of this river by the very hand of God Himself. Like a diamond held in sunlight flashed intense sparks of vibrant color with the tiniest movement, each with its own beauty, so this moment sparkled with one realization upon another of what God was doing in their midst. No wonder so many were more silent than usual, carried away in thought. Change was breaking forth. It could be thrilling and good. It could also be disastrous, and everyone knew that.

Stories that had been only words carried from ancient days now transformed into reality. No matter how one considered it, this arrival at Jordan was precisely what the Lord had announced five hundred years earlier to Abram, when He had told them He would make a great nation of their descendants and then lead them to a land He would give them.

In the ancient beginning when people were few, God spoke directly to Adam and Eve, Cain and Abel. As time passed and man's numbers increased and spread over the earth, God had elected to communicate to mankind through certain people, prophets or leaders, whom He then told to record His words and pass them along to others. He corroborated these messages with details of future events that later came to pass in the world exactly as He had predicted. This was now happening right before Matthias's and Jerusha's eyes. These somewhat bedraggled travelers were about to step into a new life of victory and abundance. Much had happened on this five hundred year journey from Abram's day to this day at Jordan.

The journey had begun simply with words spoken to Abram, a wealthy, successful man in antiquity in the prosperous but pagan city of Ur, near the Euphrates River in Mesopotamia (modern day Iraq), often called the "Cradle of Civilization." God's first recorded words to Abram in Genesis chapter twelve were, "Leave your country, your kindred, and your father's house, and go to a land I will show you. I will make of you a great nation, and I will bless you, and make your name great, and you shall be a blessing. I will bless them that bless you, and curse him that curses you, and in you shall all families of the earth be blessed." So much brimmed in those few words. Abram would think about them for a long time. "In you shall all families of the earth be blessed" encompassed the entire world. How could this be? What was God telling him? It was too large to comprehend for the moment, but for now Abram would believe those words and consign the fuller understanding of them to some future time. God had a plan that would bless mankind, a perfect plan that He was announcing on this day. What man could not do for himself God would do for him. Man's part was to accept. Abram had no way of comprehending the vastness of what God was setting in motion. Yet what he heard he believed, and God said, in effect, "Good enough." The scripture recorded, "And he believed in the Lord, and He counted it to him for righteousness." Think of the import of those words—the Creator of heaven and earth speaking to him and announcing that simply because Abram believed what he said, God would impart to him "righteousness." God could do that because, even though He saw all humans as corrupt descendants of the fallen Adam and Eve, He had a plan to remedy their condition. He would do for them what they could not do for themselves. He would take the penalty for their condition upon Himself, satisfy its death edict by suffering it for them, and then stand up from it victorious because He was stronger than death. He had kept His word that Adam and Eve would die if they ate the fruit of that tree. They instantly died a spiritual death and years later a physical death. "Righteousness" simply for believing God would become a concept to reverberate through all of scripture.

This story was old, but it had its roots in the much earlier story of Adam and Eve, their fall into disfavor with God and His promise to Eve that a "seed," or descendant, would be born to her that would rescue them from the evil that had come into the world. When her first son, Cain, was born she mistakenly thought he was the seed, but that "seed" would actually be Jesus, who was born two thousand years after God spoke to Abraham. He would do for mankind what he could not do for himself, repair the relationship between God and man. Certainly Abram could not fully understand on that day the import of all that God spoke to him.

After Jesus's time, the Apostle Paul in writing about salvation referred back to Abraham. His words carried the same idea: "For what says the scripture? Abraham believed God, and it was counted to him for righteousness" (Genesis 15: 6; Romans 4: 3). The message was the same from the beginning until Jesus's time and until today. Paul taught that "believing" God's words brought forgiveness and new life to a sinner. The message never changed because it was true from the beginning. When Adam and Eve accepted the animal skin clothing God made for them to cover their "nakedness," the openly seen result of their rebellion against him, they, like Abraham, were "believing God" and accepting His help. The help came not by their efforts, but by His. Not that it was an easy fix. The innocent animals that gave their lives to provide that covering paid dearly. It cost them their lives. And so it would cost the Savior.

The Journeys of Abraham

And thus was born the nation that Abram never saw. And simply because he believed God, he was the father of those people, the millions that would be and the millions more to be reached through their influence throughout the world, throughout the ages. Abram would live in glory with his Heavenly Father forever, and so would all of those before and after him, who believed as he did.

That entrance of evil into the world was set forth early in scripture in Genesis 3. After God had brought Adam and Eve to life and placed them in the garden, He walked and talked with them daily, and they enjoyed His presence. With Him the world made sense and held joy and peace. God placed two special trees in Eden, the tree of "life" and the tree of the "knowledge of good and evil." He told them they could eat every plant and tree in the world except the fruit of the "tree of the knowledge of good and evil in the midst of the garden." If they ate of that tree they would die. It happened like this.

Eve noticed a serpent resting comfortably on a large branch in a tree and became captivated. She had seen him before and remembered that he was the most beautiful of all the creatures in the garden. So much was new that she never paid much attention to this remarkable creature. Today she paused and looked at him with wonder. Then a startling thing happened. He spoke to her with words she could understand, as Adam and the Lord had talked to her.

"Has God said, 'You shall not eat of every tree of the garden?'"

She answered, "We may eat of the fruit of the trees of the garden, but of the fruit of the tree in its midst, God said, 'You shall not eat of it, neither shall you touch it, lest you die.'"

The serpent replied, "You shall not surely die. God knows that in the day you eat of it your eyes shall be opened, and you shall be as gods, knowing good and evil.' " And here was the knife inching toward her heart. It would kill her if she did not flee its fascination. A totally new thought . . . doubting God. She had no reason to doubt Him. Such ideas had not entered Eve's mind. God was their friend. What should she do?

She looked at the tree and saw that it was "good for food and pleasant to the eyes and believing it to be desired to make one wise, she took the fruit and ate and then gave to her husband" (Genesis 3: 6), who also ate. And the eyes of them both were opened. Everything changed and the world grew darker. They saw that they were naked. Up until that time they had been completely at ease with each other's presence and their differences. Now their fellowship together was shattered and, coupled with the knowledge they had disobeyed God, they felt the need to cover up. Maybe God would not see. Nakedness was more than just their physical openness. It was that they knew that what they had done in disobeying and taking the fruit was wrong and that He could see it. Their actions were "naked" before God, and they were afraid. Hence the cover-up, hoping that maybe He would not see. With their uncanny ability to think and reason they sewed fig leaves together and made clothing to cover their nakedness.

They had not died, or so they thought. Maybe the serpent was right. Yet, having been made "in the image of God," they were unlike the other creatures of the earth. God had breathed into them "the breath of life" (something not said of plants and animals), giving them an eternal existence, capable of inestimable blessing or its opposite, inestimable suffering. Death was not an end of existence but an end of their beautiful relationship with God, who Himself was the very essence of life. They *had* died. They had been created body, soul, and spirit, and on that day their spirits lost their connection to God. He was right. They had indeed died, and there was no way back. They could not fully comprehend all that had happened, nor could they fix it, and now the way they perceived everything was different, darker, no longer bathed in light. Little did they know it would only be a matter of time until their bodies withered and died too, as when you cut a branch full of green leaves off a tree. It looks alive, but give it some time and its disconnection from the tree will become apparent. Adam and Eve had an appearance of being alive. But they were dead, separated from the life of God. The lovely relationship they had with each other was also marred. Whereas each in the past had been focused on the well-being of the other, that now changed. Adam had been concerned for his wife's happiness and wanted to please her even more than himself. Now he was concerned about himself. Eve took second place. His world had closed in and become small. His ability to think clearly clouded and prevented him from understanding his true condition. Eve conjured new thoughts. This man, Adam, that she loved with all her heart, had failed to take care of her, and for the first time in her existence she thought ill of him and blamed him for her failure. From then on she would take care of herself and be skittish about trusting him as before. Adam saw the change in her and recoiled.

He said, "Eve, we did something horribly wrong. God told us to have children, but now they will probably be like us, not like we were before. Nothing will be right anymore and our children will be flawed." Adam was right. Something was horribly wrong.

Their concern for and awareness about all the plants and animals in God's creation had shrunk to "me first." Their concern about each other had shrunk to "me first." The animals became fearful of them. A barely noticeable spirit of competition seeped in between Adam and Eve, quietly soaking into their thoughts, waiting like a serpent hidden in the dark corners of awareness. It watched, biting over and over again, not painfully or noticeably but imperceptibly, injecting venom that further poisoned their relationship. God saw all this, but they were too caught up in it to see as He did.

Then they heard the voice of God walking in the garden and hid themselves amongst the trees. And the Lord called to Adam, saying, "Where are you?" Of course God knew where they were. He asked for a different reason.

Adam answered, "I heard Your voice in the garden, and I was afraid because I was naked, and I hid myself."

"Who told you you were naked?" questioned God. "Have you eaten of the tree that I told you not to eat?"

He answered, "The woman You gave to me gave the fruit, and I ate."

The Lord did not argue with him. Instead he asked the woman, "What is this you have done?"

She said, "The serpent beguiled me, and I ate."

Observing their newly secretive and deceptive ways, the Lord engaged in no argument. Beginning with the serpent He pronounced, "Because you have done this you are cursed above all cattle and above every beast of the field. Upon your belly shall you go, and dust shall you eat all the days of your life. I will put enmity between you and the woman and between your seed and her seed. It shall bruise your head, and you shall bruise its heel." He then told the woman that childbirth, which would have been easy and beautiful, would be fraught with pain and sorrow, a reflection of the pain and sorrow the Lord himself would experience in bringing mankind back into a right relationship with Him. To the man He said, "Cursed is the ground for your sake. In sorrow shall you eat of it all the days of your life. Thorns and thistles shall it bring forth . . . in the sweat of your face shall you eat bread, till you return to the ground, for out of it were you taken, for dust you are, and to dust you shall return."

Then for Adam and his wife He made coats of skins and clothed them. His question, "Adam, where are you?" was meant to draw them to awareness of their new condition—hiding from Him. "Did you eat the fruit of that tree?" brought them face to face with their doings. Due to their poisoned condition they could not fully own up to it, and God took action to help. They were where each of us, as their descendant, is today.

Reverberating through all of scripture rang the idea that belief of God's words to man was the key to restoring a right relationship with Him, just as *un*-belief had destroyed it. Now, centuries later, God dealt with Abram on that same principle, but in a new way. The simple fact that Abram *believed* God resulted in God declaring him "righteous" (Genesis 15: 6), a notion so simple that man would barely notice it and "stumble" over it, as one might stumble over an exposed root of a huge tree on a path in the woods. Something big was connected to that root, but a careless hiker would see neither. Abram, however, understood and departed from his homeland with his wife, Sarai . . . He was seventy five years old. A few years later, as recorded in Genesis chapter fifteen, God came to him a second time in a vision, repeating the promise and adding more details. As noted above, scripture recorded that Abram "believed God" and that "God counted it to him for righteousness." These words, from so long ago and in the very first book of the Bible, protected and preserved by God from that day to this, glowed through all of history, highlighting a principle foundational to God's dealings with man. God was announcing to Abram His intention to create a great nation of his descendants and through that nation to bless the whole world. The blessing would be a restored relationship with God—and all its attendant benefits. Thus God spoke of the beginning of a nation before it existed, and springing as it did from two people too old to have children, it was miraculous, a supernatural intervention by God Himself into man's world, His way of saying, "Look at this. This never happens, but I am doing something special here." Abram had asked God how this would all work. "Lord God, what will you give me, seeing I go childless? . . . To me you have given no seed, and one born in my house (a servant) is my heir."

God told him, "This shall not be your heir. He that comes forth out of your own body shall be your heir." And He brought him forth and said, "Look now toward heaven and count the stars, if you can count them. So shall your offspring be." He further said to him, "I am the Lord, who brought you out of Ur of the Chaldeans to give you this land to take possession of it" (Genesis 15: 2-7). Details God included in this story were not accidental, and they invited careful study. One would do well to read and reread what He spoke to Abram—and then to ask Him for help in understanding. He would answer prayers like that.

He then disclosed to Abram a troubling prediction. "Know of a surety that your seed shall be a stranger in a land that is not theirs, and shall serve them, and they shall afflict them four hundred years. And also that nation, whom they shall serve, will I judge. Afterward they shall come out with great substance" (Genesis 15: 13-14). He described the boundaries of the land they would inherit. "Unto your seed have I given this land, from the river of Egypt unto the great river, the River Euphrates" (Genesis 15: 18).

As Matthias and Jerusha viewed the Jordan River and the land, they pondered how the promise made to Abraham was coming true in their lifetime. God had used Moses to lead Israel out of the slavery of Egypt. But he had grown old and died, and now Joshua led Israel. Would he be able to lead in the dangerous situations sure to come, as had Moses? Change and new adventures always carried risk. The recent years of slavery had been miserable and unhappy times in Israel's existence. Matthias had only lived there fourteen years, but they were enough to leave a bad memory. Many Israelites had become so discouraged they had long ago given up hope in Abraham's God. After all, why was everything so bad? It appeared God did not care about them. Maybe He was not even real. No one had seen Him—except Adam and Eve—but that was so long ago; maybe they were not real either. Then had come the miraculous deliverance. Great joy had erupted, only to be followed by deprivation and discouragement in the wilderness.

Yet within those difficulties God had taken care of them every single time, and the Israelites had gradually learned to trust Him and count on His care. One by one those problems unfolded into blessings as they saw the Lord turn troubles into bounty and happiness. Many Israelites had continued to trust God's promises to Abraham and had cried out to him for help. Now their willingness to believe those old promises and follow their leading had brought them to this place and this moment. Egypt had been the most powerful nation in the world. Their pyramids, some now over four thousand years old, reflected engineering skills and construction abilities attained by only a few civilizations in the world. The exquisite sculptures, the colors and gold work discovered more recently in hidden burial chambers in the earth or deep within the pyramids were stunningly beautiful. That Israel escaped the grip of such a kingdom was more miraculous than people of today realize.

Israel's history and emergence into the world, even amidst heartache and multiple difficulties, was proceeding in accordance with God's plan. Their story would become emblematic of God's dealings with all mankind. Moses and Joshua, among many others, were key figures in that story. They lived and acted in Israel, but their significance extended to all the world. Some of the ancient nations, such as India, China and Egypt, have survived until today. Yet the Lord used the much smaller nation of Israel to carry His message to those nations and all the world. The release from Egypt represented God's rescue of man from the power of a world corrupted and held captive by the sinister influence of evil, that deceptively beautiful, mysterious, invisible power that ruled everywhere and held man in merciless captivity, subject ultimately and bitterly to death. Israel's story depicted the checkered past and tiny, barely noticeable beginning of the nation God would one day use to provide salvation to all citizens of the world who would respond to Him.

Their new freedom and anticipated taking of the land promised by God illustrated a further step in man's escape from the overwhelming power of evil. First was deliverance from the enslavement of a cruel master's complete grip on their lives. Next would come enjoyment of the blessings God had prepared for them. Today's journey, now undertaken with Joshua's leadership, was the reality of that plan set in motion with those words God spoke to Abraham.

Springtime wildflowers in the river valley had burst into color, brilliant color, and splashed happily on its overflowing banks, nurtured day after day by a life-giving sun in a hopeful blue sky. Each day new events blossomed, and though Moses, the remarkable man who had led them out of Egypt and through the wilderness these past forty years, had died, an entirely new venture was developing. In Moses' place this younger man, Joshua, appointed by Moses, and evidently by God, was now leading them. Could he lead as Moses had, a man who had displayed such a close relationship to God, daring under His guidance to walk uninvited into the presence of Pharaoh, king of Egypt, the most powerful monarch in the world, and tell him to "Let God's people go?" It had been a terrible contest of wills, but in the end the enslaved Israelites came out of Egypt free from Pharaoh's maniacal grip and, furthermore, possessing enough gold, given willingly to them by Egyptians frantic for them to leave, as payment for the years of slavery. How could Joshua continue in the tradition of one such as he?

That generation of adults who had accepted God's deliverance was for some reason later unwilling to follow God to the Land of Promise that He had sworn to give them. As a result they had gradually died off over a forty-year period wandering in a wilderness, a journey that could have ended two years after leaving Egypt the first time God led them to the Promised Land. The older generation had been afraid to follow God into the land occupied by others, where lay possible danger and warfare. Now the younger generation, having been impressed as children and teenagers with God's miraculous deliverance from Egypt and then His continual care of them in a hostile wilderness, had grown up, visibly more willing to trust God. Recently Joshua had been appointed as their new leader. Would they be more successful at letting God lead them into their promised inheritance? Time would tell. Many Israelites held vague fears that God had abandoned them. Mainly they trusted God, but when threatening circumstances confronted, fear silently welled up in their hearts. Circumstances changed daily, often bringing anxiety and fear, but one thing remained constant. So far, they had to admit, the Lord had taken care of them in every instance. *But . . .* would this time be different? It was always easier to look back and realize God *had* taken care of them. Trusting Him in the present moment was considerably more challenging.

They had learned, through one trial after another, to *mostly* trust God to protect them, and as their trust grew their anxiety disappeared. Their God had a way of continually stretching their faith through new and daunting circumstances. Learning to trust Him at such times and to walk in the strength of His promises was the heart of the intertwined stories of Moses and Joshua. It is what true believers in every age face, trusting (if for no greater reason than that God had *told* them so) that He is with them and will guide them—at this moment. As God's words were fulfilled exactly as He had said way back then, so they can be fulfilled in us today. Our part, like Israel's, is to hear them and believe. It is about learning His Word and then letting it guide us. Sometimes it told believers to take action. More often than not, it told them to sit still and relax, to simply behold Him through His Word and, with a believing heart, ask His help and watch Him work. As Israel did so their trust grew and they learned, little by little, to let Him guide amidst their circumstances. Those who learned exerted an influence in the world that reaches into eternity. Their hearts and their attention, however, like ours, often wandered off in wayward directions and led them into trouble larger than they could handle. Even though they reaped the consequences of their actions God did not abandon them. Whenever they called out humbly to Him for help He answered and took them under His wing.

The Israelites could talk themselves into a fright very easily. Usually some wiser believer, be it a wife or a husband, an elder, a friend, and sometimes even a child, would calm them by reminding them to think on God's faithfulness and just relax and trust Him. If God were not leading them, even at this moment, how had they arrived at this very spot at Jordan in keeping with a five hundred year old promise? Indeed, one of the most convincing arguments that the word of God was true was the fact that so many of the things He spoke to man concerned events far in their future, some in the immediate future, only days or weeks away, some years into the future, and many of them centuries off. Most of the future predictions presented in the Bible have been fulfilled today. Most but not all. Some still await fulfillment.

Israelites did not yet know it, but the events they were about to experience would fit into a larger story, setting forth the way in which one who becomes a child of God can learn to walk in fellowship with Him and partake in victories only God could provide. This story of Moses and Joshua is more than just their story; their failures and victories are a real life illustration to future believers of how to "walk by faith." Fifteen hundred years later, the Apostle Paul would write, "For whatsoever things were written aforetime were written for our learning, that we through patience and comfort of the scriptures might have hope" (Romans 15: 4). Paul learned by studying them and so can we.

CHAPTER 2

ANCIENT PREDICTIONS OFFER HOPE DURING DARK DAYS

(Genesis 15-17, 21)

If Matthias and Jerusha were full of anticipation, so was Joshua as he paced back and forth in a secluded spot out of sight of others. Unlike those of us today born in a free country, Joshua was born an obscure Israelite slave in Egypt and grew up under the harsh rule of a nation and its king that despised all Israelites and secretly feared them because of their rapidly growing numbers. Though he and many of the Israeli men were physically powerful due to the rigors of the daily work they performed and could have, in many cases, overpowered the Egyptians abusing them, they had learned not to fight back nor attempt to defend themselves. Doing so invited the imposition of greater force by Egyptian leadership. And while several Israelites joining forces could likely have fought off the next wave of retaliation, the pressure of the entire Egyptian kingdom would ultimately be brought to bear, and the rebelling Israelites would be crushed. Discretion dictated a wiser course of action. Yet patiently bearing Egypt's cruelties carried a further price, the crushing of their spirit by having to give in to the humiliation of Egyptian domination without fighting back. Their dignity and self-respect suffered in silent misery. Many had come to accept slavery as their only lot in life. That would change sooner than they expected. God had told Abraham that one day his descendants would be a blessed nation in their own land. Countless years of captivity in Egypt had pushed that promise to the background and made it seem, for so many, that such freedom and blessedness could never come true. Yet many cherished an underlying belief that the words God said somehow rang true. Even though their daily lives were hopeless and miserable, a glimmer of hope existed in what God had told Abraham. This miserable captivity had been foretold by him. That part of the promise had come true so far. Would not the rest of it? Just because they could not understand all that happened did not mean that the promises were untrue.

Scripture later said, "He remembers our frame, that we are but dust" (Psalm 103: 14). God took pity on mankind and sought to rescue him. And, as in Abraham's case, the beginning step to finding God's blessings was to hear His words and then believe them. Those promises assured them he cared about them and blessing would come at some point. Belief was like a valve in a pipe that, when opened, allowed whatever was in the pipe to flow and perform its function. Each person had control of the "yes" or "no" belief in his heart. Those who have truly believed God's words at some point in their lives have experienced that God's words are true. They may become confused at times in their lives, but that initial connection with God ensures that He is now the one taking care of them. Those who have abandoned all hope in their own ability to take care of themselves and reached out to God for help have found His help. The experience of these Israelites would demonstrate how that worked. God had promised great blessing to them, and through them, to all the world. It would happen as certainly as tomorrow would come.

Daily life in Egypt was mainly hard work, frequently exhaustingly hard, but overall, bearable. They had food and tolerable homes. However, if one worked too slowly or with not enough eagerness, the "crack" of a fiendishly aimed and invisibly fast end of a whip bit bare flesh like a lightning bolt of misery. Or the alternative, a beating with a hard wooden rod, taught a bitter lesson. It was difficult to tell which was worse. And so they passed their days, alive but not free, existing but seldom enjoying. They had been in Egypt longer than anyone could remember; their first years under the brilliant leadership of Abraham's great grandson, Joseph, were prosperous and peaceful. But after that, things changed. New kings arose who despised and enslaved Israel (fearing that they might become too numerous and powerful). The surlier parts of human nature took over in the Egyptians as their leadership allowed them to treat the Israelites any way they pleased. Soon they saw them as less than human and treated them with no regard for their right to exist. Some had revolted at this treatment and talked secretly to others likewise dissatisfied with their cruel treatment. Eventually it was too much for them to take, and about twenty of them banded together and agreed that the next time one of them was treated cruelly he would shout loudly for help. The others would drop what they were doing and rush to his aid. They would kill the Egyptian and any unfortunate enough to come to his aid. Their pent-up anger and hatred would carry them on, and more Israelites would join them. In their desperation they believed in their hearts the plan would work.

One day they revolted and killed several Egyptians, but something went wrong. Egypt was too well organized to permit such behavior. A head taskmaster saw and called in help, and very quickly a small army of guards arrived and slew most of those twenty. The remaining few were captured and questioned about the identities of the families of those rebels. Torture finally got them to speak. Wives and children of the rebels were rounded up and executed that very hour. "Who else wants to be executed?" asked the chief guard. "Go get your families." Nothing more needed to be said. The mangled bodies were left for Israel to bury. Such was the life of a slave.

A further indignity was that women were sometimes taken by one or two Egyptian masters to a place where their cries for help could not be heard and returned hours later, bruised and disheveled, dropped unceremoniously at their own doorstep. Joshua knew. It had happened to his mother. He had seen the pain and smoldering hatred in his father's eyes and felt in his soul the anguish and inhuman humiliation poured out in his mother's shaking, uncontrollable sobs. Some days were horrible and left their mark on the soul.

One glimmer of hope existed for the captive Israelites. Though this present misery had existed for almost four centuries with no intervention by God, nor any word from Him, His words spoken to ancestor Abraham all those centuries before were still true. They made mention that Israel would serve another nation four hundred years and afterward come out free and with great substance. As bad as things looked, those four hundred years had elapsed and the time of their release must be near. The young man Joshua, the more he thought about it, became convinced it would happen soon. Nearly a thousand years later the prophet Isaiah would write, "That they may see, and know, and consider, that the hand of the Lord has done this, and the Holy One of Israel has created it" (Isaiah 41: 20). No one knew this, but God's words were stirring in Joshua's heart as he "considered" God's promises to Abraham. From then on they would guide his actions. It has been the same for thousands of other believers since that time.

Many now had given up hope while living through their seemingly unending world of captivity and had concluded that Abraham's story was simply not true. In bitterness they had said, "God does not care about us." Others said, "I don't even think He exists. Why would a God who cares about us leave us like this? There are many other gods in this world. Who knows if one is better than the other? Maybe Egypt's gods are the ones with all the power. After all, they are ruling over us. Maybe their gods are better than all the others." With such words they influenced each other to morbid hopelessness. Others countered with arguments reminding of God's faithfulness to Abraham in the miraculous birth of his son Isaac, and finally of Joseph, whom God used to feed and preserve Israel and even pagan Egypt during a seven year famine. In those first years in Egypt Israel was held in high esteem and honored with Pharaoh's blessing and gift of the finest land in Goshen. They further argued that the small family of Israel, that had rapidly grown while in captivity in Egypt to over two million people, had sprung miraculously from two people too old to bear children. "None of that is true," argued the naysayers. If God were really taking care of them, why had He abandoned them to this horrid slavery, they bitterly complained. Could He not see the cruelty of the Egyptians?

Joshua had listened with keen interest to the stories. Though centuries old, they were fascinating and had been preserved by many in writing and memorization, then passed from generation to generation. Countless storytellers could recite them word perfect to those who took an interest and listened. Part of its interest was that several of its unlikely predictions had surprisingly come true to the finest detail. When those words were spoken to Abram (at age seventy-five) he had no child and the nation of Israel did not exist. A few years later Sarai still had never conceived a child, and they both wondered why. A few years after that, his wife told him, "The Lord has restrained me from bearing. Go in to my maid. It may be that I shall obtain children by her." And so it happened. Sarai's maid, Hagar, conceived and bore Ishmael to Abraham. This, by the way, was Sarai's plan, not God's, borne of her and her husband's impatience and unclear understanding of God's faithfulness. Friction developed between the two women. Abram was now eighty-six years old. The ancient forefathers and mothers were not always as perfect as later generations imagined, and yet the Lord never abandoned them.

Finally when Abram was ninety-nine the Lord appeared to him again and said, "My covenant is with you, and you shall be a father of many nations. Your name shall no longer be called Abram, but Abraham, a 'father of many nations.' I will make you exceeding fruitful, and I will make nations of you, and kings shall come out of you." He further added, "The land in which you are a stranger, all the land of Canaan, will I give you and your descendants after you, for an everlasting possession." Then God instituted the rite of circumcision upon every male child as a "token" of the agreement "between you and me." He said to Abraham, "As for Sarai, your wife, you shall not call her name Sarai but Sarah (Princess) shall her name be. I will bless her and give you a son by her, and she shall be a mother of nations. Kings of people shall be of her." Then Abraham fell on his face and laughed, and said in his heart, 'Shall a child be born to him that is a hundred years old? and shall she that is ninety years old bear?' And Abraham said, "O that Ishmael might live before you!"

God said, "Sarah your wife shall bear a son indeed, and you shall call his name Isaac . . . " Sarah, inside the tent, heard and also "laughed within herself" at the human impossibility of it. The Lord rebuked her, saying, "Is anything too hard for the Lord?" Sarah in fear denied, but God knew human hearts—even of those who follow Him. God assured her that within the year she would have a son.

Within the year a son was born, and they named him Isaac. His name, in their language, meant laughter. Who would not laugh? First Sarah laughed when she heard God say that now at age ninety she would bear a son. Now that name became a tender touch as Sarah smiled in her heart at the antics of this little boy she never believed would be. Truly, he brought laughter to their hearts. Her barrenness and old age and even her unbelief of such a staggering promise could not prevent God's original promise from coming to life. Did not that prove God's ability to keep His promises, no matter how improbable, to Abraham—and His promise to one day deliver Israel and bring them into a land of blessing He would give them?

Joshua pondered all these things, and one day remembered a story he had heard in his youth that stirred his curiosity. An Israelite man named Moses had, by the strangest turn of circumstances, been raised in the wealth and splendor of Pharaoh's court and by equally strange circumstances, had been drawn as an infant from the river by Pharaoh's daughter. Bathing at the river, she heard a baby crying and found him tucked in a floating woven reed basket she called an ark. Her father, fearing the Israelites would become too plenteous and powerful and a threat from within to Egypt, had issued an order to kill all Israel's male children by drowning them in the river. Realizing the baby was an Israelite child who had somehow escaped her father's death edict, her heart nonetheless went out to him, and she prevailed upon her reluctant father to keep him as her own. Maybe because of the special way daughters have of convincing their fathers to grant their wishes, she won his permission. She hired an Israelite woman (who turned out to be Moses's real mother) to nurse and care for him until he was old enough to live permanently at the palace. As he grew amidst the luxury of Pharaoh's court, many Israelites regarded him as a turncoat against his own people for accepting such extravagances. Then at age forty, as part of royalty and possibly in line to become the next Pharaoh, he had unexpectedly attacked an Egyptian who was openly abusing an Israelite. His action was so swift and his hands so skilled that the Egyptian was dead in an instant. Maybe years of anger focused in those blows. The next day Moses vanished. No one ever heard from him again. Had Pharaoh's elite security personnel eliminated him? No word and no news of him ever came. Joshua, intrigued, had determined to search out all he could learn about Moses. He began with searching for Moses's parents to check out the story for himself. One day he learned of their whereabouts.

Who were these parents who dared defy Pharaoh's death edict, who had witnessed all this transpire with their son? Would they talk to him? Such people who had acted on their beliefs in the midst of danger held great interest for him. And what kind of man, with an upbringing as he had experienced, had Moses grown to be? Though some criticized him as a turncoat, others admired his attempt to help Israel in the end, even though it had gone badly and Moses had had to flee for his life. No one had heard a shred of news about him since, for over twenty years. Most likely he had been surreptitiously tracked down and killed somewhere. Pharaoh could do that. Joshua rightly perceived that the pressures on Moses had been great from both directions, and he hoped his parents could shed some light on it.

At their home he found them agreeable to talking about their son. It had been a heartbreak that they had never heard from him. If he were alive maybe he was protecting them, as they could truly say they did not know where he was should they be questioned by "authorities." They reflected a quiet confidence that the God Who had saved their son from the river so long ago was still in control. Amram and Jochebed had abandoned themselves to God's care when they set that little boy adrift, and God had rewarded their faith that very day when Pharaoh's daughter claimed him as her own and hired Jochebed to nurse and care for the baby. In his earliest years Moses's eager acceptance of his parents' teachings was a joy to their hearts. They knew their son walked a tightrope between two worlds. Whether he were alive today they did not know, but they knew that God knew all about him, and they were content with that. They openly admitted that they had been angry at God more than once since Moses had vanished, but, like Abraham who had also failed miserably on many occasions, their trust in God had gradually grown as they thought deeper on His promises. "Trust in the Lord with all your heart," said the writer of Proverbs (five hundred years later), and they were living and demonstrating what that poet distilled and put into words, “and lean not on your own understanding. In all your ways acknowledge him, and he will direct your paths” (Proverbs 3: 5-6). For the past many years God had directed them into peace, and they had followed him there. Joshua sensed he was in the presence of humility and greatness here in this humble home in the land of Goshen, in the land of Egypt. Such people were Joshua’s teachers.

More years into the future when word came that Moses, after all this time, had returned with a remarkable message from the Lord, Joshua knew he had to meet this man. A crowd made it difficult to get near Moses, who had asked to meet with the elders. Hundreds of onlookers gathered as well, trying to get a glimpse of Moses and to hear what he had to say. Because of his swift disappearance long ago and then complete lack of any news about him, he had become something of a legend. Joshua would persist and finally meet Moses face to face.

Now, years later, Joshua, like Matthias and Jerusha, contemplated Jordan and, across it, the Promised Land. Swollen with spring runoff and a stronger than normal current from the melting snows of the distant mountain tops, it presented a formidable obstacle to further travel. Yet within the next few days Israel would be on the other side and stepping into a new chapter of their lives. When Jerusha had seen the river she raised her hand in front of her mouth and whispered quietly, “Oh my . . . no bridge . . . no boats.” Most likely many younger men and teenagers could swim across, but small children and older people could not. It was as though the river would be death to anyone trying to cross at such a dangerous time. How would two million people get across? Matthias had no idea, but the God who had miraculously nurtured them through years of trials had led them here, and they had been slowly learning to trust that when He said something he was fully capable of making it happen, even if he did not explain all the details. Having seen so many improbable things happen over the last forty years they had learned to relax in the Lord’s care—most of the time anyhow. Maybe that awful wilderness had actually been a training ground, preparing them for the victories they were about to experience. The invisible God had provided them water in desert places and food day after day when they had no time nor ability to grow crops in such a dry, barren land.

In the past weeks God had led them to triumph over two kings and their armies who stood in the way of reaching this land. Moses had chosen Joshua to lead these battles. Not only Israel but the world was taking notice, waking up, so to speak, to Israel's existence. Something extraordinary was happening.

Jerusha and Matthias were of the generation that would walk in to Canaan-land. The word "walk" was possibly somewhat of an understatement as this "walk" involved one life-threatening battle after another. Yet, as Israel had been learning, God would lead them in these battles, fight for them and give them improbable victories. As teenagers, Jerusha and Matthias had watched their parents, who had experienced the Lord's miraculous deliverance from the slavery of Egypt and had partaken of His care for them day after day in the wilderness, fail to trust his ability to take them safely into Canaan. They had accepted His deliverance from Egypt, had trusted Him enough to paint blood on their doorposts at the "Passover," which protected them from the death angel who killed all the firstborn of Egypt. They had accepted His further deliverance through the Red Sea but now would not trust Him to lead them into a new land of blessing. It puzzled the children. They could not understand the reluctance of the older ones to trust God. They would have trusted Him. After all, they had seen Him work and had come to believe in His power. Soon they would get their chance.

In the wilderness, years had passed and all the older generation had died—except for two, Joshua, their new leader, and Caleb, both now eighty years old and somehow in marvelous health and strength. Every generation had heard about this land their entire lives, but during the centuries of slavery in Egypt it had begun to seem like God had forgotten about them because so much time had passed without a word of hope from Him. Their parents and grandparents had told them about their ancestor, Abraham, who claimed to have been told by God that He would make a great nation of him, give his descendants their own land and, further, bless the entire world through them. The reality today was that, even though they had grown into a small nation and had been delivered out of the grip of Egypt, the promise seemed to have stalled. They still had no land of their own, having instead wandered for forty years in a wilderness. They *wanted* to believe God's promises, but so far nothing had come to pass. Thirty-eight years earlier God had brought them to the border of the land, and it seemed like they would go in. Moses had sent twelve spies, one from each of Israel's twelve tribes, to spy out the land. The report they brought, of walled cities, prosperous and powerful-looking large populations of inhabitants, and fierce-looking warriors, so frightened them that they recoiled from any desire to enter that land, that is, except for two of them, Joshua and Caleb, who counseled to go in. "God will surely give us this land," they said. "He promised, and He will do it." But fear ruled the day. God honored their choice and made them one more promise. Since they would not trust Him to care for them and prosper their way, they could spend the rest of their lives wandering in the wilderness until they wore out in futility and died, a foretold prosperous and fruitful part of their lives wasted. It was their choice. After thirty-eight years of that, the last of them had finally died—except for Joshua and Caleb. Generation after generation had awaited this moment, and now here *they* were.

Matthias was deep in thought. Would they too fail as their parents had when brought to the edge of the land, to the moment when everything became real? When it came right down to it, would they trust God? Jerusha studied her husband's face, which to others would have looked expressionless, and saw his barely noticeable furrowed brow. Guessing his thoughts and mirroring them in her heart, she spilled them into words almost without realizing it. "If ever there were a moment to trust the Lord, this is it." Matthias looked up, somewhat startled, hesitated a moment while looking into her beautiful eyes, and nodded. They did not know it yet, but the Lord had spoken to Joshua, who would soon be sending word through the entire camp to be ready, for they would be crossing over Jordan and beginning to take possession of the land.

God tells of events long before they happen. The story of God's promise to Abraham, of future servitude to a foreign country (Egypt), and of deliverance had been preserved for them. The details were beginning to make sense.

The four hundred years' service to another nation had certainly come to pass. The lavish amounts of gold necklaces, rings, bracelets, pins, ankle bracelets, and even gold idols now possessed by every Israelite were the "great substance" God had mentioned and now became a continual reminder of God's supreme knowledge. There was more. The God who had spoken to Abraham had preserved word of the earliest times, before even the flood that inspired fear and legends amongst every family and nation on earth. The stories preserved by God had roots all the way back to Adam and Eve. In these God told of man's fall by his free will into the sinister influence of the master deceiver, Satan, and the loss of his intimate relationship with God. Many on earth remembered the flood but lost remembrance of these details. They set forth man's current condition, that of inheriting Adam's fractured relationship with his Creator: ". . . in Adam all die" (I Corinthians 15: 22). He had also predicted that the "seed," or descendant, of Eve would crush the head of the seed of the serpent who had influenced them to disbelieve God. In very few simple words that story revealed where man came from and the nature of his relationship to God, and that God, not man, would be the One to repair the relationship.

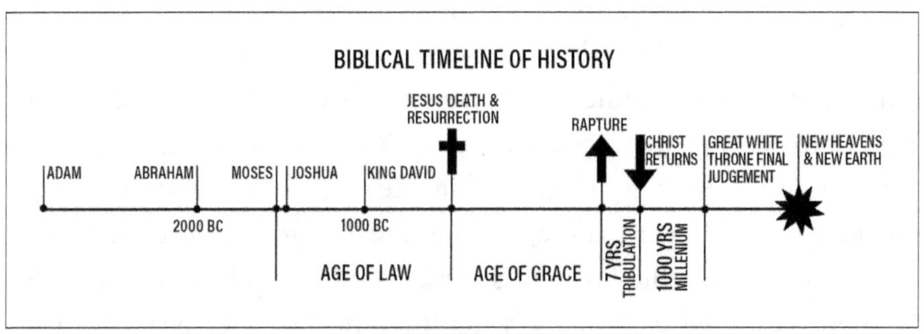

History Timeline

Joshua struggled for years to figure out what all that meant. On the surface it seemed like Moses's defeat of Pharaoh and of all the power of Egypt had been a fulfillment of that, and yet, at the same time, why was there no Promised Land? Maybe God was using Israel to picture an even larger view of history, that evil had a deeper and more permanent hold on the world than man comprehended. It was not going away easily nor all by itself. Evil wrapped itself like tentacles around the power centers of the world and then, further and invisibly, to the very fibers of man's heart. There must be a more complete destruction of evil and Satan still to come. Certainly God had understood the plight of man far more deeply than had man and had set a plan in motion to tackle man's problems and deal with Satan for his influence on man's misery.

Israel's expansion had continued, in many ways unnoticed in Egypt and the wilderness, like an ever-growing tree, into Joshua's time, nurtured by God, who cared about not only Israel but all mankind. His words and pronouncements, made so long ago, about the future now began blossoming into reality as one day followed another. God had spoken to Joshua, and the soon-to-follow conquests in Canaan would send an ever-spreading message to the world. As Israel conquered, shockwaves radiated far and wide. Physical battles and victories caught everyone's attention, but behind that an invisible battle, a spiritual battle, transpired. Satan was put on notice that his destructive influence in man's heart and the world owned by God was being overruled. Through Adam Satan had managed to infect all mankind with his diabolical schemes and their miserable consequences. Now God's wisdom purposed that through Adam, the very mankind Satan attacked, one would be born who would destroy Satan and his schemes.

The master deceiver had been invited into the world, and mankind was defenseless to his incessant workings. Wayward portions of certain civilizations had followed his influence so completely they now attempted to thwart Israel's progress in the world altogether. Israel would conquer each soundly and miraculously in battle. Israel's part was to see that the battle was a spiritual one, and the only way to win it was to accept God's guidance and help. Joshua, through the years, had become the man who could lead Israel in such a way. Aware of Moses' key part, he was beginning to realize his own key part.

CHAPTER 3

GOD SPEAKS TO JOSHUA

Deliverance from captivity and slavery in Egypt was recorded in the Book of Exodus, with further details explained in the next three books, Leviticus, Numbers, and Deuteronomy. The Book of Joshua follows and details Israel's entrance into the new world promised by God. The Lord Himself spoke to the new leader, Joshua, who had been Moses' minister: "Moses my servant is dead. Now therefore arise, go over this Jordan, you and all this people, to the land which I am giving to them . . . Every place that the sole of your foot will tread upon I have given you, as I said to Moses." As they say, "God buries His workmen but His work goes on." Moses had led Israel, now emerging as a nation in its own right, from obscurity and captivity in Egypt, whose cruel influence was miraculously overpowered by the strength of God, who all the while was breathing life into them. Moses was also used by God to deliver the Law to Israel. As God used Moses to represent the law He also used him to represent, since he broke the law himself and would not be allowed to enter in, the inability of the law to carry man to spiritual victory. He would use an entirely new operation under Joshua to lead Israel into the Promised Land.

Then God described to Joshua the area He had first described to Abraham, a huge land stretching from the Mediterranean Sea to the Euphrates River, and from Lebanon in the north to Egypt in the south, about three hundred thousand square miles. Israel in its heyday claimed only about thirty thousand. Nonetheless, God offered it, and the offer still stands today. The land Israel conquered and possessed reflected their faith. God gave far more than man took. The same is true for all believers today. God has promised man far more blessings than he ever actually takes hold of and possesses. The Apostle Peter later wrote that God's "divine power has given to us all things that pertain to life and Godliness . . . whereby are given to us exceeding great and precious promises" (II Peter 1: 3-4). The Apostle Paul wrote that God "has blessed us with all spiritual blessings in heavenly places in Christ" (Ephesians 1: 3). Blessings and power are ordained for us from God's very throne in heaven.

As Creator of the earth He had the right to give the land to whomever He chose, and His decisions were based on far more information than we have. According to scripture, one day He will set up His kingdom on this world, as He was now doing in a smaller way in Canaan—which would become Israel—and govern in a type of righteousness never yet seen. In the meantime Satan, who deceitfully obtained entrance into the world when Adam and Eve believed his words, remains here by God's permission, awaiting imprisonment far in the future. In the end all will see the true and horrible effect of Satan's selfish and destructive thoughts. With Joshua's impending victorious entrance into the Promised Land, the world and Satan were put on notice that God's original promise to Eve and Abraham was continuing on to fulfillment. Israel's victory, though tainted with human imperfections, pictured God's complete, total, and perfect victory in His future kingdom and in today's crooked and dark world.

His words to Joshua continued, "No man shall be able to stand before you all the days of your life. As I was with Moses, so I will be with you. I will not leave you nor forsake you. Be strong and of good courage, for to this people you shall divide as an inheritance the land which I swore to their fathers to give them . . . observe to do all according to the law which Moses my servant commanded you. Do not turn from it to the right hand or to the left, that you may prosper wherever you go . . . Have not I commanded you? Be strong and of good courage. Do not be afraid nor be dismayed, for the Lord your God is with you wherever you go" (Joshua 1: 1-9).

God gave marching orders for a new era of victory. After some four hundred years of captivity and slavery something new was about to happen. Israel had strayed and erred many times in the past years, yet

God would not forsake them. It was a tall order to go in and take the land which their fathers had feared to enter. The last few words, "for the Lord your God is with you wherever you go," provided the key to victory. The original King James version of the Bible, translated to English in the year 1611, uses the older word "whithersoever" where we now say "wherever." In a way, that old word more beautifully conveyed God's meaning. "Whithersoever" was more colorful, meaning that God would be with them no matter where or what.

Some over the years have focused on God's word "*command*" in these passages, emphasizing the fact that if it is a command it *must* be done. True enough. It seems noble to champion God's commands, and doing so puts one on God's side. But a problem exists in that notion. Israel had proven over and over that they were not very good at performing God's commands. Even when they seriously wanted to please Him they, in one way or another, often failed. Then there were times when they had *knowingly* ignored God's commands. What did one do with that? Focusing on the fact that God would be with them "whithersoever" provided the comfort that even when one failed, he could come back to God.

"Whithersoever" meant that, no matter where they went, God would always be with them. How could that be? Was he telling them it was okay to fail? No. He was telling them they *would* fail because of what they were. They needed to accept that. If they did and then came to Him for help, He would help no matter what they had done or "wherever" they went. It did not depend on their goodness but on God's goodness and on His acceptance of the sacrifices they brought to the tabernacle to cover for their sins. "Whithersoever" meant all that.

The original promise given to Abraham was "unconditional," meaning "no strings attached." There were no conditions for man to fulfill to make that promise come true. It was going to happen no matter what man did. God had said, "Get out of your country, and from your kindred, and from your father's house unto a land that I will show you . . . Unto your seed will I give this land," and because He said it, it was going to happen (Genesis 12: 1, 7). Fulfillment of the promise did not depend on Israel's ability to obey nor to fulfill certain of God's "conditions." God placed *no* conditions. He would bring this nation and its blessings for the world into existence. Because He was God He could look ahead and see that there would be those who would refuse to follow Him and those who would choose to follow Him, even if imperfectly or sporadically. Many years after that promise to Abraham, God gave the law to Israel, but that promise was "conditional," meaning that the blessings of the law would come only to those who followed it perfectly. Fifteen hundred years later the Apostle Paul wrote, "The covenant [to Abraham] that was confirmed before of God in Christ, the law, which was four hundred and thirty years after, cannot disannul, that it should make the promise of no effect. For if the inheritance be of the law, it is no more of promise, but God gave it to Abraham by promise" (Galatians 3: 17-18).

Man could not dig himself out of his sin-cursed condition any more than he could escape Egypt. Israel's existence, captivity, deliverance and inheritance of the land were all a part of God's plan. Joshua understood this because he studied the old stories, learned from Moses and read his writings. He understood that if he simply followed what God told them, God would give them the victory. He did not *want* Israel to fail, but if they did it could not prevent His promise from coming true. Failure on Israel's part always invited "correction" or "discipline," but discipline was not punishment. Rather it was "correction" designed to bring God's children, of their own will, into alignment with His will—how encouraging.

Some of God's promises were "conditional," dependent for fulfillment upon man's meeting certain conditions. For example, the Ten Commandments when given, were "conditional," that is, blessings would be given *if* you kept the commandments. If not you would be cursed. God's promise to Abraham to lead Israel into the Promised Land was different. It did not depend on their reliability or faithfulness. God announced a plan He would carry out on His own, without man's help. And so the word to Abram that a great nation would descend from him came true in spite of the several failures recorded about him—pretending on two different occasions that his wife was his sister to protect himself rather than being truthful and trusting God to protect him; fathering the illegitimate son, Ishmael, when God delayed in giving him and his wife their own son. That original promise, or covenant, to Abram was "unconditional." God would gain for them the victory. And so He did, in spite of their lapses and failures. Their part was to keep that in mind, enjoy His presence, and see Him work. No matter what, even when they failed, He would be with them. He could lead them out of the failure whenever they looked to Him. Great comfort lay waiting to be exploited in God's promise to be with them "whithersoever." As Israel realized that it was God Himself, the Creator of heaven and earth, telling them to enter and take the land, it made a difference. They knew the obstacles and how to deal with them. He would lead, and if Israel would follow, He would be their strength. Israel's part was simply to believe and walk in His promises.

Joshua, who had spent years in the Tabernacle studying God's Word and learning from Moses and the priests, quickly grasped what God was telling him. As he and his fellow believer, Caleb, had been ready to enter the land thirty-eight years earlier at Kadesh-Barnea, they were ready today and would set the example for the younger believers. Following God, they would take the land. He knew it in his heart. This movement was bigger than Joshua, bigger than Israel. It was God's plan, and they were part of it. Joshua's confidence inspired others who wanted to trust the Lord but were not quite as certain of God's help as he. He passed God's word along to the officers of the people, telling them to "prepare" because within three days they would cross over Jordan to go in and "possess" the land God was giving them. The people heard and prepared.

Seeing the river and contemplating crossing opened up memories of another crossing forty years earlier at the Red Sea, and that, in turn, brought up memories of Moses and what God had done through him in Egypt. Joshua had worked closely with Moses for the last forty years, and Moses had taken time to teach him how after fleeing Egypt the Lord had taught him, through many disappointing failures and trying situations, to follow Him. Thoughts of what Moses's brave mother must have taught him in his youngest years opened in his mind during this time and guided him. Joshua drank in Moses's words and teachings like water, and they nourished him. One of the chief things Moses had had to learn was how to respect God's will more than his own. A case in point was his early action in Egypt that forced him to flee for his life. He had truly thought he was serving God by helping an Israelite slave against an Egyptian master. What he had learned through the failure, though, was that the plan had been his and not God's. The Lord let him fail because He had a better plan in mind. Moses would have to learn to quiet his own will down in order to hear God's will, to trust that God's plan would work better than his own. It took time to learn—forty years, in fact. The number forty showed up often in God's Word, and it represented a time of testing. Forty years in the wilderness was a time of testing for Israel. The Flood of Noah's day began with forty days of non-stop rain. Jesus was tested for forty days in the wilderness after He had been identified as the Messiah (a test which proved Him sinless and able to handle Satan). Years of listening to Moses's teachings and following the Lord Himself had prepared Joshua for this moment. Now was time for action. Joshua was ready.

CHAPTER 4

THE SPIES AND RAHAB

(Joshua 2)

Privately Joshua detailed two men, Matthias and Nathan, to spy out Jericho, the first city they would encounter after crossing Jordan. It was well fortified, approached only after a tiring uphill walk, having been designed ages ago by a very cunning people—then surrounded by a thick stone wall entered only through a giant gate, almost as strong as the wall itself, that could be closed and locked in less than a minute. The city was formidable and it would pay to know as much about it as possible. "Every place the sole of your foot lands will be yours," the Lord had said to Joshua. Everything their feet touched would be theirs. "No man will be able to stand against you all the days of your life" (Joshua 1: 3-5). Joshua took these words seriously and envisioned Israel marching victoriously through this vast land. At the end of his life he could look back at a string of victories that few, if any, to the present time could match. Believers today are given the same promises that God gave Joshua and Israel, to guide and be with them if they, like Joshua, would learn God's will and learn to follow. Potentially any of us could be a victorious soldier in the army of the Lord. Joshua could be you.

Both of these men had displayed the ability to keep their wits about them under pressure, and Joshua deemed them suitable for such a dangerous mission. Of course, they would be noticed as strangers, but their aim was to pass as visitors from a neighboring city. If anyone ascertained their true mission they would surely be killed. Matthias and Nathan took a few moments to say "goodbye" to their wives. They might be back in a day, or they might be gone several days. Or they might never return.

Jerusha looked long at her husband. "Be careful," she was about to say but realized that, of course, he would be careful. They looked into each other's eyes. Their lives together, their meeting in the Red Sea, their children, their grandchildren, all blended together in that moment as their eyes brimmed almost to tears. Given the danger of this mission it could be the last time they ever saw each other. Suddenly fear rose up in Jerusha's heart, a horrible fear of impending doom. It was as though she knew the future and that for certain Matthias was stepping into disaster. Somehow she *knew* she would never see him again. Was God punishing her? Was He going to make her pay for the stray, rebellious thoughts she sometimes had that no one else knew about? The Apostle Peter, far in the future, would write, "casting all your care upon Him, for He cares for you" (I Peter 5:7), comforting words for a fearful heart. Jerusha, in all her thought about the old stories and Moses' writings, had learned this about the Lord, that she could cry her worries to Him and He would hear and take care of her—very comforting when sudden fears rose up. The Apostle John also wrote (after having been with Jesus daily for three years), "There is no fear in love, but perfect love casts out fear, which has torment. He that fears has not fully understood God's love. The truth is we love Him because He first loved us" (I John 4:18-19). It is not the other way around. When we fear it is because we have not really grasped the boundless love our Father in heaven has for us. Those who have understood relax. These ideas, not yet formally written in scripture, had nonetheless been worked into Jerusha's heart through the teachings of Moses, accompanied by the countless trials they had endured. She might be momentarily touched by sudden fears but was not permanently swayed by them. The God Israel believed in was bigger than any problems facing them. Little could she know that the problems she and Israel endured would become lessons for later generations, and the successes they captured would teach many others.

Joshua had discussed the dangers privately with Nathan and Matthias before ever finalizing his decision to send them to spy out Jericho. He did not want to force anyone nor shame them into going. He also reiterated the Lord's promises to give them this land, to be with them, and that no man would be able to stand against them all the days of their lives. Joshua was confident in the Lord's words and was ready to step out by faith himself. He needed men who thought like him, and Nathan and Matthias assured him they were ready. They too were well aware of the dangers but also of the Lord's faithfulness. Their eyes and their hearts might show them the dangers and even terrify them. God's promises gave them the message they chose to believe. That was the essence of walking by faith. As Matthias left, Jerusha remembered that, though they had been frightened for their lives many times, the Lord had always been there with them. This was a new test.

The gate was wide open when they walked through. They tried to study its construction and that of the walls without being too obvious about it. It was a busy city. Carts loaded with fabrics, fresh vegetables, honey, wheat, spices and handmade utensils moved in and out of the gate. People selling grocery items jammed a marketplace, and customers bartered over them, sometimes in heated words, pretending the other was cheating them. It was good it was so busy. That made it less likely Matthias and Nathan would be noticed. Music reached their ears, and out of curiosity they followed it to a small crowd gathered around three dancers who swayed smoothly to the fascinating beat of tambourines and a deep-toned drum whose rhythms were accompanied with the soothing sounds of flute-like instruments. Enchanted listeners occasionally dropped coins into a wooden box near them. Jericho brimmed with activity. Continuing on they encountered a few shrines to various idols men had carved. A particularly chilling one was an iron statue of a seated god with arms held in front as though ready to hold something. They had heard reports of such statues, which would be heated in fires until nearly red hot. Live children would be bound and laid on those arms as a sacrifice to their god to gain victory over an enemy or rain to nourish their drops. Matthias and Nathan recoiled in a mixture of horror and anger as they imagined the ceremonies that had been held there. Except for the outlandish costuming and jewelry of several, these people looked normal. How could they do such a thing?

Gradually, they walked around most of the perimeter of the city, apparently attracting little attention, stopping occasionally to look at goods for sale. The stone wall they surreptitiously inspected revealed no areas of weakness. Late in the day and as darkness was closing in, a rather nice house, built on the north wall and appearing to be a business of some sort, attracted their attention. It looked like a place to gather information. A few men had come and gone, and it seemed busy enough that no suspicions would be aroused. Fresh flowers adorned the entrance, inside and out, creating an inviting atmosphere. A very attractive woman took note of their arrival, finished a conversation with a customer and, introducing herself as Rahab, questioned, in a manner that somehow set them at ease, "You are visiting Jericho?"

"Yes, we are from east of here," they offered. Her dress was of very fine fabric, scarlet colored with yellow accents, stylishly designed and very comfortable looking, though somewhat risqué and loose fitting. At their answer a look of alarm flashed across her face, though only for the briefest instant. "Come with me," she invited in an intimate tone, and turning, disappeared through an inner doorway decorated with hanging beads. Not exactly certain why, they followed. Her somewhat overdone makeup and familiar manner led them both to realize at the same moment, "We're in the home of a harlot!" Quizzically, they looked at each other. "Now what?"

Leading them into a private chamber, she turned to face them, and fastening them with a most sober gaze, donned to mask her fear, challenged, "I know who you are." The large circles of her silver earrings dangled and sparkled in the few last rays of sunlight filtering through a high, partially curtained window as she bravely faced them. The set of her beautiful chin was firm, almost defiant. She was a brave young lady. "You are Israelites!"

Their hearts almost stopped. There did not look like any easy way out of this house, and if she called for help, half the town might show up. No matter how fast they could run or how skillfully they could fight, the odds certainly were not with them. Now was no time to panic. Their faces betrayed no emotion; they knew their lives depended on calm nerves and rational thinking. Matthias remembered other times he and Jerusha had faced frightening circumstances and how it always came into their minds that the Lord was in control. His anxiety subsided, his emotions settled down, and his thinking cleared. Then a remarkable thing happened.

"I know that the Lord has given you the land," she confided in hushed tones, "and that terror of you is fallen upon us, and that all the inhabitants of the land faint because of you."

Nathan and Matthias looked at each other, intrigued and puzzled at the same time. Just then footsteps shuffled in the entry room and a rather official, unsympathetic sounding voice boomed in a demanding manner, "Anyone here?"

"Follow me," she whispered and quickly led them to a back stairway, brought them to her rooftop, and showed them a place to hide. Assuring them they would be safe and that she would return in a few minutes, she disappeared back downstairs. Having no other options, the men hid—and waited. Men of action, they studied the area for possible escape routes.

The king of Jericho, with his network of informants, had been apprised of the 'spies' and had sent men to Rahab's house to bring these strangers to him. As Rahab descended the steps she formulated a plan. She had met them face to face, this dreaded enemy, this hated people. Not often did one get so near the enemy and have the chance to observe close up, look them in the eye. Their countenance was not cruel but rather reflected resolve and a composure not readily unraveled. Two men in a dangerous situation in the midst of a hostile people had communicated to her in those moments not fear but power. Was this what the true God engendered in His followers? Quiet confidence? Was she beholding the very power of God veiled in human form? Before the interruption she had dared to look for a long moment into Matthias's face. Behind his unflinching gaze she saw, she knew she had seen it, kindness. She decided in that moment what she would say to these men when she went back up to them. God had brought her face to face with the opportunity to escape certain destruction. Maybe these men could actually help her. Why her? She was no good. Not that anyone cared. Life was cheap in Jericho. No one's heart was safe from being violated and trampled upon. Even as a young girl her happiness had been destroyed so many times by the cruelties of others. To be honest about it, she had just as blatantly deceived, taken advantage of, and hurt others. But that kindness in Matthias' eyes drew her in. Something there called to her heart, a kindness beckoning from somewhere deep within, maybe even beyond Matthias. And pure. That hard shell around her heart cracked a little and let in a little light, a comfortable light, a welcome light. She would help them. Her quick instinct to hide them had been correct. Now she would seek their help!

First she must get rid of the king's men. Rahab met them and told them that two men had indeed been there and had "left about the time of the shutting of the gate, when it was getting dark," and that she had no idea where they went. She told them to "pursue quickly" and they would overtake them. So the men pursued all the way to Jordan. She was a master at "explaining" things in a manner that suited her purposes.

In addition to "explaining," Rahab was highly skilled at bargaining and making deals, and that was how she now approached God. Returning to the rooftop, she said, "We have heard how the Lord dried up the water of the Red Sea for you when you came out of Egypt, and what he did to the two kings of the Amorites, on the other side of Jordan, Sihon and Og, whom you utterly destroyed. Hearing these things our hearts melted and we lost all courage because of you. I know the Lord your God is God in heaven above and in earth beneath. Now please, I pray you, swear unto me by the Lord, since I have shown you kindness, that you will also show kindness to my father's house and save the lives of my father and my mother and all my brothers and sisters and all that they have, and deliver our lives from death." The Red Sea! Egypt! That was forty years ago. And people were still terrified? When the enemy tells you that you are going to defeat him, it is a good sign. The Lord had shown them much today. Jericho would certainly be theirs.

"Our lives for yours," they said. "Keep this quiet, and when the Lord has given us the land we will deal kindly with you." She made ready to let them down by a rope through her window on the outer town wall and counseled them to hide in the mountains for three days, until the searchers gave up looking for them. Then they could return home safely. The rope she used to let them down was scarlet in color. Most of the things she had were colorful. They told her to leave that scarlet rope hanging from the window so they could identify her house when they returned. Whoever was in her house would be safe. Any that left would die in the streets. It would be certain. "If you tell anyone of this, the deal is off." God did not love her for her wretched self nor for her ability to make deals. He loved her because that was how *He* was. He accepted her because she realized His power and His ability to destroy her—and she had called out to Him for help.

Such details matter in the Word of God, in the scripture God has preserved for man to read. No matter where in the world nor what language anyone speaks, word of that scarlet line becomes safety for all who reach out and grasp it—even to a condemned prostitute in a condemned city in a condemned land in a condemned world in a condemned human race. Its scarlet color speaks of the blood of Christ, given for all humans everywhere. Mention of His blood spilled for us is scattered throughout scripture, there to be found by the searching heart, like silver, gold, and gems scattered throughout the earth, treasure hidden in its soil.

"So be it," said Rahab. When she came back down the stairs her demeanor was changed. That kindness she had seen in Matthias's eyes and his complete lack of fear were totally unexpected. He was the first person she had ever seen not totally immersed in taking care of himself. Early in her life she had learned how to flirt and use a smile to get her way, how to speak in a manner that put others at ease. She tuned in to others' feelings quickly and displayed genuine affection for all she met, or at least was adept at giving that impression. In our modern times she would be admired for being so "open" and "accepting," "non-judgmental," as it were, for having such a "big heart" and "positive" attitude. She knew that taking an interest in others and their comfort always put them at ease and would help her get her way. Somehow this drew others to her. They felt comfortable. Behind her cheerful countenance, though, lay a certain unhappiness, an impatient dissatisfaction, a searching for more, that rendered her, for all her "openness," distant, her true self hidden away in some safe place, a shell she had built around her heart, like a hard eggshell that no one could break into. No one could touch that part of her and there she was safe. She knew the king of Jericho. He operated the same way, and she understood him. Strong and capable, he mostly had everything he wanted—but it was not enough. He too was on the prowl, always looking for more. "Is that all there is?" his jaded manner seemed to say. Deep in his heart welled up constant longings for possessions and pleasures the world could bring him. Yet the joys were more in the conquest of beating someone in a conflict, or in gaining a new possession, or devouring a sumptuous meal. Then, in a few hours, the joy wore off, and new longings crept up. The actual object no longer brought the same joy, and the search would begin all over again. The king did not really perceive what drove him on relentlessly, nor bother to think about it, but he was looking to fill an empty space in his heart, a space that lurked in every human heart descended from Adam and Eve far back in Eden. Mankind had been prowling through life ever since. On the surface the king looked extremely successful, and his manner and strength attracted people. Many sought to be in his "inner circle" for the wealth and privilege it could bring. His favor went to the highest bidder and was continually up for grabs.

That joy and inner peace sought by the king was what Rahab had suddenly tapped into on the rooftop with Nathan and Matthias. Up until today, as Rahab saw it, no one really cared about anyone but himself. She had watched peoples' actions, pondered them deeply, and that is what she, in her own private search for truth and meaning to life, saw. It had always been that way as far as anyone in Jericho knew. No one was really safe in this world because there was always someone looking to cheat you out of your goods or to take advantage of you and use you to satisfy their own pleasure. When they were kind to you they were getting something out of it. If someone despoiled you of your possessions there was no one to help because the king himself operated that way and was in no position to enforce any laws to protect people. It was a gray and bleak world she inhabited, full of self-centered people and no hope of anything changing. Most of the world coped with its despair by pursuing one distraction after another, desperately searching for peace and happiness. It was chilling and depressing to look at it that way, so Rahab, like many others, was glad for the hustle and bustle of the city and its colorful attractions. Throwing oneself into its endless activity, one could enjoy it and stifle out the depressing parts. Such was Rahab's world.

But that was before. When she came down from the rooftop that hardness of heart was gone. The futility and emptiness she perceived, the shadow of death under which she lived, had been replaced by a promise from Israel's soldiers to come under their care and protection, a promise, in reality, from their God. She had been with many men before but none had ever touched her heart as these two had, and all they had brought was words, words that had calmed her fears. She had taken the news of Israel's God seriously, the news of his power over Egypt and her king, news of the Red Sea parting, and now news of their unstoppable approach in her direction! Their God seemed to be a merciless judge of the evil of mankind—coming very soon to destroy her and all those in her city! Everyone knew about it, and she assumed others were as worried as she was. Judgment and destruction were coming. Yet that powerful God had helped the Israelites, who in reality were no more special than anyone else, taking pity on them and freeing them from the enslavement of the Egyptians. He appeared, now that she had seen the kindness of these men, to care about people and to do things for their own welfare in a way she had never seen before. God was most certainly judging people. He had overthrown the Egyptians, and now He was overthrowing the people in her land. She had heard that even some of Pharaoh's advisors and wizards had recognized his power and reached out to him for mercy all those years ago. God knew who each was and accepted all who took His help. Though Egypt as a nation was judged, individuals within that nation had seen and believed in God's power, and God would honor that. Scripture tells that far off in the future she will honor God and be a blessed nation dear to His heart.

Deep in her heart Rahab had been terrified by her impressions of God's power, but until God brought these men to her she had never allowed them to surface where she could see them more clearly. Things had come into focus in an unexpected way for her. A whole new world had opened up, one in which this "horrifying" and "merciless" God had reached out to her and drawn her to Himself, somehow accepting her in spite of her complete, self-serving, conniving wickedness.

She had cast herself upon His mercy by asking these men to spare her, and, to her surprise, had been granted mercy with the promise that her life would be spared. It was too much. Such mercy touched the deepest part of her heart. She wanted to know more about this God. Why had God brought these men to her house? In those few moments with the spies from Israel, her aching heart began to heal.

In the coming days those who knew her well noticed the change, for after this day she was peaceful and warm, truly open-hearted. Her impatient nature was replaced by an accepting demeanor difficult to offend. Her face almost shone. It probably did not, but somehow that impression came through. Maybe she radiated an inner happiness. She would make sure her family and friends would be in her home when danger came. Like Noah of old, she told all who would listen, imploring them to flee to safety as she had. Rahab became an ambassador for God inside the walls of Jericho. Many of her friends believed her words and, when the feared Israelites encircled their city, sought within the walls of her home the peace and refuge she had found.

Meanwhile Joshua's two spies were navigating their return from Jericho. They found the mountain Rahab had mentioned, hid three days, and then crossed safely to Joshua and told him all that had befallen them. His penetrating eyes studied them with an intensity that could have melted rocks as he considered their words, but for some reason neither Nathan nor Mathias was overly intimidated. They knew Joshua. He was a powerful man who had led people in life and death battles, a man sure of his purposes and given to action. Yet, as swift as his actions appeared, they were not foolish or impulsive. His manner always was to think ahead and carefully consider the possible outcomes to an action. His reactions may have seemed quick to those around him, but his habit of thinking far ahead prepared him for situations others did not bother to think about. This powerful man, listening carefully to their words, saw them looking back and forth to each other to corroborate their remembrances, wanting to get the details right. He had picked the right men, men not given to exaggeration nor hasty conclusions about what they saw. As they stood in front of him and finished their story, he put a hand on each one's shoulder, and with a squeeze of appreciation communicated to them his heartfelt thankfulness for risking their lives to bring him this report. They knew he did not take these risks lightly, as he himself had risked his life many times for Israel. Joshua was alert to find men like them among the warriors of Israel, men who dared walk by faith. A deeper kinship settled in between these three men. In a way it could be said they had not really risked their lives. After all, they had God's promise that "no man would be able to stand against them," so what was there to be afraid of? When they focused on that there was no fear. At the same time they were human and could fall prey to their own emotions and indulge fear. God's words had taught a distinction between the viewpoint of fallen man and the viewpoint of a righteous and loving God. Those who accepted God's words as true embarked on a path of seeking to know Him more completely. All three understood that. Another realization they shared was that all the battles they faced were bigger than they could handle or even comprehend. Each had dared to trust the Lord in the face of overwhelming opposition, and no matter how failure-prone or imperfect each of them was, they had each seen God protect them. Joshua had made them feel like equals. They were all in the same battle, each with a certain and important role to play. It was the Lord, the Unseen Captain, who was leading them. Their lives were in His hands, and the horrible battles they would face on an almost daily basis rendered them continually aware of that. Joshua told them to thank their wives on his behalf for allowing their husbands to go on this dangerous mission.

"Truly the Lord has delivered into our hands all the land, for all the inhabitants of the country are terrified because of us," they said with an exuberance befitting the situation.

No one had really seen Nathan and Matthias enter quietly into the camp, and now each headed home. Matthias saw Jerusha before she realized he was present. Her long, dark hair partially shrouded her downcast face as her posture revealed her to be deep in thought. She heard his footsteps and looked up. Her face lightened like the sunshine that reappears after a storm cloud has passed, and her radiance warmed his heart like it always did—this girl he had met so many years ago on a day in the Red Sea.

CHAPTER 5

JOSHUA REFLECTS ON ABRAHAM AND ISAAC

(Genesis 20 through 22)

News from the spies confirmed the decision Joshua had already made about their next steps. It was as though the Lord was encouraging them that they were on the right path. That news would help some of the Israelites who were not as strong in their faith as Joshua and the many he had selected as leaders and captains of his army. Conquering and possessing the Promised Land would be the final segment of an important portion of the story of Israel that had begun with God's words to Abraham. That story would continue from him to the slavery in Egypt, to their deliverance, to their entrance into the Promised Land, and then to great strength and prominence under kings David and Solomon and several later kings, on to the birth of the Messiah. He would be rejected by His own people, crucified, and raised again to life three days later. It would continue to His second coming at the end of this present age of grace and the conquest of His enemies, and the establishment of his kingdom.

As Joshua contemplated this move into the Promised Land he was keenly aware of the history that had gone before. Knowing that history gave insight into what he faced in his lifetime and showed him how he fit into God's plan. That principle would be true for all time. Moses' life and actions were a fulfillment of circumstances rooted in the stories of Abraham and Isaac, and now Joshua's leadership of Israel was a further extension of God's plan announced to Abraham. Joshua studied these stories diligently, pondered them deeply. He saw how God first spoke to Abraham, Isaac, and Jacob and then guided them with His presence. He took those stories, and now Moses' writings, as God speaking to him and determined, like them, to follow what they said. Oddly enough, this thirty-five hundred year old story helps us today as well. We saw the promise God made to Abraham about making a nation through him. That nation still exists today in the exact same area God gave to Abraham, and its existence in the world is still miraculous. Throughout much of its history other nations have sought to destroy it. It spent many centuries under the harsh rule of the Roman Empire. When Jesus came into the world and announced that He was the Messiah for whom they had been waiting, many Israelites accepted Him as such, including many of the Temple leaders. But the bulk of the nation and their accepted leadership rejected Him and, in fact, pushed for His crucifixion. Seventy years after that rejection of Jesus as the Messiah, Rome demolished Israel's temple and scattered its citizens—and for the next two thousand years they had no land or nation. They existed as strangers in other nations, often looked down upon and persecuted. God turned their rejection of the Messiah into blessing for the rest of the world as the "age of grace" offered salvation to all mankind through belief in the Savior Israel had rejected. At the present time He is not finished with Israel, as many have believed. His promise to Abraham to use Israel to bless all mankind is still true and in operation. Recently, in 1948, Israelites re-took part of their land, and, in spite of the world's efforts to destroy them, most recently under Adolph Hitler, became a nation again. Though many individual Israelites have believed in Jesus, nationally they still do not honor Him as the true Messiah. One day in the future they will realize that Jesus, whom they rejected, was the Messiah. That day is approaching but not yet here. But the promise God spoke to Abraham is still true: "I will bless them that bless you and curse them that curse you." It is remarkable that a nation as small as Israel today in this world somehow manages to occupy a noteworthy part of the world's news, far beyond that of dozens of other similarly sized or even larger nations.

Abraham, while in the land to which God had led him, encountered famine, and here were recorded some of the not so glamorous events in his life. God did not sugarcoat His account of Abraham. When famine came in that land, Abraham could have asked God what he was supposed to do, since God had sent him there. But he did not do that. Instead he journeyed to Egypt, where food was more plentiful. Evidently women back then remained beautiful well beyond the childbearing years, and Sarah must have been so because Abraham feared that the king of Egypt would see her and take her for himself—killing him to get him out of the way. Abraham concocted his own plan, which involved telling the Pharaoh that she was his sister (and insisting to Sarah that she corroborate his story). So, rather than killing Abraham, Pharaoh gave him gifts as a dowry for his "sister." God told Pharaoh, "You're a dead man. You took a man's wife." Pharaoh took the words very seriously and, in the end, restored her to Abraham. Thus God protected Abraham in spite of his foolishness. It was very interesting that in the land to which God had led Abraham a famine occurred. Was it a mistake? No. Even God's chosen people encountered the troubles of a sin-cursed world—like all people in the world—but God would take care of them in the midst of it.

"Restore the man his wife and he shall pray for you," God told Pharaoh (Genesis 20: 1-14). God protected Abraham and Sarah, and here we see an example of God's *unconditional* promise to Abraham. The covenant with Abraham would be kept because, being unconditional, it did not require Abraham's obedience. Ultimately, Sarah was unharmed and Isaac was most certainly born in accordance with God's promise.

Years later when Isaac was grown, God spoke some very puzzling words to Abraham: "Take now your son, your only son, whom you love, and go to the land of Moriah and offer him there for a burnt offering upon one of the mountains which I will tell you of."

(Note: A respected Bible teacher, J. Vernon Magee, states, "We are walking on mountain peaks in this book of Genesis. Chapter 22 is the account of Abraham's offering of his own son. God commanded him to offer Isaac on the altar and then restrained him at the last minute when He saw that Abraham was willing to go through with it . . . This was the last test He brought to this man." He further said Genesis 22 was among one of the ten greatest chapters in the Bible. It clearly revealed so many things: that human sacrifice was wrong and not approved by God, that God required a life be given up in order that He might save sinners, that none among the children of men was worthy to take that place. God's son was the only one. It is interesting that Paul said, "God spared not His own Son," but you might add that He *did* spare the son of Abraham and did not let him go through with the sacrifice of Isaac . . . Not only in the birth of Isaac, but now also in the sacrifice of Isaac there is a strange similarity to the life of our Lord.)

Human sacrifice was common in the world, but that the Lord asked this was surprising. Abraham had learned over time that the Lord always had the details considered and worked out in what He said, so he left the next morning, taking Isaac and the wood for the burnt offering, trusting that God had some good reason for this strange request.

"Then on the third day Abraham lifted up his eyes and saw the place afar off." He told his helpers to wait there while he and Isaac went up to worship. He laid the wood on Isaac to carry, and he brought fire and a knife. When Isaac wondered where the lamb was for the burnt offering Abraham said, "God will provide Himself a lamb for a burnt offering." Arriving at the place God had shown him, Abraham built an altar of rocks, laid the wood in order, and bound Isaac his son and laid him upon the wood. Judging by the timing indicated in other passages, Isaac would have been eighteen to thirty-three years old and stronger than his aged father. The fact Isaac complied meant he did it of his own free will and in respect for his father. It must have been an emotionally charged moment for both of them—Isaac about to die, Abraham about to slay his son for whom he had waited so long. When Abraham took the knife and reached out to slay Isaac, an angel of the Lord called out to him, "Do not harm your son. Now I know you fear the Lord, seeing you have not withheld your son, your only son, from Me." And Abraham looked and saw a ram caught in a bush by his horns. He took the ram and offered him up for a burnt offering instead of his son. Here we have a father willing to offer his beloved son as a sacrifice according to God's will on a mountain in a wilderness. Years later, that wilderness would become a busy city called Jerusalem. Mount Moriah would be the site where Solomon's temple would be built and the vicinity where the Son of God would be sacrificed just outside the city walls.

God was showing Abraham (and through him, all the world) two thousand years before it happened what He was doing to rescue man. Abraham certainly understood firsthand the agony of sacrificing his beloved son, and now he was seeing (if he caught on to it) into the heart of the Father in heaven. Before God's Son could take the throne as King He must deal with the problem of sin, rebellion, and death. Here in the first book of the Bible God laid out His plan. It would be developed and explained in greater detail in time to come, but here it was, set forth in picture form long before it happened. It is said, "Great events cast their shadow before them." A miraculously born Son would be sacrificed by a Father whose heart would be pained more deeply than even Abraham's. God was showing man His heart and his plan.

This story about Abraham and Isaac was well known to much of the world well before Christ was sacrificed in that same spot. A thousand years after Abraham, King Solomon was directed by God to build the Temple on that spot, now in the city of Jerusalem. Another thousand years later the crucifixion of Christ took place near this area. No mere coincidence. If God could speak from beyond time and have such a surpassing view, compared to man's, of the world and its events, is it not "reasonable" to take His words seriously and follow them?

Jesus, like Abraham, walked through this sin-cursed world where Satan ruled, and He met continual opposition. He had left the orderliness, the beauty and perfection of heaven and entered the chaos of the world. He would endure, with mankind, the pain, horror and misery Satan would inflict upon him. He would experience the ultimate blow Satan could inflict—death—and then a horror greater than that, punishment by God, His Father, for the sin of the world. That was when he finally screamed in agony, "My God, my God, why have you forsaken me?" No torture Roman or Israeli leadership could inflict upon him, no matter how cruel and demonic, drew that response from him. Adam and Eve had no comprehension of what they invited into the world when they followed the serpent's words to that tree and its fruit. Jesus would take it all and "drink" the entire cup, as He put it.

It was Satan who influenced the Jews and the Romans to crucify him. When it finally happened it looked like a victory for Satan. Yet it took place only when God allowed it. Satan's influence brought chaos, pain, destruction, and ultimately death. His hidden purpose was to exalt himself and receive worship, as he had seen God worshipped by his creation. Unlike God he had neither created nor done anything worthy of worship. Still he craved worship and cared not who suffered as he sought it. If God was light and truth, he was darkness and deception. Yet God's plan would triumph in the end. "Be of good cheer. I have overcome the world," said Jesus just before His capture. Satan threw all his power at Him, and Jesus submitted to it, including the final enemy of man—death. Satan organized the evil wickedness that had spread throughout the hearts of humans, impelling them to mob and clamor for his death, carrying Satan's hatred to its bitter end, that of killing the Son of God. Jesus felt, He endured, the hatred of Satan and the rejection of God's own deceived creation. From His battered body, ravaged and torn almost beyond recognition, with life nearly extinguished, He cried, "It is finished" . . . then finally, "Father, into your hands I commend my Spirit." His body slumped into the stillness of death. People watched in disbelief, looking for some movement or sign of life. Nothing. Death was too real, so real it shook the earth beneath men's feet as Earth itself quaked in reaction to its master's agony.

To all appearances He was destroyed. Days of silence in the grave followed. Then Jesus stood up from death, full of life, holiness, and victory—life He would share with all who would come to him. That was the true significance of the "Abraham, Isaac" story. Isaac did not die. The sacrifice died in Isaac's place so that Isaac could live. And Jesus died so that mankind could live.

Joshua mused, reflecting on how much Abraham's story had been a part of his thinking and how Moses's teaching had broadened his understanding. As Abraham and Moses had to learn through time and experience, so he had to learn. Though painful, their failures had led them to question their own basic beliefs. Much of human learning and socialization centered around teaching a person to be self-sufficient, capable of standing on his own two feet and taking care of himself. With the Lord it was different. A balance existed between being an individual and at the same time humbling oneself before the Lord, dependent upon Him, learning to listen to Him and follow His guidance. It was said that Moses was meek: "Now the man Moses was very meek, above all the men which were upon the face of the earth" (Numbers 12:3). The dictionary definition of meekness is "quiet, gentle, easily imposed upon, submissive." The Biblical usage of the word from earlier times was more like "power under control" or "knowing one's place before God and honoring His leadership." To those who saw him, Moses was a very powerful man, certain of his purposes, persuasive among people, intimidating to many. Yet before the Lord he knew his place and willingly allowed him to lead. He portrayed the qualities the Apostle Peter (himself a strong, impulsive man of action) would write about so many centuries later: "God resists the proud and gives grace to the humble. Humble yourselves therefore under the mighty hand of God, that He may exalt you in due time" (I Peter 5: 5-6). Thus the Lord called him "meek."

Joshua, a capable warrior himself, was much like Moses, similarly willing to let the Lord guide him. Moses had been a good mentor to him, and it helped having a teacher like him. The Lord had spoken to Moses, and now He had spoken to Joshua. What would he do?

Moses had been willing to learn what God had communicated in the past to Israel and to the ancient believers before them. He had been willing to let God work in his life and had gradually learned to understand His will. Slowly Moses learned to choose God's will over his own. In aligning his will with God's he had tapped into the power and guidance that made him the leader he had become. Now Joshua was doing the same, and the world would soon see extraordinary events and victories as Israel day by day took Canaan from Satan's grip. Just as certainly, but further into the future, God will take the entire world from Satan's grip and expel him from the world.

Moses and Joshua serve as role models to mankind about how to let the Lord lead. Countless men and women have followed their example through the centuries. The writer of Hebrews 13: 7 used the words "whose faith follow" as advice for all of us, referring to faithful leaders who had spoken to them the word of God. The encouragement was to "follow their *faith,*" not necessarily to do the same things they did nor to mimic their behavior. God is the author of diversity and has different plans for different people. Humans became successful by learning to follow him.

CHAPTER 6

ABRAHAM, ISAAC, AND JACOB

(Genesis 25: 19-Genesis 33)

A brief detail mentioned in this story deserves our attention. After Isaac's mother died Abraham sent his servant to the land from which he had come to find a wife for Isaac. The servant asked, "What if she will not come with me?" Abraham responded, "If the one you choose will not come look for no other but return home, and you will be cleared of your responsibility." The servant took ten camels and left. Reaching the land of Nahor, Abraham's brother, the servant stopped at a well at the time "women go out to draw water." He prayed to the Lord, "Send me good speed this day . . . and let it come to pass, that the damsel to whom I shall say, 'Let your pitcher down and give me a drink,' and she shall say 'Drink and I will give your camels drink also,' let her be she that you have appointed for your servant Isaac." The servant, having been influenced by his master, Abraham, and knowing the Lord in the same manner, dared to pray such a specific prayer.

Before he was done praying, Rebekah, who was born to Nahor, and was Abraham's niece, arrived at the well with her pitcher on her shoulder. She was "very fair to look upon," and the servant asked her for a drink. Letting down her pitcher she gave him a drink and then said, "I will draw water for your camels also." The man, wondering at her, held his peace, whether the Lord had made his journey prosperous or not. Then he took a golden earring, very expensive and beautiful, and two golden bracelets and put them on her. Imagine her wonder and surprise at this totally unexpected action on his part. While she looked at him, struggling to understand, he said, "Tell me. Whose daughter are you?" She told him, "and the man bowed down his head and worshipped the Lord." Here is a beautiful detail hidden, like a diamond, within the larger story. Scripture said this man "worshipped," and even though he was not in a temple or a beautiful church building with stained glass windows, God was honored by his thoughts and accepted his worship. There was no music or ceremony. No one even knew, not even the young lady standing in front of him. He said, "I, being in the way, the Lord led me to the house of my master's brethren." "In the way" meant the "way" the Lord was leading and that he was following Him. He was "in tune" with the Lord and acknowledged God was leading him at that very moment. Since God called this worship, it could be said that this is the essence of worship—a realization that the Lord was present and was, at this moment, leading him. He had God's words and promises, learned from Abraham, to guide his thinking, and now the Lord affirmed His presence by answering his prayer. According to the commendation of the scripture, no greater thing could have been done than that. His simple but sincere realization of God's presence and faithfulness was more precious to God than many offerings or sacrifices. The worship of a heart truly beholding Him, seeing God for who He is and how He is close to us. The servant teaches us as a masterful teacher. Any of us could worship at any time and any place, as did he, by similarly realizing and acknowledging that God is with us and guiding us. Very simple.

Rebekah ran home and told her family of this man. Her brother, Laban, when he saw the earring and the gold bracelets on his sister's wrists, hurried to the man, whom he found still resting his camels at the well. The servant went home with him, and at supper explained who he was and why he had come. He told how he had prayed to find the right girl and how she had appeared before he even finished this silent prayer and gave him water and offered to draw for his camels. Then he said to her family, "Now, if you will deal kindly and truly with my master, tell me, and if not, tell me."

Laban and her father considered and said, "The thing proceeds from the Lord. We cannot speak bad or good. Rebekah is here. Take her and go, and let her be your master's son's wife, as the Lord has spoken." When Abraham's servant heard their words he again "worshipped the

Lord, bowing himself to the earth." You can imagine this young lady, quietly beholding this unbelievable scene and listening to every word. This was *her* life, and it was about to change. Some things were too real to grasp. God was doing a startling new thing with her. Then the servant brought forth jewels of silver and of gold and beautiful clothing of the finest fabric and gave them to Rebekah. Should she be thrilled, or should she be frightened? Then he gave also to her father and her mother precious things. Such wealth had a humbling effect and lent its own aura to the evening. It had been a very long time since they had heard anything about Abraham. Seemingly from nowhere came this man. Many had wondered about Abraham when he left his homeland so many years ago, claiming God had told him to leave and would guide him. In the morning the servant wanted to leave right away, but they begged him to stay longer. They said, "Call our daughter and ask her. So they said to her, Will you go with this man? And she said, 'I will go.'"

The journey by camel, donkey, and wagon was long. Toward the end Rebekah saw a man walking in the field toward them and asked about him. In the past days she had come to know by the servant's words, *about* him, but now the new bride would see him face to face. Believers today are called "the bride of Christ." Perhaps our meeting with Him will be like this. When our Savior comes, will we know Him? A certain hymn says, "I shall know Him by the print of the nails in his hands" (Fanny Crosby). That is one way we will know Him when He comes. This story about Rebekah made a beautiful picture of the moment we will meet the Lord (J. Vernon McGee: *Genesis Volume II,* page 90).

And so Isaac and Rebekah became man and wife. In time she gave birth to twins who struggled so within her that she asked God what was happening. He told her, "Two nations are in your womb, and two manner of people shall be separated from you, and the one people shall be stronger than the other, and the elder shall serve the younger." In scripture the firstborn was sometimes flawed, the second blessed. The first man Adam disobeyed God and fell into sin, while the "last" man, Jesus, followed the Lord and brought blessing for Adam and the human race. Firstborn Cain and second son Abel. Now Esau and Jacob. What did it all mean? Did God make a mistake? Or was it free will and its consequences? God could look ahead and see what would happen and yet, at the same time, allow man to make the decisions. When they were born, Esau came out first, the elder and firstborn, then his brother Jacob with his hand grasping Esau's heel. His name meant "supplanter" or "one who grasps and takes over."

As they grew Esau became "a cunning hunter, a man of the field," Jacob a "plain man, dwelling in tents. Isaac loved Esau because he ate of his venison, but Rebekah loved Jacob." Jacob was probably a "momma's boy," who was not as innocent as Momma thought. Here this esteemed couple, though most certainly chosen by God, was playing "favorites," which ultimately led to trouble. Most new readers of the Bible are surprised to discover human weaknesses reflected in its true life heroes. Many study books about the Bible have tended to portray its characters as "sold out" for the Lord and above the failings most of us have, making them seem far better than all the rest of us. So it is surprising to see the failures of its actors recorded in scripture. God gave the unvarnished truth about man and his flaws (one of the reasons many reject the Word). Only a few, among them Joseph and Daniel, for example, have no negatives recorded about them. Yet we can know from other scripture that, even though God chose not to record negatives about them, they were still sinners like the rest of us. "There is none righteous, no, not one. There are none that understand, there are none that seek after God. They are all gone out of the way and together become unprofitable; there is none that does good, no, not one" (Romans 3: 10-12). This was true of those men too, and those were God's words, His description of every human (except Jesus) that ever lived. Joseph was set forth as a "type" or representative of Christ, and in that regard it fit God's purpose not to record sin concerning him. The focus in nearly all Bible stories is on the patience and goodness of God more than on the goodness of the human characters. The triumphs and victories achieved by its heroes came when they were actively leaning on the Lord for His help. Their failures should be an encouragement to us in that they demonstrate that normal people with human failings can do extraordinary things when they allow the

Lord to guide them. The biblical narrative gradually shifted to Jacob and the family that would come of him. Ultimately it would continue tracing its way through the tribe of Judah, which led to king David and the generations of kings descending from him, then on to the Savior Himself as descended through both Mary and Joseph.

This was what Esau esteemed of little worth on a certain day he traded a bowl of soup for his "birthright." According to the record, Esau was a "man of the earth," a superb hunter, skillful and successful at everything he did, an adventurer busy making his way in the world. He had no use for the unseen spiritual things his father talked about. He was into the "here and now" and what the world could give him, tangible things that actually meant something. His brother, Jacob, was a sneak and a chiseler, never able to do the things Esau could do, yet always looking for a way to outsmart and cheat him. Though they were twins, Esau only tolerated his brother. That ended on a certain day when Esau, after a day of hunting, came home famished and smelled a delicious soup his brother had seasoned and cooked to perfection. He said to Jacob, "Give me some of that soup. I'm so starved I could die." And conniving Jacob saw his chance. He replied, "Not unless you sell me your birthright for it." Whoa! For a bowl of soup? Isn't that a little extreme? The birthright was the right of the firstborn to inherit the largest part of his father's estate, the honored position as spiritual head of the family, and, even more valuable, to be in direct line of the Abrahamic promise to the whole earth-blessing Savior. Esau's decision carried monumental importance.

For a moment he was quiet, and then he said, "What is that to me when I'm half starved? What good is this birthright anyhow? Give me the soup before I die!" He possessed no appreciation for spiritual blessings. He cared only for what he could see and the enjoyment of now. Jacob, a scoundrel himself, valued, at least to some degree, the spiritual part of life and the words God had spoken to Abraham. He understood the blessings of the birthright and wanted them, though he went the wrong way about gaining them. As at his birth he was "grasping after" the blessings God would give him anyhow. Five centuries later another believer, David, who as a young man triumphed over the giant warrior, Goliath, had been told by a prophet of God that he would be king of Israel. David, perhaps learning from Jacob's example, operated differently. Several years passed before he would become king, and in those years the present king, Saul, reigned and grew jealous of David. In his anger he sought to kill him. David fled to the mountains and spent more years as prey to Saul's jealousy. David on one occasion said, "Surely there is a but a step between me and death." On two occasions Saul, close to David's hiding place but unaware of his presence, slept with his army so near to David that David's men told him God had delivered him into his hands and that he should kill him and become king. "Not so," said David. "No one should raise his hand against the Lord's anointed. When the Lord wants me to become king he will handle Saul himself." And so it happened that one day Saul died in battle, and the way opened to crown David as king (I Samuel 24: 4-18). David had learned as a young man to trust the Lord and wait for Him to guide. It took Jacob many years to grow to that degree of spiritual maturity.

Jacob, not playing around, said, "Swear to me right now." And so Esau did, and that easily he traded away his birthright and his special destiny. Later on, he chafed over what he had done —and at how his brother had taken advantage of him just because he was hungry. But it was too late. He had given his word.

Years later, when their father was old, blind, and possibly dying, he spoke of pronouncing his final, unchangeable blessings upon Esau. Rebekah heard him and concocted her own plan to ensure Jacob got all the blessing. God had already said the elder "would serve the younger" (indicating Jacob would inherit the birthright), but Rebekah took matters into her own hands rather than letting the Lord bring it to pass (In that instance she was not meek.). She convinced Jacob to pose as his older brother and go in and ask for the blessing. Because he could not see, Isaac (also ignoring God's statement about the 'elder serving the younger') took matters into his own hands in giving the blessing to his favorite son Esau. And so Isaac unwittingly gave the blessings to Jacob. Isaac was wrong, and Rebekah, though she promoted the right thing, was also wrong in taking matters into her own hands and not asking for or waiting for the Lord to bring it to pass. When Esau found out he seethed in anger, vowing to kill his brother. Rebekah, hearing him, again orchestrated from behind the scenes. She complained to Isaac that, as Esau had taken a wife from among the Hittites who was a 'grief of heart' to her and Isaac, it would break her heart if Jacob did the same thing. "What good shall my life be?" With such words she influenced her husband to send Jacob away without realizing her subterfuge. The woman God had selected as a wife for Isaac was not always perfect in her doings. She had already manipulated peoples' lives, and now entangled herself further.

Isaac called Jacob and told him not to take a wife from among the local girls but from the land and family from which his mother had come, from the land of Padan-Aram and the house of Bethuel, in the city of Haran, where his mother's father lived. So Jacob, learning of Esau's anger, left quickly, and Rebekah, because of her scheming, lost her son that day. She died before he ever came back. God would have worked it out that Jacob would receive the blessing without any of Rebekah's scheming.

CHAPTER 7

JACOB—ISRAEL

(Genesis 29-35)

Jerusha, always questioning things in her mind, even while they were still teenagers, asked Matthias, "Why was so much written about Jacob? He barely gave any attention to the Lord for much of his life, yet so much of our history recorded details about him. What an enigmatic character."

"Enigmatic? What do you mean?" asked Matthias.

"Puzzling," said she, matter-of-factly.

"Why didn't you just say so?"

She gave him one of her looks and then reconsidered. "He's one of the heroes of the faith, yet so much of his life was spent seeking his own wealth, getting rich, being a success as he saw it. He is one of the most difficult characters in scripture to understand, difficult because, for much of his life he was not what one would expect of one of the 'heroes of the faith' in the Bible. He knew the Lord had told his mother, 'Two nations are in your womb,' and 'the elder shall serve the younger.' That meant that as the younger twin he would inherit the largest part of his father's estate and become the spiritual leader of the family. Yet he could not wait and let the Lord cause those things to happen. Instead he schemed and cheated his brother out of the birthright. I don't think the Lord wants us to cheat to do his will. He is no example of how to follow the Lord. What do you think?"

"You're right, Jerusha," he said weakly, not quite interested yet in her ramblings nor wanting to be drawn into the conversation.

"Jacob was a poor example of how to trust the Lord. If I were his mother I would be disappointed and give up on him," said she with a teenager's certainty. "Two very different people came from Isaac and Rebekah, and I think they were both losers. Esau was 'of the earth' and had no interest in spiritual things. Jacob valued things he had been taught about the Lord, but he sure didn't appear to take them too seriously. His name meant 'chiseler' and 'cheat,' and he spent most of his days scheming and serving himself."

"It's up to us to follow the Lord or to ignore Him," enjoined Matthias, finally giving in to entering the conversation and beginning to catch on to her thoughts. "Sometimes we go back and forth between both opinions. I do that myself, so I better not be too critical of Jacob. Maybe the Lord is giving us a picture of the human condition through Jacob. Isn't that what He's doing?" he questioned, wondering out loud. "Maybe we are more like Jacob than we realize," seeking to answer her question. "We are all 'Israelites.' Maybe we are *all* like him."

Here's what I remember about Jacob after that," said Jerusha. "While sneaking to the far away city of Haran, where his mother years earlier had come from, he slept one night along the path and dreamed he saw a ladder set up whose top reached to heaven and there the angels of God ascended and descended upon it. The Lord stood above it and said, 'I am the God of Abraham and Isaac. The land where you are lying will I give to you and your descendants, and in you and one of your descendants shall all the families of the earth be blessed. And behold, I am with you and will keep you in all places you go and bring you again to this land. I will not leave you until I have done all this.'"

Matthias chimed in, "So God repeated the promise to Jacob that He had given to Abraham and Isaac, telling him those promises would continue through him and that God would be with him always, wherever he went."

"Right," agreed Jerusha. "What would you do with a dream like that? Considering that it tied in with the things told to Abraham and Isaac, I think it would have changed my life." She fell silent for a moment. Matthias looked at her and slowly began to agree. "Then when Jacob awakened he said, 'Surely the Lord is in this place, and I knew it not.

This is the house of God and the gate to heaven.' He set up a stone for a memorial and poured oil on it and called the name of the place Bethel, or 'House of God.' This place would become a special place in Israel's history. Then he said, 'If God gives me bread to eat and clothing to wear so that I come again to my father's house in peace, then shall the Lord be my God.' This is the first place where we see Jacob call the Lord *his* God. It was a worshipful response, and Jacob's manner was different after that. Instead of fleeing from his brother, now being assured God was with him, he was looking for a new life and considered more seriously that maybe it was time to start looking for a wife. Still, he often followed his own will more than God's. That's what is puzzling. If God had spoken to him why wasn't he a changed man?"

Matthias countered with, "In effect God spoke to us in parting the Red Sea and in feeding us with manna. He spoke to us at Sinai when he gave the law. How come *we* aren't perfect?"

Jerusha saw his point and went back to telling her story. "Days later, when he came to a well and saw people watering their flocks, he asked if they knew of Laban. They said that they did and that the young lady approaching to water her sheep was Rachel, Laban's daughter. Jacob watched her, his uncle's daughter, and then helped her with the sheep. To him she was the most beautiful girl he had ever seen, and his emotions took over after all those earlier days of fear and lonely traveling. Unable to restrain himself, he drew her in his arms and kissed her. Kissing relatives was a proper greeting at that time. Weeping out loud he told her he was Rebekah's son. Rachel, totally surprised and shaken rather deeply, pushed away, though only slightly, and looked into his face, studying him in wonder. This man who had just kissed her was Auntie Rebekah's son? Her father and grandfather had spoken lovingly of Rebekah, but she had left before Rachel was born, so she had never met her. Rachel ran and told her father, and soon they were all together meeting and exchanging stories of each other's welfare. Laban welcomed him openly, and after a month with Jacob helping with the sheep, he said, 'We need to pay you. What shall your wages be?' Now Laban had two daughters, Leah and her younger sister, Rachel, who was 'beautiful and well favored.'

"Jacob said, 'I will serve you for seven years for Rachel your younger daughter.' Laban agreed, and those seven years seemed only a few days because he loved her so much. Jacob did not yet know it but in Laban he was encountering a person even more wily and conniving than himself, something he had never encountered before. Nobody ever out-smarted Jacob. Unknown to Jacob, God would use Laban to "chisel" him into the man he would later be. Always Jacob knew more about what was taking place around him than anyone else, and because of that he could manipulate situations to his advantage. Esau was tough, capable, more organized and competent than all he met. But Jacob outmaneuvered him. Esau was generally good-natured and liked most people. Even if he lost to someone it didn't bother him too much. He knew eventually he could win if he really wanted to. He had staying power. That was why he was an extraordinary hunter. He was patient enough, observant, and confident enough to continue until he won. To be bested by his younger, un-athletic brother, though, injured his pride and would fester for years. Neither boy won in Jacob's selfish cheating of his brother, and those shenanigans had forced him to flee from home."

Many Israelites knew these stories very well and were good listeners and re-tellers. Jerusha was one of them. She continued, "Jacob had gained the birthright by cheating and had obtained his father's blessing by deception, and the Lord allowed him to do that. But the Lord was also free to use circumstances to train him to follow him more carefully. Jacob was about to get a 'taste of his own medicine.' The marriage took place, and in the dark of night Jacob took his bride, with the customary veil over her face, to his tent. In the morning light it was Leah at his side, the older sister, now legally his wife. Jacob, outraged, stormed out to Laban, who calmly explained—as though Jacob certainly understood and knew this—that 'in this country the younger daughter could not be given in marriage before the older daughter' (a detail for some reason he had neglected to explain to Jacob). Laban, being a reasonable man (and an opportunist), defused the argument by explaining he was now free to give Rachel in marriage to Jacob—of course for seven more years of free labor on Jacob's part, that was, if he still wanted her. Jacob understood Laban's subterfuge and was a little surprised that he had been so skillfully outmaneuvered. In the following years he grew to despise Laban, but he tried not to show it. He really did not think anyone else could outwit him, but Laban continually did. He worked for fourteen years for Laban to procure Rachel as his wife. And now he had two wives! And was experiencing being cheated and deceived!

"Over the years Laban never changed and Jacob felt the sting of his subterfuges so many times he grew weary of the man. How could one person take advantage of and run roughshod over so many people and never seem to care who he cheated? He had seen him cheat his friends when he weighed out silver on his balance scale. His weights were slightly off from the accepted value—always in Laban's favor. Jacob had cursed Laban in his heart many times, and then one day it dawned on him. What he despised in Laban was exactly how he operated, though he resisted realizing it. Not fun to see.

"As time went by things grew more complicated for Jacob. Jealousy and rivalry developed between his two wives. Leah conceived and bare a son with Jacob. Then three more times. She had four sons and Rachel had none and envied her sister. She gave her maid, Bilhah, as a wife to Jacob to bear a son whom she would then claim as her own. And so it happened. She bare a son. And then another. Now Bilhah, in her eyes, did what Rachel could not and saw herself as more important. Meanwhile Leah ceased bearing and grew envious of her sister. She then gave her maid, Zilpah, to Jacob, and she bore him a son and then another. Then Leah began to bear again and bore two more sons and then a daughter whom she named Dinah, so there were ten sons and a daughter. Finally Rachel, the wife he loved, conceived and bore a son whom they named Joseph. Four wives, eleven sons, and a daughter. With jealousies and rivalries, it was not always a happy household, maybe even dysfunctional.

"For all that, the Lord was still with Jacob and prospered him. Laban noticed that his flocks grew larger and healthier under Jacob's care, and Jacob worked hard at trying to please his father-in-law. Laban let him keep any cattle, sheep, and goats that were speckled, spotted, brown, or had white in them, which were seen as undesirable traits, and soon

Jacob's small flocks grew more rapidly than Laban's. God was blessing Jacob with surprisingly fast-growing wealth, and yet Jacob appeared to be oblivious to and unappreciative of how greatly God was blessing him. He enjoyed the prosperity and the admiration it engendered among neighboring shepherds and owners. Deep in his heart he sensed that God was doing something with him, but he still could not bring himself to the point of openly acknowledging God's help and humbling himself before Him. He wanted to run his own life and ignore the destiny God had planned for him. He could not give in to simply following Him and living in the light of those promises to his grandfather Abraham.

"Meanwhile, Laban's sons grew angry with him, concluding that Jacob must be cheating their father. Then God once again spoke to Jacob: 'I have seen all that Laban has done to you. I am the God of Bethel where you saw a vision and made a pillar. Arise and leave this land and return to the land of your kindred.' For some reason he did what God said. He was beginning to acknowledge God's guidance, and he told his wives to pack their things for a journey back to his homeland. When Laban was away for several days tending his sheep, Jacob and his wives, his children—and his flocks and cattle—stole away.

"Remember, God had told Jacob a great nation would come from him, and now it was beginning to happen. His family was growing very large, eleven sons and a daughter, and his wealth in cattle and sheep was multiplying rapidly. Such prosperity was noticeable. Presently a long ignored problem came back to life. The last thing he knew about Esau was that he wanted to kill him. Things were about to heat up for Jacob, and it was not going to be easy to follow God's words. Many believers through the centuries had learned that following God's words often led one straight into trouble. Those who dared follow him, though, always seemed to find some kind of peace and blessing at some point, ready to blossom within that trouble. Perhaps part of God's plan was to use Jacob as an illustration of that very principle as an encouragement for future believers.

"It was three days before Laban found out about Jacob's departure. He was livid. In his mind Jacob had stolen his daughters and his grandchildren. He gathered his servants and set out in pursuit and in seven days caught up with him. However, God spoke to Laban in a dream at night, saying, 'Take heed how you talk to Jacob,' and Laban took the warning. 'Why did you steal away like this? I would have made a feast and sent you away with goods and happiness,' Laban lied to Jacob. He had cheated and taken advantage of him at every opportunity.

"'I was afraid you would take your daughters and your grandchildren away from me,' answered Jacob. 'For twenty years I have been with you and taken care of your flocks and herds. Your ewes and she goats have not cast their young, and your rams have I not eaten. When something was torn of beasts I bore the loss of it, yet you required all of me anyhow. Same when something was stolen. I had to give of my little flock. I worked so hard for you that I was hot and thirsty many days just trying to care for your flocks. Then many nights I shivered outdoors in the frost. You changed my wages ten times, breaking your promises over and over to me. Except that God was with me, you would have sent me away empty-handed.'

"'These daughters are *my* daughters,' scoffed Laban, 'and these children are *my* children, and these cattle are *my* cattle, and all you see is mine.' Then, remembering God's warning, he softened a bit and said, 'Let us make a covenant between us to do no harm to each other.' So they did, and finally Laban left.

"Jacob sent messengers to tell Esau he was coming home and told them, 'Speak to my lord, Esau: I have oxen, flocks and asses, menservants and woman servants, and I have sent to tell my lord, that I may find grace in your sight.' Calling his brother 'lord' was certainly a new approach. The messengers returned and said, 'We met Esau, and he is also coming to meet you—with four hundred men!' Now what? That could be bad or good. 'Didn't you try to find out? Are they coming to welcome me or to kill me?' screamed Jacob. 'What is wrong with you? Didn't you ask?' The uninquisitive messengers had not even wondered what it meant. Jacob was terrified and divided his people and livestock into two bands and sent them ahead separately, reasoning that if Esau destroyed one band the other might escape. Jacob was still scheming and relying on his own efforts to take care of himself, even though for one of the few times in his life he was following God's advice.

"Then he did something he usually did as a last resort. His situation was so hopeless and terrifying that he called out to God. 'O God of my father Abraham and Isaac, the God who told me to "return to your country and people, and I will take care of you," I am not worthy of the least of Your mercies and of all the truth which You have shown me. Deliver me from the hand of my brother, for I fear him, that he will come and kill me and my family.' This was a new and humble approach, one in which he owned up to his own unworthiness. The years and circumstances had gradually been changing Jacob's heart. Then he added, 'You said, "I will surely do you good and make your seed as the sand of the sea . . . " reminding God of His own promise. God could have reflected offense, but he did not. Jacob's request meant that he had at least paid attention to what God had said and taken it seriously. Many future believers over the years, including Moses and Joshua, would follow his example.

"With his family gone ahead, Jacob was left alone that night, 'and there wrestled a man with him until the breaking of the day.'"

Jerusha interrupted, "I've always wondered, who was he wrestling? Was he really wrestling with a man, or was it a dream?"

Matthias thought a few moments before answering. "First off, I don't think it was Jacob who started the fight. With Laban behind him and Esau ahead, the last thing Jacob wanted was a fight with someone else. He had enough trouble hounding him, and the trouble in both cases, was largely caused by him, a truth he did not want to admit. If it was some stranger or thief Jacob would have certainly done all he could to ignore him and get rid of him. Yet some unnamed man wrestled against Jacob, and he could not get away from this fight. The question was, who was the man way out here in the wilderness? I think God was not done working on Jacob, and He or an angel He sent was wrestling with him, bringing him face to face with his own doings. God, who had created the world, had created invisible forces like gravity and wind, could easily have overpowered Jacob. I think He wrestled him to make Jacob realize he was fighting someone far stronger and more capable than himself. He was fighting God. His life was one giant wrestling match with God. Whether it was a man or a dream, God was working on him. 'I just want to do what I want to do' was how Jacob thought deep in his heart. He just wanted the trouble to go away—Laban, Esau, and now this man fighting him. It was too much. Why wouldn't he quit?

"Yet Jacob fought on. He would not quit either. All night. And so God withstood him. He was a child of God but a wayward one. God fought against him to bring him to the realization that as one about to bring his family back to the Promised Land and into Israel's history he needed to learn to draw on God's strength rather than his own. That he had been able to outwit most people so successfully had inflated his ego, and now that was about to change. Laban had been a trial, but Jacob still had managed to obtain the wife he wanted and, in spite of Laban's cheating, had accumulated vast flocks of sheep, goats, and camels and the wealth they brought. The earlier promise to grandfather Abraham was that he would be the father of a great nation, and Jacob was directly in that line springing miraculously from Abraham. His destiny was far greater than he could envision. But for now he was in a wrestling match—from which he could not escape. His life in the past few weeks had catapulted into turmoil. And here he was. Reality. Day was breaking and Jacob still would not give in.

"So the man did something extraordinary. He touched Jacob's thigh and pushed it out of joint, and just like that the fight was over. He could have won at any time, but he let Jacob fight. Jacob the conniver, the chiseler, the deceitful fighter who had beat so many in his lifetime, encountered someone he could not defeat. Somewhere in the night he might have guessed he was fighting the Lord and God's will for his life, too stubborn to give in. We don't know. Instantly crippled by this man's touch with a pain so intense he went limp, he suddenly knew. Nobody had power or patience like that but the Lord. Jacob had been following his own will, a flawed will he had inherited from Adam, his dimly remembered ancient ancestor. It had led him to more trouble than he could handle, and God had patiently let him do it—as He had let Adam exercise his right to make his own choices, even to the point of disobeying God.

"Totally exhausted, he came face to face with his true self. He was like many of us. God could have killed him for his stubborn insistence in forcing his own will over God's. But he did not. It melted Jacob's heart, and at that moment he switched from fighting God to clinging to Him with all the strength he had left."

"I think you are right," said Jerusha, lapsing into a long moment of silence. "Why couldn't I think of that?"

Matthias continued, "Then, according to what Moses wrote, a strange thing happened. The man said, 'Let me go. The day is breaking.' But Jacob clung to him and said, 'I will not let you go unless you bless me.' Why this sudden shift from fighting the man to clinging to him and asking for a blessing?" wondered Matthias.

"I don't know," said Jerusha, "but I think you do."

Matthias studied her face, guessing she too understood. "The answer is in the rest of the story. Remember the man asked him his name, and he said 'Jacob.' Then he said, 'Your name shall no more be called Jacob, but Israel, for as a prince you have power with God and with men and have won.' In saying his name Jacob ceased arguing with God and was admitting its meaning of "chiseler" and "conniver" truly described him. An honest moment before God. Remember when God asked Adam, 'Did you eat the fruit of that tree?' Adam halfway admitted it but then twisted facts around to make it seem like it was God's fault due to giving him Eve. Jacob was now more honest than Adam, and God called that a 'victory' and gave him his new name. God wanted honesty, from the inside out. 'He desires truth in the inward parts' (Psalm 51:6). 'He that covers his sins shall not prosper, but whoever confesses and forsakes them shall have mercy' (Proverbs 28: 13). In clinging to the Lord Jacob had finally realized only God had all the strength and the blessings of life, a realization that would live in his thinking from now on. He was now 'Israel.' The sons born to him would multiply into a nation that would bear his name and persist to the future and forever. God had so promised to Abraham and Isaac, and had hinted from the beginning to Adam. Jacob, or more properly 'Israel,' began to sense the enormity of those promises to Abraham and his father he had taken so lightly. He began to realize this nation of Israel was coming not only through him but also through his eleven sons. He had been enjoying to some degree these four wives he had, though the one he really loved was Rachel. Today it began to dawn on him that he had been oblivious to

God's purposes working their way right through his family. Grandfather Abraham's stories had been true. Truer than anything he knew. For the moment Jacob, no, 'Israel,' was completely humbled. God was working through him? And on that day that realization was overwhelming. Now 'Israel' would purpose to follow God's words more carefully."

Jerusha, still thinking, asked, "But if he lost the fight why did God say he won?"

"Because on that morning a new day began. In admitting his self-centeredness and stubbornness he was really just agreeing with God about himself, taking a true look at himself and letting that be his new truth. God already knew this about him and still cared about him and had a plan for him, and Jacob clung to that. On that day he was no longer Jacob but 'Israel.' He still had his aging body with all its ways and weaknesses—and now a hip sorely out of joint—but a new understanding that God would take care of him relaxed his heart. God, to whom he was clinging, would be his new strength. He would still struggle and fail when he followed his old self, but now he 'knew' that God with His wisdom and power could guide him better, and that very realization would continue to grow in the coming years. Today he had quit fighting to gain his own blessings. Today he had 'won' by accepting that God was in control and would fight for him and the nation that would come from him—a better victory than Jacob in his old self-effort could ever attain.

"At the end of the fight," said Matthias, "Israel walked away—with a limp—from the injury in his hip that would remind him the rest of his days of his human weakness and shortcomings. Deep in his heart he clung to the One who had wrestled him to submission. The memory of God's power and faithfulness would guide him through life's moments now. The injury was real, so the One wrestling with him must have been real—and so was his deeper relationship with the Lord. I think God wants us to see that for ourselves."

Jerusha, marveling at Matthias's insight, nodded her head in agreement. "So that long story about Jacob was really about us!"

"Right," agreed Matthias. "Your 'enigmatic' story turned out to have meaning for us."

She looked at him and stared, suddenly realizing she had been taken in by his antics. "You knew all along what I meant!"

"That's what I love about you, Jerusha. You can handle being needled. Together we figured out why God wrote so much about Jacob." She quietly enjoyed the moment, content by Matthias's side.

Unknown to Matthias and Jerusha, the prophet Isaiah, centuries later, would put in clear words what they figured out that day: . . . "let him take hold of my strength, that he may make peace with me, and he shall make peace with me. He shall cause them that come of Jacob to take root. Israel shall blossom and bud and fill the face of the world with fruit" (Isaiah 27: 5-6).

"He still had to meet Esau," continued Matthias, "and face up to the results of his previous conniving. Israel reverted to acting like Jacob again (which, surprisingly, a true believer can do). As he returned now with two wives, two concubines, eleven sons and a daughter, and those large flocks of sheep and herds of cattle, Esau would be jealous and enraged and kill him, a terrifying prospect that ultimately thrust him into the most frightening moment of his life. Unknown to him, the Lord had influenced Esau to take pity on his brother and let him live. He still hated him for the sneak and phony impostor he was. Jacob had fooled his parents, but he did not fool Esau. As far as he was concerned, Jacob was a worthless person. But he was, after all, his brother, so Esau backed off. The world yielded plenty of wealth for all who worked hard and had talent, and Esau stifled his hatred and overruled his lust for vengeance. Practical Esau, the hard-headed realist, who fought his way to superiority. His disdain for things spiritual he passed on to his sons and grandsons.

"His grandson Amalek was only too willing to champion Esau's ideas, as we shall later see. He too became great like Esau and built a city, then a nation. The earth was there for the taking back then, and it went to the ones who took. The old hatred for Jacob festered in the hearts of the descendant Amalekites, who kept it alive by telling and re-telling the story of how Jacob cheated Esau. He was no good and all his descendants were like him. Most did not know why they hated Israel so much, but they allowed that hatred to live in their hearts like an endless infection. Not caring to think more deeply into the story they fed themselves over and over, nor caring to consider their own cruelty and selfishness, they became a tribe of truly vicious marauders. It was easier to hate and destroy than to face up to one's own wicked self. Though God had said he desired 'truth in the inward parts,' they were not willing to come clean and instead chose to follow the path of their own hearts—to their own destruction. Certainly there were Amalekites over the years who broke free of their great-grandfather's self-centered occupation with the world and his skill at capturing rewards from it. Some existed who paid attention to God's word and took the life and freedom He offered, even fought nobly in Israel's armies, but the mainstream of Esau's descendants wallowed in his example and followed his ways. Esau's unchecked and undisciplined self-will flowed like a river for several generations into the families he spawned."

Matthias worked toward the end of the story. "Ruled by fear of Esau, Jacob divided his family into four groups, putting the handmaids and their children first, then Leah and children, and finally Rachel and her son Joseph last. He was not accustomed to asking the Lord continually for guidance, nor even expecting His help. He sent gifts of cattle and sheep ahead to Esau to buy his favor. Finally he saw Esau and bowed himself to the ground. Esau ran to meet him and 'fell on his neck and kissed him.' What a change. Jacob had not needed to engineer the situation because the Lord had softened Esau's heart. He asked him what all this large number of cattle and people meant. He said, 'to find favor in the sight of my Lord.' Imagine Jacob calling him "Lord," but he did.

"Esau said, 'I have enough, my brother. Keep these for yourself.' All Jacob's fears about Esau had been handled by the Lord for him, and he began to relax. 'The Lord makes even our enemies to be at peace with us' (Proverbs 16: 7). Israel, even though he had purposed in his heart to regard the Lord's will as more important than his own, had reverted back to behaving as the old Jacob again. He had become the Lord's child years ago, a permanent relationship that would never be undone, and he would be Israel forever. How he behaved from day to day did not alter God's promise. He had believed the Lord's promises spoken to him by his father, but most of his life he had been so busy following his own will that he seldom followed the Lord's will. The realizations during the wrestling match had given him a fresh look at a better way to live. His heart had cried out to God for a blessing. He had not really expected the Lord to help him. He was overwhelmed by how the Lord graciously helped him in spite of his failures, and he truly was a different man after that."

CHAPTER 8

MOSES - DRAWN FROM THE RIVER

Hundreds of years passed after Jacob's journey to Egypt. The family was well nourished there and had prospered greatly in crops and cattle on the marvelous Egyptian delta soil. Seventy people had arrived with Jacob. Honored at first because Joseph's leadership had protected Egypt from a devastating famine, Israel's numbers had multiplied exponentially. Conditions worsened for them when years later a new Pharaoh, fearing Israel's growing numbers, had enslaved them and recently issued a death edict (as mentioned earlier) that all male Israelite babies be drowned in the Nile River. An unseen spiritual battle was playing out. Pharaoh, overly impressed with his status as king of a powerful country, was unwittingly led by Satan to attempt to stop God's Savior, whose exact identity and arrival time he did not know, from coming into the world. Two obscure slaves, father Amram and mother Jochebed, would parent a son who, when grown, would be used by God to deliver Israel from the overpowering clutches of Egypt. He would be one of the few remembered and influential people in all the history of the world. Israelites had heard, all their lives, the stories of Abraham, Isaac and Jacob and how God had promised to make a nation of them and give them their own land. They loved hearing those stories, which were as real to them as the fact they were slaves, over and over. Those words from God were the only ray of hope they had, and that belief led Amram and Jochebed to keep the arrival of their third child a secret to protect him from certain death in the river. She wore loose clothing to keep her large tummy from showing. When her baby was born she hid him from the Egyptian tyrants and nursed him out of sight at home. She was a slave in her life, but in her heart she was free, and, like her great-great-great grandfather Abraham, believed God and trusted that her people would one day be freed and become a blessing to the world. Little did she know the far-reaching influence her son would wield. Historians have never said so, but she and her husband were among the truly influential people in the history of the world.

Finally, at three months it became too hard to hide him, and in their misery they prayed to God for help. Not exactly getting a visible answer but trusting that he would guide, they built a tiny ark of bulrushes, and in her agony, Jochebed wept at the river's edge as she stepped into the water and floated the ark, with its precious cargo, upon its surface and into God's invisible hands. She, with her daughter Miriam, prayed, "Help, Lord. I know no other way. This child I cannot protect. Pharaoh's forces are too strong for me. Please . . . take care of him . . . " Then, the pain of her heart cried out, "My son, my son, why is this evil done? . . . Into your hands I let him go." She watched silently for a moment through shimmering tears as the ark, untied from human care, bobbed gently among the reeds. As she backed away a few steps, her balance teetered, the smooth river rocks so slippery . . . and the world went dark. In her half-conscious state the screams of other mothers whose sons the soldiers had ripped from their arms echoed in her ears. The pain of the world was too much to bear. Had God forsaken her? The child she had tried to save was torn from her after all. Then Miriam's frightened arms caught her as she collapsed—and pulled her up on the shore and back to consciousness. God on His throne saw the travail of her heart, travail that touched His heart even more deeply than hers—the misery of His beloved humans—and had pity on her, even on foolish Egypt. His heart, too, ached. For all mankind. They were all adrift in a hostile world. Pain throbbed in bringing children to life. Mothers knew this. Fathers knew it too from watching the mothers scream. From the foundation of the world He had known what He must do. Evil would not prevail.

Pharaoh's daughter found the ark and took pity on the baby. Moses' older sister, Miriam, watching from the riverbank, bravely stepped forward and offered to find a woman to nurse him for her. Pharaoh's daughter agreed, and Miriam brought Jochebed, her mother, Moses's mother. The princess offered to pay her to nurse him for a few years, until he would move permanently to the king's court, where he would eventually grow up under Pharaoh's protection, amidst the wealth, privilege and training of Egypt's elite.

For now, Miriam was as heartbroken as her mother. Though Moses was still alive and would be taken care of, he now belonged to Pharaoh's daughter. The young girl could only trust that the Lord had heard their anguished cries. Unknown to her He *had heard,* as He had heard millions of equally broken-hearted cries before this. Why did He wait so long before answering? To one who did not yet know God's heart as deeply as she later would, it was frustrating. To the believer, willing to patiently wait and trust Him, there could be peace and a deepening understanding. Man profits by trusting God's heart to do the right and best thing. In our day God often makes us wait for that very purpose, to deepen our understanding of His love and care for us and of our own impatient hearts, to bring us closer to Him as we see our helplessness and then find that He *does* take care of us. Sometimes God makes us wait because He has a larger plan and will in time make all the details fit—even our misery and suffering. David, when he became king five hundred years after Moses' time, could say, "It is good for me that I have been afflicted that I might learn your statutes (principles)" (Psalm 119: 71). Having been anointed by the prophet Samuel as Israel's next king, he spoke those words after years of running for his life, hiding in mountains and caves, away from a jealous King Saul seeking to kill him. More than once the thought "there is but a step between me and death" gripped him with its terrifying reality. But he had been delivered from those perils and experienced God's care through it all. Those trials had enlarged his heart and imparted the wisdom that would render him a wise and understanding king. When he saw those afflictions as "good" it was as one who had suffered many afflictions and then deeply seen the tenderness of God's care. Certainly many of his afflictions were greater than ours, but he is an encouragement to us as we experience trials.

The Lord always hears, and now the prayers of thousands of anguished hearts over several centuries, prayers He never forgot, would unfold into action as God moved within human history to set man free. We can trust His faithfulness. The abject misery of the centuries of slavery in Egypt, as awful as they were, mirrored to them and to the world, the even larger misery of the captivity of mankind to his own fallen nature and to the dominion of Satan. Man was trapped and could not escape—just like Israel could not escape, no matter how hard anyone tried—from the merciless and cruel grip of Pharaoh—and from the ultimate cruelty—death.

That would change, but not for many years. The princess named him Moses, "because I *drew him out* of the water," she said, which was what his name meant in her language. Little did she know that one day God would "draw" Moses and all the slaves out of Egypt and out of Pharaoh's cruel grip. For now she simply nourished this helpless child. Her brilliant, arrogant father had no idea his wealth was paying for the care and training of the Lord's deliverer—not that God needed Pharaoh's money. It was more a type of justice that He would often employ to frustrate the pride and arrogance of the human heart. Thus Moses grew up in Pharaoh's court, un-drowned and un-harmed, as one of his sons, with the best care and training the world could offer, while Moses's real mother taught her child his true identity—and got paid to do it. On the other hand, think of the unmitigated cruelty to hundreds of Israelite families who lost sons due to Pharaoh's wanton death edict. The cruelty of the human heart knows no bounds. Like fire, it never says, "enough."

Somewhere in his boyhood heart Moses had questions. Where did we come from? Why are we here? Things happened beyond our control. People died and they spoke no more, quit responding to those they knew, to everyone. Is that the end of them, or has the life in them moved on to somewhere else, somewhere we cannot go? What about me?

These were questions floating around in Moses's mind. At seven years old he had never put them into words, nor thought too deeply about them. They were just there. He was in a peculiar position. As an infant he had been snatched from his birth parents and placed with different people, the ones who now took care of him. But now he wanted to know more. Why had he not seen his birth mother for a long time? She had said, when he got old enough to understand, that he might not see her much in the future. He had seen tears in her eyes, but beyond that he could not remember much more. Did she not care about him anymore? She had nursed him in her warm bosom, and he was comfortable there. She had spoken to him words, and her voice carried to him love. He had always heard them, even before he could understand, and then gradually those words carried meanings to him, meanings he could understand. And he made words back to her. She often corrected him and made him say them exactly as she had. She knew so much more than he did, and he loved being with her and listening to her soft voice.

His other mother, the one they called "Princess," took care of him now. She told him how she had heard him crying and found him floating in a basket in the river. The basket was dry inside and he was wrapped tightly and carefully in a blanket. The moment she saw him he looked so helpless that her heart went out to him. She picked him up and drew him to her breast to cuddle and protect him and then took him home to a large beautiful place called a 'palace.' At that place also lived her father, whom many servants called "Pharaoh." The princess loved and cherished him, even though he came as a stranger from the river, and begged her father to let her keep him. When he saw how thrilled his daughter was with this child he could not say 'no.' Thus he had come to live in a kingdom separate from his birth family. Pharaoh was a little cold to him at first, but gradually he "warmed up" to this little creature because his daughter loved him so much.

As he grew, the servants told him that his father, Pharaoh, was God and connected to the unseen ones that had made the earth and ruled its forces. The servants loved Moses too—most of them, anyhow. A few, careful not to let Pharaoh see, despised him in their hearts because he was a 'Hebrew,' fit for nothing more than slave labor. In fact, the entire kingdom despised the Hebrews, and Moses grew up feeling that hidden hatred, understanding two ways of life existed in his world. One was of his birth mother and father, who nourished him at the first, and the other of his 'replacement' father and the princess, who now nourished and cared for him.

Jochebed, his birth mother, told him stories from before the time he could understand her words. As he grew and learned to understand, those stories shaped his thinking. She told him people had always had a knowledge of God traceable back through the generations to the first person, Adam. God had spoken with Adam and many others through the generations and had told them to preserve his words and pass them along. Any person on earth who so chose could be connected to God through those words.

Moses saw different beliefs between Israel and Egypt. As a youngster he just took it all in. Since grownups always knew more than kids, he figured they all knew what they were doing. But the human mind keeps questioning, trying to make sense of the world. In time he would realize the differences were major, and he asked Pharaoh about it. Pharaoh said their way was right because they were in power and controlled the world. Others had tried to rise above Pharaoh, but he had vanquished them all, and that proved he was right and his power was superior. At a much younger age he had asked his birth father, Amram, "How come we can't see God? How do we know he is real?"

He said, "God is perfect and lives in heaven. We humans are not perfect, and God cannot allow imperfect people into his presence. We cannot fix ourselves, but He has said he will fix us, and we must wait for Him to do that and accept His help. We do not completely understand it all, but the things He has told us in the past have come true, so we wait, patiently—for Him to guide us." Moses listened. He did not understand either, but he too would wait because his father said so.

Moses was trained by the finest scholars of the day in science, mathematics, and leadership skills, and also by seasoned warriors in the use of all types of weapons. He learned numbers, knowledge passed down from the most ancient people, who lived long on the earth and possessed clear and sharp memory capacity. The early people had discovered relationships between numbers that were predictable and constant and could be manipulated. They learned to measure distances and angles and used them to increase their understanding of the world and its forces. Later generations built on that. Nimrod, one of the ancients a few generations after the flood, used that knowledge to build a tower higher than any structure man had ever built. Scripture describes him as a "mighty hunter," perhaps better than all others, who could outwit and kill animals, even huge, powerful, and terrifying ones. Now he was manipulating the earth and its elements in building an imposing tower, higher than any ever built, whose "top could reach to heaven." It was a heady experience, and he and his engineers began to imagine they could build their way into heaven, to God's abode, and manipulate Him. In reality they had not a wisp of a notion how to reach the dimension in which God and His holiness existed, but their arrogance carried them on and prevented them from seeing their own ignorance. Today our airliners daily fly about a thousand times higher than Nimrod's tower, and our rockets have propelled man far out into space. One of those astronauts looked out his window and reported he did not see God and mockingly intimated he did not exist. Nimrod, who built with wood and stone, was simply unaware that one day steel would enable the construction of bridges and buildings many times larger than his earthen tower. God watched from heaven and went down and scattered mankind from their short-sighted mission. The whole earth was of one language until that day. God confused their talk and instituted the many languages we have today. Confused humans teamed up with people they could understand and wandered away. The Tower of "Babel" was named after the confusion of that day. Languages that seemed as babble to so many supplied the name. The city of "Babylon" had its beginnings in that mix-up of languages. Egypt perfected Babel's knowledge and dwarfed its tower with the construction of the pyramids, built around Moses's time and existing to the present day.

Moses learned martial arts and horsemanship, practicing until he became exceedingly skillful. As a boy he loved sword fights with other boys using wooden swords. They pretended to be great warriors and had many battles. They also grew adept at throwing spears, impaling straw targets with growing skill. His favorite weapon was the bow. He had natural ability and learned quickly, often, as he observed, more quickly than the other boys. What they complained about being difficult surprised him, as those things were easy for him. This gave him an underlying confidence in himself. With plenty of time to practice and skilled instructors to train him, he developed lethal skills in the use of skills all but lost and unheard of today. With his 'state of the art' bow he could shoot an arrow straight up into the sky and then put five more up before the first returned to stick fast in the ground. He could send an arrow fast into a flying ball in mid-air or fire an arrow while leaping from the back of a moving chariot—and hit his target. What his instructors emphasized most was the ability to shoot fast and accurately, short range, while dodging and weaving through a chaotic battlefield. This they trained into him until he became dangerously accurate. An eager student, he studied hard, learned well and gradually began to outperform his teachers. He was on his way as a serious candidate to becoming the next Pharaoh. (A few modern day experts, after studying ancient writings, paintings and sculptures of warriors from Egypt depicting methods of holding arrows in the right hand and drawing and firing rapidly with deadly accuracy, have developed similar skills. Demonstrations can be seen on YouTube.)

Pharaoh himself taught Moses the fine art of managing people and the affairs of a large kingdom. Great leaders had a clear vision of what their nation should be, and accompanying that, an ability to put skilled people in charge of important daily affairs as well as of mundane details that constantly needed attention. For example, a powerful, well-trained army needed food, equipment, and uniforms that looked smart and commanded respect in order to maintain its edge. The leader who failed to understand that would be defeated by a rival who knew how to keep his people equipped and strong. With so much to attend to one had to find and appoint able people to carry out such responsibilities and, equally as important, to pay attention to whether or not the job was getting done. The kingdom depended on it. Pharaoh drilled these concepts into Moses's thinking, and Moses comprehended. He had watched Pharaoh put his skills into operation as he taught others to help him guide his kingdom. He had also seen the human side of his father and had observed that many of his father's warriors were stronger and better with their weapons than was Pharaoh himself. Some of his advisors were as cunning as Pharaoh. Moses wondered at the ability of one man really no stronger than the others to command so many. He concluded they followed him out of respect for his position and for his fine qualities as a leader—and because of his connection to the gods.

One day he asked him, "Why do you work so hard at staying ahead of everyone else? Wouldn't they follow you anyhow because they honor you and respect your leadership?"

"No, Moses. Many would. Many would not, especially the ones who believe they are more important than anyone else—and you yourself know that many of my most capable officers are like that. They are only kept in check by my convincing them I can overpower or outmaneuver them. The truth is each person thinks he is more important than everyone else and that he should have all the world's goods, that the rest of the world should wait on him. If you look deep into your heart, you are like that too." Moses was awed once again by his father's wisdom and quietly considered his words. "You think they all respect me because they act like they do. Those people you think would follow me would take my place in a heartbeat if they thought they could. My job as Pharaoh is to know who they are and be watchful. They must never see my vulnerability. And they must never see yours either, if you are to be a great leader." Moses was beginning to see into the wisdom of the world. That was part of the skill of maintaining control over the strong-willed and aggressive ministers working for him. Such talented men were necessary in forging a great kingdom, but it took continual effort to stay a step ahead of them and prevent them from taking over. Brute force worked for a while but did not make for a strong kingdom in the long run. A true leader needed strength of character, wisdom, and a burning desire to do whatever it took to maintain his position against all challenges. If he got tired of the effort required, someone would notice and seek to overthrow him. Pharaoh perceived that Moses, this remarkable Israelite drawn from the river, was one of only a few of his sons capable of grasping such subtleties and possessing the willingness to work that hard. He had taken him at the insistence of his daughter and had allowed him to partake of the privilege and training as part of his royal family. Surprised at the talent manifesting itself in this slave person and having grown fond of him, the wary Pharaoh nonetheless kept a close eye on Moses, his "adopted" grandson. Several of his ministers advised him not to trust this son of a despised people, people of low enough birth to deserve slavery. One day this upstart would turn on him. Pharaoh perceived the self-centeredness and jealousy in their "candid" advice and remained as wary of them as they advised him to be of Moses.

Amram and Jochebed's role as a father and mother in Israel was plain and ordinary as people saw it, not nearly as flashy as that of Pharaoh and the powerful leaders under him, yet the son they nurtured and taught would one day turn the world's power system upside down. The Lord heard all prayers of those who waited on Him and trusted His promises. He did not grant immediately every request they asked. Yet he heard and did not forget. He had a larger plan, into which their lives would ultimately fit and would, for a greater purpose than they knew, allow that plan to work out. They saw no answers yet, but in the innermost beliefs of their hearts they hung on to their God. They, like Abraham, Isaac, and Jacob, believed God's promise to make a great nation of Israel. They taught young Moses, as much as he could understand, about God's working in the world and his promises to Abraham, and he treasured their words deep in his little boy's heart.

As he would learn later from his Egyptian "father," the Egyptians had a different "take" on reality. They would succeed where Nimrod had failed. He had built a tower whose pinnacle he fancied would reach heaven and, along with that, a kingdom that would rule the world. Nimrod's kingdom had a start but never a completion. In the centuries since his time human knowledge had vastly increased, and Egypt would build structures that would dwarf Nimrod's tower and last "forever." They would be perfectly oriented to the true direction of heaven and the forces of the universe. Egypt would be the pinnacle of all nations of the world, the essence of perfection. Its structures would dominate and teach the world to revere the wisdom of those who built them. Pharaoh would be the connection to the unseen gods and forces that ruled everything. When Pharaoh left this world it was not really death but a "transition" from which he would return. His body would be preserved and placed deep in the heart of a pyramid where power, drawn in from the universe by its special shape and the marvelous wisdom of the ancient engineers who conceived it, would sustain him and bring him back to life. Every Egyptian would be forever blessed. Many would even allow themselves to be killed after Pharaoh's death so as to join him and serve him, so complete was their trust in this god-like man. None ever returned from those graves to tell of their experience, so no one ever really knew. Moses was extremely fortunate to be partner to Egypt's glory.

The wealth, prestige and privilege of the world's most powerful kingdom were within reach for him. Yet when he was grown he made a quick decision that would alter his life. At least the decision had the appearance of being quick. In reality it had been stirring in his heart for years. His mother's teachings about his roots in Israel, and her unshakeable trust in God and His promise to deliver them from the slavery of Egypt always lived deep in his memory. When on a certain day at age forty, Moses saw an Egyptian cruelly beating a Hebrew slave, the injustice of it all suddenly drove him to action. He was well aware of the hatred toward him of some of the leadership under Pharaoh and had walked a tightrope all these years, having to overcome suspicions and criticisms about his loyalty to Egypt. At first, as a child, he occupied both worlds, his mother's and Pharaoh's, with comparative ease, but as he grew older the vast differences between the two grew more and more difficult to ignore. He had seen his fellow Israelites beaten or whipped mercilessly for the smallest infraction. He had seen them left bleeding and nearly lifeless lying on the ground and had heard the Egyptians joking about the beatings they gave their slaves. He had known of women abused by their masters and then abandoned, heartbroken and shattered. What agony that wrought in the entire family. He had seen so much in his lifetime and had never once taken a stand for his fellow Israelites—until today. Maybe God had been preparing him to help his people break free from slavery. Maybe God had planted him in Pharaoh's court for this very moment. Maybe God had given him all those natural talents for this moment. Moses did not know it yet, but his next actions would "blow up" in his face.

In a moment he sprang into action. The Egyptian barely saw the lightning fast blow that took his life. The shocked and confused slave stared in awe at Moses. "RUN!" shouted Moses.

CHAPTER 9

MOSES FLEES

With lightning speed he had moved in and killed the Egyptian with his bare hands, his "trained" bare hands. The slave, suddenly free, ran away, and Moses hurriedly buried the Egyptian in the sand. The next day he saw two slaves arguing and tried to tell them to stick together and protect one another. They said, "Who made you a judge over us? Will you kill us too?" Moses realized his actions were common knowledge and that soon Pharaoh would find out and have to take action against him. He fled for his life toward the far away land of Midian.

He had allowed himself to imagine that the marvelous skills he had acquired in the Temple of the Sun in Egypt could be used to deliver Israel from its cruel bondage, and he had taken action. After all, he knew how the king's court worked and had sway with its key policy makers. They respected his military skills and knew him to be a formidable negotiator. He was in a position to help Israel. He had thought God had put him in this position, had prepared him for it. Why had it not worked? Why did God fail him? This attempt had gone awry, and now he had absolutely no influence, having foolishly misplayed his hand. In truth, he had not thought it through very clearly. Nor had he checked in with the Lord before attempting to do his will.

Weeks later and hundreds of miles away in Midian he sat down by a well, discouraged and confused, and moreover, physically drained after endless days of traveling fast, ever wary for potential captors he knew would be tracking him. Finally, having traveled through small villages in the dark of night a few times and followed well-worn paths during daytime to obliterate any identifiable footprints, he had allowed himself to rest, correctly judging that no one could have successfully trailed him this far. He had thought he was finally doing God's will, but it had all gone wrong. As he would learn, the problem was that his focus was on himself and his own ability rather than on God. In reality God had not rejected him at all—only his inaccurate thinking. If he were to help Israel he would have to learn to rely on God's leadership rather than his own heart, and that would not happen in a day. So unknown to him, he was squarely in the path of the Lord's leading. The years in Midian would be spent *un*-learning the reliance upon himself, and *now learning* to rely upon God's help. Changing how one sees life and the world does not come easily, and it did not come quickly for Moses either. In fact, it would take forty years . . . But at the end of the Lord's slow but real training, training that began in the heart and gradually worked its way into Moses's behavior, he would be ready.

While he sat by a well and agonized over his failures seven young women, all daughters of the priest of Midian, came and drew water for their father's flock. Several local shepherds came and drove the girls and their flocks away and took their water. The girls disputed and tried to fight off the shepherds. Moses watched with interest, then presently stood up and moved closer to them. "Who are you?" challenged one of the shepherds.

"The women drew the water. It's theirs," answered Moses, stepping closer yet. His obviously superb physical conditioning and his years of tough practice for battle had ingrained into him a formidable presence.

"Nobody owns the water," came the insolent response, "and we're taking it."

Pointing to a spot about thirty feet away, Moses said, "You boys better go sit over there while these women let their flock drink THEIR water."

Two of the shepherd men had quietly maneuvered behind Moses while their spokesman said, "We don't like strangers coming in here telling us what to do." He leveled a menacing glare at Moses.

Moses returned his glare for a long moment. The other sensed triumph and prepared to deliver a further challenge. Moses had had enough. He spun around to the two men hiding behind him and, quicker than they could respond, delivered two rapid blows to each that dropped them helplessly to the ground. Then he casually turned around. "Go ahead, take the water," he said to the girls. The others moved closer, preparing to attack, but not one of them stepped to the front. A few of them looked at the two men still lying motionless on the ground. Moses studied them with interest while they considered their next action.

He helped them decide. Directing his attention toward the seven sisters he said, "Your flocks are thirsty. Give them water." The shepherds, rather than waiting around, shuffled off.

Moses drew more water for them. Back home the girls told their father about this Egyptian who helped them. Intrigued and wanting to meet the man, as well as to repay his kindness, he sent for Moses to come and enjoy dinner. The meeting went well, and Moses, having been invited to work for him, accepted his offer. In time the man gave his daughter, Zipporah, to be his wife, and there they lived and raised two sons.

His father-in-law took a keen interest in Moses's telling of the Israelites' plight in Egypt and of their belief in the God of Abraham, Isaac, and Jacob. The Midianites were descendants of Midian, a son born to Abraham and Keturah, the wife he took after Sarah died (Genesis 25: 2). They had retained the stories of God's promises to Abraham. These Midianites in a land hundreds of miles from Egypt, and in a world of idol worshippers, had a similar history and belief in God as Israel, but they had lost track of what had become of Isaac's son, Jacob, who had disappeared into Egypt centuries earlier. Now this man Moses appeared with his strange tales of a huge number of descendants of Abraham in Egypt and of their enslavement. Moreover, they held the same belief that Abraham's God would one day deliver them from bondage and make of them a great nation. They all had heard the same stories! Fascinating indeed!

In the coming days, then months which grew to years, Moses thought about his attempt to help Israel. He thought, too, about things his mother had taught him as a youngster, about God's promise to Abraham to make of him a great nation, about God's prediction that Israel would be a stranger in a land that was not theirs and be afflicted four hundred years, that God would judge that nation and bring Israel out "with great substance" (Genesis 15: 13-14). All of those things were God's doings. He had set the plan in motion and carried it out, just as He said. Israel was certainly under affliction and had not been delivered—yet. But just as certainly, would not God continue to keep his promises and deliver Israel?

Then why had Moses's attempt failed? It was difficult for him to understand why God had not helped him. He had been convinced his parents' God was real and would one day deliver Israel from its bondage and make a great nation of them, bringing blessing to all the world. For a long time Moses was disillusioned. Some days he was bitter against God. Was he to end his days forgotten in this strange place, his life amounting to absolutely nothing? He had had so much wealth and influence in Egypt. On his bitter days if he had had to sum up his life, he would have said that everybody was lying to him. Nothing he had ever believed was true. Egyptian finery was at its core hollow and empty, the puffed-up pride of man that in the end, was still 'every man for himself,' and worse yet, meaningless, finally succumbing to death, the cruel mocker of mankind. His parents' belief in God?—just words. Words that came to nothing. Miserable lives of sorrow and slavery followed by stupid death. It was all pointless and meaningless. He wished he had never been born. How cruel, to get a glimmer of hope in this foul world, only to have it pointlessly extinguished.

Other days he could not shake the belief that the words God had spoken to Abraham, Isaac, and Jacob were true. Had not God kept His word to Abraham that he would have a son? It took twenty-five years of waiting for that son—but look at the number of his descendants now. Still, their plight as slaves was exceedingly difficult to understand. As the years passed, Moses came to realize that his attempt to deliver Israel would have come to nothing. He had no plan, no far-reaching strategy, no idea where to take the Israelites should they escape Egypt, no ability to feed them on the way, no ability to protect them from Pharaoh's army that would undoubtedly chase to recapture them. All he had was anger toward Egypt. Now as he began to look at it, his whole attempt looked embarrassingly foolish. Maybe God had been kind to him by sparing him the embarrassment of starting a huge movement only to have it fail.

Gradually, Moses began to see a larger plan than his limited experience had previously allowed him to see. The battle was larger than it looked. Things his parents had taught him about dark forces at work in the world began to come more clearly into focus. Gradually he was understanding what the Apostle Paul would later put in words in Ephesians chapter six: "For we do not wrestle against flesh and blood, but against principalities, against powers, against the rulers of the darkness of this age, against spiritual wickedness in high places." The conflict had begun in heaven itself with Satan's attempt to overthrow God. It was over in a fraction of a second, and Satan was banished forever from his exalted position in God's kingdom. He now ruled invisibly over this world as the chief ruler of "the darkness of this age." His influence would come to an end at a time known by the Lord when He would consign him permanently to "outer darkness," the logical, far-reaching and ultimate outcome of Satan's decision to overthrow God. Since God was the source of light and life, moving away from Him or attempting to overthrow Him was a move into darkness and death. Death was not an end of existence but rather an end of existence and nourishment in the presence of God. To make matters worse, Satan had chosen it for himself.

Moses's formidable warrior skills would have little effect in this larger battle, the battle between darkness and light, between deception and truth, between death and life. Satan was not only invisible, but he had also organized layers of control, from the lowest demon to the highest dark angel. One cannot fight an enemy he cannot see, one who has vast domains of power and influence. Adam and Eve had unwittingly opened the door to let this enemy into the world simply by believing his fair speeches and deceptive words. They had forsaken God's guidance and now were powerless to undo the effects of evil they had unleashed. Moses began to understand these principles deep in his heart. Scripture would later describe him as the "meekest" of all men, meaning not that he was weak or weak-willed but that he correctly understood his place before God, that he was subject to God and should honor Him. Understanding that, he, more than most people, relied on God's help and nourishment, thus aligning himself with

God's will and allowing His power to flow through him. In that way a seemingly ordinary man was on the side of God himself, whose superiority exceeded in every way that of all powers in the world and, ultimately, of Satan. One of the great truths today is that this same relationship with God is available to all who belong to Christ, who take the time to study His Word, humbly asking for His guidance—and then step out by faith, trusting Him to do as He promised.

It was his parents' faith that had cast him to God's care in the face of Pharaoh's death edict. It was God's influence that had drawn him as an infant from the Nile years before he had any strength of his own. Moses had been too young to understand what led his parents to preserve his life in the face of Pharaoh's command, but he remembered the peace and love and so many kind words he had experienced in their care. Now, as a man, all that was still in his memory, and from his mature perspective he began to understand their actions. Their words about God being true and in control lined up with the promises made to Abraham, Isaac and Jacob, about the emergence of a nation from them, about the four hundred years of captivity to a strange people—all validated their claims about God's promises. His childhood memories made more sense than he ever could have imagined. It was God's guidance that induced Pharaoh's daughter to manipulate her father into unwittingly sparing and caring for the very person he sought to kill. God was displaying his power in barely noticeable details that would one day fit into a larger picture that all the world would see. As Moses pondered all this, his misfortunes began to take on a new light. God had been training him to have a part in this plan. He was not forgotten, nor his life without meaning after all. He laughed out loud in delight the day he realized that. He realized that if God had initiated this whole plan to make a nation out of the descendants of Abraham, God Himself would provide the wherewithal to make it continue to happen. Abraham had listened to God and followed His advice. So had Isaac, Jacob and Joseph. Moses realized that he had not been very good at listening to God. He had believed in him and been willing to act on what he believed, and God had honored his faith by allowing him to fail, painful as that was. His bitterness and disillusionment gradually diminished as he realized that, if God's will were to be accomplished, it would take believers who were willing to listen to Him, learn about Him, and follow His words.

Often powerful, influential people in the world become true believers, but when they do they need to take the position of a new child of God or, as scripture put it, "a babe in Christ." They have the "wisdom of the world" and great influence but not the "spiritual wisdom" that only comes as a result of spending time with the Lord through learning and comprehending His Word. Moses had been like that. He had been raised a prominent part of the elite ruling class of Egypt. In his heart he acknowledged the Lord, but his worldly training led him to act as he did in his first attempt to help Israel. He could not distinguish how to differentiate between the two schools of thought under which he had been raised. He gradually realized that Egypt's view of the world was different from Israel's view, but what he should do was not clear to him. From his heart he had to come to that painful place in which he admitted that he had been (like the rest of us) hasty and self-willed, even self-absorbed, and did not really know how to follow the Lord. One could almost say Moses was a slow learner because it took him forty years in Midian to "unlearn" Egypt's wisdom and re-learn God's. When God was through with him he knew from the heart how to be the man scripture would describe, how to follow Him instead of his own self-centered heart.

As a planted seed grew unseen under cover in the earth, silently expanding its life, reaching out roots and forming a stem, many days before it ever broke through the surface into the light of day, so Moses had to spend time alone with God, nourished day by day, where no one saw, before he could walk back into Egypt and be God's servant. God wanted his heart. "Surely you desire truth in the inner parts; you teach me wisdom in the inmost place . . . you do not delight in sacrifice, or I would bring it; you do not take pleasure in burnt offerings. The sacrifices of God are a broken spirit; a broken and contrite heart, O God, you will not despise" (Psalm 51: 6, 16-17). A broken spirit and a contrite heart? That was it? Was that all God was looking for in each of us? It took Moses many years to become that of his own free will. So too with us. Our strong points and skills are the areas where we have trouble letting God lead us. They become our weaknesses in the spiritual realm because we will not listen to God in those areas we are so sure we are right. Some of us are so strong-willed we cannot let anyone tell us what to do. We think we can do it better than everybody else, including God. So He patiently waits until we are ready. When He allows us to fail (because we will not listen), He is training us. As painful as failure is to a proud person, it is a necessary step in our spiritual growth, in our learning to see ourselves more accurately—as God sees us. Only then do we see how much we need His help, and only then do we begin to realize that He truly cares for us and will work in our lives, even though we are not perfect. Some learn very quickly to allow Him to lead. Most do not. Time alone with the Lord is never wasted, no matter how busy we think we are, and is what makes the difference—as Moses would learn. In time he relaxed and began to simply wait for the Lord to show him things. And on a certain day, before he even realized he was ready, the Lord called out to him.

CHAPTER 10

THE BURNING BUSH

(Exodus 3-4)

At the same time back in Egypt, "the children of Israel sighed by reason of the bondage . . . and their cry came up to God . . . and God heard their groaning and remembered His covenant with Abraham, with Isaac, and with Jacob. He looked upon the children of Israel, and God had respect to them" (Exodus 2: 23-25). This touching verse shows the Lord's heart toward Israel and, in reality, toward all the world. Humans trapped in misery of their own making and unable to help themselves were "looked upon" by Him, and He "had respect" for them. He saw them abusing and enslaving each other and had determined from the moment they erred (even before that, from "before the foundation of the earth") (I Peter 1: 20; John 17: 5, 24) to set them free from that servitude. He cared for them and would help them back to a right relationship with Him in a way they simply could not do. He had announced that plan to Abraham, referred back to it often, and had every intention of carrying it out.

And so it happened on a day in Midian, Moses was tending the flock for his father-in-law in a wilderness area when an "angel of the Lord appeared to him in a flame of fire out of the midst of a bush." When Moses saw from afar and "wondered" at the sight, he marveled that, though on fire, the bush was not consumed. Intrigued, he moved closer, but as he approached he began to fear, as though something far more powerful than himself loomed ahead. Little did he know that the Lord was ever near all his life, closer than a heartbeat. His power, like a waterfall or a frightening thunderclap, could destroy in an instant, and so the Lord shields us from it. Suddenly Moses knew he was helpless and terror overtook him. At that moment a voice called out to him and said, "Moses . . . Moses."

Moses, nearly unable to speak, said, "Here I am."

The Lord said, "Take off your shoes. The place you are standing is holy ground. I am the God of your father, the God of Abraham, the God of Isaac, the God of Jacob." It was all TRUE! The God his mother and father had told him about, the God all Israel spoke of, was speaking *to him*! Had God come to kill him for his evil heart? Was today the end of his life? The many gods of Egypt, which Moses knew about so well from his time in Pharaoh's court, never took an interest in humans or spoke to them like this. But today the God of his Israelite parents, the God of Abraham, Isaac, and Jacob, was speaking to him. "I have heard the cry of my people in Egypt, and I know their sorrows. I am come down to deliver them out of the hand of Egypt and bring them to a good land and large, to a land flowing with milk and honey. And now I will send *you* to Pharaoh to bring my people out of Egypt." Moses, who had tried before and failed so miserably, was now being *sent* by God back to Egypt! Little did he realize that he would be like that burning bush—the very power of God working through him while he, as a fallible human, was not the real power—nor was he consumed.

Moses, in stunned disbelief, said, "Who am I, that I should go to Pharaoh and bring Israel out of Egypt?" He remembered the last time he had tried to help Israel, when he had been so sure of himself. His own people misunderstood and rejected him. Now years later, Moses had lost his arrogant belief in himself, the pride of Egypt gradually pushed away by a deep and growing sense of God's power and presence in the world and in his own heart. He had taken a step on that disastrous day toward believing God and had stumbled badly. He was no more special than anyone else, but . . . he had dared to believe God, as had his parents, as had Abraham, and now God had chosen *him* to carry out a task. What would be different this time? Why would God speak to him? And why would Israel listen to *him*?

And God said, "Certainly *I* will be with you. You will see when you bring the people to this very mountain to meet with Me." That mountain he was near was Sinai. The step he had taken so long ago had led him here to Midian. Though steeped in the world's wisdom, he also believed in the trueness of Israel's God—who had been working in his heart the whole time. Moses had been gradually learning to rely on God rather than on himself. But he was still learning and did not yet understand the reality of God's power nor of His willingness to work in the hearts of men. God was pulling him onward, as He does with all believers, "drawing him out" of himself. Now Moses was so humbled he was afraid to go, and it was God's reasoning with him that began to put the last forty years' experience into focus. In so many little things Moses had learned the possibility of failure and had gradually shifted his focus off himself and onto the Lord as his helper, his real strength. He did not realize how much his thinking had changed until God reminded him. When he said, "Certainly *I* will be with you," a whole new, larger world opened. It was no longer Moses doing the work but God. What had been impossible before was now a certainty (at least in God's view), and Moses was beginning to understand. God had been preparing him, and the failure, discouragement, and hardships made sense when seen in the light of God's larger plan to deliver Israel. Moses actually rejoiced to realize his life was not a waste and had meaning he had never fully seen before.

Still, he balked. "When I come to the people and say, 'The God of your fathers has sent me' and they ask, 'What is his name?' what shall I say?" questioned Moses.

And God said to tell them, "I AM THAT I AM. Tell them *I AM* has sent you." Not exactly a real clear answer in Moses' estimation. But God said that would make an impression on them. Continuing, He said, "Gather the elders of Israel and tell them the God of their fathers appeared to you and has seen your affliction, and He will bring you up out of Egypt and into a good land. And they will listen to you and go with you to Pharaoh when you tell him to let the people go. I know the king of Egypt will *not* let you go. Therefore I will smite Egypt with my wonders, and after that he *will* let you go. Moreover I will give you favor in the sight of the Egyptians, and they will give you gold and silver and jewels and clothing just to make you leave. You will not go out empty. Egypt will pay for your slavery" (Exodus 3: 1-22).

Wait a minute—"I AM" is his name? Puzzling and of great interest at the same time. What did he mean? I AM? . . . I AM everything? One day Jesus would say, " *I am* the way, the truth, and the life. No man comes to the Father but by me." When He was in the garden of Gethsemane and men sought to capture Him for His execution, they asked if He were Jesus. He replied, "*I am* he," (the same 'I am' he had said to Moses) and the power of that word blazed out for an instant, driving His would-be captors, in helpless submission, to the ground. Jesus looked like the ordinary man they had seen teaching in Jerusalem, but where had that power come from? It was the power of the eternal Godhead residing in Him. That they persisted in capturing and arresting Him was amazing. It could never have happened had He not willingly submitted himself to their cruel will. No doubt many of them wondered at their actions in the days following.

"I AM the creator of all there is. I AM the creator of you and all people. I AM the provider of all you will ever need. I AM the one who takes care of you—for eternity." That is what He meant. The essence of God in two words that everybody could understand. They would believe Moses because *God* was sending him, and deep in their hearts his words would strike a chord they would *hear*. I AM who you need to know. I AM who you need to believe. God told him that the elders would indeed listen to him. They would be convinced and drawn to him because of the power of God's words. The whole world, including Egypt, lay in darkness and layer upon layer of deception. God was reaching in, into the very heart of darkness, and was sending this man Moses as His human ambassador. Nothing could penetrate the depth of that deception in Egypt. Nothing, that is, but the Creator's words, words that sprang to life in the fertile soil of the believing human heart. They had power to pierce anything and to reach into the stoniest of hearts. "All who belong to me will come to me," had said Jesus with an air of assurance that would never be overruled. Reaching individual hearts was God's purpose in all ages. Now He would perform a work that would convince Israel, Egypt, and all the world. "And the Egyptians shall know that *I am* the Lord, when I stretch forth my hand upon Egypt, and bring out the children of Israel from among them" (Exodus 7: 5). God was not destroying Egypt but shining light on their beliefs that they might be rescued from the deception brought in by Adam and Eve.

Moses would go. Yet, as the impossibility of the task loomed in his mind, fear and a doubt rose again, and he protested, "They will not believe me and will say, The Lord has not appeared to you." Moses had lost his arrogant faith in himself but still could not quite understand the reality that God's power would be with him, though God had said it.

And the Lord said to him, "What is in your hand? And he said, A rod. And God said, Cast it on the ground." He did and it became a serpent. Moses fled from it. Then God said, "Put out your hand, and take it by the tail." Beginning to trust, Moses put out his hand and caught it, and it became a rod again in his hand.

Still, Moses protested a few more times and finally agreed to go. Requesting permission from his father-in-law to return to Egypt, which he granted, he readied his wife and their two sons to travel. The Lord told him, "Go, return to Egypt, for all the men which sought your life are dead." They began the journey, and Moses "took the rod of God in his hand." As he journeyed the Lord told him that in Egypt he should perform the "wonders" He had shown him before Pharaoh but that Pharaoh would not let the people go. He told him to tell Pharaoh, "Israel is my son, my firstborn, and if you refuse to let him go I will slay your son, your firstborn." Pharaoh had been warned. Would he humble himself before God?

Hebrews 11: 24-27 gives a New Testament summary of it: "By faith Moses, when he became of age, refused to be called the son of Pharaoh's daughter, choosing rather to suffer affliction with the people of God, than to enjoy the passing pleasures of sin, esteeming the reproach of Christ greater riches than the treasures in Egypt: for he looked to the reward. By faith he forsook Egypt, not fearing the wrath of the king, for he endured, as seeing him who is invisible."

CHAPTER 11

MOSES RETURNS TO EGYPT

(Exodus 4-5)

The last time he was in Egypt he was running for his life, and the experience was not pleasant. The long-forgotten memory rose up unexpectedly with fresh pain. Only now, forty years later, Moses put that thought in a different perspective. He was journeying to the land that had enslaved his people and would have killed him, first in the river and then when he fled. This time he was traveling in response to words from the God of Israel, whose words had brought into existence that nation—and before that, the world itself!

As he approached Egypt, it seemed remote to him that anyone would even remember him. God had said his brother Aaron, at age eighty-three, was still alive, so he would remember. Finally reaching Egypt, he told the Israelites that God had heard their cry and was about to deliver them. Then he performed in their sight the signs God had given him. They remembered him and his sudden disappearance years ago, and as the Lord had said, accepted his words. "And the people believed, and when they heard that the Lord had visited the children of Israel, and that he had looked upon their affliction, they bowed their heads and worshipped" (Exodus 4: 31).

Journeying toward Egypt Moses remembered the awe-inspiring statues and pyramids the Egyptians had built. Indeed, the skills of that empire would reflect in the structures they left behind. Their ability to accurately measure precise dimensions for extremely large structures and to set large foundations that would remain level for centuries, then to orient them to true north, in preparation for huge buildings and monuments, cannot be exceeded to this day. We cannot figure out how they cut with such precision and moved into place the multi-ton stones of the pyramids, fitted so perfectly they needed no mortar. Greek and Roman empires displayed similar levels of artistry and skill, but they came to power over a thousand years later.

Pharaoh's magnificence was overpowering. The fabric of his robes was of a finer, smoother weave than most people ever saw. Vibrant and clear colors reflected life and power. His manner was not that of a rigid, disciplined soldier. Rather, he was relaxed, and yet somehow strength radiated from his very being. Like a huge tiger, he moved smoothly, unhurriedly, confident that what he set out to do he would accomplish. One knew all the power of a kingdom and its army resided in this man who held it comfortably under his control, this man who had triumphed over all others to gain this kingship. His manner was direct and alert, disarming, actually, as he observed these two men who brazenly dared enter his court uninvited. All who stood before Pharaoh endured his scrutiny longer than they wanted, while he studied them. Even the strongest men grew uncomfortable at such moments. Moses had been here before in this intimidating court, under an equally intimidating monarch, his foster father. He had lived here and known firsthand its ways and intrigues. Walking in here uninvited and unescorted flaunted every court manner, was an affront, and could certainly invite instant death. He knew, nay, had seen himself, that Pharaoh with a certain barely perceptible nod, unnoticeable to all but a few elite and constantly alert guards, could signal death for the one standing in front of him. Within seconds that foolish person had forfeited his life as final judgment fell upon him. His lifeless body never hit the ground, being caught as it fell and carried out with practiced skill, never soiling Pharaoh's polished granite floor.

Today he and his brother, Aaron, had walked into the headquarters of the most powerful nation on earth, perhaps the worldly headquarters of Satan himself as he chose such a place to work because of its far-reaching influence. The world at large was oblivious to this meeting, but at this time the most consequential events in the world were playing out.

Exodus 6: 26 simply says, "These are that Aaron and Moses to whom the Lord said, 'Bring out the children of Israel from the land of Egypt' . . . these are they which spoke to Pharaoh king of Egypt, to bring out the children of Egypt, these are that Moses and Aaron." Moses was no longer hiding out in Midian. Further, the Lord told Moses, "See I have made you a god to Pharaoh, and Aaron your brother shall be your prophet . . . but Pharaoh shall not listen to you, that I may lay my hand upon Egypt, and bring out the children of Israel from among them." Moses was eighty years old and Aaron eighty-three when they spoke to Pharaoh.

And now here stood Moses in front of a man whose very aura threatened instant destruction and whom he had just insulted. His incensed scowl and piercing attention demanded an explanation. The memory of all this power flooded back to him in a moment, only now as he had approached Pharaoh he had felt something new in the court, something he had never experienced before. Amid the splendor and dignity of this room there loomed a darkness, not overly noticeable, perhaps more felt than seen, but it was there, nonetheless. Why had he not seen it before? Maybe it was because he was part of this whole system the last time he had been here. His immediate reaction was fear. But there was no escape. He could not run, could not disappear. He was here, a moment in destiny from which he could not escape. Was there some way he could simply vanish? Another thought grew in his mind. The God who had "drawn him out" of the Nile, the God who had "drawn" Abraham out of the Chaldean empire, the God who had drawn Adam out of nothingness, had brought *him here* and was with him now, at this very moment, indeed, had sent him. Pharaoh fastened a chilling gaze upon him. He did not look down his nose at Moses as some arrogant leaders might. He looked straight on, as a fighter would, unafraid but sizing him up. He had fought his way to the pinnacle in Egypt and did not fear conflict as most others did. Long ago he had accepted frequent challenges as part of maintaining his position, and that attitude rendered him always ready. He would be king or die—an outlook that carried him beyond the willingness of all challengers to keep up with him so far. As he viewed these "pretenders" in front of him he searched his memory for clues about who these two might be. That he had even allowed them to continue their entrance into his presence was out of the ordinary. What had prompted him to do that? he wondered. Then he remembered his father having years ago mentioned the strange story of an Israelite child his daughter had found floating in a basket in the river. He had allowed the child to live—and even raised him—in his court. That child when grown had created some kind of disturbance and suddenly vanished. His father's surveillance teams had never found a trace of him. Could this man standing in front of him be that person? If so, Pharaoh was now dealing with a problem caused by his father's lax control of a situation that should never have been allowed to develop. A quiet anger rose in a deep place in his heart. He would never have allowed such nonsense.

Pharaoh studied the man's face. It revealed no trace of servitude or fear so common among Israelite slaves. His gray eyes looked dark, reminding him of rock, steady and unmovable, an impression simply there like a mountain. How could anyone stand before Pharaoh without some hint of fear of his awesome power revealing itself? This man was different. Pharaoh had been able to bend every comer to bow to his will, but something about this man's complete lack of fear or awe indicated no intention of bowing to him. It irritated Pharaoh.

In Moses' heart the fear that at first had bubbled up in his consciousness evaporated as he returned the gaze of this tyrant. The "King of kings" had sent him here. If that "King" wanted him dead, he would die here and now, and it would be exactly right, a strange comfort to Moses in the throes of a frightful moment. God would have allowed it, and no power on earth could stop it. Moses relaxed in that. But . . . if the "King" wanted him to live . . . no power in heaven or earth could stop that either, not even Pharaoh with his elite warrior guardians. With that realization, every last shred of fear fled from Moses's suddenly powerful persona. That moment forty years earlier when he had fled for his life after trying to help the Israelite slave took on new significance as he realized anew that God had been with him amidst that failure. The confusion over the purpose of his life cleared and came into focus. The seemingly small detail of the story of Abraham's servant realizing God was with him in the moment when he found beautiful Rebekah, the bride-to-be for Isaac, a mother to Israel, taught how God guided in every day's details. That servant had taught him to realize that God was with him in ordinary moments and answered the simplest prayers of his heart, had taught him to know how to walk with God.

God had shaped him for this moment, and here he stood, his presence projecting power, which now spoke to each participant standing in that court. Even the guards winced. Pharaoh did not know it yet, but the strength of the most powerful empire in the world was about to be overruled. As Moses looked into Pharaoh's firm, unblinking eyes he too saw hardness, like flint. A different Pharaoh than the one that had raised him all those years ago, he possessed the same strength and implacableness. But behind his father's strength lay a certain kindness that Moses had seen him reveal, on a few occasions, especially toward him. Peering long into this Pharaoh's eyes Moses saw no hint of kindness nor mercy.

He recalled his experience at the burning bush. Surpassing power radiated and compelled attention. In the voice he had heard certainty unlike anything he had ever heard before. Words spoken by God carried that effect. They originated in eternity and conveyed an understanding to Moses that whatever He said was true to its core and could never be countermanded. The seeming reality of the man-imagined gods of Egypt evaporated like so much smoke compared to the power of the true God. The One behind that voice was vastly more assured and intimidating—astoundingly powerful and able to carry out his will—than this Pharaoh standing in front of him, this Pharaoh who was, in reality, just a man masquerading as someone far more important than he really was. In this excruciating moment it was Pharaoh who grew uneasy at being studied so intensely by this man, this insolent, arrogant man, this man who dared return his fear inspiring gaze. Moses' presence held him captive and would not let him go, and Pharaoh knew that Moses was seeing into his soul more deeply than anyone had ever dared look—and perceived the truth that he was an imposter. Suddenly he hated Moses. Brewing anger flared to rage, but before he could react, Aaron's voice boomed clear and loud, smothering all other impressions in the room. "Thus says the Lord God of Israel, Let my people go," then slowly and quietly, "that they may hold a feast to *me* in the wilderness."

Pharaoh, having just been intimidated, masked his emotions and rendered his face as inscrutable as a stone. Murder flashed in his eyes for a brief instant, and Moses caught it, the ancient hatred of Satan himself ruling in this man who dared exalt himself, and who now with withering scorn said, "Who is the Lord, that I should obey his voice to let Israel go? I know not the Lord, neither will I let Israel go." With the words of his own mouth he revealed the true thoughts of his stubborn *human* heart, words for which he would give account in the future as he stood before God's throne at the last judgment. The absolute foolishness of his proud arrogance would stun him. But on this day Pharaoh ruled and would give no honor to God

With even more contempt he added, "Why are you keeping the people from their burdens? You have too much time and are idle." He had turned the tables by mounting an attack. Instructing his officers to order the taskmasters to demand of the slaves that they find their own straw to make bricks, but still deliver the same number of completed bricks, he effectively doubled their workload. Moses and Aaron turned and walked out of the court. Unexcused. Alive. God's message had been delivered. The guards in the room had seen Pharaoh intimidate and overpower all who dared challenge his authority. This time they were not so sure he had succeeded.

When the people could not gather straw *plus* make the same amount of bricks, the taskmasters beat them, and consequently the slaves found Moses and Aaron and poured out their frustration—and stirred themselves quickly to downright anger. "You are not helping us. You have made our lives worse!"

Distraught, Moses sought the Lord, saying, "Why have you done this evil to me to send me here? The people have not been delivered. Instead their lives are made worse."

Then the Lord told Moses, "Now you will see what I will do to Pharaoh, for with a strong hand will I drive them out of his land. *I am the*

Lord! I made a promise to Abraham, and I will bring you out from under the bondage of Egypt, and with great judgments upon them I will take you to myself and be to you your God and will bring you into the land I promised." What is more, God told him to tell Pharaoh, "Israel is my son, my firstborn, and I say to you, Let my son go that he may serve me. If you refuse I will slay your son, your firstborn" (Exodus 4: 22-23). God would do to Pharaoh what Pharaoh did to God's children, perfect justice that he could have escaped had he honored God. Overly impressed with himself, Pharaoh did not take God seriously.

CHAPTER 12

CONTESTS WITH PHARAOH

(Exodus 6-11)

Moses told all this to the Israelites, but they refused to hear him "for anguish of spirit and bitterness for the cruel bondage" under which they lived. "This is what we get for trusting you!" they jabbed, and it stung.

Nevertheless, the Lord told Moses to go and tell Pharaoh again to let Israel go out of his land. Moses said, "The Israelites will not even listen to me; how then will Pharaoh listen to me?"

He reminded Moses what He had told him before. "See, I have made you a god to Pharaoh, and Aaron your brother shall be your prophet. Speak of all that I tell you to Aaron and he shall speak to Pharaoh that he send Israel out of his land. Pharaoh will resist you, but I will begin to show my signs and wonders in the land of Egypt. The Egyptians shall know that I am the Lord when I stretch forth my hand upon Egypt and bring out the children of Israel from among them." So Moses and Aaron returned to Pharaoh and made demand.

With contempt Pharaoh asked to see a sign. Aaron threw down his rod before Pharaoh and his servants, and it became a serpent! Unimpressed, Pharaoh called his wise men and sorcerers, and they did the same with their enchantments, each casting down his rod which, likewise, became serpents! This seems incredible, but evidently these sorcerers tapped into Satanic power (which the Lord allowed on several occasions in history) to do this. It was an indication of the true depth of the struggle playing out here, a struggle between the powers of darkness and of light, of disorder versus order, of opposition by Satan himself to God. The Apostle Paul described such situations with his words, ". . . we wrestle not against flesh and blood, but against principalities, against powers, against the rulers of the darkness of this world, against spiritual wickedness in high places (Ephesians 6:12). The contest between Pharaoh and Moses was larger than it appeared and involved powers far beyond mere earthly powers.

Then Aaron's rod swallowed up the other rods! Pharaoh, so consumed with maintaining his power, could not appreciate what he had just seen and was not moved. He chased out Moses and Aaron. Still alive!

The God of creation had made a simple request to Pharaoh. He had the power to crush Pharaoh on the spot but chose to appeal to his will instead and give him the opportunity to comply, to bow to superior power and wisdom. How Pharaoh responded was up to him. It was a test, and God was giving Pharaoh every opportunity to take his rightful place before the One who had created him. Pharaoh had made his decision. He was not accustomed to anyone commanding him.

God told Moses, "Go to Pharaoh in the morning when he goes out to the river to refresh himself. Stand at its edge as he approaches and say, "The Lord God of the Hebrews has sent me to you to say, 'Let my people go.' If you refuse you will know that I am the Lord when I strike the water with the rod in my hand. The water will turn to blood, the streams, the rivers, the ponds, all the pools of water, even the water in wood and stone vessels, and all the fish will die.." Moses and Aaron spoke these words to Pharaoh and his attendants, held out the rod, and all the waters turned to blood! The Egyptians worshipped the river and its water as the givers of life, and God was displaying to all His power as vastly superior to that of the river. He could control and change it at will. The fish died, the river stank, and no one could drink its water. Pharaoh's magicians did so also, and he dismissed Moses and Aaron as unimportant, meaningless subjects of his. Seven days it continued. All of Egypt was affected, and word leaked out about the Israelite Moses's confrontations with Pharaoh. All of Egypt knew, and now the neighboring nations began to notice. Egypt's leadership and their gods were beginning to look foolish, and it was becoming difficult to hide. Pharaoh took none of this to heart and ignored the request to set Israel free—as if he owned those people and could do as he pleased.

God sent Moses again, this time to tell Pharaoh to let the people go or he would bring frogs upon the land, frogs that Egypt worshipped as gods. He would send so many they would invade houses, jump into their cupboards and cooking pots, everywhere, even their beds. So frogs covered the land until people hated them. Pharaohs' magicians showed their power by duplicating the miracle. As if Egypt needed more frogs! Pharaoh called for Moses and Aaron to pray to the Lord to take the frogs away. So they prayed, and the frogs died where they were. The Egyptians gathered them into piles and the land stank. Egypt was reaping the fruit of Pharaoh's decisions. Still no cooperation from Pharaoh. In his own eyes he was a god, and the power over nature with which he was confronted—the frogs, the river—did not pierce his consciousness. "Fools pass on and are punished . . . The fool rages and is confident" (Proverbs 22: 3; 14: 16).

So God told Moses to stretch out his rod and strike the dust of the earth. It became lice over all the land and crawled upon man and beast. Again the magicians tried to do so with their enchantments—but they could not! They told Pharaoh, "This is the finger of God." Imagine that! The magicians knew. Pharaoh refused. He never admitted to anything.

So God stepped up the pressure and the next day sent Moses to tell Pharaoh, "Let my people go. If you will not I will send swarms of flies upon you, your servants and your lands, into your homes and over all the ground. I will sever the land of Goshen where my people live, that no flies be there to the end that you and *all Egypt* may know that I am the Lord in the midst of the earth." So the Lord sent flies, unbelievable amounts of flies, into Pharaoh's house, his servants' houses, and all the houses of Egypt—except the Israelites' houses. All of Egypt was experiencing firsthand the power of the God of Israel, the *true* God of all the world. Pharaoh appeared to give in and begged Moses to pray to his God to get rid of the flies. He agreed to let Israel go but not to the wilderness they had requested, a compromise. Then Moses told Pharaoh, "I will go out from you and pray that the swarms of flies would depart, only let Pharaoh not deal deceitfully any more in not letting the people go." God destroyed all the flies as Pharaoh wished. Every single fly disappeared, but Pharaoh changed his mind and would not let the people go. God had shown his power over even nuisance flies. These situations revealed the stubbornness of Pharaoh's heart. Each of these plagues was an opportunity to humble himself before the Lord. Pharaoh could make all people in the land submit to him, but he was not God. He should have had respect for God's superior power, but he WOULD NOT, even in the face of God's triumph over any force the world possessed.

A fifth plague would come if Pharaoh would not relent, one that would fall upon the cattle in the field, horses, camels, asses, oxen and sheep of Egypt, and kill them. None in Israel would die. In reality, God could have killed all the Egyptians. He had that power. Instead He gave Pharaoh another chance to escape destruction. To signal them that judgment was coming, every plague got worse. God was showing the world not only His right to judge but His power to judge. An implicit message was that all mankind was destined for judgment, and God had the power to bring it to pass. One day each human would die. No possible way existed to escape it and the judgment that would ultimately follow, just as Israel had no possible way to escape the slavery of Egypt. "It is appointed to man once to die, and after this the judgment" would later be written in Hebrews 9: 27. Pharaoh and Egypt could give in now and escape the judgment. That was not what happened.

God repeated His request to Pharaoh, adding that if he refused He would send a plague upon all Egypt's cattle, horses, asses, camels, oxen and sheep. The Lord appointed a set time, saying, "Tomorrow I will do this thing." So it happened on the next day as He said, except that "of the cattle of Israel nothing died." Pharaoh found out that Israel was spared, but he still refused to let them go.

So God told Moses to take ashes from a furnace in the sight of Pharaoh and scatter them toward heaven. This was the first plague to directly affect humans, as it became boils upon man and beast—deep, horribly painful sores. Now the magicians could not stand before Moses because of the boils. Pharaoh, instead of giving in, resisted even more stubbornly.

These plagues constituted a systematic dismantling of the faulty thinking of the Egyptian people and of the powerlessness of the idols they mistakenly worshipped. God was appealing to their reason and calling the Egyptians and all the world back to Himself as much as He was reaching out to Israel. Many times when He sent Moses to Pharaoh He included the words "that all the world may know that I am God."

The seventh plague would be hail mixed with fire and rain. According to Exodus 9: 13-18 the Lord told Moses, "Rise up early in the morning, and stand before Pharaoh, and say, 'Thus says the Lord, Let my people go that they may serve me. I will send all my plagues upon your heart and upon your servants and upon your people, that you may know there is none like me in all the earth . . . in very deed for this cause I have raised you up, to show in you my power, and that my name may be declared through all the earth. As yet you exalt yourself against my people by not letting them go.'" God was graciously allowing this man who, in reality, was no more special than anyone else and who, like them, was completely in the hold of death and judgment, another opportunity to respect and honor God's authority and escape judgment. "Tomorrow about this time I will cause it to rain a very grievous hail such as has not been in Egypt since its beginning until now." Imagine Pharaoh's thinking process over the next twenty-four hours. His authority was being challenged. Who were these upstarts anyhow, Moses and Aaron? Low-life slaves, not worthy to be called humans. Why had he not killed them right at the beginning? They had brought so much misery to the entire nation of Egypt. All this trouble was their fault. River turned to blood, frogs, lice, flies, death of cattle, boils, then hail to destroy crops and cattle.

God advised Egypt to gather their cattle into barns for protection, as any man or beast in the field would die by the hail. Many of Pharaoh's servants and subjects heeded the warning and were protected. Those who regarded God's words as empty talk ignored the warning. The next day Moses held up his rod toward heaven, and the Lord sent thunder and hail and fire that ran along the ground. Fire mingled with the hail as it beat mercilessly all the land of Egypt, destroying man and beast in the field, the growing crops and even trees. There was no hail like that since Egypt became a nation! In the land of Goshen where Israel abode there was no hail.

Pharaoh called for Moses and said, "I have sinned this time. Pray to the Lord to stop this, and I will let you go." Yet when the Lord stopped the rain, hail, and thunder Pharaoh changed his mind and would not let Israel go. Pharaoh's confession was superficial and not a true admission that he had been defying God by pressing his own will over God's.

The Lord told Moses He had suffered Pharaoh's display of self-centered ego to reveal the depth of the rebellion in his heart and to show His own mercy in allowing him and all Egypt one opportunity after another to relent and give in to God. Further, Israel could tell their children and grandchildren what things God had done in Egypt, that they too could know that God is the true Lord.

God would not lose this contest. He sent Moses the eighth time to Pharaoh to say, "How long will you refuse to humble yourself before me? Let my people go. If you refuse I will bring locusts to your coasts, and they will cover the earth so that the ground cannot be seen. Anything that escaped the hail will be eaten. No one has ever seen locusts like this." Moses turned and went out from Pharaoh. Pharaoh's servants said, "How long will this man be a snare to us? Let them go. Do you not yet know that Egypt is destroyed?" Pharaoh called them back, offered a compromise and then drove them out.

It could be argued that God *forced* Pharaoh to believe Him. But careful thinking could arrive at a different conclusion. Since God is the Creator of the world and its occupants, He has the right to judge it and make changes. He has the right (and the power) to pass judgment on each person and to deal with each as He sees fit. Until that day came He gave many, many opportunities for Pharaoh to honor him with respect for who He is. God could have destroyed Pharaoh on any of these occasions, but He did not. One day the opportunity for Pharaoh to humbly come to God of his own free will would cease. He would bow and believe God's power but it would be too late. He would see how graciously God had been calling him—too late.

When the locusts came the surface of the earth was dark with the black backs of the locusts, and every green thing, all the crops earlier beaten down by hail, in all Egypt were eaten. In Goshen where Israel lived no hail fell and no locusts came. Many Egyptians saw this, and Pharaoh's demonic hold over them was beginning to crack. They no doubt wondered how long it would be before God might step up the punishment to the point of killing them, and they began to fear.

A ninth plague brought three days of thick darkness over the land, so frightening that no one dared leave home. At the end Pharaoh offered to let them go—on his terms. An argument ensued, ending with Pharaoh driving them out of his sight, saying, "Take heed you see my face no more. In the day you see my face you will DIE!"

Moses weathered the onslaught and in a soft voice answered, "You have spoken well, I will see your face again no more." The power of God residing in Moses rendered him bold and deadly accurate in his prediction. Pharaoh was not yet wise enough to be terrified of God's power.

The Tenth and Final Plague — The Death Angel

The Lord said to Moses, "Yet will I bring one more plague on Pharaoh and upon Egypt. Afterwards he will let you go. In fact he will thrust you out altogether." Now Moses had grown very great in the land of Egypt, in the sight of Pharaoh's servants, and in the sight of the people (even greater than he had been forty years earlier when, as a favored son of the previous Pharaoh, he had tried to help Israel).

He told the Israelites, "Here is what the Lord has said: 'About midnight I will go into the midst of Egypt, and all the firstborn in Egypt shall die, from the firstborn of Pharaoh that sits on the throne, to the firstborn of the maidservant behind the mill, to the firstborn of beasts. And there will be a great cry throughout all the land of Egypt, such as never was, nor will ever be. But against the children of Israel will not even a dog move his tongue, that all may know how the Lord puts a difference between the Egyptians and Israel.' Further, Pharaoh's servants will come to us bowing and begging us to leave. Then will we go" (Exodus 11).

Pharaoh, this "king," was resisting a man who was sent to him by God. He was resisting the message sent to him through these overpowering plagues. Pharaoh was nowhere near as great an individual as he fancied himself and would do well to humble himself before the

Lord—before it would be forever too late. "God resists the proud, but gives grace to the humble," states I Peter 5:5, and God had given countless opportunities to this man—who was listening to his own inflated pride more than he listened to anything else—to humble himself. He was continuing in a very dangerous direction and God's dealings with him were about to change. "He who is often rebuked and hardens his neck, will suddenly be destroyed, and that without remedy" (Proverbs 29:1). A day comes for all who ignore God when opportunity is past and judgment falls.

Back in his court Pharaoh called for his wise men for one grand-scale effort to get rid of Moses and all this trouble he caused. The darkness that still smothered the land rendered it difficult for these men even to meet. They were to pray to ALL the gods at once and even to the one true god behind all of them, the one who never bothered to get involved in human activities because they were not worth his time. Moses could never stand up to all these gods at once.

Pharaoh's wise men, many of them visibly frightened and waxing uncharacteristically bold with their advice to Pharaoh, reminded him that every single one of those gods had been soundly defeated and exposed as powerless before the God of Moses. There would be no real strength in the uniting together of a large number of defeated gods. Then a division appeared between the wise men as one dared say, "We know these gods are only pretend anyhow, with no magical power or intelligence to share with us. I learned *that* as a child playing with frogs and swatting flies. They are stupid creatures. Our ancestors conjured their supernatural powers out of their own imaginations." No one had ever dared to speak such things before. Many in their hearts knew this to be the truth, but none was ever brave enough to speak what he really thought. It could mean death, and many chose compromise over truth. Even Pharaoh's most honored advisors, honored with wealth and respected position, were held captive by fear. The splendor of this magnificent kingdom was a hollow shell of pretense, another deception of Satan, who liked to portray himself as an "angel of light." Generations far into the future would revere the majesty of Egypt, not knowing the inner emptiness of a people that, like their ancestor, Ham, had wandered far afield from the true God. Now this God Moses claimed to represent had destroyed the power of these so-called gods and was intensifying the pressure. He was about to kill people. Where would it end? "Would we all be dead?"

"Enough," thundered Pharaoh with a rage suddenly frightening—terrifying, really—in its ferocity. "Kill that man!" he ordered to no one in particular, intending that the guards move in and act. Asking a guard to kill a wise man was like asking him to kill Pharaoh, his own king, the giver of life. Tension escalated in the room as the guards stood paralyzed with fear, afraid to even look at each other. Pharaoh glared at them all. Never had anyone defied him so openly and vilified the gods. They may have questioned some of his ideas, but it was always delicately, with a great deal of respect, and seemingly only as a helpful suggestion for Pharaoh to consider. Certainly no one had ever dared question the "reality" of the gods before. Pharaoh's divine right to rule flowed from the belief that the gods were real and gave their power to the king. To prevent this opposition from gaining strength, Pharaoh snatched a sword from one of the guards and ran it himself through the heart of the wise man—and then cowered the determination of all those in his presence with a glare straight into each one's eyes that said, "Who is next?" His ferocity shocked. No one moved a muscle. No one spoke a word. All, including Pharaoh, were stretched to the breaking point. This man from Midian had troubled the land. Egypt lay ruined, with crops destroyed, fields ravaged by grasshoppers, cattle dead of disease, people diseased. The gods Egypt worshipped, the creatures and forces, absolutely powerless before Moses's God, were not gods. They were ideas, deceptions of the mind fabricated in the hearts of individuals not interested in acknowledging the true God. And God gave them freedom to follow these. Some would see the futility and return to Him. Egyptians had foolishly bowed and worshiped these, built their nation upon the deceptions of their own hearts, all the while terrified of death and futilely hoping to conquer it. Their mummified bodies, still waiting to rise four thousand years later, were as dried up and silent as the sand in which they were buried. Would they acknowledge the foolishness of their ways and turn to the true God?

Would Pharaoh? Now the sun god Re had been shackled in darkness. What would be next? Would Moses's God kill all the Egyptians?

"As I said," breathed Pharaoh in a flat, measured tone, "let us all pray together to the gods here and now to destroy this Moses and his deceiver of a god, to undo his disruption and the trouble he has brought upon our land. He has insulted their power and all the care they have given us." They all prayed. Some even cut deep lines in their skin, allowing blood to drip on Pharaoh's hallowed floor, to show how serious they were. "Now go home and wait for the gods to speak," ordered Pharaoh.

Pharaoh was pretending he had power to protect the nation, but fear was creeping across the land and many began to wonder where this would all go. Would God start killing humans, and if He did, how many would He kill? Would ordinary citizens die because of Pharaoh's hard-hearted obstinacy?

CHAPTER 13

DEATH ANGEL AND PASSOVER

In the Israelites' homes each family was conducting its own Passover feast, killing the lamb and painting its blood on the doorposts using a small bushy branch of a hyssop plant as a paint brush. Then they roasted and ate its flesh, thus accepting God's instruction and care, daring to hope as they waited for what He would do next.

In the Egyptians' homes a solemn quiet prevailed. The awful blackness of the past three days had struck fear into their hearts and left a horrible sense of foreboding that something worse was about to come upon them. It hung like a thick cloud, like dread, over the entire nation. Many wished Pharaoh would have given in long ago and acknowledged Moses's God as superior. Everything was out of control. The relative comfort of life in Egypt had been turned upside-down. Even the power of the noonday sun bowed to the power of the God now communicating Himself to the world. A boy told his friends they were going to paint blood on their doorposts to protect from the 'Death Angel.'

"Shouldn't we all do that?" asked another boy. By candlelight in the dark his parents looked at each other, wondering.

Darkness of night crept deeper through Egypt, yet very few found comfort in sleep, and as it is written in Exodus chapter twelve, "It came to pass at midnight that the Lord struck all the firstborn in the land of Egypt, from the firstborn of Pharaoh who sat on his throne to the first born of the captive who was in the dungeon, and all the firstborn of livestock. So Pharaoh rose in the night, he, and all his servants, and all the Egyptians, hurt to the heart and terrified. And there was a great cry in Egypt, for there was not a house where there was not one dead." Then

Pharaoh called for Moses and Aaron and said, "Rise, go out from among my people, both you and the children of Israel. And go, serve the Lord as you have said. Also take your flocks and your herds and be gone. And bless me also." The Lord had sent an Angel of Death, who struck at every house except those with blood on the doorposts. Those he "passed over" and touched no one, even some Egyptian households who had grown to respect the Lord. Following that, Egypt literally chased them out, fearing that soon "we will all be dead." The Lord had told the Israelites to ask the Egyptians for articles of silver and gold and clothing, which the terrified Egyptians gladly gave them just to get rid of them. God's gave them back wages for the years of slavery. Thus they plundered the Egyptians.

Israel left Egypt that night, having been there for 430 years. They could not fully understand the reality of it all. The promise made to Adam and Eve that God had a solution to their nakedness and sin, the promise narrowed further to Abraham that all the world would be blessed through a "seed" descending from him, was not really in the forefront of their mind. The misery of that captivity and slavery that had been their life longer than anyone could remember seemed to be coming to an end that night. They would be coming out of darkness. Only slowly were they waking up to the reality of their new freedom. In the next few days God would drive that truth deeper at the Red Sea. For now they were occupied with just "going" before something changed for the worse.

1. (Note: Centuries earlier Ham, the son of Noah, journeyed to the African continent where his numbers grew explosively, populating more and more geographical areas and giving rise to nations. Among the northernmost developed the large, powerful and influential country of Egypt. Many times the Bible referred to that area as the "Hamites" or the "sons of Ham" and also as "Mizraim" because Mizraim was the particular son of Ham to settle that area.)

Thus occurred the first Feast of the Passover, the greatest of all the Jewish traditions. It was a night to be remembered, and the Lord told them to observe this Passover feast in all future generations as a way of remembering year-by-year what He had done in Egypt. A great work done *once.* The surrounding nations knew what Israel's God had done in Egypt. Although they might forget, Israel was never to forget and to be a continual light to the world. Though done ONCE, the deliverance from Egypt burned into the world's awareness and was subsequently written into many nations' histories and, chiefly, into Israel's history. There it was preserved and passed on through the centuries for all to see, though man has sought to ignore it. The Passover would be a memorial of Israel's deliverance from Egypt and of God's adoption of them as a nation. They had gone into Egypt as a family and come out as a nation. Their deliverance was by blood and by power. Deliverance by blood transpired through the blood on the doorposts and was the sole condition used by God in determining whether or not the Death Angel would strike that house. It did not matter who was in there or what kind of people they were. If blood was on the doorposts everyone in the house was spared.

God had reached His hand into the dark world of uninterested mankind and rescued. Satan schemed and hoped to distract people from ever reading about it. He used (and still uses today) the world to keep man spellbound with its attractions, so caught up in useless nonsense that it is difficult to figure out what is going on, to understand what is truly significant and what is simply the meaningless activity of wayward man. God's written Word and his ever-present Holy Spirit are the silent guide to the heart of each who cares to listen and learn.

Deliverance by blood was a concept worked deeply into Israel's consciousness as it now took on a prominent role in gaining Israel's freedom from the grip of Egypt. Indeed, New Testament writings would explain that "almost all things are by the law purged with blood; and without shedding of blood is no remission" of sins (Hebrews 9: 22). When the blood was shed, the life of the sacrifice was given up, the total self was given, and that was what paid for sin.

In case no one got the message it was presented twice. Deliverance by power would be demonstrated even more visibly in the coming days as God continued to lead his people and deal with this Pharaoh who would never truly relent in his efforts to smother and enslave Israel. "There was never a night like that in the history of the world, nor shall there be anything like it anymore." The Egyptians, now terrified, kept pushing the people to leave immediately, fearing that soon "we will all be dead." They left in a hurry with little but what they could carry. Many Egyptians also left with them. Moses took the bones of Joseph, as he had directed Israel so long ago with a solemn oath, saying, "God will surely visit you, and you shall carry up my bones from here with you." The Lord went before them in a pillar of cloud by day to lead the way, and by night in a pillar of fire for light. So God himself led them every step of the way.

CHAPTER 14

ESCAPE NOT SO EASY

(Exodus 14)

Days later the Lord told Moses that Pharaoh would assume that Israel was tangled in the wilderness and, chafing in anger about letting Israel go, would change his mind. And so it happened that Pharaoh pursued with all his horses, chariots and army and caught up with them at the Red Sea, the place to which God had led them. It had steep, unclimbable hills to the left and right, the Red Sea ahead, and a vast trail of footsteps behind.

Someone looked back in that direction and shouted. Miles away, just above the distant horizon, a tiny cloud of dust appeared in the sky. What could raise dust with no noticeable wind to stir it up? Horses' hooves! Hooves of horses ridden hard! And chariot wheels spinning fast, flinging dust as they sped. From far away trouble was bearing down on them, big trouble. They were trapped! How long would it take until the pursuers caught up? Those rocky hills on either side completely prevented escape. Fleeing into the sea would be ridiculous. Heading backwards toward Egypt meant death, or at the least, capture and brutal treatment by a stirred up and angry enemy. This whole thing had been a horrible mistake! Old people, children, babies and women taking care of babies, could not outrun an army. As the Israelites comprehended their plight they moaned out loud. Moses heard the cries, which rapidly intensified as fear multiplied itself like a hungry brush fire burning itself through the anguished hearts of the people. They scared each other into a near panic with their own noise. Fists waved in Moses's direction, and the two million strong crowd appeared to him as a turbulent sea, waves splashing noisily every which way at once. An especially loud crowd of fifty or so shoved its way to the fore and burst out in front of Moses. Frantic women, fearing for their children and grandchildren, pushed from behind, gnashing at Moses with a rage even those men could not hold back. One voice leaped suddenly above the rest. "There weren't enough graves in Egypt, so you led us out to this desert to die!" The words stung. These people almost deliberately misunderstood and threw accusations around, as if they themselves were righteous. God later told Moses to write this down for all the world to see.

Three of the front-most men, the passion of the moment poisoning their reason, stabbed toward Moses with clenched fists. "Didn't we tell you in Egypt to leave us alone? We never wanted to come to this wilderness. You forced us here to kill us!" The crowd smelled of sweat. Their clothing was caked with dust from days of travel in this barren place. Hatred put a nasty edge on their words that cut at him and seemed like teeth, tearing viciously into him. Moses remembered a time when, as a shepherd in Midian, he had heard a pack of wolves tear apart a living sheep he was supposed to protect. Its pitiful screams continued far longer than he could have imagined as he ran toward the lost sheep's voice. The wolves never quit, tearing and consuming that pitiful creature while it lived. Now the wolf-like nature of mankind lunged at him, just as merciless, just as vicious.

Those front men stopped short, however, when they drew near enough to see Moses's face and powerful stance at such close range. The effect froze them where they stood. One man against two million—and he was not afraid. They saw the eyes of a man who had stared death in the face too many times and had experienced the Lord's power. Those eyes beheld this unkempt mob with an anger stronger than theirs and brought them up short. His face was set like flint. He had walked into Pharaoh's palace, into his very presence, into the throne room of the power of Egypt, into the presence of armed guards ready and able to strike down any threat to their master, and looked into Pharaoh's eyes. He and his brother Aaron had spoken, with a firmness emanating from eternity, the very words of God: "Let my people go." God had sent Moses to that place.

"NO!" had thundered Pharaoh. "I know no other god but me." His unbridled self knew no listening to words other than his own, and he never backed down. Pride. Naked and ruthless. His words and the power of his presence always overcame any in the kingdom he ruled, and on the rare occasion they did not work, his rage pushed it far enough to work—until the day God said,

"NO!"

When for the tenth time Pharaoh had refused to acknowledge God's superior power and to humbly bow to His words, God, who could have crushed him on the first meeting, simply over-ruled him. Pharaoh was a man like all others, flawed from the heart and in need of God's help. God had allowed him, for a season, supreme success on the earth, but his pride, a pride that reached to heaven, clouded his vision and prevented him from seeing correctly his own weakness. In the face of powers vastly beyond him he still withstood, standing proud. That very night God abased him during the Passover and forced him to let the people go. Days later he would abase him further at the Red Sea. Pharaoh had so many chances to give in to God, but he WOULD NOT!

This Moses who had withstood Egypt and its king possessed an iron resolve. Underlying that, God was with him. The people rushing upon him had suddenly encountered that steadfastness and stopped in their tracks. They beheld strength in this man who was more interested in truth, in being honest with himself before God, than in popularity or in the passion of the moment. He did not need the will of the crowd to stand with him, and, if he died on the spot, he would die honorably, true to his Lord. Moses knew the Lord was in control and would always do the right thing. The crowd, ruled by fear, saw the complete absence of fear in this man, and it had the strange effect of quieting theirs.

Moses had observed the fickle hearts of this people and, knowing this moment would come at some time, was prepared. He had replayed in his mind God's words at the burning bush when He told him he had heard the cry of the children of Israel, had seen their oppression and would now send him to Pharaoh to bring his people out of Egypt. He had seen, firsthand, the utter truthfulness of God's words, which he had at first doubted, and the utter helplessness of the people. Now he saw the fear ruling this disoriented mob. In the midst of the panic, he had heard today while facing the impossibility of the situation, the still, small voice of God whispering to him, "I am with you." He remembered his mother, who, in his almost forgotten, earliest memories, in the softness of her bosom, had comforted him with the milk of life and the tones of her voice. She had told him about the God of Abraham, Isaac, and Jacob. He remembered too the words of older men, passed down through the ages, of how God would make of them a great nation and through them, bless the whole world. He remembered the example of Noah standing against the ancient civilization, of taking seriously God's words concerning the judgment to come, and of his deliverance through that judgment. Always, God kept his word. Not all the people knew that yet, but he knew.

"You took us away to die in the wilderness!" a hard heart farther back in the crowd protested. "Why have you so dealt with us? Did not we say, 'Let us alone that we may serve the Egyptians?' It would be better than dying in this . . . this . . . wilderness." The Israelites were certainly no shining example of strong faith in the Lord. They were fickle, unthankful, impatient. Moses, the man taught by God for forty long years in the wilderness, now became a voice "crying in the wilderness." That voice boomed above the crowd, "Fear not, stand still now, and see the salvation of the Lord, which he will show you today. The Egyptians whom you see today, you shall see again no more forever. The Lord will fight for you, and you shall hold your peace." He paused, and the crowd fell silent. "The Lord is delivering you this day from Egypt . . . from death itself. Will you accept it? You must decide. You can go back to Egypt, or you can walk with him to freedom. The Lord brought you to this moment. It is your choice."

And the Lord said to Moses, "Lift up your rod and stretch out your hand over the sea and divide it. The children of Israel shall go on dry ground through the midst of the sea." God told Moses that Pharaoh and his army would follow them into the sea, and "I will gain honor over Pharaoh and over all his army, his chariots, and his horsemen. Then the Egyptians shall know that I am the Lord." Then the Angel of the Lord moved the pillar of the cloud from in front of Israel to behind, stopping the Egyptians. It became a wall of fire and darkness to Egypt and a light to Israel. The waters divided and a strong east wind came up, drying the sea bed, the waters being a wall on the right hand and on the left. Rather than going back to Egypt Israel accepted God's deliverance and walked that day into the midst of the sea on dry ground, the way He had prepared—long before he spoke to Abraham, long before Adam's time according to Revelation 13:8, " . . . the Lamb slain from the foundation of the world." The Lamb of God, the Savior Jesus, was invisibly guiding Israel. One day He would join the human race visibly through this nation of Israel, all according to plan and in the protection of Almighty God. It was He who led them to escape miraculously through the midst of the Red Sea, not only from Egypt, but in a larger sense, for all mankind, from the world and its pain of sin and death. Israel on that day, in the path through the sea and on that shore, accepted God's deliverance. No power on earth or in heaven could prevent that deliverance. God confirmed, made permanent, each person's decision to accept His help.

CHAPTER 15

IN THE DEPTHS OF THE RED SEA

(Exodus 14)

Through the night they walked, into the day. They were walking safely through what would have been certain death for anyone else, through the depths of the Red Sea, with Pharaoh held at bay on the shore behind by the fury of a black cloud placed there to block his path. Pharaoh should have known that One who could use the very powers of nature as a skillful tool in his hand was no one to be trifled with. His delusion of power and belief in himself was soon to be dealt a crushing blow. And all the world would see. The Satanic power that influenced him would be thwarted, and though Satan himself would escape destruction on this day, he was sent an undeniable signal that he was no match for the Lord's power and would ultimately be destroyed at an appointed moment. Satan deflected all such messages, maniacally clinging to the belief that one day he would overthrow God.

Among that crowd escaping through the Red Sea walked fourteen-year-old Matthias. He knew many of the boys and girls who had lived near him in Egypt and had good friends among them. But these last few days had seen changes that would alter their lives. All had left their homes behind. A huge number of people—no one had counted, but it was over 2 million including children—was on the move. All were meeting other Israelites they had never even seen before. Walking in wonder between tall walls of water on either side, Matthias pondered, what if the walls collapsed? Would God do that? They would all die instantly. He had heard, back in his earliest memories, grownups talking about God's promise to deliver his people from slavery after 400 years. Well, it had been about 400 years and that was happening—right now! Matthias decided that if God had foreseen and predicted all this with such accuracy and had kept His word so faithfully, He would not let the walls collapse. He began to relax. It was then that he noticed her, a girl his own age he had never seen before, walking just a few feet off to his right and a little ahead. He knew many kids his age, so why should he notice her with a special kind of interest he had never known before? Maybe it was the way she walked over the sand and small pebbles, gracefully and effortlessly. Her long brown hair and smooth, tanned skin struck him as beautiful. What was happening? He had never thought of any girl as beautiful before. He mostly tolerated them. They liked to play with dolls their mothers had made for them out of old fabric, pretending they were taking care of them. Most of them could not run or jump or climb as he could. Some of them were too bossy. Some teased him too, and he did not like it. They could not throw spears as well as he and the other boys, and did not seem to care either. And many of them were not as "grown up" as he was beginning to fancy himself. But this girl seemed more mature and responsible—qualities for which he found himself striving. He walked a little faster to move ahead and see her face more completely. Now much closer to her, he saw her dark eyes sparkling with life, a stray wisp of hair dangling carelessly over one cheek, both cheeks glowing, ever so slightly, with a reddish tan from days of walking in the sun. Captivating. He had to force himself not to stare.

"Jerusha," her father's voice called out. "Help your little sister." Her sister, tiring beside her, appeared to be about six. So that was her name . . . Jerusha! A perfectly beautiful name. Jerusha's hand reached out and took her little sister's hand in hers. On they walked, Matthias pretending the crowd had pushed him so close. Many of the grownups, putting the fear and panic of yesterday behind them, were talking as they walked to freedom, about the wonder of it all. By following Moses into this path through the Sea they were accepting God's deliverance from Egypt, a further evidence of the miraculous deliverance effected at the Passover. They could not help staring at the walls of water over and over, trying to understand all that was happening, vertical walls, translucent blue, and tall—probably three hundred feet, here in the midst of the sea—and marveling at the sheer power that held them there, a sight so striking that none could forget as long as they lived, and, unknown to them, the world would not forget either. What would happen tomorrow or to Pharaoh they did not know, but for now they were safe and were daring to believe in their newfound freedom, to believe more completely in their God who was taking care of them. Here and there shouts of joy erupted. In fact, these were moments *filled* with joy and happiness here in the midst of the Red Sea, a place where no one could go and survive, but on this day a place of protection by God. Old things, captivity and slavery, had ended—a reality they were cautiously daring to believe, still not convinced it was true. A new life, hard to imagine, was dawning for all. A few weeks ago they had known only slavery. The one who delivered them from bondage was delivering them now from Egypt and its awful hold on them.

Years in the future the Apostle Paul would describe an experience similar to this about all who embraced the Savior he himself had lately come to know, about joy and happiness that flooded into all who found new life and hope in their Savior. "If any man be in Christ he is a new creation. Old things are passed away, behold, all things are become new" (II Corinthians 5: 17). Much was happening here in the Red Sea, not only today but for all time, an event reaching beyond time to eternity. For now, Israel was simply experiencing and enjoying deliverance.

Matthias was walking next to the little sister when she stumbled. He grabbed her free hand, steadying her. Jerusha glanced over at him, her eyes asking, "Who are you?" He did not care. All he saw was a girl he wanted to know—forever. What Jerusha saw was a boy who, being near her side, had kindly helped her little sister. He gazed at her so long she wondered, "Do I know him?" Embarrassed, she looked away. But she too was captivated.

"It's a great day," he managed to utter finally, lamely. "Escaping from Egypt, I mean." She could not answer. They walked on in silence amidst the occasional cheers of the joyous older people. Fourteen-year-olds have deep feelings and both of theirs had been touched. Matthias did not mind her not speaking. He was happy being beside her.

The distance through the Red Sea was great. Matthias had rejoined his family, walking on for miles. Each step was part of a new life they had never enjoyed before—freedom! The sea bottom was strangely dry, with hard packed sand littered with small pebbles and occasional corals. He looked back, and far in the distance through the path in the sea the roiling cloud stood still at the water's edge, holding back the ruthless power of Pharaoh's army. This pathway through the heart of an ocean was the *way* to freedom. The power of God Himself was leading them through it and setting them free.

He had to see Jerusha again. Her family must be somewhere ahead in this huge crowd. He walked a little faster and caught glimpses of her tall father. Then her long, dark hair and slave girl dress caught his eye. He had found her! That dress was no different than all the others, but somehow it was beautiful on her. Maybe it was how she wore it or how her mother had fitted it for her. Maybe it was how she moved in it, picking her way over the pebbles, seeming comfortable and confident, so young and yet so grown up. He had been thinking about how they were not slaves anymore, and it was still hard to believe. They were set free. He wanted to tell her and wondered what she would have to say. Again he was beside her when she saw him. Her eyes sparkled and a smile lit up her face. He had so much to say, but neither said anything. They simply walked, both happy, looking straight ahead, pretending not to notice each other. Finally he said, "We are not slaves anymore. Not us, not our parents. We are free!"

Jerusha listened and paused rather long before she spoke, the first time ever he heard her voice. "We'll never forget this moment." Her gaze lingered on him, this boy who today appeared in her life. Suddenly she looked ahead and pointed. "Look, there is the other shore. We're almost there." Excitement gripped them both. Matthias stretched out his hand and took hers. It was warm and he felt her fingers in return close with his.

She's right, he thought. *We'll never forget this moment.*

In the coming days Matthias kept close track of his new friend and made sure to be near her often. It seemed that she watched for him too. Gradually their shyness melted away as they learned to talk to each other. She spoke of the grownups' conversations about God's promises to Abraham and how it was all coming true in their young lives. "God is going to lead us into the Promised Land," she said confidently. "We have exciting days ahead of us." Matthias had thought about this also, but teenagers rarely gave voice to such thoughts. It was as though Jerusha's way of saying things helped him see more clearly. And when he spoke she listened intently and seemed to know just what he meant. He liked being with this girl. A relationship was budding that would last a long time.

Far back on the shore behind them the Lord lifted the cloud that had blocked Pharaoh's path . . .

CHAPTER 16

REACHING THE FAR SHORE

(Exodus 15)

Walking up the shore to higher ground and out of the sea, the Israelites looked back and saw a scene developing that would burn itself into their memories forever. A dust cloud slowly rising on the far shore indicated that, though still too distant to see, something big must be happening. Hundreds of horses running fast and chariot wheels spinning at high speed could throw up dust like that! Pharaoh's chariots were racing furiously toward them—and into the path God had made for them! As Israel watched for a long time, barely daring to breathe, the leading chariots came gradually into sight, still several miles away! Their joy at deliverance turned to terror. Was their freedom finished as quickly as it had come? Would they be stabbed with spears or slashed with swords and rendered dead in the dust in the next few minutes? Or would they be captured, punished and dragged back into miserable slavery? What emotions they had experienced the last twenty-four hours: first fear, then joy at escaping into the sea, and now terrifying fear again, plus fatigue from having walked many miles. They were spent, drained of strength, and felt like collapsing, all hope lost.

The Lord told Moses, "Stretch out your hand over the sea, that the waters may come again upon the Egyptians, their chariots and their horsemen." Moses did so, "and the Lord overthrew the Egyptians in the midst of the sea. None escaped, not so much as one" (Exodus 14:28).

The giant walls of water let go and water so deep and heavy crashed upon the chariots and soldiers. It flushed over them with power none could fight. Boisterous waves filled what had been a safe path for Israel, muffling the screams of dying men far below the surface. The angry waves mellowed to swells that gently lapped at the seashore and gradually leveled to a quiet stillness, the sea returning to her normal appearance as though nothing unusual had happened. There was no wind. Only a smooth, quiet calm, and with it, *silence.* God had just spoken. Remember the first time Moses had told Pharaoh, "The Lord God of Israel has said, 'Let my people go, that they may hold a feast to me in the wilderness?'" And Pharaoh said, "Who is the Lord that I should obey his voice to let Israel go? I know not the Lord, neither will I let Israel go" (Exodus 5: 1-2). Arrogance that reached to heaven! Pharaoh could have spared Israel and himself much trouble had he heeded God's request.

God allowed him his opinion—for a time—and granted him many, many opportunities to change his mind. Pharaoh never gave in, even when the Lord demonstrated to him with miracle after miracle that his power was no match for the power of God. He and his top "yes men" were too proud to give in, and now their pride and stubborn self-will had led them all to their deaths and a watery grave in the deep, dark quiet where no ray of light could even penetrate. Sealed at the moment of death, each person's destiny became permanent on this day. Each now awaited the long promised judgment that man hated so much but ultimately proved powerless to avoid. The days of free will ended as God rewarded each with the outcome of his beliefs. Pharaoh had stepped into his "long home," his *eternal* destiny, chosen by him in this lifetime—luxury, power, and the comfort of servants waiting upon him being more important to him than truth. Pyramids and exquisitely carved, richly decorated burial vaults, like those of many Pharaohs, were nothing more than a rebellious insult to the God of all creation, a fist shaking itself with impunity in His face. A meaningless mountain of work, impressive to the world, held in contempt by God. This Pharaoh's body would not even be found to give him a royal burial.

The Israelites were stunned. The freedom they had rejoiced in while walking through the Red Sea was real! Pharaoh and his entire army had vanished in a moment into permanent destruction. Presently a few lifeless bodies, warriors who had almost reached the shore, floated to the surface, no doubt men who had struggled free of their armor and thrashed hopelessly for the surface, drowning, just like those far behind, in the overwhelming depths. The water had brought deliverance to some, death to others. Exodus records it this way: "Thus the Lord saved Israel that day out of the hand of the Egyptians, and Israel saw the Egyptians dead upon the seashore. Israel saw the great work that the Lord did upon the Egyptians, and the people feared the Lord, and believed the Lord, and his servant Moses" (Exodus 14: 30-31).

Let us back up for a moment and view the same scene from Pharaoh's position. Held back by the fiery cloud from attacking Israel, Pharaoh's anger built into a rage, intensified by the fact that he, king of Egypt, was being thwarted by this God of Israel and made to look powerless in front of his own soldiers. Perhaps some of them were beginning to question his ability to lead. Were cracks developing in his kingdom? He tried to force his horses to charge with his chariot into that cloud, but even the cruel cut of the whip tearing bright red wounds into their necks and hindquarters availed not. His rage boiled. His supremacy was being challenged, and it was becoming difficult to keep others from seeing it. Always he had been able to force others to his will through physical strength and skill or through his superior intellect. He had convinced them he was a god and could not be withstood. He had convinced himself—and was *not willing* to let that idea go. He liked being looked up to. He liked being worshipped. Now all of that was beginning to unravel, and he had to do something to maintain control or, at least, give the appearance of being in control. He turned an almost demonic face to his generals and issued orders to tell the army to stand down and wait but to be ready for his next order to action, which made it seem like he had a plan and would buy him some time. But his anger could not be contained.

Like a vicious dog, snarling and baring its teeth, lunging to kill, leaping at its chain, nearly choking itself, Pharaoh, straining to charge ahead, was held back by the impenetrable cloud set before him by the Lord. His generals who tried to calm him were batted away and threatened with death. His hatred whirled into a frenzy as they watched. Israel's God certainly knew how to use pressure to strip away the layers of deception and expose the true heart. They were not so convinced anymore of the wisdom of following this man and pursuing Israel. In fact it could be a disaster. God had already destroyed Egypt, its crops, its cattle, its life-giving river, the light of the sun, and now their firstborn. What would happen next? Would he send lightning to consume them in an instant? Should they not bow to his power? Terror gnawed at their hearts as they waited patiently on their tired horses. Egypt's beliefs and fraudulent gods wilted before the blazing power of God. The defiant and strong-willed monarch Pharaoh would not give in. Weeks ago many had advised him, "Don't you know Egypt is destroyed? Let them go." But here they were. Their duty was to follow Pharaoh and do his will. Now his claims of deity were wearing thin. He was a man supremely capable and strong-willed, but in reality, just a man, pushing his own selfishness and lust for power. To oppose him meant death but it was beginning to look like following him meant death as well. They were doomed. Their own ambitions and drives for power would soon be cut short and disappear, forgotten like so much smoke vanishing into the relentlessly drifting invisible air currents.

Maybe not, for then a miracle happened. The cloud lifted! God was losing His power! The path into the sea was open! Those miserable Israelites would be recaptured and forced to pay for all the damage they had done, and, if they resisted, they would be killed, right there in the sea. Justice would be done. A screaming shout and the crack of Pharaoh's whip sent his army careening into the open path, emboldened with renewed hope. The Lord in heaven watched as the most powerful man on earth sent, with colossal stupidity, his army, his power, Egypt's finest chariots and elite soldiers, charging headlong into the wide path through the Red Sea, the path He controlled. The Lord could have collapsed the sea in a moment, but he let them go, racing far into the deepest part. In time he allowed the ground to become just a little muddy, and then the horses began to strain as chariots bogged down. Whips cruelly snapping their backsides forced every ounce of strength from the horses. Drivers tried to turn around and flee back to the shore. Chariot axles cracked and wheels broke off. It was no use. It was too far, and now mud clung to the horses' feet. Warriors forced to follow their fanatical leader panicked as the hopeless realization they were in a trap dawned on them.

"The Lord is fighting for Israel," screamed a terrorized Egyptian. Then the tall walls of water caved in. There was no swimming to the top. It was too deep and too violent. As they were drowning, the once proud, powerful soldiers realized they were utterly helpless against Moses' God and that Pharaoh, too, was helpless. This God that could use an ocean as an obedient instrument to do his bidding had power so far beyond man's that the word "invincible" barely described it. Why had they not seen this before? It was all so obvious now. *What about my wife back home—and my children?* many thought.

A gracious God was giving them a few more moments to reach their hearts out to Him for help. They had all seen His power displayed over and over the past few weeks in systematically overpowering Egypt's false gods. "That *all Egypt may know that I am God,*" He had said with each miracle, seeking people to come back to Him of their own free will. He would honor and not violate each person's free will, even if it meant their ultimate rejection of Him. Selection of each person's destiny belonged to that person alone, a responsibility so awesome it literally meant eternal life or eternal death. Man liked to pretend it was not so, but judgment was destined for the earth and every human on it and was as certain as tomorrow's sunrise. Any Egyptian who reached out from his panicked heart to God would have found Him.

"As I live, says the Lord God, I have no pleasure in the death of the wicked, but that the wicked turn from his way and live" (Ezekiel 33:11). The Lord is "longsuffering toward us, not willing that any should perish, but that all should come to repentance" (2 Peter 3:9). "Who will have all men to be saved, and to come to the knowledge of the truth" (I Timothy 2:3-4). Having seen God's power back in Egypt they had also seen His mercy to Israel, who had honored Him as the true God. They had seen Israel spared the misery of the last few plagues. They had seen Israel delivered from the death of the firstborn by applying the blood of a lamb to the doorposts of their houses. There was hope to any willing to allow in his heart that Israel's God was the Creator of the earth and each person on it and, further, willing to "believe" this God's words. The threat of imminent death was God's final call, after all of His displays of power, to these perishing soldiers. Did any reach out to Him? We will never know—not while we are on this earth anyhow.

The weight of the water was heavy, crushing. Many screamed in absolute terror, but the water muffled all sound. No one heard the screams. Panicked gasps for air brought in choking amounts of salt water, and suddenly the world faded to a deep sleep. Each person, though in the midst of an army of others, faced this last struggle alone, completely alone. His next appointment would be, at a certain moment in the future, known only to God, face to face with him to explain his actions in life. "It is appointed unto man once to die, and after this the judgment" (Hebrews 9: 27). As with the death in the Red Sea there would be no escaping that future terrible moment. For them nothing else would happen until that terrible day, no "reincarnation," that false hope invented by man's imagination, no second chances. There had been thousands of second chances during their moments on earth. The final score stood. Now all that was left was God's judgment about it and the sentence to pronounce and execute.

And so Pharaoh, the ruler of the most powerful nation on earth, who had defied God at every opportunity and had maintained the lie that he was more powerful than God, was stripped of his power and glory that day. Whether or not he died in the Red Sea with his army at this time cannot be determined with certainty from the text. Scripture tells us that "the LORD overthrew the Egyptians in the midst of the sea. And the waters returned, and covered the chariots, and the horsemen, and all the host of Pharaoh that came into the sea after them; there remained not so much as one of them" (Exodus 14:26-28). All that chased Israel into the sea drowned, yet scripture does not tell us explicitly whether Pharaoh was among them.

He may have watched and given commands from a high vantage point on the shore, as was typical of kings and generals leading a battle. In that case he witnessed the destruction of his army and would have returned home alone, powerless and humiliated. With no army to protect him, he would not have been much esteemed by the Egyptians whose nation had been ravaged under his leadership, and he would have been hated by the wives and children of the soldiers whose deaths he had caused. All Egypt would know Israel's God had proven himself to be the true God. As the

Pharaoh during Moses' infancy had drowned untold numbers of Israelite baby boys in an attempt to destroy Israel and its coming Savior, it was a touch of God's justice to drown Pharaoh's army in the sea. Possibly watching it happen was a worse punishment for him than drowning. No one really got away with mocking the Lord. He would return their own miserable schemes upon their heads. Moses recalled Pharaoh's mocking arrogance at their very first meeting: "Who is the Lord that I should obey his voice to let Israel go? I know not the Lord, neither will I let Israel go" (Exodus 5: 2). He also recalled God's initial words to Abraham, before Israel ever was. "I will make of you a great nation . . . bless you and make your name great . . . I will bless them that bless you, and curse him that curses you, and in you shall all families of the earth be blessed." (Genesis 12: 2-3). God's words had rolled over Pharaoh like an ocean. *Now* Pharaoh knew who the Lord was. Would he ever give in to the Lord? Would we?

It could also be that Pharaoh indeed led his army into the sea, in which case he would have drowned with them, breathing his last at the bottom of the Red Sea, all his splendor, his fawning servants, themselves fakes, all left behind. His plans and dreams of expanding his power and glory vanished with him. An intelligent and powerful man had died a fool. "How are they brought into desolation, as in a moment! They are utterly consumed with terrors" (Psalm 73: 19).

The sea had swallowed wickedness, with none left to tell about it except possibly Pharaoh and a few of his attendants. For now their land lay in ruins, food and cattle destroyed, their gold and silver given to Israelites. The Pharaoh in power centuries earlier when Jacob and his twelve sons journeyed to Egypt honored them greatly, giving them the best of the land. Indeed, his entire nation had been blessed through Jacob's eleventh son Joseph, who had correctly interpreted a dream God had given Pharaoh, the dream in which he had shown him how to prepare for a future famine. He had believed Joseph and followed his advice. Egypt and Israel together were blessed. Egyptian history records a fifty-year period around this deliverance in which the country was so weak that other nations came in and marauded. This small nation of Israel was capturing the attention of the world.

Jerusha and Matthias, simply beholding, stood hand in hand, near Matthias's family. In the last few hours they had experienced events that would alter their lives forever, and in that silence no one said anything. All were too exhausted. Having just escaped death at the hands of the enraged Egyptians, they had, moments before, allowed fear to terrify and overrule reason and had forgotten that God was with them. Before that had been joy at escaping through the Red Sea and leaving behind a life of miserable slavery. Before that, terror as the Egyptian army caught up with them at the shore. Their emotions had been whip-sawed back and forth for weeks now, and after walking all night they were spent. Two million people just stood there. Some looked at Moses with wonder and newfound respect.

In humbled amazement, Matthias's father said, upon seeing several no longer powerful Egyptian soldiers wash up dead on the shore, "We were born into slavery, lived in it all our lives. We had no idea how it crippled our thinking. We thought like slaves and had given up imagining we could ever be free. We knew nothing else and had no hope. Sure, we knew the old stories about Abraham, but they came from so long ago. It seemed like God had forgotten about us. And now this . . . I cannot take it all in." Matthias, still holding Jerusha's hand, and with a growing attachment to this young girl, watched his father in silence. The moment was too big to understand.

Jerusha, trying to understand, put her thoughts together. "We were in the heart of the sea, and it should have been death. Instead it was deliverance, deliverance from Egypt, from Pharaoh, from slavery." Matthias squeezed her hand in agreement. They were beginning to understand each other, to be comfortable together.

"And there I met you," said he with a touch of awe in his voice. After many seconds of silence he said, "There was death there too, death to our old life and the slavery holding us captive, death to all we were—and death for that awful army chasing us. When the Lord sets you free he really sets you free." Jerusha looked at him, seeking to digest his words, admiration setting in.

Moses too was overtaken in wonder. He thought back to God's call at the burning bush and of his own reluctance to believe Him. He remembered his first attempt to help Israel forty years earlier. It had met with disaster, and he had had to flee for his life, leaving all behind. He had wanted to follow God, to serve Him, but did not know how. For all the disillusionment, heartbreak, apparent waste of time, and seeming failure Moses had experienced, God had been leading him through it all. And had, moreover, honored the faith of his parents. God also remembered His words to Abraham, Isaac, and Jacob, His plan to use Israel to bring deliverance and blessing to mankind. It was He who had chosen Moses to bring word of this deliverance, who had protected him from death in the Nile and nurtured him and brought him through the experiences that would prepare him for the task. Few knew—as Moses knew from firsthand experience—the cunning skill and ruthlessness, the absolute power held by Pharaoh. There was no standing up to him. Now Moses thought back to God's words at the burning bush. He had wanted Moses to make demands to Pharaoh! The supreme confidence Moses had held years earlier had been tempered by life and by God's special school of hard knocks and frustrating failures. He had had to slow Moses down and teach him to hear and follow Him. Those forty years were not a waste after all. Deep in thought, Moses realized how all the details in God's promises to man meshed and that today was a day of joy.

In the crowd stood another man, a man named Joshua, forty years younger than Moses and in awe. He was not sure if he should be in awe of Moses or of God who was guiding him. He rightfully leaned toward being in awe of God. Months earlier he had managed to meet Moses face to face, who himself had taken notice of this energetic young man and enjoyed his relentless questions.

Presently a lone voice sang out: "I will sing to the Lord. He has triumphed gloriously. The horse and his rider has he thrown into the sea." It was Moses himself singing. "The Lord is my strength and song and is become my salvation. He is my God and my father's God, and I will exalt him. He is a man of war. Pharaoh's chariots and his army has he cast into the sea. His chosen captains are drowned, and the depths have covered them." A woman raised up a tambourine and its sound blended with Moses's voice. It was Miriam, his older sister, who eighty years earlier, at her mother's direction, had floated her baby brother into the river in defiance of Pharaoh's death edict. She remembered the horror of that wicked order from Pharaoh. Every male baby born must be thrown into the river and drowned. There was no escape. Pharaoh had so much power, and his heartless enforcers were everywhere, obeying their heartless master. She had adored her baby brother, so cute but so helpless, and loved helping her mother take care of him, delighting in holding him every chance she got. And now this baby must be taken and brutally murdered. Why? What had he done? Why must he die? Her young mind could not comprehend. She was thrilled when her mother and father told her they would hide Moses and that God would show them a plan for protecting him. Pharaoh had all the power of his kingdom, but they had the power of God Himself and the assurance of the promise He gave to Abraham, and they were willing to pit that against Pharaoh's commandment. Pharaoh feared that the Israelites, should they keep growing in numbers, would sooner or later overpower him. Thus his plan to limit their growth—no matter how much it hurt anyone else. He must protect himself. After all, was he not the embodiment of all the gods Egypt worshipped, and thus more important than all others? In reality Pharaoh had gone so deeply into sorcery and submitting his life to the power of his "gods" to find extra ways to magnify his kingdom that he had unwittingly come under the control of Satan himself. Thinking himself great, he was a tool for Satan to use to accomplish his purposes in this world, the greatest of which was to destroy Israel and prevent the Savior, who would ultimately cast him into the lake of fire, from being born. Less powerful leaders pushed people around and forced them into submission, manipulating them for their own purposes. Superior leaders manipulated events, behind the scenes, and got their own way without anyone even knowing. True evil operated invisibly. It controlled Egypt without Egyptians knowing, with Pharaoh sensing but barely knowing. It controlled the world without mankind knowing. But Moses knew. He had learned in God's 'school of hard knocks' in his years in Midian. "You shall know the truth, and the truth will make you free," later wrote another of God's students, quoting the Savior Himself (John 8: 32). Moses knew the truth: that the real battle was against evil in high places. Centuries later the Apostle Paul wrote, to explain in words, what Moses knew and stood upon: "For we wrestle not against flesh and blood, but against principalities, against powers, against the rulers of the darkness of this world, against spiritual wickedness in high places. Wherefore take unto you the whole armor of God, that you may be able to withstand in the evil day, and having done all, to stand" (Ephesians 6: 12-13). Moses, a meek man, stood upon a rock far more sure than the supremely powerful Pharaoh. Today Moses still lives with the Lord. Pharaoh's body lies, long ago corrupted, at the bottom of the Red Sea, or maybe hidden lifeless within a splendid pyramid. We do not know. His spirit, in chains of darkness, awaits a day of judgment before the throne of the God he defied. Israel's life, like a spear, had cut a path into his kingdom. Israelites did not even know how important they were nor how big a battle lay in their path.

Satan knew not exactly when this Savior would come, so he worked continuously to eliminate Israel. As long as Pharaoh was useful to him, Satan would keep him in power. When he was no longer useful he would discard him. Of these larger issues the young Miriam was not aware. There was always more going on in this world than met the eye.

The four thousand-mile-long Nile, the longest river in the world, which should have been death for Moses, was his deliverance. Miriam had seen it with her own eyes, had seen Pharaoh's daughter find a crying baby in the ark in the river and take him to be her own. Today Miriam was overcome with wonder. A helpless infant had been cast into God's care. Look at him now, a persuasive leader of a group of slaves who had engaged the most powerful king in the world—and won. Moses' mother taught her son the history of God's dealings with man, telling him of Adam, Noah and the ancient civilization, of Abraham, Isaac and Jacob, of slavery and deliverance, of future blessing to the world. She had taught him respect for God's word and made it real to him because she herself believed it and respected it. She had taught him to listen to God's promises and think on them, believing that in them he would hear God's voice—to him. Miriam had plenty to sing about, for she had seen all this. Her mother and father had been right. And Moses, because of his mother's training, had heard when God spoke to him at the burning bush.

That heart-wrenching moment when they set Moses adrift at the river's edge eighty years earlier was as real as though it had been only moments ago, and she joined her brother in singing from the deepest part of her heart. Many of her friends, who had shared in this drama with her as a child, began to harmonize with her voice and shake their tambourines, and soon the song was picked up and repeated, then added to by others, until all Israel was singing. Moses' voice was overshadowed. He too was overcome with wonder. The best songs in all the world spring from deep within, from life and suffering, and cannot be stopped.

This was a rare moment in the long life of Israel. They had truly grasped the reality of God's care and love for them, and it overwhelmed. Other days they would forget the reality of these blessings and their painfully learned lessons, so easy it was to slip off God's clear path. It was part of living in a dark world with a human heart plagued with rebellion and sin.

But today the women danced and sang, "Sing, all of us, to the Lord, for he has triumphed gloriously." Joy and happiness flooded their hearts. It just happened spontaneously as they realized God was taking care of them. The essence of true worship. He had brought them out of Egypt; he had brought them through the Red Sea. Delivered them from slavery. Delivered them from death. In truth, they were thankless complainers, but he had done it anyway. His kindness melted their hearts, and, for the moment, they humbly adored him. There is a verse, simple and sublime, that captures it perfectly: "Be still, and know that I am God" (Psalm 46:10), and for that moment, Israel knew. The Lord gave nearly the whole chapter of Exodus 15 to recording their song.

CHAPTER 17

WILDERNESS

(Exodus 15-17)

In the days that followed, God had led them through a wilderness, a barren place of deprivations that drove them to rely on him daily for their needs. The hot, prickly land offered little comfort to weary travelers, and after three days' travel their water ran out. When they finally found water it was too bitter to drink. Thirsting and sweltering in the heat and complaining under their breath, they cried angrily to Moses, "What is going on? What shall we drink? This trip is a failure." He understood God's faithfulness better than they did and reached out to the Lord for help. One would think that, had they thought seriously about God's ability to deliver them out of Egypt, through the Red Sea and now into this wilderness, they would have realized He had the ability and the willingness to take care of them. Maybe He delighted in having them come to Him with their problems and ask for His help. But then the human race did not necessarily have a good track record at following the voice of reason over the emotion of the moment.

God "showed Moses a tree which, when he cast it into the waters, they became sweet" (Exodus 15: 22-25). Many Bible teachers believe that this tree represents the cross of Christ that, cast into the midst of a bitter, dark world and a dying humanity, changed everything so that life could be made sweet to any who would drink of the new water of life. God was leading Israel through a land tainted with evil, deprivation and death, a land ruled, since the fall of Adam and Eve in the garden, by Satan, called by God Himself "the god of this world" (II Corinthians 4: 4). The dominion over the earth God had given to Adam transferred to

Satan the moment Adam followed his advice over God's. Adam and all those who descended from him fell powerlessly under his control.

Years earlier Moses had learned that the only help lay in ceasing to trust his own ability and calling on the Lord for guidance and help. And the Lord never let him down. Over the weeks and then years following the Red Sea deliverance, Israel too, especially the younger generation, gradually learned, like Moses, to trust Him.

"We're on our way to the Promised Land!" The words spilled from Jerusha's happy heart and found a ready home in Matthias's ears. So much was new. Even though it had been two months since their departure from Egypt, it took time to get used to their new freedom. Their lives of slavery were over, but the memory of those awful years was so fresh and so real that it sometimes seemed hard to believe that their new freedom was true and permanent. Possibilities abounded. "We don't have to serve cruel masters any more, Matthias. We'll be free like the Egyptians. No—better than that—we have the Lord taking care of us."

"I wonder what He will do next," offered the equally exuberant Matthias.

"More walking, I'm sure," she said. "The land God gave Abraham is many, many days away from here."

"If God announced all this over four hundred years ago, and now it is coming true exactly as he said, I am sure He has a plan," reasoned Matthias.

Israel journeyed onward, coming near to Mount Sinai. On the fifteenth day of the second month after departing from Egypt they hungered. Again the whole community of Israel complained against Moses and Aaron. "If only we had died by the hand of the Lord in Egypt! There we sat around pots of meat and ate all the food we wanted, but you have brought us out into this desert to starve us to death." They were certainly singing a different tune from a few days ago.

Then the Lord said to Moses, "I will rain bread from heaven for you. Gather what you need each day. On the sixth day gather twice as much so you can rest on the following day." That evening the Lord sent quails into the camp, and Israel had more meat than it could eat. In the morning something new lay on the ground, and Moses told them it was "bread from heaven" and called it manna. God told them to gather all they wanted but not to save it overnight as He would give them new each morning. They ate all they wanted, but some saved it overnight. In the morning it bred worms and stunk. Moses in anger chided them for not trusting that God would give them a new supply each morning. On the sixth day they did as God had said and gathered double. The next morning it did not stink nor did it have worms, and there was no manna on the ground either. Moses told them this was the Sabbath, a day of rest for them. Israel ate manna for forty years, until it ceased when they entered Canaan. There He fed them a new way with the "corn of the land."

Jerusha and Matthias had found an inviting spot to sit comfortably and talk, away from the crowd. It was a time to digest what had been happening and of wondering how their experiences related to what they knew of Israel's history. After all, they were part of the nation of Israel too, and they were growing more and more aware that they were God's people, and he was guiding them. Was their life a continuation of the story?

They pondered what they knew: God's promises to Abraham; Isaac's long-awaited birth, so out of the ordinary for a person of Sarah's age; the prophecy of serving another people in a strange land; the amazing story of Joseph; the foretold deliverance; and within it all, the idea that "believing God" was the key.

Matthias reiterated some of the examples of belief. "Abraham left his homeland because he 'believed' what God spoke to him. Then he believed God's statement that he and Sarai would have a son even though they were old. When after several years no son came he began to doubt but after twenty-five years their son, Isaac, was miraculously born. When Isaac was grown God told Abraham to offer him as a sacrifice on Mount Moriah, a place to which God would lead him. Though Abraham had strayed from God on several occasions, he had also seen that God's words always worked out, so again he believed God and took Isaac to Mount Mariah. Then came that miraculous deliverance from sacrificing Isaac when God called out to him and provided His own sacrifice instead."

Matthias mentioned Jacob's encounters with God, the fabulous blessing in Egypt that later turned to slavery, Moses's training, first by the world in Egypt, later by God in a strange land and without the power of Egypt at his fingertips. God prepared Moses to lead Israel out of Egypt. Now, as Matthias realized, Israel's stubbornness against recognizing God's care for them, and their refusal to trust Him going forward began to look very foolish.

"Day after day we travel through this wilderness. Some days we walk, some days we stay where we are. We follow this pillar of smoke that rises from the Tabernacle," breathed Jerusha, deep in thought and hardly realizing she spoke out loud to Matthias. They sat side by side on a gentle slope a little way off from the camp. There they could talk together, uninterrupted and unhurried, yet still in view of the camp. From here it looked different, and it afforded them time to think, think about their lives and what they were doing. They looked forward to these moments together and were always refreshed by their little talks.

"Remember that day in the Red Sea when we first met?" questioned Matthias. "Do you think God Himself brought us together?" They both knew the answer, but they discussed it anyway, pondering it anew from a later point in life.

"You know he did," assured Jerusha. It was their way of reminding themselves that, as God had invisibly led them then, He was just as assuredly leading them now. They needed this time together to sort things out.

"I am sure thankful that God brought us together, Jerusha," said Matthias after a long, unhurried silence.

"Me too," she answered, leaning a little closer upon his shoulder. They sat quietly as they looked toward the busy camp, cherishing these moments. After a while she spoke again. "I have been thinking, Matthias . . . "

"Oh, that's a surprise," he kidded. "What have you come up with now?"

"I think God is pulling us along, teaching us to trust Him and to get used to realizing He is with us and will always take care of us. And we have a hard time simply letting Him do that. We always get worried thinking that something will go wrong. Then we complain. How do we forget so soon that He led us here, and that He has never abandoned us? Remember at Marah when we were so thirsty from walking in that burning sun? The land was just dry and crusty. No water in sight. Finally we came to that pond and were so thrilled. Then when we scooped some up and took a drink. It was bitter and gagged us."

"How could I forget? It was discouraging. No, it was downright maddening."

"And then what did we do? We complained to Moses. We blamed him. Here was a man following the Lord, never dreaming in the first place that he would be leading two million people through a barren wilderness—a wilderness God chose—and we blamed Moses for the hot sun and our weariness. Did you ever stop to think how discouraging that would have been to him? He never asked for the job. God sent him to do this. And he inherited all the criticism. We never stopped to think that God had led us here . . . and that maybe He knew we were thirsty and had a way of taking care of us."

"Some people even swore at Moses. Their anger made them cruel," remembered Matthias.

"And then Moses prayed to God. Why didn't we think of that? He told him to throw a branch into the water, and when he did it became clear and sweet. That was a miracle, Matthias." Matthias nodded in agreement. "Did you ever wonder how God viewed us at that moment?"

"It must have been discouraging to Him . . . If God could ever get discouraged," he added after thinking that one over. "I think He was showing us what we are like."

"And what He is like too," continued Jerusha. "After we had behaved so badly He could have just abandoned us, but He didn't. I think we should never worry, Matthias. Hasn't He shown us so many times that He will always take care of us?"

CHAPTER 18

THEN CAME AMALEK

(Exodus 17)

The wilderness walk continued. All believers, as we are about to see, experience God's training in learning to walk by faith as they encounter situations into which God leads them. He promises He will not lead them into situations "beyond that which we are able to bear" (1 Corinthians 10:13). Though a large number of believers exists in the world, each person is special to God and has a unique purpose. God loves variety and delights in guiding those who will listen to Him. Abraham, though very wealthy, was an ordinary man who had a special role to play in the history of mankind. So too was Joshua, and each passed through a rather long period of training on the way to greatness. Their success lay in that they listened to God and "believed" him. Here we will see part of Joshua's training. It was not necessarily fun, but it was where God led him. He does the same for each of us.

"Then came Amalek." Brief but ominous words recorded in Exodus 17. On this journey led by the Lord the new nation of Israel walked through a hostile world. They had not gone far when a band of fiercely painted warriors carrying spears and swinging glistening swords wildly in the air rushed at the rearmost of them. "Amalekites," shouted someone. Who were they, and why were they attacking? Moses knew. Joshua, as the emerging leader of Israel's military power, did too. They were descendants of Amalek, grandson of Esau, Jacob's twin brother from four centuries earlier. It is good to know history. Those descendants had multiplied into a small nation, and the hostile contention between Jacob and Esau smoldered still in Amalek. Old hatreds die hard and insinuate their way into future generations. Moses and Joshua (and all Israel) faced the revenge that had simmered in Esau's heart for too much of his life, a hatred he unwittingly passed on to his descendants as he nursed his anger.

This angry mob should have respected Israel, through whom God would ultimately bless the world. Yet here was Amalek, attacking to kill. It was hard to understand, but there was no time to think. The battle was on, and Israel needed to defend itself. Someone said, "In the midst of a battle for your life the 'nuances' disappear." It is defend yourself or die. Moses was on to them. With their practice of attacking stragglers of any group unfortunate enough to cross through the land they thought was theirs, they could inflict damage and take spoil with little risk to themselves. On this day, though, they were especially riled up due to their age-old hatred, because Esau's brother, Jacob, was walking through their land. Their spies had been tracking Israel's progress, watching for the opportune time to attack, keenly aware of Jacob's past treachery to Esau. Esau had more or less forgiven his brother by the time they met at Jacob's return later in their years. More or less. There were moments when remembrance of Jacob's manipulation of events to cheat Esau out of his birthright pushed into his memory, and when they did he wallowed in pity for himself. Though a "man of the earth" he spent little time thinking about such things, but he had never *really* completely forgiven Jacob, nor had he asked God to help him forgive. Unwittingly he had passed his hard-hearted bitterness on to his children and grandchildren. That attitude drove them on this day.

Using the ancient practice of the war dance around a huge fire, they danced a fanatically wild, hostile dance driven by fierce pounding drums. It had whipped them into a murderous frenzy. They ate extracts from certain plants to add to their ecstatic behavior, and now, with faces painted in grotesque and hideous designs that broke up the patterns of faces and bodies, they were almost unrecognizable as humans. In such a state of mind they felt little pain and were indeed formidable. In a way they terrified each other and found a secret, god-like thrill in that. These men were cruel, with no limits shackling their imagination to work evil, sold out completely to some ancient, dark inner strength.

Moses called upon Joshua, here mentioned for the first time in the Bible, to lead the fight against Amalek's attack. First mentions of persons in the Bible are never random. They provide a key to understanding their character, and here we see Joshua as a warrior—and victorious.

Joshua nearly lost his life—more than once. Moses told Joshua that he would stand on the top of a nearby hill, with two men, Aaron and Hur, and hold his hands up to heaven and pray for victory. Evidently he thought his army—and Joshua—vulnerable to this vicious band of attackers. Accustomed to dealing with trouble, Joshua reassured Moses that he could handle the situation and that there was no reason Moses should have to make the difficult climb up that steep hill. "Bow your ear, Son," Moses rebuked Joshua, "and do what I say. The battle is larger than you know." Joshua at this point, and because of his own skill, was much more confident than Moses and felt belittled by this lack of confidence in him. He would fight with all his might and prove Moses wrong. Sword in hand and in the thick of the battle, Joshua and his men prevailed at first. But the enemy kept coming, and the battle grew more and more difficult as men, filled with hate and violent energy, almost superhuman strength, attacked in wave after wave. Why were they attacking Israel? What had they done? And where did all this hatred come from? Joshua knew, but on this day the reality of human nature, even of his own, would become more clear. In the years leading up to this battle Joshua had fought many smaller, seemingly insignificant battles in the quiet moments with himself, battles no one else saw. In seeking to follow God's words, the principles he had heard in the ancient stories, he encountered the waywardness of his own heart, which wanted to follow its own path and was drawn to the pleasures of the world. God's words seemed more important and more true than his own ideas, yet it was his own ideas he followed much of the time. That made no sense, but that was how it was.

The truthfulness of the Word weighed on him each day. On those moments when he gave attention to it, it drew him beyond himself, and he began to understand and enjoy what he found. Centuries later another believer would write, "Thy words were found and I did eat them, and they were to me the joy and rejoicing of my heart" (Jeremiah 15: 16).

Such experiences gradually changed Joshua into the man he was in this wilderness. Those stories of God's promises to Abraham, Isaac, and Jacob, and the even older ones of Adam and Eve and how they brought death and misery into the world had stuck in his mind and caused him to seek to know God better. All those little moments in which he could pay attention to those ideas or to the ways of the world had been opportunities to draw closer to the Lord. The more he followed God's words the more real they became to him, and they were what had led him to this leadership role in the battle against Amalek. Victory in the little battles led to victory in the larger battles. No one grew into a successful warrior overnight. His daily decisions had led to this battle today under Moses, another listener. Joshua could not know it, but his story would become an inspiration to millions of future believers. But today Amalek was coming for his life.

The Lord had led them out of Egypt, through the Red Sea and now into this wilderness. Joshua was certain God was with them, but this made no sense. If God were with them why all this hatred and trouble? They had no homes or great possessions to take as spoil. Maybe Amalek wanted their cattle—or the gold jewelry (considerable amounts) the Egyptians had given them. Who knew? At the moment Israel had to defend itself or die.

As the battle raged, a vicious warrior, leaping from somewhere, landed squarely in front of him, face painted and twisted in a demonic scream, and struck instant terror into Joshua's soul. He was seldom afraid of anyone, but all he could do now was to hold up his sword in front of him for protection as the man, both hands on his sword, swung at him before he was really prepared. That sword slammed his with such violent force it shook him to the bone, knocking it out of his hands. Never had he felt such power and hatred aimed at his life. The grotesque man used the end of that stroke to set up for the next, a violent swing that would take his head clean off! And Joshua had no sword! This man knew how to fight. Joshua dove to the ground and rolled toward his sword as the enemy blade slashed over him. It missed and he was still alive! Grabbing for his sword he saw out of the corner of his eye that others of his men were similarly outmaneuvered. They were losing this fight! That horrible man was lunging for him again, and he used every ounce of his strength to squirm out of the way. It was not enough, at least not fast enough for what was coming next. Suddenly Joshua was scared like he had never been scared before. This man was stronger than he was, faster than he, and about to kill him, and he could do nothing about it. For the first time in his life he was completely unable. All he believed in, all he lived for, all he ever wanted to do in his life, all was coming to an end. He had finally encountered a man he could not beat. That hideous, awful monster of a person was taking his life from him. Why had God brought him out here to die like a fool in a horrid battle? Confusion flashed through his mind, and he puzzled about God and everything he knew about Him. Evil hung over the scene like a dark, malevolent cloud. What a waste.

Helpless, he knew he was no match for this dark evil everywhere around him, in these wretched people. It had hunted him down and conquered him. Scripture had told him about the evil in the world, and he had refused to believe. Moses had told him, and he had refused to believe. Now he was about to die.

It was then Moses's words boomed in his head: "I will stand on top of the hill and pray." Joshua, in the brief instant while his enemy set up for the next blow, turned his eyes toward that hill—and saw Moses holding his hands toward heaven. Blessed Moses. That scene burned itself into Joshua's mind.

Then something unusual happened. Time seemed to Joshua to slow down, and he saw his life, the life of Israel, and the life of God Himself there with them and realized God was beholding, from eternity, this scene and was pouring life into Israel through Moses's outstretched hands. That life had power over evil, as light could dispel darkness, and drive evil from its presence. Joshua realized in that instant that God, the God of Abraham, the God of Adam, had been with them all the time, but he, too sure of himself and proud of his own strength, could not see it. The force of God's ancient promises hit him as real in that moment as they had hit Abraham centuries before. If God said He would lead them into the Promised Land, He would. No force in this world could prevent Him. A supremely clear realization. All of this flashed into Joshua's mind as quickly as lightning bolted from sky to earth. The Amalekite had no clue what God had just done in Joshua's heart and was shocked to see Joshua grab his sword and spring to his feet. A quick sword slash cut the surprised warrior so deep in the neck just above his armor breastplate that he dropped helplessly to the ground, life draining out of him with each spurt of his blood. His shocked, wide open eyes began to glaze. Taking no time to savor the victory, Joshua attacked the next closest enemy, then the next, and then remembered to encourage his men—only to discover they needed no encouragement, as they too attacked with renewed energy and fierceness. Those frightful faces did not look so terrifying as their limp and lifeless bodies dropped into the dirt. The hideous, grotesque expressions, exaggerated by the war paint, looked like the foolish efforts of the misguided soul who had indulged himself in their creation, all coming to nothing, vanishing to death. Joshua's men were prevailing, now destroying this violent enemy. He for the first time had seen his utter helplessness, and not until then had he seen the clearly superior power and unwavering faithfulness of the Lord's presence among them. Another lesson worked so deeply into his heart that it would never leave.

Still, the power of evil never quit, devouring with insatiable appetite, wasting, destroying, all in its path, so the lesson was not yet over. Many believers have come to the point where they think, *This is so bad it could not get worse.* Then it does. As time wore on, Joshua's hands began to cramp on the sword handle, so difficult now to even hold, let alone to strike a blow. He began to focus on the struggle that loomed larger with each moment. He forgot the Lord—again. His legs and arms felt heavy and hard to move. Fatigue sapped his strength to hopeless weakness, and now the battle began to turn against them. Would this enemy never quit? Carnage everywhere, the attack raged on. He even had blood on his feet from stepping on gouged, dying bodies. Out of the corner of his eye he saw some of his men displaying similar signs of fatigue and beginning to drift backward, pushed by the relentless onslaught of enemy swords. More Amalekites kept coming to replace the dead ones, cruel and fierce as the first, hungering for murder, lusting to destroy, ravaging like fire with an appetite that never said, "Enough." Driven by passions untempered by thought, their power raged on and on and on. In the thick of the battle, death as close as the next swing of enemy sword, Joshua fought so hard he forgot the Lord again, so fierce was the battle. Now fatigue ate at his courage.

The skill and strength of moments ago drained to nothing, all over again, only worse this time. In the midst of this vicious battle for his life he finally cried with his heart, "Lord, help me!" not realizing his lips also cried out loud. He no longer cared who heard him shout in weakness and fear. He needed help. Quickly. Visions of losing this horrid battle tortured his mind. His warriors' wives and children would be taken and brutalized, maybe even cruelly murdered. In the thick of the battle, and while desperately employing his sword, that thought came up again. This Amalek, who should have been a friend and, more than that, a close relative, was a hate-filled enemy, descended from their same great-great . . . grandmother, Rebekah, now attacking them. It was difficult to understand, and there was no time to dwell on it. Joshua was the leader, and losing was his fault. He was at the end of his strength once again when he had called out in desperation to the Lord. Yet the way his men heard his frenzied call was not that way at all. They heard a reliance on the Lord so resolute it injected renewed strength into their hearts. Maybe God had made his voice sound like that.

Satan, the real force behind the Amalekites, was a dirty fighter, wearing Israel down with relentless pressure, sadistically scheming to humiliate and destroy. Warriors had poured like ants from a stepped-on anthill. Something hit Joshua from behind across the shoulders and lower neck with an audible thud, something heavy and solid, perhaps a club, and he saw stars as the sheer force of the blow smashed him flat to the earth. The wind was knocked out of him and he could not breathe. In the next moment again a sword would run him through or remove his head! He tried to move out of the way of the death blow he knew was coming, but he felt heavy and numb, about to lose consciousness, so tired he did not even care anymore and could not move. Once again he faced the end of his life and there was nothing he could do about it. Every few minutes death rushed to him, so close he could feel it. Yet his words had flown to the One stronger than death! Craning his neck and in utter weakness, he looked up and saw Moses—still atop the hill—his weakening arms now held skyward by Aaron and Hur, blessed Aaron and Hur. Faster than the speed of thought, Moses's prayer and God's power flooded his heart with courage. With explosive strength he leaped once more to his feet and spun around, sword in hand, angry for victory. Seeing the club in the man's hands he narrowed his eyes and focused the wrath of God upon this vicious, drug-influenced, powerful man. Somehow this fool perceived the power now arrayed against him, but not before Joshua's sword, in a blaze, slashed his club in two! The startled man now held only its useless handle in his hands. He dropped it, turned and ran, attempting to disappear into the mob. An Israelite saw him coming and, planting the butt of his spear in the ground, held the sharp point up to meet him. The Amalekite, with all his strength, impaled himself.

Joshua had again understood something he would never forget. His own formidable strength, like that of the powerful, skilled warrior Moses, was no match for Satan. And Satan was no match for God. Moses's faith, Joshua's faith, Joshua's cry, had tapped into God's power. Israel carried swords and spears, but it was God who guided their movements. The battle finally came to an end with the Amalekites routed, destroyed by their own hatred and foolishness. Joshua was stunned by how instantly the Lord had reached out and helped them. Maybe He had been waiting for Joshua—and Israel—to see their helplessness and dire need in a deeper way and for that cry from a hopeless heart. Then He would show them how close they were to His heart and how willing He was to help them. He had used the Amalekites to drive them to that point. The "furnace of affliction" forged many new warriors that day, realistic battle-hardened men with a deep-seated trust in the Lord.

Moses had been right. He was wiser than Joshua. This battle was too big for any of them. The vivid scene of Moses atop the hill, a needy human figure silhouetted against the sky, hands outstretched to heaven, was one more thing to live in Joshua's memory. In the midst of future battles with a cruel enemy bent on killing him and all his people, Joshua would remember those scenes—part of the wisdom that would serve him the rest of his life. It pointed him straight to the Lord, the true source of his strength.

He did not know it yet, but in fighting this battle he was taking one more step toward becoming the one who would lead Israel into the Promised Land. God's method of teaching all his children is first to communicate His ideas through His Word and then to teach them through experience in the world through which He will lead them. Everything in a believer's life is special in the Lord's eyes and serves a good purpose, maybe not yet understood by the believer, but understood by God. Joshua had put his life on the line today and had entered into the arena of the Lord's teaching, a place where the lessons drove so deeply they were never lost.

Moses had learned in an earlier season about his own need for God's help and could now teach Israel. During the forty years in the desert of Midian, tending cattle for his father-in-law, the glory of his position as part of the royal family in Egypt had evaporated into the desert air. He had gone through a dark time after fleeing Egypt. Yet the forty years in Midian turned out to be a better school than Pharaoh's privileged courtyard, and God would eventually use him mightily to lead Israel out of Egypt. Only now they were stuck in a wilderness fighting for their lives. Today Moses was not easily blown off course by the winds of the world. He clung to his God—and it was that simple. Now his example was teaching all Israel.

Joshua won the battle that day. In the process he had met Amalek, and now, with time to think about it, this battle should never have been. When the attack came it was so intense it took all his attention. Now that it was finished, at least for a time, he reflected on it. Something was pushing up in his mind, something hard to put his finger on. Amalek, as a grandson of Esau—twin brother of Jacob, the father of all Israel, was a close relative. They came from the same mother and father, Rebecca and Isaac, the son of Abraham and Sarah, from whom sprang this new conquering nation of Israel. The family was chosen by God to carry His Word to a humanity held hostage in a dark world, a world of suffering humans sitting "in darkness and the shadow of death" (Luke 19: 10). More than that, this family would give birth to the very Savior of all mankind. Amalek should not have been an enemy but a beloved brother! Why did he hate Israel?

It was like Cain and Abel. Coming from the same two parents they should have loved and cared for one another. All the world was theirs, so much space and provision for every need. Limitless abundance existed for each. Yet Cain was so angered by his brother's acceptance by God that he killed him! The first children born to the first people had the seeds of their own destruction deeply embedded in their hearts. That was the human condition revealed in the record God preserved for mankind. Cain's hatred still existed and manifested itself through Amalek. It was a truth so deep it could not be ignored. Cain could have been forgiven like his brother, but he got angry and chose instead to cling to his own way, his anger. And Joshua knew the same selfishness and hatred existed in his own heart. He had seen it at many moments in his life. His own pride in thinking he could win this battle—even when the Lord said they would need His help—was the same resistance to God reflected in Cain, Esau and Amalek. And Joshua knew it. It was always easier to see error in others than in oneself. Amalek was a grim reminder of the evil buried deep in his own heart, an evil inhabiting every human heart, an evil man sought to ignore, to pretend did not exist, to work hard at overcoming, all to no avail. He could hate the evil in Amalek but not in himself because he would not let himself see his own faults. Only today Amalek had forced him to see.

And now Amalek had come right out in the open and attacked to kill, when Israel was alone in the wilderness with no one to help and no place to hide or escape. Amalek fought dirty and never bowed to superior force. Only death would subdue his twisted will. God had already pronounced judgment upon Esau and Amalek: "Jacob have I loved but Esau have I hated . . . Shall not the judge of all the earth do right?" (Genesis 18: 25). Esau's refusal to value any mention of God or His right as Lord over him was what God hated. He worshipped his own ideas. "Humble yourselves in the sight of the Lord, and he shall lift you up," said scripture (James 4:10). God's word further said, "at the name of Jesus every knee shall bow . . . and every tongue confess that Jesus Christ is Lord (Philippians 2: 10-11). We do this willingly in this life, or unwillingly at the final judgment of God. To be called to that judgment without Christ as one's protector and defense is a horror beyond the worst tragedy that can be imagined. The brutalities of the worst dictators and marauding warriors would seem like insignificant previews compared to the horrors of hell. No escape will exist at that point. God created us with an eternal existence, and in this life we select whether that existence will be in God's presence or apart from it. Judgments pronounced on that day would be final and forever. (The famous French philosopher, Voltaire, an atheist who hated God to the point that he spearheaded efforts to rid the earth of Bibles, reportedly faced death screaming in terror. His home was later purchased by an organization that used it as headquarters for distributing Bibles in Europe. Ironic.)

Joshua realized his own inner ambitions often ran counter to what he knew God's will to be. On this day in fighting Amalek he saw his own pride spurn God's help and then, going down in defeat, saw his own utter helplessness more clearly and unforgettably than ever before. Now he learned to scrap his own efforts and take God at His word. Like the priests stepping into Jordan carrying the Ark, he saw that taking that first step of trusting God's advice was what unleashed God's power in his life.

In the days after the battle and the victory, Joshua shuddered many times to remember how closely they had come to losing. Sometimes, while fighting for one's life, one had no time for fear, only time to act. Later, fear would rush in as one realized how close death had suddenly reared. That would have been the end of the promise to Abraham—but it had not happened. Joshua had rather brazenly dashed into battle, proud to be the one trusted to lead God's army, sure of himself and his ability to conquer. That grotesque man who had smashed the sword out of his hands had changed all that in an instant.

Joshua fought two battles that day, one against an army of vicious Amalekites and one against his own proud, self-assured heart. In the thick of the battle, and while desperately employing his sword, a thought began to form in Joshua's mind. This distant relative Amalek was like his own heart, working against him, never completely bowing to God's will and always wanting to go his own direction. Joshua was seeing in a new way his own incorrigible heart and, beyond that, the hearts of all humans. Incorrigible because there was a part in every heart that would never change, a part that doubted God and resisted Him all the time. It refused to believe His words or to bow to Him. The prophet Jeremiah would say it this way in chapter 17: 9: "The heart is deceitful above all things, and desperately wicked: who can know it?" No matter how hard one tried to reform it and make it good, it would NEVER change. It would make one think it had, but that was part of the deception. Joshua would not believe how truly needy and helpless he was in the face of the powers of the universe until he had seen it firsthand, as had Moses, when all hope and all strength were gone.

CHAPTER 19

SINAI

(Exodus 19-34)

Israel continued its journey into the wilderness, and on the fourteenth day of the third month after they had come out of Egypt, they arrived at Mount Sinai, where the Lord would use their very pride to humble them and teach them a lesson. Joshua stayed close to Moses, and Matthias stayed as close as he could to Jerusha. He cherished each moment with her. Sometimes he just gazed upon her face. Often it sparkled with joy or enthusiasm at simply being with him. Other times it bore no expression as she silently observed happenings around her. Matthias knew her well enough by now to know she was taking everything in but revealing no indication of what she was thinking. When she did finally say something, her conclusions were often more astute than his. He did not mind. She was his partner, a helper in his life, and he knew she respected him as much as he respected her. Besides, she kept him on his toes.

Israel set up camp near the base of the mountain, and Moses went up unto God. He called out to him, saying, "Thus you shall say to the house of Jacob, and tell the children of Israel; You have seen what I did to the Egyptians, and how I bore you on eagles' wings and brought you to Myself. Now, therefore, if you will obey My voice and keep My covenant, then you shall be a special treasure to Me above all people, for all the earth is Mine. And you shall be to Me a kingdom of priests and a holy nation. These are the words which you shall speak to the children of Israel." Moses came down from the mountain and relayed all the words.

In reminding them of their deliverance from Egypt God was reminding them that, when they had no strength to help themselves and escape from Egypt, God had done it all for them. The plagues that demonstrated his power over every force and false belief in that nation were all God's doing. Forcing Pharaoh to let them go was God's doing, with no help from a single Israelite. Destroying Pharaoh's power and his merciless army at the Red Sea was God's doing. Yes, He had "borne them on eagles' wings" in carrying them out of Egypt.

What He told them today was a departure from what He had told Abraham. The original promise to Abraham was unconditional, meaning that God's plan for Israel to be a great nation and a light to the world had no strings attached. God would do it in spite of Israel's human weaknesses—as He had done in the deliverance from Egypt. The "if" in "if you will obey" changed everything. It made this new promise "conditional" upon Israel's obedience, that is, they would now only be and blessed "if they obeyed Him." Moses could have respectfully asked God why this change to the blessings now being conditional upon their obedience.

But Moses did not do that. Neither did Israel. Instead their response was, "All that the Lord has spoken we will do." It was man's natural tendency to believe in himself and to think that he was better than he actually was. God understood this about man. It had been present in Adam when he sewed fig leaves together to cover up for his failures. Now Israel carelessly told God they would obey Him at all times. Adam was reluctant to believe how thoroughly depraved he had become, and, like him, so was Israel. God rejected the fig leaves (the world's first religion—man trying to make up for his own sin), and now He would be giving a set of commandments in the next few days which would set forth God's extremely high standards of behavior to which man should compare himself. A true understanding of them would convince one of his own inability to make himself righteous before the Lord.

What followed was the famous "giving of the law." God told Moses to tell the people to get themselves ready, even wash their clothes. A special day was coming. On the third day he would come down upon Mount Sinai in the sight of all the people. The people could watch but not come up the mountain. Anyone who even touched it would be stoned or shot through with an arrow. On the third day thundering and lightning shook the mountain and a thick cloud covered its top. A trumpet sounded so loud and long that all the people in the camp trembled. Moses brought the people to the foot of the mountain to meet with God. Smoke rose high in the sky, and God descended in terrifying fire to its top. The entire mountain shook in great earthquakes, and the trumpet blast grew louder and louder. Then God called Moses and Aaron to the top of the mountain, and spoke to them the ten commandments, and thus began the Age of Law. As the people saw the thundering and lightning they trembled and moved away, telling Moses, "You speak with us . . . but let not God speak with us, lest we die."

Moses said to them, "Do not fear. God has come to test you, that you may respect him and not sin." One would think that after an absolutely earth-shaking display of God's all-consuming power no one would ever sin again. Moses wrote all the words of the Lord and the next day built an altar at the base of the hill and twelve pillars, one for each tribe of Israel. Then he read those words to all the people so that they heard them too. He detailed men to offer burnt offerings and peace offerings of oxen to the Lord upon the altar. Then he sprinkled the blood of the sacrifices on the altar and on the people. One can imagine the effect of bright red fresh blood splashed on your clothes and of seeing it on the clothes of others. A very visible signal from the Lord.

Following that the Lord told Moses, "Come up to Me in the mount, and I will give you tables of stone, and a law, and commandments which I have written that you may teach them." Additionally, God gave instructions concerning the tabernacle, the priesthood and the sacrifices. God called Moses into the thick cloud, and he remained on the mountain forty days and forty nights.

In the meantime the people grew restless and gathered together to Aaron, saying, "Make us gods to go before us, for this Moses has disappeared and we don't know what has become of him." So Aaron told them to give him their gold earrings and jewelry, which he then melted down and remade into a golden calf. They worshipped it as the "god that had brought them out of Egypt." Aaron was the brother who accompanied Moses to all those conflict-ridden meetings with Pharaoh and secured victory. As the first official priest designated by God, the entire priesthood of Israel was named after him, the Aaronic priesthood, and all the future priests descended from him. But we see Aaron caving in to the will of the crowd. God certainly did not sugarcoat the failings of his beloved people. Man tends to glorify those from the past who did great things, maybe because he wants to think better of himself than is really true. God recorded the failures along with the successes. "Why did not God pick someone better than him?" one might ask. The sad answer was that there was no one better.

Forty days ended, the Lord told Moses, "Go, get down! Your people whom you brought out of Egypt have corrupted themselves. They have made themselves a calf and worshipped it. I have seen this people, indeed it is a stiff-necked people!" He further said, "Let Me alone that My wrath may burn hot against them and I consume them. Then I will make of you a great nation."

What an offer to Moses. An entire new nation would arise from him, and he would be the head of it, definitely a difficult offer to turn down. Moses' answer was touching. "Lord, why does Your wrath burn hot against Your people whom You have brought out of Egypt with great power and a mighty hand? Why should the Egyptians speak and say, 'He brought them out to harm them and consume them off the face of the earth'? Turn Your fierce wrath and relent from this harm to Your people." Moses had seen the power of God and understood and absorbed something of His character. Knowing Him and his kindness gave him the confidence to reason with Him.

"Remember Abraham, Isaac, and Israel, your servants to whom you swore by your own self and said to them, 'I will multiply your descendants as the stars of heaven, and all this land I have spoken of I give to your descendants, and they shall inherit it forever.'" Many of the ancient believers dared reason with God on the basis of His own words, His promises. God seemed to enjoy it and always honored such requests. Moses here reflected a love for God's people and a respect for God's reputation. And God, rather than reacting in anger at him, honored Moses' respect for His words. He granted Moses' request and relented from the harm He had threatened against His people.

Moses walked down from the mountain carrying the two stone tablets of testimony. Joshua, waiting farther down, joined him, and when he heard the noise of the people clamoring in the distance, he said to Moses, "There is a noise of war in the camp."

Moses said, "No . . . it is the sound of singing I hear." When they came near the camp and saw the calf and the dancing, Moses, in anger, cast the tablets out of his hands and broke them. Then he ground the calf to powder, threw it in water, and made them drink it. After that God called Moses up the mountain again and said, "Cut two tablets of stone, like the first ones, and I will write on these the words I wrote on the first tablets which you broke." The Lord met him there again, and once more he was there with the Lord forty days and forty nights. When he came down from the mountain with the new tablets, Moses did not know that the skin of his face shone. The people moved away from him in fear, but he called them close and gave them the tablets and instructions. From then on when he spoke with the people he put a veil on his face. The glory of the Lord and the intense fire of his presence had caused Moses himself to glow!

CHAPTER 20

MATTHIAS AND JERUSHA DISCUSS LAW

Matthias and Jerusha, at their young age, had beheld this Mount Sinai experience—the terror, the people's worship of the golden calf, the wild, immodest dancing, Moses' wrath, and his instructions.

Now, almost a year later, Jerusha was troubled. She lamented, "I know we said, 'All that the Lord has said we will do,' but I have been thinking about it . . . we don't really do what the Lord says."

"What do you mean?" questioned Matthias.

"Well, one of the commandments said to honor your father and mother. I know I have talked back to them many times, even yelled at them when I was mad. I know I have broken that one. What do you think, Matthias?"

"Hmmm . . . but you're a good girl, Jerusha . . . and I love you. God does too."

"Is that all you have to say? I'm scared, Matthias. Then I said something mean about my little sister just to get her in trouble. It was a lie. And I did it on purpose. Now there is nothing I can do to fix it. I already did it. I didn't mean to do wrong, so God could overlook that, right?"

"I don't know, Jerusha. You think too much. Just let it go. You're no worse than anyone else."

"You're no help! I'm worried."

Matthias put his arm around her, trying to comfort her, but she would not be comforted. He had not seen her like this before.

"Remember," she said, "Moses told us God also told him to 'be holy, for I am holy' and not to turn to idols and worship them? How can we be as holy as God? And then about idols . . . the Egyptians had idols and we knew they prayed to them. We thought them foolish because our God was the real God. But we did not know how real He was. Now, after the Red Sea, it is all different. He *delivered* us from Egypt. He is more real than we knew! We don't even know how to honor Him or put Him before all other gods as He commanded."

"Like I said, you think too much, Jerusha. You are confusing me with all these complicated thoughts."

"It's not complicated, Matthias. When you look to something to help you, you are worshipping it. Can't you see that?" Matthias listened, having a hard time following her. "When the Egyptians put their hopes in those dumb idols, they were worshipping them. God had no place in their hearts. They thought *we* were foolish. They prayed for their crops to grow, for happiness, for money . . . and they thought their idol could make it happen."

"So the idol was their god?" questioned Matthias.

"Right . . . I don't have a carved stone idol like they did, and yet what I think about most of the time is myself and my plans, the things I want to make me happy. I don't think about God that much, or what He cares about. I think about me! Isn't that worshipping myself? Aren't I my own idol? I used to think I was a good person, thoughtful of others, respectful to God. Now that I see His holiness, His pureness, His truthfulness, His commandments more clearly, I don't feel so good about myself."

Matthias was becoming uncomfortable with the whole conversation. He watched her talk, half bored, half interested. *Why doesn't she just drop it and quit worrying about it?* he thought to himself.

"I'm just as bad as those Egyptians that we hated so much. I cannot even keep the first commandment. Is anyone else as bad as I am?" She paused for a moment, and Matthias saw tears glisten in her eyes. In the painful silence she thought about the inconsistencies she had observed in other people. "Even children . . . "

"What about them?" interrupted Matthias. "You're not going to find fault with them too, are you? They are so innocent and lovable."

"I can't help what I see, and you know I'm right."

"What do you see, Jerusha? C'mon."

"Many times I have seen one take another's toy right out of his hands—and then hit him over the head with it and walk away leaving him crying—and he doesn't care either! Even children are self-centered sinners. It's how we are born. All we care about is ourselves. Nobody can keep God's laws," she sobbed finally.

"You dishonor God, Jerusha. He *wants* us to keep them. What's wrong with you? You're just giving up and pretending you can't help sinning? So you're not even going to try. Do you think God *wants* us to sin?"

Her voice rising in anger, she blurted, "*You* can't keep it, Matthias! You're a sinner like all the rest."

"At least I *try*, Jerusha—not like you. You don't even care! I've never seen you so disrespectful."

"At least I'm not stubborn." Her words pricked like a thorn as she glared at him in defiant silence.

Matthias fidgeted. This conversation had gone sideways and out of control. "You need to at least try, Jerusha," he offered in a conciliatory tone. Then, without thinking, he countered with, 'You're looking for an excuse to sin. Do you think God does not even want us to try not to sin?"

"I don't know, Matthias. I'm confused about it all, and you have no sympathy for what I'm going through. You're a sinner but you don't want to think about it or even talk about it."

"Girls shouldn't speak up like that. Wasn't Eve the first to sin? It's your fault, Jerusha. All women. If it weren't for you this world would be a better place," countered Matthias, suddenly seeing a way to triumph in this argument. Proud of himself, he had punctuated those last words with disgust, inching farther out on a limb that was about to snap. At that moment he heard her mother call her to help with supper. "I have to go now, Jerusha," he snarled opportunely as he turned his back and stalked away. "Why does she always think she's right?" he muttered to himself but quietly enough so she could not hear.

Now Matthias was troubled. Walking home, he could not help thinking about the commandments either, but so far he had always quickly put them out of his mind, as they made him upset, and he did not want to be bothered. Now she had dredged them all up again, and as he thought about it he realized he could not even keep the first commandment either. "Love the Lord your God with all your heart . . . " Nobody can do that. He knew he had not always put God first in his thinking. In truth, he probably *never* did. Now he was bothered too. What had Jerusha done to him? He had been content until he talked to her. He found his way back to his family, but his steps were no longer carefree and happy.

"What's wrong with you?" asked his father.

"Oh, nothing." He did not want to get into another painful discussion. The more he thought about it, the more he realized they were all guilty, even his parents. Maybe even Moses. His thoughts raced. "All I care about is myself. I can never put God first. I can't even keep His first rule either, let alone the other ones. Back in Egypt I was jealous of the Egyptians and all the privileges they had. I hated them. Why did they have everything? What made them better than me? I'm better than they are. We are God's chosen. We don't deserve to be slaves. And now God says it is wrong to be jealous. What does He want anyhow? Nobody could keep all those rules. Maybe God just hates everybody and wants to make us miserable and find an excuse to punish us. Maybe He is going to kill us too, like He did the Egyptians. We are in a giant trap. What kind of ocean will cave in on us? I hate you, Jerusha." He hated God too, but he could not bring himself to say it. At least he was not *that* bad.

Meanwhile Jerusha sought out her friend, Abi, whom she found passing time with their other friend, Tamar. Hoping they might have some insight to help, she re-explained her concerns to them both and how she had talked with Matthias, but he did not seem too concerned and did not want to think about it. Abi understood Jerusha's misgivings and let on that she too was troubled over the high standards demanded by the law. But she had no answers either and in her mind backed off and waited, hoping time would help her understand it better. Tamar chided, "I don't see what the problem is. If that is what God says, just do it and quit making things so complicated." Tamar saw herself as reasonable and, beyond that, practical. You could waste a lot of time questioning things from this direction and then that and in the meantime getting nothing done. Both looked at her, wondering how she could think it was so easy to keep the law, but they were not up to arguing, especially when they knew her to be a little "bull-headed" about her opinions. She mistakenly took their silence as an admission that they really weren't interested in following God. "I do what God says, and that's it. You should quit fighting Him." Jerusha sensed a lecture coming. "Most people just don't want to obey Him. We would do a lot better if we just did what He said."

"Tamar, I didn't say we shouldn't try to keep the law. I said the law demands such perfection no one can keep it."

"So you are saying it's okay to sin? Do you think God is in favor of us sinning? He hates sin, so I am going to be as good as I can be. I know God will accept that."

"You're not as righteous as you think, Tamar. Nobody can live a perfect life, not even you." Abi watched these two with interest but said nothing, concluding that she had nothing to offer that would help the conversation. Tamar looked to her for support, but at this point Abi nervously bit her lip and said nothing.

"Are you saying God is not powerful enough to help us?" Tamar countered. "I trust Him. Don't you?" A standoff ensued and Abi suggested they go find something to eat.

That didn't go very well, Jerusha thought to herself later after they parted. *They're no more help than Matthias. I thought that no matter how hard I tried, it was not possible to keep the law every minute of every day my whole life—which is exactly what the law demands. Even if I kept the law perfectly for many years and then broke one law one time, it would make me a lawbreaker, like a break in a rope would make the whole rope unfit. Tamar does not even know what I am talking about.*

"From what we saw at Sinai," pondered Jerusha, "lawbreakers could not come near to God who is pure and holy and a devouring fire. That whole time was terrifying. The mountain was on fire on top. The earth shook at God's presence. I thought it would fall down and crush us the way the ground shook. We were all scared. No one could go near. God said anyone who did would be killed on the spot. Only Moses could go up there—because God called him—and then used him to bring that awful law back to us. We were so foolish as to say, 'All that the Lord has said we will do.' What a joke! If anyone was really honest about it, they would have to admit they failed enough since the first day to deserve death. Instead of the law being a good thing, it was a death sentence for us. We do not have a chance of seeing God by keeping the law. Tamar only *thinks* she can keep it and then looks down on me for being a lawbreaker. Are all of us that crazy?" Jerusha, in her agitated state of mind, found no comfort anywhere that day. Then she bitterly wondered why God delivered them from Egypt if there was no chance that they could ever please Him. As surely as God had judged Pharaoh and Egypt, He would have to judge her too. And everybody else in Israel.

CHAPTER 21

MATTHIAS IS TROUBLED

That night Matthias had a hard time sleeping, and once when he awoke, an idea came to him. After delivering the commandments to Moses, God had spoken of more, something else that amongst all the details, Matthias had overlooked, about a "Tabernacle," a structure to be erected where God said, "And there I will meet with you." God had given Moses lengthy and detailed instructions, almost too confusing to understand, about constructing a tent-like room, a giant walled in area. At its entrance stood an altar for offering burnt sacrifices to God. As Matthias thought about it he remembered more than he thought. Beyond the altar stood a room called the "Holy Place," and connected beyond that another smaller room called the "Most Holy Place," housing the Ark of the Covenant. It was a wooden box covered inside and out with gold and containing the very stone tablets Moses brought down from the mountain, inscribed with those awful commandments.

The words on those stone tablets spoke to man of God's character and holiness and His expectations for man in order for him to be acceptable to God.

Then more revived in his memory. The Tabernacle's outermost walls would be of "fine twined linen" and the outside of those covered with rams' skins and a roof over the top consisting of badgers' skins. The plain appearance from the outside gave no indication of the fabulous treasure within. The value of this structure, with so very much gold lining its surfaces and the stone tablets from the hand of God, would be impossible to calculate. This entire Tabernacle was a message from God to man. Looking so plain, it would nonetheless yield its message to anyone willing to look inside and search for answers.

Now that he was thinking about it he remembered something else God had said that suddenly seemed important. He had detailed several types of sacrifices to be offered on the brazen altar at the Tabernacle's entrance. Those had to be offered before anyone could enter. No entrance without a sacrifice. That was when things started to clear for Matthias. In the most holy place above the Ark, he remembered, stood two golden figures of angel-like creatures, and that was where God's presence would dwell and where He would "commune" with man. The brazen altar at the entrance to the Tabernacle signified that the only acceptable approach to God was through a sacrifice at that altar, through judgment of one's own unholiness before he could ever be accepted by God.

In offering a sacrifice for himself that would be killed he was admitting he was a sinner deserving of death. The beautiful part was that God was communicating to man that *He* would provide that special sacrifice for man. Those who did not value God's advice would never bring a sacrifice or at best would bring a diseased or otherwise worthless animal. The offeror was to place his hands on the head of the animal which, in God's own words, transferred his sins to the animal. The animal was then killed at the altar, signifying God's complete hatred of sin and its effect in his world. The entire process was a clear picture of God's view of sin and mankind—man was marred and deserved to die. That sacrifice would die for him. Matthias thought back to the story of Adam and Eve and how they fell into sin. He knew the story so well because as a child he and his friends had acted it out, taking turns with who would play Adam, Eve, the Lord, and the serpent. At one time or another he had played every part. Tonight that story took on new meaning for Matthias (Genesis 3). Now that he thought about it, that story seemed to picture the same thing as the Tabernacle, that the sacrifice of an innocent substitute was God's way of dealing with man's fallen condition. *We were all so stuck on the law and trying to keep it that we missed what the Tabernacle was showing us,* he thought to himself.

God would deal with man's sinfulness for man, because man was not capable of remedying his condition himself. Those innocent animals pictured the sinless sacrifice God would provide for guilty man. "Who would that sacrifice be and when would he come?" he wondered to himself. "That sacrifice must picture the 'seed of the woman' about whom God had spoken to Eve and Adam, a human descendant God would send in the future to deal with the serpent." As Matthias thought about it, that message was given to them immediately after their first sin. When they took the fruit of that tree, something changed instantly in their relationship with God. They of their own will had forsaken His words and instantly experienced, at least in part, the "knowledge of good *and* evil" about which God had warned. Now there was no way back, and they could neither understand the depth of it nor do anything about it. The light in the world suddenly dimmed noticeably, and for the first time in their existence they felt fear, a new and unwelcome emotion. When they heard God's voice, instead of moving toward Him in delight as before, they feared and hid. That was where God had approached them—hiding in fear.

For some new reason their nakedness now shamed them, and they covered themselves with fig leaves to hide it. God questioned them not to find where they were hiding but to get them to realize and admit what they had done. They partially admitted it but made it look like it was someone else's fault. Adam said, "The woman *you* gave me made me eat," thereby blaming Eve and God. Eve said, "The serpent deceived me," blaming the serpent and making herself look innocent. Now, like Satan, they were deceivers. God did not argue with them. Nor did He question the serpent. He instead pronounced judgment on him. Rather than argue, God gave them a special lesson about their new condition. Rejecting their fig leaf covering, He Himself provided special clothing for them made of animal skins. It could be said those fig leaves were the world's first religion, which was *man's* way of covering up for his sin and making himself acceptable to God.

God's way meant an innocent animal died to provide covering for them. Matthias made the connection instantly to the brazen altar. It was the same message from the beginning of human existence. The path back to God was through the sacrifice of an innocent substitute. Those animals had not sinned as Adam and Eve had, yet they died because of them. A startling message to man was communicated in that brutal slaughter to make their clothing. Maybe the "seed of the woman" who would come would be an innocent person who would be the actual sacrifice that would both cleanse man and please God. It did two things. It took care of man's sins and with them gone, man was now clean and acceptable to God. Secondly, it aligned with the truth of God's statement that one who ate of that tree would die. In fulfilling that statement it showed that God was true to His word and was 'right' or 'righteous' in keeping it. The sacrifice meant more. It went beyond death and meant God was not leaving man there. From Adam's point of view he was made acceptable. From God's point of view He could righteously now accept Adam because the sacrifice had made him clean and holy, and God could be "satisfied" with that. What was impossible for man, God did for him. Man's part was to admit his guilt and accept God's help. These ideas lay imbedded, though not yet clearly seen, within this story. Nonetheless, like diamonds they lay waiting to be discovered. Matthias sensed all this but could not exactly bring it into focus. He thought on. If God could meet with Israel at the tabernacle, would that not mean that God accepted that sacrifice and somehow the sin was taken care of? That was the answer to the breaking of the law. The death of the innocent sacrifice seemed to satisfy God's dissatisfaction at breaking His laws. Matthias' mind was whirling.

He remembered a certain sacrifice God spoke of that was a "continual burnt offering," which was "one lamb" in the morning and "one lamb" in the evening, "day by day continually throughout your generations, at the door of the Tabernacle" (Exodus 29: 38-42). And then God had said that He would "meet with them there," and "dwell among them." *How could he condemn us for breaking the law and then dwell with us in the Tabernacle? God was telling us two different things, so how could both be true? The law proved to us undeniably that we were sinners. No matter how hard we tried we could not rid ourselves of sin. Yet when we offered the sacrifice He required, God could "meet with us" and dwell among us."* Hard to understand, but there was hope. Matthias remembered stories that, often in the past, God's people had offered sacrifices on stone altars and fire had come down from heaven and consumed the sacrifice completely. That too meant God accepted the offering and there was hope. Didn't it? The thought crept into Matthias's mind that maybe God knew people would break the law. Maybe He gave that law as a way of showing man how out of tune he was with God. On his own there was no hope for him. He could *never* be as good as God expected. That must be what God meant when he rejected Adam's fig leaves. But then *he* provided a covering for them. God had a way of making them acceptable to Him again. Strange as it seemed, the sacrifice was a way of dealing with the problem. Else, why would He prescribe the altar if there were not a need for it and if it would not work? (Note: The coming of the Savior Jesus was announced by God in the sparest of detail after the first sin. It was clear from the beginning that sin brought death into the world and that God would deal with it for man by sending someone to take care of it for us. Exactly who that was and when He would come was gradually revealed over the coming centuries. From Adam's time and continuing through history people offered animal sacrifices for their sins—an indication that many understood what God had communicated to man. In the Book of Job, probably the oldest book in the Bible, Job, a non-Jew and contemporary of Abraham, stated, "I know that my Redeemer lives," indicating that in his time it was common knowledge in the world that a redeemer was coming. Abraham was given the message that a descendant would come through him who would be a "blessing to all the families of the world." The law and instructions for the Tabernacle were given to Moses at Mount Sinai, over four hundred years after Abraham's time. Five hundred years after that, King David wrote, "Blessed is the man whose iniquities are forgiven and to whom the Lord will not impute sin," indicating that David understood that admitting one was a sinner and giving the specified offerings at the Temple absolved a person of his sins so completely that he could proclaim himself as "righteous.")

It was still hard to understand, but somehow the answer was in there. He had to tell Jerusha. Maybe together they could make sense of it—and her troubled heart would be comforted. He was not angry with her any more.

CHAPTER 22

MATTHIAS AND JERUSHA CONTINUE

Both a little standoffish and embarrassed at their hot tempers the previous day, they meekly peeked at each other's expressions for some sign the fight was over. Matthias motioned toward a place to sit near one of the scrubby trees so common in the wilderness. She accepted the invitation, and they began to relax. He told her his thoughts about the Tabernacle, that maybe there was hope for them after all. Those sacrifices of an innocent animal had been performed since Adam's time. They were a gruesome, messy thing, puzzling to think about. Why had God chosen to do such an awful thing? Then, as Matthias thought about it, God had not chosen it— Adam and Eve had. Having never seen death, they were not sure what God meant when He told them not to eat the fruit of the 'Tree of the Knowledge of Good and Evil,' but the way He had said it, they knew it was not good.

Then he explained about Job, another believer back around Abraham's time, who referred to the "seed" promised to Eve as the "Redeemer." So far a redeemer had not come into the world, and yet Job and very many others believed that one day he would come, even if not in their lifetimes. (The Book of Job is thought by many to be the oldest book in the Bible.) As surely as Isaac had been born in accordance with God's prediction, that "seed," foretold so many years earlier, would come and deal with Adam and Eve's transgression, a condition they passed on to every human descended from them. Matthias told her his thoughts that the sacrifices God called for were His way of showing us that somehow He would provide a way to deal with our sin for us.

That meant God KNEW we could not stop sinning and we could not keep the law!

He knew, but we did not. We brashly responded with "All that God has said we will do," not really having any idea about the depth of the evil that occupied our hearts. He gave the law to show us the impossibility of gaining His favor by our good behavior. So many operated under the perception that if they tried hard enough and were sincere, God would certainly accept their efforts and welcome them into His presence. Every sacrifice made on an altar since Adam and Eve's time and now at the Tabernacle should have dashed that notion. The Tabernacle and the glory that filled it displayed God's presence among them. Yet God could not be approached without first encountering that awful altar and offering an animal sacrifice to be killed for their sinfulness. To pretend one was not a sinner was tantamount to spitting in God's face.

Jerusha perceived his meaning and semi relaxed. "God can accept us *because* of those sacrifices?" she replied tentatively, patiently, letting the thought develop.

"Right," he continued. "Somehow our sins are transferred to that animal, and when he is sacrificed on the altar, God accepts it. The spilling of blood at the altar, the death it brought of the innocent animal, the consumption by fire, all speak of God's attitude toward sin. He hates it and He will abide none of it in his kingdom. It has infected mankind and cast him into an abyss." Matthias paused . . . then added, "Do you see what he was showing us, Jerusha? Before God can forgive any sin He first has to deal with it in a manner true to Himself. When He told Adam, 'In the day you eat of it you shall die,' it was true; He meant it. If He said they had to die, they *had* to die. God is not like us, who often say things we would later have to correct. If the result of counting God's word not worth following is death, no way for man to correct it exists."

"What do you mean they died?" questioned Jerusha. "They were still alive."

"They *looked* alive, Jerusha, but inside they were dead. They had lost their perfect relationship with God. Remember at the beginning of Genesis it said, 'God created the heaven and the earth?' And then it said, 'the Spirit of God moved upon the face of the waters.' God was God, and he had a Spirit, and when he created man he said, 'Let us make man in our image, and in our likeness,' and he 'formed man of the dust of the ground and breathed into his nostrils the breath of life, and man became a living soul.' God did not say that about any other part of creation, not even the animals. They had physical life but did not share in that spiritual life. Only mankind had that kind of connection with God."

"You're going too fast for me, Matthias. I don't think I can follow all this."

"Just listen and think about it later. It will begin to make sense. Their spirit died; their connection to God, to real life, was broken. The "breath of life," the Spirit of God, could no longer dwell in the heart of man, who had allowed sin into his heart, who had spurned God's Word, so He left. Their bodies were physically alive but were beginning to die from that day forth, so yes, they did die; they died spiritually the moment they took of that fruit, and there was nothing they could do about it. They passed that spiritually dead condition to the rest of us through their children, and we cannot help ourselves either."

"So what does all this have to do with the Tabernacle and all the offerings?" questioned Jerusha, trying to keep the conversation on track, and then fell silent. While she sat there thinking, a few things began to click in her mind. "The reason we can't keep God's law," said she with silently igniting excitement, "is we're not like Him. He gave us the law to prove that to us. Just like Adam and Eve, we have a hard time admitting we are wrong, and that we can't help ourselves. That's what the sacrifices are about. They are our admission we can't help ourselves but that God has a way of dealing with our sinfulness for us."

"Right. We don't know exactly how it all works. Job and the people of his time thought the 'seed' promised to Eve was a special person who would come, whom he called our 'Redeemer.' I think so too. God was showing us that His Word, His message, has gone out to all the world, through all the ages. In our pride we fancy this old story to be the exaggerations of ancient people far less wise than we. Maybe they were closer to truth than we are. We don't know exactly who this Redeemer is or when He will come or what He will do, but whenever He does come I think people will recognize him."

"Wait," said Jerusha. "What about trying to be good, like Abraham, Isaac and Jacob, the fathers of all of us, of our entire nation. They set the example for us with their righteous walk, or so everybody thinks. But it was not their 'righteous walk' that mattered. The old stories recorded all sorts of their failures. It was their 'belief' in what God said that made all the difference."

Matthias nodded in agreement. "So then the keeping of the law could never make us holy or righteous in God's sight. We are made righteous the same way our father Abraham was, by 'believing' what God said. It is so simple. How could we miss that?"

"Why would the Redeemer, in the power and holiness of His life, come to us in our dead condition in this world and become one of us if we were such sinners," continued Jerusha, "and take that death for us unless it would help? God could accept that, couldn't He? He has not come yet, and we don't know who He is or exactly when He will arrive, but those innocent animal sacrifices speak of Him and show us what He will do. It is good news, isn't it? He says He accepts anyone who offers that sacrifice! It does not matter what he has done. No matter what it is, it is *sin*—and that is what the sacrifice covers! . . . And MY sins. He will take care of them. Right? The answer was there all the time. We just never saw it!" She looked at him, and Matthias was amazed. She had strung words together in a way that made his thoughts clear.

"Jerusha, you made sense out of it. We figured it out together. He is guiding us every day with that smoke and fire above the Tabernacle. The peace that can come from following Him is right in front of our eyes. It is different than struggling to keep the law. There's no hope in that. We need to accept that fact. But we can follow Him. That's what we are doing right now by following the cloud! He knows we will fail, but He will even take care of our sin—if we let Him. He took us at our lowest point. He knew all about us and still cared for us. He knew we were helpless slaves. Worse than that, He knew we were slaves to our own sinful hearts. If He understood our complete sinfulness then and still rescued us, would He abandon us today if we sinned again? No! He understood our hearts far better than we did. He knew every bad thing about us, and He still loved us."

"I think He is kinder and more loving than we ever realized," agreed Jerusha.

"And I think He has a plan for taking care of us forever. He led us out of Egypt and is taking care of us today in this wilderness where there is hardly any food or water, certainly not enough to feed a few million people. We are where He led us with the cloud. Can't we accept that and relax in it? Peace lies in trusting Him—no matter where we are. He was with us in Egypt and He is with us now."

He paused, in a newly relaxed manner, and looked at her. After a few moments she lifted her gaze to his hopeful eyes. Her face lit up again with that radiance he had first seen in her on that day in the Red Sea. Her joy spilled over to him.

CHAPTER 23

KADESH-BARNEA AND MORE WILDERNESS

(Numbers 9-27; Exodus 40)

After receiving the law and setting up the Tabernacle the Israelites continued their journey through the wilderness. It had been set up on the first day of the first month of the second year after leaving Egypt. On the fourteenth day they kept the Passover, and on the twentieth day the Lord lifted the cloud from the Tabernacle and began leading them out of the wilderness of Sinai. He led Israel by it from then on, and whether it was two days, or a month, or a year, when the cloud rested on the Tabernacle again, they rested in their tents. When it was taken up they journeyed. Imagine being led *every single day* by the Lord himself. You would always be in the right place, the place where He had led you! If the journey were difficult you would still know that it was where He had led you, and that He would take care of you no matter how difficult the circumstances. Because He *promised.* In truth, He did not even have to promise. His words were not spoken haphazardly. If He said something, He meant to keep His word.

Though God chose Israel to carry His message to the world, it did not mean they were better than everybody else. In fact, God created a nation from a childless couple, Abram and Sarai, from the pagan city of Ur of the Chaldeans to be the bearer of His message and the people from whom His Savior would emerge. By his own words He did this "because He loved them" and because He would "keep the promise" He made to Abram.

In time Israel hungered and wept and complained, "Who shall give us meat to eat? We remember the fish we ate freely in Egypt, the cucumbers, the melons, the leeks, the onions, and the garlic, but now we have lost our appetite. All we have is manna . . ." Moses heard the people weeping throughout their families. He complained to God, "You have laid the burden of all these people on me. It is too heavy. Did I conceive them? I cannot feed them! Please kill me now if I have found favor in your sight—and do not let me face my own ruin."

The Lord said to Moses, "I will give you meat and you shall eat . . . not one day, nor two days . . . nor ten days, nor twenty days, but for a whole month, until it comes out of your nostrils and you loathe it because you have despised the Lord who is among you and have wept . . . saying, 'Why did we ever come up out of Egypt?'"

Moses said, "Shall flocks and herds be slaughtered for them . . . or shall all the fish of the sea be gathered for them?"

The Lord said, "Is the Lord's arm too short? Now you shall see whether what I say will come true for you." Then a wind came up from the sea and brought quail that covered the ground about a day's walk in all directions. While they ate the wrath of the Lord was "kindled against them" and a plague developed, killing a large number of the complainers.

From there the cloud led them to the edge of the Promised Land, to a place called Kadesh-Barnea, eleven days' journey away (Deuteronomy 1: 2). The Lord had told Moses to select one leader from each of the twelve tribes to form a party to search out the land of Canaan. Upon returning they reported that the land fairly "flowed with milk and honey," and they brought samples of its luscious fruit. Two of the men, Joshua and Caleb, counseled to go in immediately and the Lord would give them the victory. The other ten reported what they deemed a more "sober" assessment, that many cities were fortified and walled and protected by capable armies, and what is more, some of the cities were populated by "men of great stature. And there we saw the children of Anak, which come of the giants! And we were in own sight as grasshoppers, and so we were in their sight" (Numbers 13: 21-33)! There was no way they could take this land. With such words they stirred fear into the hearts of Israel, and Joshua and Caleb were overruled. The people wept that night and complained about Moses and Aaron, saying, "If only we had died in Egypt or in this wilderness . . . Did God bring us out here to fall by the sword and that our wives and children should be a prey? It would be better for us to return to Egypt! Let's make a captain to lead us back to Egypt."

Moses and Aaron fell on their faces before Israel and Joshua and Caleb tore their clothes in abject frustration. They repeated, "The land we searched is an exceeding good land. If the Lord delights in us He will bring us in. Only rebel not against the Lord or fear the people of the land. Their defense is departed from them, and the Lord is with us. Don't be afraid of them."

But all the congregation shouted to stone them with stones. Then the glory of the Lord appeared in the tabernacle and all Israel saw it, and the Lord said to Moses, "How long will this people provoke Me? How long will it be before they believe Me for all the signs I have shown them? I will smite them and disinherit them and make of you a greater and mightier nation."

Moses spoke a most remarkable answer: "Then the Egyptians and other nations will hear. If You kill them they will say You were not able to bring this people You delivered into the land You promised them." He continued, "Let the power of my Lord be great, and as You have said that You are long-suffering and merciful and forgiving of iniquities, pardon, I beg You, the iniquity of this people." This was an astonishing prayer by Moses, a prayer he could only make because he had been in the Lord's presence and had come to understand his character over the years. Moses, though offered an exalted position, was more concerned about God's reputation and the people than he was about himself! This was the kind of prayer the Lord would honor. God's character had made a deep impression on Moses and shaped his thinking. It was how the Lord would view the situation.

He said, "I have pardoned as you asked. But as truly as I live, all the earth shall be filled with the glory of the Lord. These people which have seen My glory and My miracles and have tempted Me now these ten times shall not see the land I promised to their fathers. But my servants Caleb and Joshua, which had another spirit within them and have followed Me fully, will I bring into the land." Then God told Moses to tell the rest of Israel, "Your carcasses shall fall in this wilderness, all of you from twenty years old and upward which have murmured against Me, except Caleb and Joshua and your little ones which you said would be a prey, them will I bring in. You will wander in this wilderness forty years, according to the number of days you searched the land, even forty days, a day for a year, while you waste and die in in the wilderness. I the Lord have said it, and I will do it." God honored their free will to choose, yet they would bear the fruit of their decision.

In the next few years, Matthias came to realize his moments with Jerusha were special, and he did not want them to end. The thought of growing older and possibly losing her as their lives might follow different directions seemed too painful to endure. He thought she felt the same way and decided to ask her. That afternoon he told her he had been "thinking" that since he was getting older he "should find a wife." The way he worded it instantly brought a troubled expression to Jerusha's face. Did Matthias love someone else? Was he telling her he was leaving her?

"Did you have someone in mind?" she questioned tentatively, almost fearing to hear his answer.

Matthias looked at her with wonder. "Of course I do, Jerusha . . . YOU! Will *you* be my wife?"

"You do surprise a girl, Matthias," she replied, pretending nonchalance. She too relished the moments with Matthias. "That is a whole new life," she said in her common-sense manner but then paused and looked up at him, unable to speak . . . Matthias saw the answer glistening in her eyes. His heart warmed with relief, yet he waited. He had asked, and it was her turn to answer. That was his way.

She knew he had perceived her answer, but she hesitated, sensing the gravity of the decision, knowing her answer would make it permanent. She may have been young, but she knew what they were saying. "Yes" would be forever. Hoping he would say more, she continued to stall. In silence his eyes searched hers, but he said nothing. "Yes," she finally breathed. They both stood motionless for several moments. Then he touched her hand, his wife to be, and drew her close. "You will have to ask my father . . . but I know he likes you and has always welcomed having you around us. I think he likes you better than he likes me," she teased.

"I will," said Matthias. And so he did, and in time, a new family came into being in Israel, in the wilderness, the barren wilderness, the cruel wilderness—where new life sprang up. The relationship that had begun on the day of deliverance in the Red Sea continued. God had brought them near each other and then watched as they found and kept seeking each other's company. The Lord knit their hearts together as they talked and learned to realize he was with them. Some moments they enjoyed doing nothing except being together, sort of pulling each other along as the months went by. They would continue in the same manner the rest of their days.

The trek through the wilderness was long, wearying for some, joyful and expectant for others. The Lord reminded them their shoes did not wear out nor their feet swell, and the diseases of Egypt had not afflicted them.

Still, near the end of the forty years of wandering, the older generation who had not yet died off complained again against Moses. "Why did you bring us out of Egypt to die in this wilderness? There is no bread, no water, and we hate this manna." The Lord sent fiery serpents among the people. One bite would kill, and many died. Now the Israelites were a little wiser, and they told Moses, "We have sinned by speaking against the Lord and against you. Pray to the Lord that He take the serpents from us."

Moses prayed and the Lord told him, "Make a fiery serpent of brass and set it on a pole. Every one that is bitten, when he looks upon the serpent shall live." Moses did so. From then on if one was bitten he could look at that serpent of brass—as God had instructed—and live! How simple God's remedy was! Poisonous snake bites are usually a quick death sentence unless some kind of medical intervention is immediately available, which is usually not the case. The simplicity of looking at the brass serpent and receiving instant healing made a perfect picture of the salvation God still provides today. Simply looking to Jesus for healing from the death sentence of sin acknowledges a need (I'm poisoned and dying!). With no help from us He does the rest and gives new life instantly to us.

The years of wandering continued. Many more died, Miriam among them, and were buried in the wilderness. At one point the water gave out. The people complained to Moses and Aaron, "Why have you brought us into this wilderness that we and our cattle should die here? There are no figs or pomegranates here, or vines, and there is no water to drink."

Moses cried to the Lord, "What shall I do with these people? They're ready to stone me."

The Lord said to him, "Go before the people, and take the elders of Israel and your rod, the one you held over the river in Egypt, and stand before the rock where you are and strike it with your rod and water shall come out."

He gathered all the people and said, "Hear now, you rebels, must I fetch water for you out of this rock?" In his anger he hit the rock twice with his rod, and water came out, rushed out, so that all the congregation drank, and all their animals.

Moses made a grave mistake here. In his frustration with one complaint after another for years on end, his anger took over and he made it sound like he, not the Lord, was the one supplying the water. The Lord graciously caused the water to flow anyhow but told Moses, "Because you misrepresented this situation to Israel you will not bring this congregation into the land I promised them. Yet you shall see the land, though you will not go in." Sometime later Moses went up from the plains of Moab to the top of Mount Pisgah, and the Lord showed him the entire land and said, "This is the land I swore to Abraham, Isaac, and Jacob and told them I would give it to their descendants. I have caused you to see it with your own eyes, but you shall not go into it."

Truly, Moses was one of the great leaders in the history of mankind. He led God's people, Israel, out of the slavery of Egypt. Doing so, he foreshadowed Christ leading mankind out of bondage to the captivity of sin and death, setting free any who would follow Him. Later Moses ascended Mount Sinai, where the Lord spoke to him and gave him the law written on tablets of stone. So Moses became the representative of God's law to mankind. The New Testament confirmed this: "For the law was given by Moses, but grace and truth came by Jesus Christ" (John1: 17). That verse also set forth the idea that the law was one thing and that "grace and truth" set forth by Jesus was another. That concept would progressively be revealed over time.

Now, drawing near the Promised Land, Israel encountered Sihon, king of the Amorites. Joshua asked permission of him to pass through his land on the way to Canaan, promising to take nothing and do no harm. Sihon refused, and instead attacked them. Israel sought the Lord's help, and thus began the era of conquests. Their path through the world as they followed God's leading to His blessings subjected them to unexplained and irrational hatred. But if He had led them into this situation, would He not be able to take care of them in the midst of the trouble they now faced? Though they would certainly experience fear, would He not know how to reach into their hearts, help them to understand the situation, and calm them with the peace of knowing He was in control? To those desiring to follow the Lord, the world is a hostile place with difficult to understand hatred and opposition. The Lord revealed to Moses that the opposition came from Satan, the one who had opposed God Himself, and, having been thrown out of heaven, insinuated his influence into this world. Amazingly, Israel smote Sihon's kingdom with the sword and took their land, all their cities and villages and all their belongings. Sihon and his kingdom of rebels were fools. Now dead fools. God was beginning to reveal more of His power over His enemies. No longer slaves and underdogs in a world fraught with confusion, Israel was emerging as a conquering force. They were children of God, led by Him in the midst of this dark world and, what's more, victorious in it. Barely known to them, they reflected light to the rest of the world. This thing was not done in a corner. The rumor-mongers of the world took notice, added their own exaggerations to the news, and spread it like wildfire.

The drama continued. Next on their way lay Bashan. Its king, Og, came out and warred against them. Another opponent. The Lord told Moses, "Do not fear him, for I have delivered him into your hand, and all his people and all his land. You shall do to him as you did to Sihon." After forty years in Midian, the encounters with Pharaoh, the Red Sea, and the Passover, Moses knew how to trust the Lord. So they smote Og and his sons, and all his people until there was none left alive, and they possessed his land. Israel's successes had begun. The world would take notice and mount its own reaction. It is still doing so today. Opposition pops up mysteriously, like weeds, for no readily seen reason, all over the world. The frantic influence of evil. One power will emerge as stronger.

CHAPTER 24

CROSSING JORDAN

(Joshua 3-4)

After returning successfully from the spy mission in Jericho and reporting to Joshua, Matthias returned home to his wife, whose expression of relief revealed her concern. The Lord had brought him back as part of His ongoing promise spoken so long ago that they would inherit the land. When they were alone he told her about their remarkable discovery in Jericho. They, like Joshua, pieced together that experience with the old stories, the promises to Abraham, the 400 years serving another nation, their deliverance from Egypt, and now God's most evident leading to Jordan and the land He had promised to give them. It was about to happen. How could God tell about it 400 years earlier—before it ever came to be? Aged and barren Abraham and Sarah had little inkling of the burning and shining sunrise, a light so bright no darkness could extinguish it, about to rise through them into the darkness of the pagan world.

Suddenly, word coming down from Joshua interrupted their musings. "When you see the Ark of the Covenant of the Lord your God and the priests carrying it, then follow after it. But do not come near. Stay back half a mile and watch, as it shows you the way to go, for you have not passed this way before." What was the "Ark of the Covenant?" It was a wooden box, covered inside and out with gold, containing the two tablets of stone on which were written the Ten Commandments given to Moses by God forty years earlier. It had accompanied them on all their journeys through the wilderness, signifying God's presence among them and His continuing leadership as they journeyed. Today it meant God was with them in their midst as they walked through the river and into Canaan land. Matthias and Jerusha looked at each other, knowing each other's thoughts after so much time together, as a new adventure opened. They were ready.

Joshua spoke the command to take up the Ark and start moving toward Jordan. God had led them *out* of Egypt and slavery. Now He was leading them *into* new territory, the very land Abraham had walked centuries earlier. Those who came out of Egypt never went back. Nor did Egypt chase after them, that is, after the Red Sea. They had been soundly and irrevocably defeated. Deliverance was once and forever. They had seen the Egyptian army unceremoniously drowned in the Red Sea. The power that loomed far greater than them, had conquered and enslaved them, was destroyed before their very eyes. The fear of them had been so great it almost made it hard to believe the truth of their freedom. Yet it was so.

The Lord had told Joshua, "This day will I begin to magnify you in the sight of all Israel, that they may know that, as I was with Moses, so I will be with you." He passed the message on to the children of Israel. "Come and hear the words of the Lord your God. Today you will know that the living God is among you, and you will without fail drive out from before you the Canaanites, the Hittites, the Hivites, the Perizzites, the Girgashites, the Amorites and the Jebusites, seven peoples. The Ark of the Covenant of the Lord of all the earth will go before you into Jordan. The priests will carry the Ark to Jordan, and when the soles of their feet touch the waters of Jordan, the waters coming from upstream will stand in a heap and the waters below will flow away." Israel's action in taking the land was much more than just them moving on their own to procure land on which to live. It was God's plan to *give* this land to them, and it was His words that led them to action.

So the priests carried the Ark to Jordan, swollen with spring runoff and a faster than normal current. When their feet touched the water (and not until then), the waters from above stood in a heap, backing water miles upstream to a city called Adam (*see footnote). Imagine the trust in the Lord those priests displayed to step into a river with two million people watching. What if the river kept flowing? The priests would look like absolute fools—and so would Joshua. This entire venture would have been a colossal failure. But it was not, and, as all the surrounding nations had heard about the Red Sea, they would soon learn about Jordan drying up for their passage. How could those people not be impressed with the Lord's power and turn to Him for help? With help like that, who could stop these people? Would it not make sense to honor their God as Rahab had? It was difficult to understand why more peoples did not attempt to make peace with Israel. A chilling truth embedded in this story is that every human heart possesses that capacity to ignore and rebel against his own Creator. To not believe is to rebel against God's assessment of us.

(Note: Many centuries earlier a certain people had built this city and decided, for one reason or another, to name it "Adam." Such details in the Word are never an accident. Now the river was backing up to that city as though God's dealings with man were reaching all the way back to Adam. His dealings would reach downriver to the future too.)

The priests continued to the center of the river and stopped there holding the Ark while all the people crossed. The Ark was a box about four and a half feet long, two feet wide and two feet high, made of durable acacia wood, then covered, inside and out, with gold—given to them by the terrified Egyptians to get rid of them before something worse happened. (Looking back at it later, it could be seen as the justice of God paying them for their slave labor in Egypt.) Inside were the two stone tablets inscribed with the law of God, the Ten Commandments, God gave to Moses on Mount Sinai forty years earlier (**see note). That law represented the character and perfection, as well as the very presence, of God, who was now leading them on a miraculous journey through the river and into the land promised to them five hundred years earlier.

**(It is unknown today whether the Ark still exists. Some think it was hidden and remains so. Movies are made about it. If it does and could be found, its value would be inestimable. The value of the gold alone would be very large, yet eclipsed by the Ark's historical importance. That particular gold would have been the jewelry worn by ancient Egyptians and then given to the Israelites the night of the Passover. Imagine the misery and anguish of the Israelite slaves represented by it. Even more valuable would be the stone tablets inside. That Ark was kept safely in Israel's midst, known to the world, for over a thousand years. No doubt God protected it as long as He wanted it there.)

The Lord works on a very long time fabric anchored in eternity and in wisdom which far exceeds man's. His plans work their way out through many generations of finite human beings. Man can know of them because God announced them before they happened and commented on them through the ages. Moreover, anyone can participate in God's plan by paying attention to His words and believing them.

As the priests stood still in the midst of Jordan, holding the Ark, the people crossed over. Matthias and Jerusha remembered a day similar to this 40 years earlier in the midst of the Red Sea—where they had met each other for the first time, two young people with so little experience. A connection had sparked that never let go. There they realized their deliverance from the bondage of Egypt and had become aware of the presence of the Lord and His power to take care of them. Together they had stepped into a new life. They had known of Him in Egypt and had heard the stories of Abraham, Isaac and Jacob, and their destiny to inherit the Promised Land, but never before had they realized with such clarity the utter truthfulness of the tiniest details of His words. Matthias, scanning the whole scene, finally said, "Remember the Red Sea? When we first arrived there, Egypt chasing us from behind, miles of deep water ahead. We were sure we were all about to die—or be carried back to slavery. People all around us mourned in misery. We had those few days of hope after leaving Egypt, and then everything collapsed. Remember the miserable fear at the shore? We trembled, and Moses stood strong and held his staff out toward the sea. Remember that? A huge wind came and opened a path right through the blue waves. The waters parted to the left and right and looked like a curtain on either side. We saw the bottom of the sea. It sloped gradually out to the deep. Here and there were corals and small stones studded in the sand, a few seaweeds flattened out on the ground—and it was already dry. Moses told us to walk in, and so we did."

"I remember like it was yesterday," answered Jerusha, calling up the picture in her mind.

"And there I met you," continued Matthias and then fell silent. Jerusha, simply looking at this husband the Lord had given her so many years ago, felt her heart warm at the memory. "I can still remember your face," he added, "and how I couldn't quit looking at you. I think it embarrassed you, but I didn't care. Now, forty years later, with four children and six grandchildren, I still see the same beautiful girl." She looked back at him, remembering the boy who had appeared out of the midst of the crowd. Their years of memories and experiences together had shaped how they now saw life, and they relaxed in peace.

That day shined in their memory as they strode through Jordan and approached the western shore, the Promised Land. Today a second miraculous crossing was taking place. As with the Red Sea experience, this would happen one time in the world's history. Both were too noteworthy to forget. It took several hours for all the people to cross, babies carried in parents' arms, children of all ages, grownups and, except for Joshua and Caleb, no one was older than sixty. The priests stood still in the middle of Jordan the entire time, holding the ark. As the people finished crossing, Joshua chose twelve men, one from each of the tribes of Israel, instructing each to pick up a large stone from the river bottom where the priests stood, hoist it to his shoulder and carry it to the far side, where it would be set with the others as part of a monument at the place they would lodge that night in the new land. Since humans were prone to forget, these would be a reminder in time to come when children would ask their fathers, "What are these stones for?" The parents were to teach their own children that the waters of Jordan had been cut off before the Ark of the Lord at this exact place, when it passed through Jordan. Fathers were not asked to send their children to the priests for answers. They were to teach them themselves. These stones would become a memorial for future generations. The Lord himself wanted each generation to tell the next of the Lord's workings in man's history so the words would come alive in the minds of future children. Before moving on, Joshua set up twelve other stones in the midst of Jordan in the place where the feet of the priests stood, and those stones had never been moved at the time of the writing of the Book of Joshua. Perhaps they are still there today.

When all was done Joshua told the priests bearing the Ark to come up out of Jordan. As soon as they stepped onto the shore the waters of Jordan resumed flowing, overflowing its banks as before. One can imagine what it must have been like to watch as their path was re-flooded. Matthias' friend, Abijah, and his wife saw him and Jerusha standing there watching the river flowing again as though nothing had happened.

"I guess there's no going back now," he said to the quiet couple, who were realizing the same thing. "It would be easy to get frightened right about now." Matthias nodded his head in agreement.

They walked on a short distance, to within two miles of Jericho, and set the twelve stones there and camped at Gilgal. "On that day the Lord magnified Joshua in the sight of all Israel, and they feared (respected) him, as they feared Moses, all the days of his life." Abijah spoke again. "When Moses died we didn't know what to think. The Lord showed us today. He is with Joshua as He was with Moses—and He is still with us too." Both Jerusha and Abijah's wife, ever watchful, ever observant, pondered his words.

It was the tenth day of the first month (the Hebrew month Abib, correlating to our spring months of late March to early April). The Lord had told Moses forty years earlier in Egypt at the first Passover, "This month shall be to you the beginning of months. It shall be the first month of the year to you." That first Passover in Egypt forty years earlier also began on the tenth day of the first month, culminating on the fourteenth day when the lamb was killed and its blood put on each home's doorposts so that the angel of death might "pass over" and not stop at any home so protected. A new phase of life was beginning for these travelers. Matthias remarked, "I have a hunch we have been watched all day by spies from Jericho. I can't see them, but I know they are there. When Nathan and I 'toured' Jericho we discovered they were terrified of us." In truth no one entered or left Jericho on this day nor tarried outside its wall. Its gate was locked tight and guarded from inside by armed but trembling warriors.

Joshua 5:1 states, "when all the kings of the Amorites, to the west of Jordan, and all the kings of the Canaanites by the sea, heard that the Lord had dried up the waters of Jordan for the children of Israel, their hearts melted and they lost their spirit to face Israel." The Ark going before Israel typified the presence of God in their midst, leading them in this new portion of their walk through life on this earth. They were doing what their parents had failed to do, which was to take God at His word, trust that He would actually be with them, and move forward believing that He was giving this land to them. All they had to do was to walk in and claim it. Sure, they had to wield a sword many of those days and be willing to do battle with it, but God Himself gave them the victory against stronger and bigger armies. In the coming months, as they experienced God's help over and over, they grew to trust Him and rely on Him in a way they had never done before. Battle-hardened warriors gained a confidence untried soldiers did not know. In Israel's case, and under Joshua's leadership, their confidence in the Lord's power to work in them grew along with their skill in handling weapons and waging war. Winners of battles learned details of war and weapons the losers never learned. Joshua's continual challenge to them was, "Remember it is the Lord that fights for you," knowing man's tendency to struggle so hard with the battle would pull his attention off the Lord and on to himself. Then his true strength would falter. A leader who could direct their attention to the Lord in the midst of battle rendered them a remarkable and unstoppable force, and Joshua knew that. His self-discipline to operate in that manner enabled him to instill that same quality into his warriors, and they retained that knowledge into the future, even after Joshua later passed away.

As the Israelites would discover, the forces arrayed against them as they ventured out in faith would grow substantially. So it is today. When any believer steps out by faith he will meet opposition, and in every case the opposition is bigger than humans can see. The more effective a warrior he is, the worse will be the opposition. We have Joshua's example today to guide in the midst of our battles. Quiet study of his story in precious moments on our own guide us later in the heat of the battle and gives the Holy Spirit something to work with in bringing God's Word to our remembrance at just the right time. Every believer who operates like that wins. He eventually learns that even if he dies in battle he still wins. Satan can touch the body—if the Lord allows—but not our new self in Christ nor our position in heaven. Death for the believer is the doorway into God's loving presence, and it will never happen until God allows. When God allows it is right, and there is peace in that.

With the inhabitants of the land terrified of Israel, human wisdom dictated now to be the perfect time to attack. God's previous miracles with Israel and this latest event at Jordan had rendered these nations completely vulnerable. It would make sense to keep the momentum going and attack immediately. But the battle was bigger than what man could see. Humans saw struggles between nations over land and the wealth it could bring. The Book of Ephesians in the New Testament is said by many Bible scholars to be the counterpart to the book of Joshua in the Old Testament. It states in chapter 6 verse 12, "For we wrestle not against flesh and blood, but against principalities, against powers, against the rulers of the darkness of this world, against spiritual wickedness in high places."

"Spiritual wickedness in high places" would be Lucifer, the highest created angel, living in God's very presence, beholding His glory and still rebelling against Him, his own creator. If he could overthrow God, the source of life, he would be destroying himself at the same time, an action that made no sense. Lucifer evidently did not reason it out, but God did and understood its ramifications. He judged immediately and banned him from his presence. Lucifer, who became Satan, had seen firsthand God's glory and majesty, His wisdom and power, and made a serious miscalculation in succumbing to pride and attempting to promote himself. He would be held responsible for the thoughts of his heart. Jesus said, "A kingdom divided against itself cannot stand." Had God been weak enough to tolerate Satan's ideas, his kingdom would have gradually consumed itself and devolved back to the very chaos and darkness out of which God was creating life.

The earthly battles between Israel and the nations they would conquer reflected the larger conflict in heaven. The battle to drive out the wicked inhabitants of Canaan and give that land and its blessings to Israel was God's demonstration to Satan, His angels, and all mankind of His supreme power over all forces in existence. Part of the message to the world was "judgment is coming." The miraculous overthrow of Egypt was a warning to Canaan and the rest of the world they should have considered very seriously—as had Rahab. This judgment upon them foreshadowed a larger judgment that will come at an appointed time in the future, upon the whole world, and will root out evil and set up His kingdom.

Part of Israel's duty was to accept God's judgment that these people they were displacing were so totally given over to evil that there was no possibility they would turn to God. What remained for them was judgment, and Israel had to know God well enough to realize He would judge fairly and accurately. The conquest of Jericho would be the first of many, and immediate attack was the logical choice. But God had a different plan.

CHAPTER 25

DELAY BEFORE JERICHO

(Joshua 5)

God told Joshua something else was more important than attacking Jericho. It involved their own relationship with the Lord. God was using the nation of Israel to deal with the world, but a nation is made of individuals, and God was looking for it to be populated with individuals who responded to and cherished their relationship with Him. A good leader could guide a nation in a proper direction, but it was far more effective when the people within that nation shared the same vision as the leader. God had given a specific instruction to Abraham that had now been neglected.

He had first told him when he was seventy-five years old that he would make a great nation of him and that all the world would be blessed through that nation. At age ninety-nine he still had no child with his wife Sarai, and no nation seemed remotely possible. God again appeared to him assuring him that his covenant, or agreement, would be with him, that he would certainly be a father of many nations, and that kings would come from him. That covenant would reach to the generations that came from him and would be an *everlasting* covenant. A son would be born to him and Sarai, and a nation would come from that son. To remind Abraham and all future generations of that covenant God instituted the practice of circumcision of all males born to Abraham and his descendants. Their son would be born within the year (Genesis 17: 1-17).

Circumcision was a painful reminder to Israel of God's view of the human race but also of the special blessings God promised to them. That something had to be cut off and discarded was a message about man's flawed condition. A perfect God was making an agreement with imperfect man. It would come true even if man failed, an *unconditional* promise. The sign of circumcision served as a reminder of that promise. Now in Joshua's time, nearly five hundred years later, that sign had carelessly been neglected by the generation that came out of Egypt. They had experienced the miraculous deliverance from the power of Egypt and the stupendous miracles leading up to it and yet remained almost completely oblivious to God's plan and work in their midst and to the marvelous part they were playing in the world's history. To them life was just one day after another with no particular significance. Yet God's Word was as true in Joshua's time as it was in Abraham's. The Israelites were too busy living life to think about it.

God wanted Israel to remember His unconditional promise made to Abraham over four hundred years before the law (a *conditional* promise) was ever given. The original promise made in Genesis 12 that "I will bless them that bless you, and curse him that curses you, and in you shall all families of the earth be blessed" still stood. The ultimate descendant who would make possible the blessings for all mankind to come would be Jesus of Nazareth (two thousand years after Abraham's time). Acts 4:12 would state, "Neither is there salvation in any other, for there is no other name under heaven, given among men, whereby we must be saved." God used Abraham (whose chief virtue was that he "believed" God) and the nation that sprang from him and the Savior that came through that nation to reach out to all the world and bring blessing to any and all who would do as Abraham had done, to "believe" the things God said. God used Abraham to make the family that would give birth to the Savior. Abraham came from a pagan family in Ur, a prosperous and advanced city in the "Fertile Crescent." He was no better or no worse than any other family of the world. What distinguished him was his "belief" in what God said—which any pagan in the world could do if he so chose.

God told Joshua that the men under his leadership needed to be circumcised because this had been neglected for all those born in the wilderness the past forty years. Submitting to this was meant to remind them of God's promises to Abraham and, further, to indicate they accepted His judgment of their evil human condition. God, as "discerner of the thoughts and intents of the heart," was the ultimate judge. In any case these Israelites complied. The impurity of human nature had to be laid aside along with a recognition of its inability to generate the promised seed. That seed would be a joining of God with the human race, His birth a miraculous work of God in our midst, a judgment and a blessing at the same time. They were about to bring God's sword of judgment upon certain nations God had judged and should be willing to use the sword on themselves first before using it on others. That meant admitting they themselves were wicked and worthy of being cut off from God's kingdom and His presence and at the same time a reminder of God's blessing to come. The animal sacrifices they made on stone altars were meant to enhance their understanding that God would accept the sacrifice of an innocent in their place as a way of dealing with their guilt before God. Many times God consumed the sacrifice with a bolt of lightning or flash of fire—indicating that He accepted the sacrifice. Not everyone thought very deeply about it, but that was the message.

Those who would admit their need and ask for help would receive God's help and be accepted. If they would not, nothing remained for them but judgment. This was about to happen to these Canaanites who had spurned all of God's pleas to accept His help. In truth there was no difference between themselves and the Canaanites, other than that they had been willing to listen to God and to accept his remedy for their sin. God had told Moses long before that He had not chosen them because they were so good but because the nations they would drive out were so evil. Judgment was serious business and must be carried out with deep respect for God's holiness.

Moses had written, and now Joshua reminded them what he said: "The land into which you go to possess is an unclean land with the filthiness of the people of the lands, with their abominations, which have filled it from one end to another with their uncleanness . . . give not your daughters to their sons, neither take their daughters for your sons, nor seek their peace or wealth forever . . ." (Ezra 9: 11-12). This was advice from God. He was dispossessing certain people from the land and giving it to people he chose. Centuries earlier the Canaanites and Amorites had hardened their hearts against the Lord, stopped their ears from hearing His words, turned away and gone their own way. They, without ever checking with the Lord, took the land He had created. Because He had given them free will to choose their path in life, He honored their choice. It was not the destiny he had planned for them, as it led to death, but he allowed it. At the end of their path He would take no pleasure in their death. Thus the warning to Israel not to be tainted by an interest in what those people did or how they lived and worshipped—and not to intermingle with them as they could only lead Israel astray—and force God to judge them as well. A sober message on the eve of their victories.

The caution about judging other people would be echoed in the future in Jesus' words: "And why do you behold the mote that is in your brother's eye but do not consider the beam that is in your own eye? You hypocrites, first cast out the beam out of your own eye. Then shall you see clearly to cast out the mote in your brother's eye" (Matthew 7: 3, 5). Israel was going to carry out God's final earthly judgment upon the nations in Canaan Land. It would only be right for them first to judge themselves. Two ways existed to face judgment. One was to heed God's words telling us we were sinners worthy of death and to take the remedy He offered. The other was to ignore His words and warnings and continue on to ultimately face His judgment. God did not want anyone to face that awful judgment on his own, yet each person was free to make his own decision. Such freedom was magnificently beautiful, but also carried with it responsibility for the outcome of one's choice—eternal responsibility. Circumcision represented God's view of man in his natural condition. Man inherited Adam's guilt simply as one of his descendants. He also inherited Adam's fallen nature, which led him to commit acts of sin. Three things then required God's judgment:

1—belonging to Adam's condemned race
2—possessing a nature like Adam's that had the capacity to sin and that neither Adam nor any man or woman coming after him could fix
3—personal acts of sin

God wanted us to know our true condition before Him. We could escape judgment by accepting His evaluation of us, admitting our guilt to ourselves and to God, and accepting His remedy for it. His remedy was to honor God's original word, which said that one "taking the fruit of that tree" against God's advice would "die." God's remedy was that His Son would come into our world, take our nature upon himself and then take the punishment that our sin required, which was death and banishment from God's presence and from His blessings. The discarding of the flesh in circumcision pictured all that. It also reminded of God's covenant or promise to give the nation arising from Abraham their own land and, further, to "bless those who bless Israel" and to "curse those who curse" Israel, and further yet that "all the world would be blessed through them." That blessing would come through the "seed,, or descendant, born to Eve. That "seed" was Jesus, born two thousand years after that promise to Abraham. Scripture declared many times things before they happened so that when they took place mankind would know that God's words were true and transcended history.

Circumcision had a deeper meaning too. Deuteronomy 30: 6 stated " . . . the Lord thy God will circumcise your heart and the heart of your seed to love the Lord your God with all your heart and with all your soul that you may live." Man's heart, his inner thoughts, were what really mattered to God.

CHAPTER 26

THE UNSEEN CAPTAIN

(Joshua 5: 13-15)

Such words describe a mother eagle with her children in the nest. Having become comfortable with her regular feeding, and unaware of their own growth and the magic of their wings, they have no desire to leave the nest. On a certain day mother "flutters over her young," stirs and chases them until they fall out of the nest. Terrified, they tumble through the open blue sky. Mother watches a moment and at the right instant dives headlong, streamlined for speed, toward earth, swoops under them and catches them on top of her wings, a dazzling mid-air rescue. They are safe and, for the first time, feel and understand how her wings carry her so smoothly and effortlessly in the blue sky. The next day she pushes them again out of the nest. Only this time they stretch out their little wings, like mother did, and suddenly they are not falling to the earth but soaring, soaring a little out of control, but still soaring. This is more fun than the nest! If they curve their wingtips the tiniest amount it alters their flight. Soon they fly wherever they please. Mother flew by, and they copied how she flapped her wings, slowly and gracefully. As they did, they moved with her to new heights. Like the mother eagle, the Lord kept teaching his children to travel in their newfound power. When they feared, He gave them a nudge, guiding them day by day, even as they stumbled and fell.

Israel was moving. Warriors were sensing the excitement of victory as power swept them along. Their new leader, Joshua, stood alone, viewing Jericho in the distance and, closer to him, the tents of the twelve tribes of Israel. It would be difficult to command this huge number of people and not be a little proud. In many ways he was an ordinary man, brave and skillful with weapons (as were so many others), but in reality not too different than those under his leadership. Yet the Lord had chosen him to lead. He had been a faithful minister to Moses, content to follow for many years, and had learned much from Moses' mentoring. In truth he also had led on occasion as commander of the fighting forces in the wilderness, but still under the overall command of Moses.

As he surveyed it all, his pride swelled more than he expected, as would the pride of most any man in such an influential position at the head of two million people. Unexpectedly, a man appeared, a powerful looking man, standing with a sword drawn in his hand. How had an armed warrior entered their camp unhindered? Did not he have guards posted? As was his manner, Joshua unhurriedly studied the man, taking in details, assessing the threat. Coming under Joshua's scrutiny and piercing, battle-hardened gaze was enough to wilt the courage of most any person. Not so with this man. His arm and neck muscles and powerful chest radiated strength as he looked back at Joshua. The polished steel of his sword blade glistened just at the moment his eyes met Joshua's. *This man is obviously a warrior, but why is he here?* thought Joshua to himself. The man's stance spoke strength, but with no threat of violence, nor was it the rigid, disciplined posture of a young officer trained for war. This was a man at ease with his own power and ready to meet whatever would come. Maybe this man was not an enemy. Maybe he came to help. Joshua remembered God's words to him that no man would be able to stand against him—even a man this powerful.

With his own sword still in its sheath at his side, Joshua strode over to him and with a menacing tone, questioned, "Who told you to draw a sword? Are you for us, or for our adversaries? Speak for yourself." Joshua, the man of action, faced trouble head-on.

An even more assured voice answered, "Nay, but as captain of the army of the Lord am I now come." Joshua, due to his years of learning in the Tabernacle, of reading Moses' writings, of talking with the priests, of talking with Moses himself, realized at once who stood in front of him. Those days and hours of beholding the Lord through His recorded Word and through the words of others who knew Him had gradually changed Joshua to think like the One he focused on. Recognizing the presence of the Lord, he suddenly saw his pride for what it was and how it had taken hold of him. Then this strong warrior's knees buckled, and he collapsed in a heap to the earth. Drained of his own strength, he worshipped, remembering, all too clearly, his own helplessness in a certain battle against Israel's merciless foe, Amalek, long ago in the desert. The passage of years and his pride led him to sometimes forget that day, but now the memory of his teacher Moses, standing atop the hill with arms outstretched toward heaven while he himself battled in the valley below, took its place in his mind again. The One to whom Moses had reached, who caused them to win when Joshua had lost all hope of even living out the next minute, let alone of winning the battle, now stood in front of him. *I am just a man,* thought Joshua to himself, *with many failures. Why does the Lord of all the earth appear to me? Is he going to kill me?* While he was still wondering in his mind, the warrior spoke to him.

"Nay, but as captain of the host am I come, to guide you." Entering Canaan and proceeding against Jericho was a larger battle than Joshua had comprehended. The Lord Himself was signaling Satan and all his demons that he would be taking back the world He had created for Himself and for mankind whom He loved. Satan, through deception, had maneuvered the very first humans into disobeying their own Creator and forfeiting the life and blessings God had given them. God would use men willing to listen to Him and believe Him to turn Satan's wicked devices back upon himself. The wisdom of God's way would be astounding to all. The destruction Satan had imagined for God's kingdom would return upon his own head, and the victors would comprehend the fruit of Satan's ways. Joshua saw anew that the Lord was with them and would fight this battle for them. An understanding opened in his mind. Here was that One to whom Moses reached on the hilltop, now standing in front of him. His years of meditating on the Word and putting it into action in his life had led him to this moment. In the clarity of the moment God's power was so overwhelming that every ounce of strength drained from him. The Lord and his angels were the real power and leadership guiding

Israel. God would use Joshua both to lead Israel as he followed and also to teach others the way to follow Him. The story of his conquests and real-life trust in God would influence countless future believers. God spoke to Joshua in an actual appearance, and he, in turn, passed on to Israel what he had heard and what he himself followed. These stories were written, preserved for future generations, and thus that one appearance passed to all who would hear, including those living today. The same God who appeared to Joshua and stood with him all of his life stands with us today who, like him, listen and hear.

"What does my Lord say to his servant?" answered a humbled Joshua.

The captain of the army of heaven told him, "Remove the shoes from your feet, for this place is holy." Joshua did so. Joshua remembered the promises God had recently given that he would be with Israel to give them the land and that "no man would be able to stand against them," and further, that God would be in charge of guiding Israel and fighting for them. Joshua's true leadership was that he understood his role as part of a bigger plan and was willing to let God guide him in that. Taking and possessing the Promised Land was the visible part of a spiritual battle the rest of the world did not see. Understanding his own weaknesses, Joshua had learned to quickly come back to the Lord when he failed. He was not too proud to accept the Lord's forgiveness—over and over.

Wherever the Lord met with someone, His presence rendered the place holy. When God spoke to Moses at the burning bush in the desert it became holy ground. When we read his Word, God says He meets with us, and that occasion is special. The question is, are we willing to communicate with Him? Reading or listening to His Word is the beginning. Jesus said countless times, "He that has ears to hear, let him hear." Most days our part is to listen. What God has to say to us will be more helpful to us than what we have to say to Him, not that He does not want to hear from us. One of the best things we can say to Him, however, is when from the depth of our heart we say, "I believe You. I believe You are present with me. I believe that You spoke to people You chose long ago and told them to write Your words. When I hear them today they are as real and alive as the day you spoke them." That was what it means to "come to Him as a little child," as Jesus would later teach, simply basking in His presence, listening to His words, enjoying knowing Him. That is what can grow into the power that "overcomes the world." Parents who teach their children to listen are doing them and the world a great service.

The Unseen Captain reiterated to Joshua that Jericho, its army, and its king were given into Israel's hand. Then He detailed to him the plan for taking it. Joshua listened.

CHAPTER 27

JERICHO

(Joshua 6)

Now Israel was ready. God had spoken to Joshua and given him the plan for the conquest. Jericho was locked up tight for fear of the Israelites. No one came in and no one went out. They knew how the river had opened up for them and were terrified. Israel was camped at Gilgal, not far from the river, not too far from Jericho. Joshua passed the plan on to Israel: "Take all the men of war and march around the city once a day for six days. Carry also the Ark of the Covenant behind you and let seven priests go before it with seven rams' horns. On the seventh day march around the city seven times sounding the trumpets, and at the end make a long blast with the horns and shout with a great shout. The wall of the city will fall down flat. You can then take the city" (Joshua 6:5). He told them to be ready at daybreak to head to Jericho.

Matthias woke very early the following morning, long before light. Jerusha rested at his side, also awake. For forty years they had anticipated entering the Promised Land, and now they were here. They talked quietly between themselves for a while and then arose and readied themselves for the day. A messenger from Joshua passed word along that the walk to Jericho would shortly begin.

In the increasing light, this army of people got their first close up look at Jericho, a very old city standing strong on a hill carefully chosen to make enemy approach difficult. The stone wall reaching to the sky seemed to be shaking its proud fist in the face of God. Long ago it had been built by people, skillful and intelligent, who had, in their 'wisdom,' repudiated God for so long they had hardened themselves to any mention of Him. They fenced him out of their lives and replaced him with idols of their own making, idols they had fashioned with their own hands and made of wood or stone or silver. To these creations they actually knelt down and worshipped, though there was no breath in them and they had no power to do anything. God had warned them and their ancestors for centuries to come back to Him and listen to Him, as the way they were choosing would lead to destruction. Instead they built this proud city.

No Israelite talked or made a sound as they began their first journey around the city, seeing from all sides the complete invincibility of that wall. The more they saw, the more impossible the situation looked. Terror poked at the hearts of a few—many, to tell the truth. Pursuing victory was one thing. Arriving on your own two feet at the battle was another. These formidable walls had withstood every single attack over the last several centuries and still stood strong, very strong. Ancient know-how had built them. What would make Israel think they could conquer where no one else could? The attention of a few Israelite warriors was so fixed on the hard stony surface of the walls that all they could think about was that. And they feared. Someone noticed a scarlet rope hanging from a window on the north wall and quietly pointed it out to the others. That rope would remain there each day that they walked around the city.

Faces gradually began to appear atop the wall as nervous citizens of Jericho struggled for a look at this army. They had no idea what to expect—only that it could be devastating. But nothing happened! Finally the army had walked all the way around the city and then, without incident, headed back to Gilgal. What was happening? Maybe the walls of the city would protect them after all. No one else had been able to penetrate them. Now that they saw them, these Israelites were not so fearsome. Just regular people. Why had they been so terrified? Fear had fooled them, and, seeing that, their pride began to reassert itself—carefully.

The gate would be the weakest spot, but Matthias and Nathan had reported that it was constructed of massive timbers swung on even stronger iron hinges. Making the approach even more difficult was the climb up the hill to get there. A massive battering ram could, no doubt, break through the gate, but anything that big would be extremely difficult to carry up the hill, and those attempting to move such a heavy timber or tree trunk would be easy targets for arrows shot from the top of the wall. Then, too, according to the spies, there was a second wall inside that first one, also protected by that same upward sloping ground. Anyone getting past that first wall would find himself in a dangerous "no man's land" designed intentionally as a death trap. Such defenses had rendered Jericho an impregnable and prosperous city. Additionally, the vigilance of its leaders protected it from more insidious foes, those who posed as friends or allies to gain a foothold to attack from within. That had almost happened twice, but each time the impostors had been found out and put to a very cruel, sadistic, public death. Still, Jericho was unsure how much to fear Israel.

That evening in Israel's camp a few warriors whispered their fears to one another. Ever alert, Joshua caught wind of it and gathered the warriors and priests around him. "You saw the enemy and their fortress up close today." Ears perked up as he went silent and let that thought sink in. What would he say next? That they should reconsider and leave Jericho alone? "Remember who brought you here. Many of you think it was me—or Moses—and are ready to complain, now that you have seen those walls. I am the leader you see . . . but remember the one I told you about the other day, the 'Unseen Captain,' the leader of the invisible armies, the armies of the Lord. He revealed Himself to us to encourage us, knowing that we would fear . . . and that knowledge of His presence among us would help. It was He who broke Egypt's grip on us and led us to freedom. It was He who opened the Red Sea, who fed us every day in the wilderness, miraculously, with manna. It was He who opened the path through Jordan a few days ago and then appeared to me that I might encourage you. It will be He who leads us into this battle and gives the victory. Think about this. In all those instances did it not look like we were in an impossible situation?" All but a few panic-stricken men understood Joshua's reasoning and began to follow his thinking and see this battle in a new light.

"And then God took care of us—every single time. It is the same now. Jericho looks impossible to take." Joshua looked at this large force of warriors gathered in front of him. Some looked visibly worried and fearful. Some looked like they were ready to attack right now. Some looked down when his gaze caught them. Hard to know what they thought. Others returned his gaze, waiting for his next words. Joshua remembered his earliest battles, times when he had been uncertain but dared to trust Moses's advice and move ahead in spite of his fears. Moses's certainty of God's protection had strengthened him and set an example for him. Joshua had realized over time that it was not necessarily Moses who had the wisdom. His wisdom was to follow God, and after all his failures he had learned to do that. A 'sin-plagued' human had learned to submit his own will to the will of God, most of the time anyhow—a "treasure in an earthen vessel" (2 Corinthians 4: 7). Joshua's leadership now rallied these men as Moses's leadership had guided him. A powerful leader stood before them. Yet Joshua, like Moses, realized that he was not the power. It was God reflecting Himself through him as Joshua had learned to bow to God's will and let Him guide. He remembered the time years ago in first fighting Amalek how his first instinct was to wield his sword and his spear with his natural strength and skill. The Amalekites so overpowered and fatigued him that he came within a step of losing his life—several times—in that battle. In those moments he had seen, clearly, that God's power would help him, in spite of himself. It took a few close calls but the lesson had gradually sunk in, and today that knowledge lived on in this powerful warrior's heart. Many of these warriors would learn that too, and this army would be an unstoppable force sweeping into Canaan.

Joshua had seen God keep His word time after time, and for years now he had held an implicit trust in his promises. "Remember what God told us: 'On the seventh day make a long blast on the ram's horn and shout with a great shout, and the wall of the city will fall down flat!' The Lord will give you victory over the city, its king and its occupants. Everything in it will be cursed except Rahab the harlot and all who are with her in her house. They shall live because she hid the messengers that we sent. Take the silver and gold, brass and iron for the treasury of the Lord but nothing else for yourselves. It is all cursed. That is what will happen, and you will see it. It is certain." Joshua's unflinching certainty communicated power and victory to the hearts of his men. "You will learn, too, that no one will be able to stop us when we are walking in God's will, as we invade this land and take it back for the Lord's purposes." The words made sense to his listeners, and in their hearts they assented to following Joshua, to the death if need be, trusting that however God guided would be right.

The next day Israel compassed the city again and returned to its camp. On the third day some of those in Jericho had grown bold and shouted insults to Israel, mocking their weakness and inability to breach their walls. They threw garbage and rocks but Israel was slightly too far away to hurt. Each day the Israelites saw anew the strength of that wall and understood the impossibility of getting past it—unless they had help. All in all, the more one looked at it, the stronger it looked. It was as though the Lord wanted them to see the impossibility of taking that city. For six days they continued like that.

On the seventh they compassed the city seven times. By now, large crowds of Jericho's citizens were watching from the wall and shouting insults at Israel's weakness. But this day waxed different. Israel did not return to its camp. It marched around again. And then again, and again and again. The wiser watchers in Jericho quit shouting insults. At the seventh time and with the priests blowing the trumpets, Joshua cried triumphantly to the people, "Shout, for the Lord has given you the city." He had told them to take absolutely nothing from the city, no spoil, no food, no weapons. They could take the gold and silver and vessels of brass and iron for the treasury of the Lord, and that was all they could touch. In the commotion they were to find and save Rahab and all with her alive. Beyond that, the city would be regarded as accursed and finally burnt with fire.

The people shouted with a great shout, and as they watched the wall, the earth trembled almost imperceptibly beneath their feet, a low-pitched rumble, too faint to know for sure if it were happening. They sensed it almost more than felt it. Had the earth itself moved? Everyone in the city and in Israel knew something was happening—something big. Very deep in the earth a long-hidden force stirred, and cracks appeared in Jericho's walls. Then dust and rock chips exploded out of the cracks with loud, sharp pops, reflecting tremendous but unseen internal forces. The walls shuddered and collapsed with a groan that further shook the earth with their monstrous weight. The great number of onlookers on the wall fell with it to a brutal, crushing death. In one quick moment the brilliant engineering that designed the walls and the skilled craftsmanship that built them succumbed to superior wisdom and power. We do not know how God did it. He may have sent an earthquake, or he may have spoken to the atoms and molecules and told them to let go of their hold on each other for a moment. Scripture says, ". . . by him all things consist" (are held together) (Colossians 1: 17). The forces holding the very molecules together may have let go because the Lord said so, freeing the walls to tumble to a pile of rubble, laying waste the supremacy of this pretentious little kingdom.

The city lay wide open and exposed, and the Israelites walked unimpeded into it, falling on its inhabitants with sword and spear. According to Joshua 6:21, "they utterly destroyed all that was in the city, both man and woman, young and old, ox and sheep, and ass, with the edge of the sword." Years' worth of warnings from God, ignored by those in Jericho, culminated in this horrific end. People ran this way and that, screaming in utter terror. A few brave men drew swords and attempted to fight the Israelites but to no avail. Israelite warriors with uncanny skill could see, as though in slow motion, every movement of the enemy swords, deflect their thrusts, and in the split second following, return a stroke dealing a deadly wound. Mercifully the terrorized screams faded quickly until only a few remained, and then, one by one, they too went quiet. An ox lying helplessly on its side heaved its rib cage as it bellowed a last, weakening moan, sighed, and moved no more. A silence so deep one could hear his own heartbeat pounding in his ears followed. The warriors' own heavy breathing was the only audible sound. Where moments before screams of terror filled the air as women and men ran for their lives, now motionless bodies littered the street, many with one, two, or three arrows stuck fast in them, others with wide open, ugly, life-draining slash wounds where death-dealing swords had cut deeply, lifeless bodies that had fallen back to the dust from which they were taken. No movement, no sound came from any. Even the bright red blood had stopped flowing from their gaping sword wounds. No bleating of sheep, no lowing of cattle. All lay dead. The judgment of God had fallen, and it was severe and final.

The conquering Israelites said not a word as they observed the completeness of the destruction. It was the most sobering scene any of them had ever witnessed, and their hands and their weapons had done it. Even the young men who had been anxious to prove themselves in battle and exult in glorious conquest matured far more than they expected on that day. This was no game. Lives ended, a tragedy, a dismal tragedy, of deep proportion. In that quiet moment many of the Israelite warriors looked at each other. They realized these dead could have easily been them. They knew that in the depths of their hearts they were not much different than these people they had just annihilated. Why had God commanded them to do this? Why had God spared them and destroyed the Canaanites? That was what the circumcision was about. It meant that in God's view, we were worthy of being cast off from God's presence, a truth so difficult to accept. It also reminded of God's unconditional promise to Abraham to use that nation that would spring from him to shed blessing on the entire world. It was God who had visited the human race and given a son to the aged Abraham and Sarai. It was God who had preserved the family growing from them amidst the darkness and corruption of a world at enmity with God. Man was at war with God due to the fire in his heart, planted there by the deceitful influence of Satan, an influence that God would ultimately destroy and remove from the heart of man. Joshua's conquests in Canaan were part of that plan. They pictured an even larger victory to come in the future when the Son of God would assert his ownership of the world and defeat Satan at the cross.

It was God who had brought them to this moment, to the land he had promised. It was God doing the work in their midst and a warning to the world that judgment was coming for mankind and the world. As Jericho could not avoid it, neither could the rest of the world. Any who would take God's warning seriously and seek safety in his protection would be spared—as was Rahab. Man's part was to pay attention to what God said, ponder it, believe it, and then to walk in the light of it. This movement in the world, led by Joshua and Israel, was far larger than it appeared.

"As I live, said the Lord God, I have no pleasure in the death of the wicked, but that the wicked turn from his way and live" (Ezekiel 33: 11). God had called all humanity back to Himself many times. He had told Abraham he would give these Amorites and their generations four hundred years to give heed to His calls and come back to Him. After that it would be judgment. Proverbs says, "There is a day to plant and a day to harvest," and yesterday was the last day of the 'growing season' for the inhabitants of Jericho. Today was the 'harvest.' Like Rahab, they knew of God's magnificent power and dominance over every deceitful, imaginary god man had ever invented. They knew of his power over each person's life and destiny. Unlike her, they had chosen to ignore it. We all live on the "knife edge of eternity" and could slip out of this world at any moment, some at a young age, some after a very long life. God had the right and the wisdom to decide. To leave this life having spurned and ignored one's Creator was the saddest tragedy possible for any human being. As Esau, Jacob's brother, carelessly sold his birthright, the right to father the nation of Israel and the family that would eventually give birth to the Savior, bargaining away eternal blessing for a momentary bowl of soup, the inhabitants of Jericho had done the same with their precious lives by ignoring all of God's attempts to call them back to Him and to an eternity of blessing. He would not call them and be ignored forever. A time would be allotted to each fully grown person, and the amount of time would be right. After that would be judgment by the Creator of life, the One who made the rules, the One who had the right to make the rules, the One who had the power to make the rules.

And thus perished an entire city and its people, after thousands of warnings, an end that came swiftly, in a day—nay, in an hour. As Matthias looked at the carnage, the strewn, slaughtered, lifeless bodies, he was repulsed and started to become sick. For a moment he wondered why God ordered such destruction. At the same time he realized he was calling God's wisdom into question. He recalled Abraham's words, "Shall not the judge of all the earth do right" (Genesis 18: 25)? He also realized that his limited view of the world and life was different from that of God, who saw centuries' worth of mankind's behavior and actions and knew intimate details of his thoughts. For Matthias this horrible scene would live in his memory. So this was the end of these people . . . an end that did not have to be. Tragedy only partially comprehended by even the wisest of men. In his mind he pictured Eve reaching for the fruit of that tree in Eden. That little act led to the mayhem and carnage of this moment. No wonder God had said not to eat of that tree. The freedom God had given man had led to rebellion against Him. Yet God had given him that freedom.

Freedom carried with it the responsibility for the outcome of his choices. We throw around the word "accountability" quite cavalierly today. The blood soaking into the dust of the streets of Jericho was "accountability," final, true accountability. Far in the future the tears and tortured screams of Jesus on the cross in the hours of darkness were accountability too, accountability He took on willingly for man as His blood dripped into the dirt for mankind.

The Israelites remembered the sobering words of Moses, spoken before his death, as he recounted God's dealings with them. He cautioned that, as their "herds and flocks grew large and their silver and gold multiplied in the land God would give them, they should be careful that their hearts be not lifted up to forget the Lord that brought them up out of Egypt and bondage into this land of prosperity." They would be tempted to think "the power and might of their own hand had gotten them this wealth" (Deuteronomy 8: 12-18). Then he reminded them that it was "not for their righteousness, or for the uprightness of their heart" that they were possessing these lands but for the "wickedness of these nations that God would drive them out," and that He "would keep his promise to Abraham, Isaac, and Jacob" in spite of the fact Israel had been "stiff necked and rebellious since the time they had departed Egypt" (Deuteronomy 9: 4-7).

Joshua broke the silence by directing Nathan and Matthias to locate Rahab's house and bring her, all those with her and all they had, out to safety, as they had promised. Seeing the destruction in the streets, they too were horrified, the reality of it so devastating, complete and final. People who had been alive an hour earlier were dead, quiet, motionless, faces ashen with open eyes looking at nothing.

Then they burned the city and everything in it, except for the silver, gold, brass and iron, which they put into the treasury of the house of the Lord. (Note: Jericho has been rebuilt more than once over the ages, sometimes at a small distance from the old location. One site unearthed by archaeologists revealed a layer of char from fire, beneath which were found many large clay storage vessels containing grain, quite unusual in that conquering warriors would always take such food stores as prizes of war. This find, however, fits with the narrative in Joshua in which Israel had been instructed to take nothing as spoil, or prizes of war, except for the silver, gold, brass and iron. Additionally, great piles of rubble exist where the outer walls would have been, except for one area where the wall still stood—perhaps the home of Rahab). So Joshua saved Rahab the harlot alive, and her father's household, and all that they had, and they lived in Israel the rest of their generations. News of Joshua's conquest spread like wildfire throughout the neighboring countries.

Unknown to the rest of the Israelites, a certain man of them named Achan took and hid for himself some of the captured gold meant for the Lord's treasury. Like Eve's seemingly minor act, this would have a devastating effect on the entire nation.

CHAPTER 28

AI AND ACHAN...UNDER THE INFLUENCE...

(Joshua 7-8)

Israel's march into the Promised Land continued but took an unhappy turn. As happens so often on the journey to success, pitfalls and problems line the way and threaten disaster. Israel, having been delivered from the captivity and slavery of Egypt, had been learning, through the years in the wilderness, to "walk by faith."

The word "walk" in scripture refers to daily conduct. As they trusted God's guidance by the cloud and His words to them, they were "walking by faith" and presented a picture to those hearing the story of how to do that. Here God records an example of how *not* to do it.

As it happened after such a resounding success, Israel fell prey to its pride. They *knew* the impossibility of taking Jericho, and they also knew that it could be possible to take it with God's help. So with that mindset they had followed God's strange instructions and had been shockingly victorious. At the evening campfires throughout the camp they sang to the Lord's glory and danced, enjoying their freedom and this astounding victory. Happiness pervaded the atmosphere. Several reveled, "Those people of Jericho couldn't do a thing against us!" The trials of the wilderness and its crusty, barren land were behind them. This new land was lush and green, full of promise and abundant with fruits, vegetables, milk and honey.

In their elation over the victory their emotions took over and led them gradually to forget God's part and to yield to the happy belief that they had won the victory on their own. At first the severity of God's judgment upon Jericho made a deep and shocking impression on every warrior. For most it was hard to understand that God had done this, and yet He had. They would consider it in their hearts for a long time, and as they did so their understanding of God's hatred of evil deepened. They had learned much during their years in the wilderness about letting the Lord guide them and provide for them. Now their very success rendered them vulnerable to their own pride. God's people, the Israelites, were humans with human failings. What made them successful—when they were—was letting God guide them. Humans were ever prone to follow their own will over God's and to believe they knew best how to run their own lives.

God loved them in spite of themselves and allowed them to make their own decisions as part of His teaching process. Even mature believers made mistakes, and Joshua and Israel were about to do just that. Their nature, inherited from Adam, ever sought to take over and exert its will in place of God's. It is difficult for people, even God's people, to comprehend how corrupt are their own hearts. The prophet Jeremiah, centuries into the future, would crystallize into words what Israel was learning through its battles: "The heart is deceitful above all things and desperately wicked. Who can know it" (Jeremiah 17: 9)? That old human will is hostile to God and will never surrender nor be reformed. It is a reflection of Satan's influence and its lasting effect and will be with man all his days on earth. It will only be left behind when one leaves earth to be with God. Until then victory lies in following God's advice over the yearnings of the flawed human heart. Centuries after Jeremiah's time the Apostle Paul set forth this conflict in his letter to the Galatians: "For the sinful nature desires what is contrary to the Spirit, and the Spirit what is contrary to the sinful nature. They are in conflict with each other, so that you do not do what you want. But if you are led by the Spirit you are not under the law" (Galatians 5: 17-18). God Himself leading man through His Holy Spirit can guide man to a worthwhile, pleasing to God, fulfilled, happy life.

Jesus announced after His resurrection that He would be ascending to heaven in the near future, and when He did He would send His very Spirit to live within every person who believes and be present to guide. In Joshua's time that Spirit resided in certain leaders like Moses and Joshua and various kings and prophets that God chose. When one followed those leaders they were following God.

When Joshua sent men to view Ai, the next city in their path, they were so thrilled over the Jericho victory that they began in their own hearts to take credit for it. They imagined they had made it all happen. Returning to Joshua, they told him they would only need to send two or three thousand men to take Ai because, compared to Jericho, it was a small city. Why make all the men go and work so hard? They were about to suffer a severe blow to their pride, a necessary but painful part of spiritual growth. Their approach would illustrate the principle that humans are ever susceptible to being drawn off track from following the Lord, especially after a spiritual victory. Such failure does not have to be for those who remain alert and continue looking to their Lord. In Israel's time and still today most do not learn the easy way. God uses their failure and this story to show believers their own weaknesses and to reveal to them how to avoid calamity. Israel's tendency was to let their guard down and enjoy the moment. Then pride could move in and convince them to make their own plans and lead them astray.

Though Ai was a small city, it was part of the kingdom of Satan and the battle was far larger than it appeared. Man in his own strength is no match for Satan and is soon entangled and defeated by him. Satan had watched man through the ages become proud and too headstrong to hear any warnings. It was easy to just watch and let man ensnare himself. That was what happened here. Joshua and Israel forgot to check in with the Lord. They acted on their own, and without realizing it, had shunned the Lord. So He let them go—without His help.

Joshua sent a small contingent of three thousand men, and the battle went shockingly badly. They fled before the men of Ai. Thirty-six Israelis died—the only time any deaths were recorded in all of Israel's battles. Warriors from Ai then chased the remaining army for miles, harassing them all the way. What had gone wrong? Had God brought them out here to make fools of them?

Joshua and Israel's elders tore their clothes and fell on their faces to the ground before the Ark of the Lord. In complete bewilderment Joshua cried out to the Lord, "Why did you bring all of us over Jordan only to deliver us into the hand of the enemy to destroy us? Now I wish we would have been content to remain on the other side of the Jordan and be at peace. What can I say when we turn our backs before our enemies? The Canaanites will hear and descend on us and kill us, and what will happen to your great name?"

Many of the Israelites began to wonder, "Is God really leading us?" Some said, "Maybe the Canaanite gods are stronger than our God." Matthias heard that and said, "You ought to know better. You know our God is the true God. Those miracles in Egypt showed us His power and that He will take care of us.

Others said, "We can't go back. We have nowhere to go back to. The land on the other side of Jordan was barren and dry. It would be so hard to get there, and then . . ."

Another chimed in, "Right, we'd have to cross Jordan with all these people and all the children and babies. All I see is confusion. We're stuck! Joshua is certainly no Moses!"

A child said, "Daddy, I thought God was with us and guiding us."

Matthias' friend Nathan told him, "Everywhere people are murmuring. Everything looks like it is going wrong for Israel. But God made a path for us through Jordan, and I know He is with us."

Another perplexed Israelite lamented, "Wait till the other Canaanites find out what we did to Jericho. They'll come after us with a vengeance."

The Lord said to Joshua, "Get up. Why are you lying on your face? Israel has sinned and transgressed my covenant, taking gold for themselves and now have hidden it with their things." Israel had two issues. They were unaware of the sin in their midst, of Achan's deeds, and they did not comprehend the depth of the sin in their own hearts. The Lord continued, "That is why you could not stand before Ai. You have sin in your midst, and you acted all on your own, without Me. Remember Jericho? That was such a strong city you knew you could not take it. But you followed My advice, and I conquered it for you, knocking down the walls and giving you easy victory afterward. You were thrilled, and in your joy made your own plan to take Ai—but you forgot to check in with Me. The enemy was stronger than you thought. I would have given you victory, but you followed your own ideas and got hurt. Tomorrow gather every tribe of Israel and every family in each tribe and present yourselves before me. You cannot stand up to your enemies until you deal with your own evil."

Joshua was praying now, but he and Israel should have prayed *before* the battle. Then God would have revealed to them a better way to approach Ai, as he had done with Jericho. Even though Israel was unaware, Achan's sin was there, and it had an effect on their progress, like when an orchestra played music and one trumpet blew wrong notes. The whole presentation was ruined. God wanted them to become aware and deal with it. Unfortunately, that was not how it went.

Jerusha asked Matthias what this meant. He struggled to understand it himself. This part of the story showed that the sin of one believer had an effect on the others and could ruin the entire operation. How could that be? For some reason the Lord allowed Achan's sin to lead to loss of an important battle and the death of thirty-six men. Why? It was not all of Israel's fault, yet many paid a terrible price for Achan's failure. Sin, even if unknown, affected the entire operation. Did God demand absolute perfection on our part before He would help them? Maybe God was teaching man to be more sensitive to the reality of sin, to become aware of its invisible hold on us, to understand the need to lean on the Lord at all times for His fellowship and help.

He told Joshua to systematically bring each tribe, then the families of the chosen tribe, to present before him. God singled out one man, Achan—meaning He knew exactly where the problem was. Imagine the effect on the other Israelites as they saw God's thoroughness. Each knew he did not always follow the Lord in his heart. *Am I the guilty one?* many no doubt thought. Would they become more aware of their own failures of heart and their need to follow the Lord more seriously?

God told them to stone Achan for the sin which had led them to ruin. They had foolishly assumed they could do this on their own, without God's help—so He withdrew His help and let them fail, not because He hated them but because He wanted them to know their neediness. It demonstrated God was able to properly assess the situation. Though each Israelite was imperfect, Achan's action was a flagrant violation of a direct command. God would use it as an easy to understand warning to the others. He wanted the whole group of Israelites to sense their own neediness and to work together and be in tune with Him so He could guide them. In truth every Israelite deserved to be stoned. Did they become a little more aware of this as they hurled a rock at Achan and realized their own sin?

Achan's attention had been drawn away from God when he grew more interested in taking care of himself than in letting God guide him. He was like an infection in Israel's midst. Like leaven, his independent, self-centered attitude could spread to others. God's standards were higher than that. He wanted all looking to Him, each taking responsibility for himself. God's severe judgment revealed His attitude toward sin.

Perhaps Jericho was disease-ridden and God was protecting them by not letting them take clothing and goods belonging to diseased people. We don't know and scripture does not say. However, God always wanted the first fruits of the harvest. He would give them the spoils of battle in due time. Had Achan waited, God would have made him far wealthier than he could have imagined.

Joshua and Israel were following the Lord on this journey into the Promised Land, and there was more to learn as they did so. The superior knowledge and sinister designs of Satan easily wrought havoc in Israel's midst on this occasion. No way existed that Joshua could defeat an unseen enemy who could deceive and mislead their thinking. God allowed them to fail, yet he did not abandon them. Instead he turned their failure into a learning experience. Achan's story shed light on man's three foes: his natural nature, the world, and the devil. Here man followed his own human nature to calamity. Satan rarely has to deal singly with a person. He chooses rather to deal with kingdoms and power centers influencing large numbers of people. He simply lets man deceive and entangle himself under the influence of his own rebellious nature. For those who get past that, he uses the world to distract their attention from the Lord. On the rare occasions those fail he takes notice and attacks, either brutally or subtly, by orchestrating events to derail unwise humans.

No one knew what was in Achan's heart nor what he was doing in their midst as he secretly disobeyed a direct and easy to understand command. Achan had become a follower of God, but on this occasion he was catering to his human, selfish nature. The plan looked good to Achan, but with God, who judges from a much higher vantage point and a larger view of reality, the plan leads to destruction. So even though Achan was part of Israel and a child of God, he became a lesson to the rest of Israel—and to us. Any child of God could sin and move in wrong directions. God wanted Israel to become aware of this. In Achan's case he forfeited his physical life but not his eternal soul. As a child of God his sins were covered by God's plan of offering a substitute in the offerings taught to Israel. God wanted Israel to understand that success lay in learning to let God, and His words, guide their daily walk.

Many Israelites grew to understand what God was teaching through those sacrifices, but later the New Testament book of Hebrews explained it more clearly: ". . . in those sacrifices there is a remembrance again made of sins every year. For it is not possible that the blood of bulls and of goats should take away sins. Wherefore when he [Jesus] came into the world He said, Sacrifice and offering you would not, but a body have you prepared for Me. In burnt offerings and sacrifices for sin you have had no pleasure. Then said I, Lo, I come (in the volume of the book it is written of Me) to do your will, O God . . . By whose will we are sanctified through the offering of the body of Jesus Christ once for all . . . For by one offering he has perfected forever them that are sanctified [set apart by their belief] . . . And their sins and iniquities will I remember no more. Now where remission of these is there is no more offering for sin" (Hebrews 10: 1-18). Those sacrifices did not actually pay for sins; they pictured that a different sacrifice would come, the true sacrifice, who would be Jesus, the Son of God. He was the one who paid for sins.

Neither Satan nor man put Christ on the cross. God's own words did. "In the day you eat of it, you shall die," He had said, and the words were not spoken lightly. Man's lack of understanding and failure to follow God's advice resulted in certain death, spiritual death, which then led years later to physical death. God had no intention of annulling His words, and now His love for man carried Him a step beyond. He entered, through his Son, into that death for man and took the full brunt of its punishment. The power of His life, greater than the power of Satan, death, and darkness, lifted Him up victorious over it all. Now with the legal right and power He could take all who would accept His help into new life. That life is planted into the polluted heart of any human who will hear his word and respond to it. Though they still have that old self-loving nature, they also have God's own life residing in their hearts, and that life is under the care of God Himself. "We have this treasure in earthen vessels," declared the scripture (2 Corinthians 4: 7), meaning that God has planted new life within the heart of anyone who will simply believe Him and accept that life as a gift. Israel had accepted that life and payment for sin at the Passover in Egypt. Their deliverance from slavery and the power of Egypt was further demonstrated in their miraculous deliverance through the Red Sea into a new land and life. No matter what people thought about it, that was what scripture said. That was how a true believer could sin. He could listen to the promptings of the old life, which was rebellious to God, or he could listen to the Word of God. Achan, a believer in the Lord, listened to his old Adamic nature—to the ruin of his earthly life.

He was "under the influence" of the world that hated God and of his own "man-centered" nature. In the weeks and months to come every Israelite would gradually reap more and more earthly blessings as they took possession of all the goods, homes and lands of the cities they conquered. Achan, so concerned about gathering goods for himself, was oblivious to the blessings God had in store for him. Had he been patient enough to wait and let the Lord provide for him, he would have been far richer than the hidden gold would have made him. And he would not be lying dead under a pile of rocks.

Of interest is the detail the Word records about discovering the guilty one. In that huge number of people the Lord knew precisely where the guilt lay and brought it to Israel's awareness. Jesus said, "A sparrow cannot fall to the ground without your Father knowing about it" (Matthew 10:29). Nothing can be hidden from the Lord, and in the end He will deal with all human activity. Of further interest is the lack of awareness on Israel's part of sin in their midst. A necessary part of our spiritual growth is becoming aware of our own sinfulness. As children of God grow spiritually, they see more and more deeply the utter corruption of their own hearts. Often they suffer discouragement, thinking that as they grow spiritually, they are growing worse. What really happens is they pick up the Lord's viewpoint and become more aware of the sin lurking in their hearts all along. They see what He is trying to show them. Instead of going backwards they are growing.

Israel also grew in their appreciation of what their future Savior would do for them in paying for their sins. The greatest—and most humble—leaders, such as Abraham, Joseph, Moses, Joshua, King David, the Apostle Paul, and many others were deeply aware of their own inner corruption and found their strength in casting themselves upon the Lord for his mercy and his help.

A Second Chance for Failed Believers (I John 1:9)

Then the Lord said to Joshua, "Do not be afraid. Take all the men of war with you and go to Ai. I have given into your hand the king of Ai, and his people, and his city, and his land. You will take it as you did Jericho, only this time take all the spoil and the cattle as a prize for yourselves. This time you will set an ambush behind the city and lie in wait." Achan should have waited. God would, over the years, give far more blessings than Achan could ever steal.

When God had explained the plan, Joshua chose thirty thousand "mighty men of valor" and sent them away to the ambush. Then he told the plan to the remaining men. It was to attack as they had done the first time, and when the warriors of Ai came out to fight they should flee as though terrified. Bartimaeus, one of the men who had counseled Joshua to take only a few men against Ai, now spoke up. "Maybe we should wait and not be so hasty. We could get into trouble all over again."

Joshua looked at him and the others around him. "The Lord has given us a new plan. Do you not think He accepts our admitting of our failures and looking to Him again?"

"Isn't it too soon? Shouldn't we wait a few days to prove we are sincere?"

"Listen to yourselves. Are you going to pay for your failure by feeling bad and punishing yourselves? You are operating by your own feelings again, just like all of us did about Ai in the first place. You don't pay for sin. We can't. He does. It's beyond our ability. If God says He accepts us and took care of our sin, shouldn't we listen to Him and accept what he tells us? It's that simple."

Bartimaeus countered, "God can't just forgive us so easily. I still think we should wait."

"All that time I spent in the Tabernacle years ago at its beginning, I read Moses's written words over and over. I observed the animal sacrifices over and over, day after day. And I thought about them. What was God showing us? I talked to the priests. I talked to Moses and asked him questions. Those things showed us we can never pay for our sins. Someone else has to. But something inside us tells us to keep trying to do it our way, and that's our big failure, over and over. God would do that for us, but we won't let Him." Joshua looked directly into Bartimaeus's eyes, hoping he would understand. "We could never measure up to God's standards. He is holy. We're not. But He cares about each one of us, and the words He speaks to us are true. We need to pay attention—and think. He said someone will come and 'crush the serpent's head.' He is not here yet, but when He comes his work will be so sure and so powerful that God can forgive us even now, at this very moment. Our sins are covered now, even before He comes, because it is certain that when He comes His payment for sin will be good for all time."

"I still think we should wait," worried Bartimaeus.

Joshua said, "No, this time we will follow God's plan." His words overpowered those who attempted to argue, and he bent their will to his. And so they attacked. When the king of Ai saw them run he called for every man of the city to chase after them. There was not a man left in the city to defend it. Then the Lord told Joshua to stop and "stretch out the spear in your hand toward Ai." As he did, the men of the ambush rose up and entered the city, took it and set it on fire. When the men of Ai saw Israel stop and stand still they looked behind them and saw smoke rising from their city. Fear took hold, and then panic, as they realized they were in a trap. In that moment Joshua's men attacked, and as the men of Ai ran, those who had ambushed the city came out of the city and attacked from behind. The rout was complete. Israel finished the conquest, took all the spoil and cattle, and finished burning the city with fire. As God had said to Joshua, "No man will be able to stand against you." Failure could only come by not following the Lord. When Israel became aware of their sin and dealt with it, God made a new plan for them and led them from the midst of their failure to victory. That is His way with all His children, no matter how often they fail. If they come to Him admitting their sin he forgives them and gives them a new start. "If we confess our sins, he is faithful and just to forgive us our sins and cleanse us from all unrighteousness" (1 John 1:9).

The brutal and severe penalty exacted on Ai, and Jericho, can be difficult to understand. Israel, in carrying out the destruction of these cities and peoples, was following God's instructions. It was God taking action through Israel, and while the world could be critical of Israel, it is really God they are criticizing. The miraculous means he used, such as the Red Sea, Jordan stopping its flow, Jericho's walls, were designed by Him to get man's attention. People today are extremely sensitive about being "judged" and are critical of anyone attempting to do so. "What gives you the right to judge me?" one often hears today. Maybe more than questioning God's "right" to judge, we should be concerned about His "power" to judge. What these stories show is God's power to judge and overthrow Pharaoh and his army, and then the cities of Jericho and Ai. He used the forces of nature to accomplish His purposes. True wisdom would stand in awe of such power.

A rebellious human race was heading, of its own free will, for eternal destruction, seemingly oblivious to the incalculable worth of their own souls and of their responsibility to flee to their Creator for His help. They had debased the value of their own lives and of the lives of others by the nonchalance with which they lied, stole each other's goods, and killed those who stood in their way. Truth to them altered as needed to fit their wants. God had warned there would be a day of reckoning, and for Jericho and Ai it had come. As there comes a day when a man building a bridge declares it complete, or a sporting event ends and the score is final, so there comes a day when a person's life on earth ends and the score is taken. Deliverance from Egypt and the victorious march into Canaan were God's judgment and intervention into the affairs of this world and should have a sobering effect on humans of all ages. Israel's existence as a people and a nation for the last four thousand years should provoke thought. It survived as a nation without its own land and scattered throughout the world from the destruction of its temple in A.D. 70 until 1948, when it reclaimed some of its original land. All other nations that have been similarly destroyed have disappeared. Is not that a continuation of God's promise to Abraham? We do well to take note.

Achan brought failure to the whole nation. God used him as a warning to Israel and all the world and at the same time as an encouraging lesson. God has a plan for each of us that includes leading us into greater and greater blessing, even after we fail. First we, like Achan, need to admit our sin to ourselves and to the Lord, agreeing with God that what we have done is sin. Then He will lead us from our failure into a new plan for victory, as He now led Israel to a victory over Ai.

CHAPTER 29

TREATY WITH GIBEON

(Joshua 8-9)

A humbled Joshua wondered in awe at the resounding victory over Ai. The sting of the defeat days earlier had been overshadowed by the Lord's mercy in granting them a new beginning after acting in their own pride and failing to look to Him for guidance in their approach to Ai. Joshua felt firsthand the kindness and forgiveness of the Lord in a way he had never quite experienced before. He built an altar of whole stones, untouched by human tools, just the way the Lord had said to do it, and offered upon it burnt offerings. Then he wrote on the stones, while Israel watched, a copy of the law of Moses and, following that, read all the words of the law, the blessings and curses, to the people. He read every word that Moses had written to all the congregation, to the men, the women, the little ones, and the strangers among them that could understand their language. Because of the victory and because of experiencing firsthand the Lord's mercy in such a stirring way, it was a day of happiness for Israel. It would become a principle though, that after a spiritual victory man would sooner or later take the glory to himself, imagining he, rather than the Lord, had won the victory and that he could do it again, all on his own. As at Ai, man was vulnerable all over again after a victory.

Here was how it developed. A ragtag group of men showed up at the camp and asked to speak with Joshua. A truly weary looking bunch, they had traveled from a far country. They made a point of showing him their bread, which they explained they had taken hot out of the oven the day they began their journey. Now it was dry and moldy. Their goatskin wine flasks had been new but now were old and torn, as were their shoes and clothing. From their far country they had heard how the Lord had guided Israel to defeat Egypt and then the two kings of the Amorites, Sihon and Og. Their leaders respected Israel's power and wanted to make a league with them.

Joshua and the men of Israel met their words with skepticism. God had told Joshua to make no league with any inhabitants of the land. Joshua challenged, "Maybe you are from a tribe around here. How shall we make a league with you?" The travelers were quick to counter with, "We are your servants."

"Who are you? Where do you come from?" They repeated their story about coming from a far country and showed them again their moldy bread and worn-out clothes. Joshua and the elders and princes could have asked the Lord for guidance—but they did not. So they made peace with them and let them live. Not expecting an attack so soon after the Ai and Achan debacle, Joshua had relaxed and let his guard down. That whole event had been terribly trying to the soul, a life or death moment that had looked like Israel's advance into the Promised Land was doomed and unraveling. Satan had studied human reactions for centuries and in his sadistic manner knew when people would be vulnerable. That was when he set snares for man and would fiendishly watch as man entangled himself. Not that he was happy. He was simply spreading his misery. Israel was about to suffer another hard lesson. These ragtag men were not what they seemed. It is like things that come into our lives. Things just appear. Sometimes they look good, and they truly are. But sometimes they are really just a trap. How do we ever know? How do we judge what is right or wrong? The answer is to ask the Lord. We can ask God to guide us. Even if we don't get a clear answer we have God's assurance that "I will guide you with my eye."

Unknown to Israel, five kings of powerful cities and lands to the south, hearing of Jericho and Ai, gathered themselves together to destroy Joshua. Satan does not stand idly by when believers step out by faith. He used these pagan kings to mount an attack, and little did Israel know the awful power arrayed against them. Word of the alliance spread, and when the city of Gibeon heard of it they had developed a different plan, a plan spawned in the heart of Satan, taking another approach—subterfuge and deception—that appeared on the surface as harmless. Second Corinthians 11:14 reveals that "Satan himself is transformed into an angel of light," which means that Satan can disguise himself as a friend or a harmless person, hardly noticed, like a serpent who moves ever so silently and just "happens" to show up at an opportune time. His friendly appearance sets others at ease, and they let their guard down. His unexpected bite carries certain death. King David wrote of a former close friend, "The words of his mouth were smoother than butter, but war was in his heart. His words were softer than oil, yet they were drawn swords" (Psalm 55:21). He too had been deceived by persons who appeared to be friends.

Gibeon's plan was to trick them into making peace with them, having heard that Israel placed great importance on "keeping their word." Then Joshua did something a man of his wisdom and maturity should not do. He failed to check in with the Lord, even though he had recently failed in exactly the same way at Ai. As Joshua 9: 14 recorded it, they ". . . asked not counsel at the mouth of the Lord." The same mistake they had made at Ai. But it all looked so plausible. An attack by a large army would have been threatening enough to impel Joshua to seek the Lord's advice. A small number of ragged travelers did not seem threatening, and Joshua, letting down his guard, made peace with them. After three days they heard the truth about Gibeon. Dismayed, the elders of Israel said, "We have sworn to them by the Lord God not to harm them, and we cannot break our oath. We will let them live but make them hewers of wood and drawers of water." At that time in history great portions of mankind placed far more emphasis on keeping their word than we do today.

Joshua called for them and said, "Why did you beguile us? Now therefore you are cursed and shall always be servants to us."

And they answered Joshua, "Because we know how the Lord God commanded you to destroy all the inhabitants of the land from before you, therefore we were afraid for our lives because of you and have done this thing. And now we are in your hand. Do to us as it seems good and right to you to do." So Israel let them live and made them hewers of wood and drawers of water. Their presence in the midst of Israel was a snare to them over time. Yet centuries later some of King David's chief supporters and soldiers were Gibeonites. Perhaps the respect on the part of some of the Gibeonites for God's power was an indication of their belief even though they used deceptive means to try to protect themselves. We will not understand fully until we meet the Lord in heaven. One of Joshua's strengths was his understanding of the Lord's character, and of his own. He knew the Lord was merciful, and he understood deeply his own weakness and tendency to wander from the Lord. He had learned to own up to it and quickly turn back to the Lord, admitting his failure and humbly taking His help. Discovering his failure was discouraging, but he had learned that at such moments it was more important to dwell on the Lord's mercy than on himself and his failures. That was what he did, and as we shall see, the Lord once again turned failure into victory for the one willing to be honest with him and accept his help.

In the New Testament the Apostle John wrote words setting forth the same concept. "If we confess our sins (admit them as Joshua had) He is faithful and just to forgive us our sins and to cleanse us from all unrighteousness" (I John 1: 9). This became a principle for maintaining fellowship with the Lord. Sin, or even simply following our own imagination in a wrong direction, takes us out of fellowship with God. It does not remove us from our status as His children. It rather removes us from our harmonious moment by moment relationship with him. As Joshua had, for the time being, neglected awareness of his relationship with God, so we also do the same. God allowed him to make a mistake foolish enough to cause him to realize he had left his Lord behind. God did not forsake him, though he did let him reap the consequences of his doings. The "treaty" with Gibeon led to difficulties both immediately and long term. Joshua quickly owned up to it, and God used his failure as a springboard into a new, successful plan. This is encouraging to those of us who also make mistakes. According to John, admitting our failures leads to forgiveness and removal of them as obstacles to our fellowship with God. Joshua, knowing from the lesson of the Tabernacle sacrifices, could move ahead in confidence knowing that God was serious when he said our sins were "covered" by them. God's enabling of his, and Israel's, startling victories was proof that God accepted them and was with them.

CHAPTER 30

JERUSHA AND RAHAB WASHING CLOTHES

In the few days of relative peace that followed, Israel took time to assess all that had transpired in the recent weeks: the defeat of the two kings, Sihon and Og, who withstood them on the other side of Jordan; the fabulous wealth they collected from their conquered kingdoms; the miraculous crossing of Jordan that reminded them of the Red Sea crossing forty years earlier; and the conquest of Jericho. They were sorting and dividing out all the things they had captured—food, clothing, weapons, jewelry, furniture, silver, gold and other precious things. The Lord had given them much.

While they worked, Jerusha was kneeling with her daughter, Tirzah, by the waters of a clear brook, helping her wash clothes and take care of her little baby. An older grandchild was scooping up wet sand and piling and carving it into the shape of a fortress, to her an imaginary place to live. Jerusha and Tirzah had invited Rahab to come with them, and they were getting to know each other. Rahab told them her parents were overwhelmed by their own miraculous delivery from certain death. They had responded to the pleadings of their outlandish daughter to seek shelter at her house when the Israelites began approaching. They had stayed there a whole week as Israel marched daily around Jericho. So insistent was she, and so certain that Israel would take their city, they could not help but pay attention to her. She plagued them with all this strange talk of how merciful Israel's God was. She pleaded day after day with any who would listen to come to the safety of her house, and many did. It was common knowledge that the spies had briefly visited her place of business, so she could tell them a little of what she had discovered about their God and how His mercy would protect them. She had been careful to say as little as possible about her plans. Indeed, it had been her parents who years earlier had given their five-year-old daughter a different viewpoint about this menacing tribe of Israel. Word around town was that they were cruel marauders out to destroy all other peoples and set up their own kingdom, and that their God somehow had already destroyed Egypt, having overpowered its gods.

Jericho was terrified and so was young Rahab. Her parents, different than most others in Jericho, had reasoned that, if Israel's God had all this power, maybe He was the one they should honor as the true God. They had no idea how to do this but had planted this idea in each of their children's thinking to calm them. Truth was where one found it, and sometimes it was found in very unlikely people—even in this land of Canaanite pagans. God dispersed His Word throughout the world. The most important thing any human could do during his life was to recognize it when he encountered it and respond to it. The intricacy and order observable in creation pointed to the existence of a creator with wisdom far beyond ours. Like it or not, that was a piece of logic God would use in His final judgment of each person. He says so in Romans 1:18-20: "But God shows His anger from heaven against all sinful, wicked people who push the truth away from themselves. For the truth about God is known by them instinctively. God has put His knowledge in their hearts." From the time the world was created, people have seen the earth and sky and all that God made. They could clearly see His invisible qualities—His eternal power and divine nature. That is what God will tell those who protest that He is unfair in judging them for never responding to him. "I called to you over and over, and you never responded to me," He will say at the judgment.

"When did you call?" they will say.

"Did I not display My power over every single idol and false belief in Egypt with the ten plagues? Did I not destroy Pharaoh's army in the Red Sea after I had delivered Israel through the Red Sea—all in accord with a promise I had made to them hundreds of years earlier? You knew about it, but you never bothered to consider it in your hearts or to ask for more information. I warned Pharaoh and all Egypt many times that they were in danger of My judgment. Some were too stubborn to give in to My words. Some simply ignored Me. Many responded, even some of Pharaoh's magicians and warriors. I *never* judge without first warning. The wise hear, and the simple pass on and are punished. I never force anyone to come to Me nor to enter My kingdom. Up until this final day of judgment, I look for them to come of their own free will, and all are free to come. Those in My kingdom are those who have chosen to be there. That is My way."

The Apostle Paul wrote, "Whoever believes on him will not be put to shame" and "whoever calls on the name of the Lord shall be saved" (Romans 10: 11, 13). The Apostle John, citing Jesus's words, wrote, "The one who comes to me I will by no means cast out" (John 6: 37). Now Rahab's family were here safe in the midst of Israel, thanks to her pleadings and God's own mercy!

A bewildered Rahab was somehow at peace and happy in her new home. The fear she and the rest of Jericho had been living under had been replaced by a whole new aura of love and happiness as she experienced acceptance by the people of Israel and, beyond that, by their God. A feeling of God's power to set free and deliver from fear and bondage pervaded the camp and, beyond that, a sense of peace—an odd thing in the midst of a nation embroiled in one conflict after another and characterized as a band of murderous marauders. Nonetheless, that is what Rahab observed. God's actions upended the noisy opinions of the world. He had not only delivered them from Egypt's power but was now giving them land and blessings He had so long ago promised. He was with them and guiding them each day, and now Rahab herself was part of it all. By her own decision she had become part of an ancient plan. God was seeking from an errant mankind any and all who would come to Him of their own volition.

She had been trying to put her finger on what was different about these people. They seemed to care about her, but why should they? She had many friends in Jericho who loved her, but something was different here. This seemed deeper. These new relationships had a permanent dimension; they were anchored in Israel's God, their Creator who inhabited eternity.

When He said something it was true from all angles, springing as it did from the depth of eternal truth. In His wisdom He could speak words that could stand the test of time and answer all arguments against it. A man who thought much about it once gave a simple definition of love, stating that love "does what is best for someone for the longest time." For example, giving candy to a child may make him happy for the moment, but feeding him nutritious food will profit more over time, the more loving thing to do. In Jericho people could be kind to people they liked, but that kindness had no permanent attachment to anything, no truly lasting significance. It all wore out sooner or later, or changed when one offended another. For those who could make it more lasting, it eventually faded to nothing at death. Rahab had been disappointed, double-crossed, and hurt often enough to know that that was the unpleasant truth. Love amongst believers in the Lord was different, anchored to the Lord Himself and protected and maintained by Him, in spite of human failings. Those who belonged to the Lord on the earth had a connection to Him and through Him to each other. It transcended what the people of Jericho had, and that was what Rahab was discovering. The people she had seen as the enemy had done the greatest good for her. They had rescued her and given her a brand new life. God had long ago seen the response in Rahab's heart—and her parents—to the news about Israel's crossing through the Red Sea and their miraculous preservation. While others tried to dismiss it as hysterical exaggeration or reacted with such fear that they would not even think about it, Rahab's family had pondered it in their hearts and wanted to know more about this God who could do such things. And so he guided Matthias and Nathan to her.

Rahab learned about Israel's law, and it was shocking. Her whole life had been built around what God called sin. She had heard of Israel's God and the astonishing power he had. Why had he spared her—and her family and friends? Her parents had introduced her to the way of life she lived. They told her about the attraction between men and women and how she could use that to help earn money for the family. Thus Rahab was introduced to the grownup world. Later her mother showed her how to dress in a way that would make men more likely to notice her and be attracted to her. Other women taught her to adorn her face with makeup in a certain way that attracted men. It worked well, and those men would pay her or barter with her for her companionship. She could make enough money to help her whole family—and she could keep much of the money for herself. The plan worked, and she soon found that many men asked to be with her. One man hurt her and seemed cruel. She told her father, and he quickly found that man and afterward assured Rahab that he would never come near her again. One of her girlfriends a few years older than her told her she could use her power to control men and manipulate them. Rahab at first was not interested in such power as much as she was in the money. Men liked her for not abusing her power over them. She saw possibilities for great success, and a doorway to prosperity opened to her. Her friend had been right. Manipulation of people led to more power and wealth. Rahab, with her intellect, refined it to "subtle" manipulation so that few of her subjects ever caught on to how successful she was.

She had been pregnant twice in spite of all her attempts to avoid it. She disciplined herself not to let her heart attach to that baby. She had connived to contract with the officials of one of the temples in Jericho to give her baby to them as an offering. It would be taken from her the moment it was born and she never had to see it. What they did with the baby she would never let herself think about. Her self-discipline helped her to harden her heart like that.

She was playing wantonly with the wellspring of life, the deeper relationship of a man and wife enjoying life together. That a new life sometimes came into being silently and unconsciously from such activity was unappreciated by her. Her cold-hearted refusal to pay any attention to those tiny, helpless persons emerging within her deepest self, insulated her for years from the pain of acknowledging their life. She ignored them out of existence.

That all ended when she began learning about life from God's point of view. In learning about the commandments God gave at Mount Sinai she learned her life of prostitution was condemned by God as sin. Same with her method of stretching the truth to fit her purposes. It was lying, lying about others and condemned by God as "bearing false witness" about her "neighbors." She could not even keep the first commandment, which said to put the Lord above everything else. She had probably never done that. Well, maybe she had once when she believed God had the right to judge her and then asked the spies for help. Suddenly a clear realization of what she had been harpooned her newly awakened heart, and there was no way of escaping it. Her own wickedness loomed before her mind as monstrous and inescapable, as the naked and horrible truth that rendered her fit for destruction. A silent scream of horror tore through her heart. And in the midst of that an even more powerful truth emerged—God had spared her! Why? Like a still, small voice a thought came into her mind that began to silence all the guilt screaming against her. God knew her true nature long before she did and had moved, unknown to her, to rescue her, had cut loose that awful harpoon. He was taking care of her, and the fears began to evaporate. She was experiencing what one day would be written clearly in scripture, freedom from the guilt of what she was. Israel's Savior took the penalty for all her wretchedness, a Savior who had not yet arrived on this earth but who was perfectly represented in all the innocent animal sacrifices in the Tabernacle and the earlier stone altars. "In due time Christ died for the ungodly," wrote the Apostle Paul (Romans 5: 6). And she was certainly "ungodly." She had been learning that since hearing Moses's writings. Because she had faced up to her own ungodliness she had opened herself up for God to show her more. The bad news set the stage for the good news to enter. God could forgive her and accept her because a substitute would give His life to pay for her sins. That truth melted her heart and healed years' worth of suppressed pain, invisible pain, invisible even to herself. In truth she was beginning to understand more now what had happened to her on the roof of her house when she determined to help Nathan and Matthias, the day she realized the Lord would spare her.

Was this what Israel knew, that God was taking care of their sin? No wonder they could reflect peace. This God of theirs was not only their God—He was hers. The more she learned about him, the more she wanted to learn. A deep change had taken place in her heart.

Little did she know it, but more than just her lifestyle was condemned by God. She would learn in the future months and years that the very heart she had inherited from Adam and Eve was devious, deceitful and corrupt. She had deceived herself with that wicked heart into thinking she could please the pagan gods by sacrificing to them. Now that she knew the true Lord she began to realize that no matter how hard she tried she could not stop her heart from coming up with evil thoughts, ill-will toward others, hatred for certain people, or lust for stylish clothing and jewelry. She could not even squelch her tendency to lie when others guessed her evil motives. All of this came from the recesses of her heart, and she could not stop it. It was as though God had turned the lights on about the inner workings of her heart. Not fun to see. Her first instinct was shame, and the next was to hide it.

So, not only had much of her past life been in direct violation of God's commandments, she now realized her uncontrollable heart was condemned by Him too. God had told them that if they ate of the fruit of that certain tree they would die. They ate, and sure enough, their intimate connection to God instantly vanished, and then many years later, their bodies died and slowly turned back to dust, the atoms of the earth. The children born from them, said to be "in *their* image," in contrast to Adam and Eve, who were made in God's image, had likewise all died, as had all their descendants, every single one of them except those alive at the present moment. They too would die one day. Not one person escaped that outcome. Futility was the way of life in Jericho. A bitter, miserable end. So man was condemned by God two ways—for his actions and for the wicked condition of his heart, and humans could fix neither. She had survived in Jericho by never thinking about any of this.

Still, it was worse. Simply belonging to Adam's race meant she belonged to a race of people that was condemned before she was even born. Her actions and her heart had nothing to do with it. Scripture summed it up in just a few words, crystal clear: "In Adam all die" (I Corinthians 15: 22). Guilty three ways: by being in Adam's race, by sinful actions, by possessing a flawed heart. She had been on the 'broad road' to destruction, floating down the river of life, a river that led to death. There was nothing she could do about any of it. People would later ask Jesus, "Who then can be saved?" His answer was "With men (or men's efforts) it is impossible, but with God all things are possible" (Matthew 19: 26). Adam and Eve's fig leaves could not hide nor undo their wrongdoings or make them acceptable with God. Yet God could literally "clothe them in righteousness" with the clothing *He* made for them. He had a way of dealing with the unrighteousness their actions had brought upon them. Man could not work his way out of death. But the Savior, the Redeemer, the Messiah, could do it for him.

In Jericho everyone was clawing for more. It was ruthless, each trying to outdo the other, taking things before someone else got them. There never seemed to be quite enough to go around. In Israel God was giving them all they needed, and no one had to take from another. They had collected more food and grain than they needed. Crops planted by someone else were suddenly theirs, as were oxen, sheep and cattle. Even gold, silver and other precious things were left behind by those they conquered. The Israelites seemed to understand that God was giving them all this and taking care of them day after day. Growing up in the wilderness had taught them to trust in His care years ago, as they had collected manna daily from the grass of the earth where it had appeared like dew each morning. God had told them to collect all they wanted—there was more than they could ever use—but to use it all that day and not to keep it overnight. At first many, worried about running out, collected huge amounts and then hid it away for future use, to make sure they had enough for tomorrow. A mistake. It bred worms and stunk terribly the next morning! They had to throw it away or bury it to get rid of the stench. But here was the thing the Lord was showing them—there was a brand new supply the very next morning, free for the taking, fresh, and, again, more than they could use. He would always take care of them, and they did not have to hoard. And so it was, day after day, all the while they were in the wilderness. His continuing kindness made them realize that, by hoarding manna, they were actually refusing to trust Him to provide for them. Would it not be better to simply relax and enjoy God's care for them? Daily manna never ceased until they came into the Promised Land, and then the Lord used a new source, the fruit of a fertile land, to feed them. There was so much no one had to scramble to get his share ahead of anyone else.

And little by little Rahab understood. The Lord was taking care of them, always, and the people knew it and had relaxed in it. Being a keen studier of human nature as she was, Rahab had observed different types of behavior, or maybe levels of understanding, amongst the Israelites. Some seemed to have very high standards of conduct and knew how to live on a higher plane than everyone else. They seemed to never fail or do anything wrong. Subtly it made Rahab feel inadequate, as though she could never measure up, and her previous life was so selfish and abominable that she could never overcome her past. It was almost as though it were a competition over whose behavior was the most God-like.

Then there were other Israelites who also appeared to love their God but had had failures in their lives that, curiously, did not seem to haunt them or drag them down. Yet they did not hide them either. They did not seem proud of such failures, nor brag about them, but were not afraid to admit them. They too had the audacity to think that God completely accepted them. How could they dare be so sure God accepted them? It was the height of pride. Plus, they were hypocrites. She had seen them fail, display foul tempers and attitudes and do foolish things on several occasions. As her mind puzzled over the different attitudes, Rahab began to see it all in a different light. These "failure types" had a humility about them. A deep sense of their own failure to measure up to God's standards was detectable in them, but along with that, a peace. Jerusha was like that. So were Matthias and Nathan. So was Joshua—as far as she could tell from the distance from which she had observed him—and she was more comfortable around them. She had met Joshua personally only once when he had asked to meet her. Her impression of him was power mixed with humility and gentleness, an odd mixture for sure. He had touched her hand with his powerful, calloused hand, the hand that could wield a sword with deadly precision, welcoming her into their care, their midst. Their confidence, as she had discovered, was not really pride over their own ability to be "good," but was confidence in the Lord's ability to deliver them from their own weakness and failure.

They had faced up to their own inner failures to meet their own standards, or the infinitely higher standards of God, and had been so overcome that they had nowhere else to turn but to God's mercy. When they had, they had realized that God had somehow dealt with their failures for them through the animal sacrifices He had taught them to perform and through the future "Redeemer" to whom those sacrifices pointed. It was not totally clear how it all worked, but the sacrifice carried the message that God was dealing with their shortcomings in a manner that made it possible for Him to declare them righteous. It was a deep inner lesson that somehow persisted and provided comfort, even when daily life with its relentless activities and multiple impressions layered their hearts over with confusion. When scripture said, "Abraham believed God and it was counted to him for righteousness," they had caught the sense of it, that their status of "righteousness" was ascribed to them by God Himself simply because they, like Abraham, "believed" the things he said to them. When they quit "trying' to behave and finally collapsed in God's promises to take care of them, accepting His help, they found peace. The peace came when they realized He would keep His word to them. *His* efforts would deal with their sin. Perfectly—as their efforts could not. Somehow it was so easy to see—but also so easy to miss. As they saw over time more clearly what God was doing for them and how much He loved them, their hearts changed on the inside, and as that happened, their outward behavior began to change.

The religions of the world centered around man working to please God while what Rahab was seeing in Israel was the exact opposite, God doing the work for man. Despite all the variations of the religions of the tribes of the world, they were all faces of the same idea, man working to become acceptable to God. To Rahab, it began to look extremely simple: man's ideas versus God's revealed way, which was to admit your guilt and then accept God's help. Those were the only two ways, man's way versus God's way. Man's way failed for the Egyptians, and it failed in Jericho, and somehow, Rahab had recently latched on to the right way.

CHAPTER 31

STILL AT THE BROOK

Later that day Rahab asked Jerusha to explain more about the sacrifices, and Jerusha had tried to explain. Now, as she absentmindedly watched Jerusha scrub and rinse an article of clothing on a flat rock in the brook, she saw the water carry the dirt away and leave a clean fabric. Somehow it reminded her of those animal sacrifices. "What in the world?" She explained her observation to Jerusha, who picked up the same thought. The sacrifices were like this clean water that removed and carried the dirt far away. Water could penetrate into the very fibers of the cloth in a way other human efforts could not and at the level of the tiniest, invisible particles of soil, dislodge them and wash them away, leaving a clean fabric. Somehow the sacrifices spoke of God's ability to reach into a human heart stained so deeply within with ungodliness and wickedness that no amount of human effort could cleanse. God's action could accomplish what man's could not. He saw man's failure, comprehended it, and then dealt with it. God had instructed to put one's hands on the head of the animal he was offering as a sacrifice for his sin. This action transferred his sin to the animal. Then it was killed and offered. Many times, God had sent fire from heaven to devour the sacrifice, indicating His judgment had fallen upon it and that He had accepted the offering. Legally, punishment for sins transferred to the innocent animal. God could rightfully pronounce the offending sinner clean because the sin had been properly punished. If the worth of an animal to pay for sin did not quite measure up to the value of a human life, the value of the life of the Redeemer, or the "Seed" promised by God to Eve, certainly would. At least that was how Matthias and Jerusha, and now Rahab, saw it.

Thus when God pronounced something clean it was clean according to the highest court in the universe. "Who can say, I have made my heart clean, I am pure from my sin" (Proverbs 20: 9)? No one could. It took an outside force, the water, or the sacrifice, and, ultimately, the work of God Himself.

Then Rahab asked about the Tabernacle, a giant tent-like structure she had seen.

Jerusha said, "It is the place where God meets with us. It was built around the Ark, the chest in which the stone tablets containing the law given by God are kept. The law was written in the stone by the finger of God at Mount Sinai thirty-eight years ago, on those very stone tablets. The law shows God's perfection and holiness and also His presence in the heart of the Tabernacle. Before anyone can enter the Tabernacle, God expected him to be as perfect and holy as the law demands. Additionally, it reminds of God's *agreement* with man that He will *bless* all who make themselves holy by keeping the law perfectly. At the entrance to the Tabernacle, though, stands a brazen, or brass, altar on which animal sacrifices are offered daily. These deal with one's own wickedness and breach of the law. Strange thing. If man is supposed to obey the law, what are the sacrifices for? If keeping the law makes you perfect, why does anyone need to bring a sacrifice?"

"It is confusing, Jerusha, isn't it?" asked Rahab.

"Yes. And there is more. These animals were innocent. They are not the guilty ones. They have not rebelled against God nor broken his commandments, but they are dying because of the humans' problems. It does not seem fair, not for the animals anyhow. They are not lawbreakers but are dying a lawbreaker's death. What does it all mean?"

Rahab partially understood but was still laboring to figure it out. "Why can no one enter the Tabernacle without offering at the brazen altar?" It seemed like God was forcing everyone to think.

Jerusha said, "The Tabernacle is God's way of meeting with man and of teaching the way back to Him, and the way back is through the offering He said to bring. It means we are admitting we are poisoned with sin and need His help. We cannot come near Him unless we are first cleansed—and it means we will accept *His* cleansing."

"I think I'm beginning to understand, but it's going to take more time," said Rahab, still puzzling in her mind.

"We are still learning too, Rahab. We understand it a little better than we used to, but still not completely," answered Jerusha. "We have asked God to help us understand. You can do that too."

God certainly was not impressed with any natural goodness in man, not even the Israelites! Rahab, coming in as an outsider, had a keen interest in these strange practices. Having been told of her acceptance by the true God himself in spite of her unworthiness, she had been puzzled. Yet those who struggled over its meaning gradually gained a deepening understanding of God's relationship with man. For those who did not like to think or reason, the Tabernacle was a meaningless structure, something to worship. Sacrifices were just something they "had" to do. Some never wondered why. Scripture would later say, "A prudent man foresees the evil and hides himself, but the simple pass on and are punished" (Proverbs 27: 12).

Jerusha, sensing Rahab's struggle, explained more, but at first it only further confused her. "We all have an out-of-control BEAST inside of us," she said. "that we inherited from Adam. We knew so from the ancient story of Adam and Eve, the story God preserved for us. You could never really control that beast, and you could not get rid of it either. It was the spirit of the serpent who was really the spirit of Satan, of rebellion, of deception and death, to whom they opened the door when they believed his words. Believing him let him into their hearts and from there into every heart of every person later born to them."

"Wait a minute. A beast? Inside us? You're not like that. None of you are. You rescued us. You are good people. You are losing me, Jerusha," objected Rahab.

Jerusha, returning her gaze, sat silently while those words hung in the air. "We all like to think we are good. It is difficult for us to accept that the pure goodness we all thought we had is not as good as we thought. That's what God was showing Adam and Eve. That's what that story from so long ago showed us. And we did not want to see it any more than they did."

Rahab studied her but said nothing. At the moment she had no words.

"God was giving us the answer," continued Jerusha. "That evil nature inside us was out of control. At least *we* could not control it. Oh, we might control it for a while, but it never rested. It never went away. It lurked . . . and waited. It fooled us into thinking we were good. But it was a deception."

"Then there is no hope for any of us. This whole thing is make-believe."

"It might look like that, but remember the story, Rahab. God came to Adam and Eve right after they had fallen for Satan's lie. He did not abandon them—and He gave them hope."

"How so?" asked Rahab.

"Remember, God told them a 'seed' would come who would bruise the head of the serpent's seed. That meant a child born to Eve would overcome and destroy the effects Satan had on the human race, then and in the future. It was not clear at the time, but that seed would be a child born many generations in the future."

"All of that was in that story?" wondered Rahab out loud.

"Remember who told the story, Rahab—the Lord Himself, the Creator of the world. He could tell a story that contained many details hidden in its words and would accomplish what He wanted. He wanted us to listen and think about it and then believe it—as Adam and Eve had 'believed' the serpent's false words. Now *believing* God's words from our broken position would be our rescue."

"What do you mean 'believe?' Doesn't God want us to *do* something?"

"God did not accept Adam and Eve's fig leaves because they did not really fix their problem. It only covered it up. Nothing they could do would undo what they had done. And nothing we can do can fix our sin either. God gave them one way. Their unbelief of God's warning had brought their downfall. Their *belief* in what God was showing them was the way back to Him. Belief is not a physical action others could see. It is an invisible reaction to what one saw or heard and is more important than action. Belief came first, and action comes out of belief. That is what God was interested in—man's beliefs. He revealed that when He said, 'Abram believed God and God counted it to him for righteousness.' Abram did not believe God about everything nor all the time, but on that day when God spoke to him Abram believed what he heard—and God could work with that."

Jerusha paused, wondering if Rahab was following all this. It had taken her a long time to learn. Why should Rahab comprehend everything in one day? She observed Rahab's rapt attention and continued. "In fact that was why you were spared, Rahab. Satan's sinister influence, once allowed in through the doorway of belief, wrapped itself into and around every fiber of man's heart. Then it would invisibly pass itself on from parent to child through every generation ever to come. Once they had opened that door, whatever had come through could not be pushed back out. It was too powerful, like letting a dragon into your house, and they could not get rid of his presence, his influence, nor of the death that he brought that now infected all mankind. It was like opening the door when a hungry lion growled outside," she added, using a second example. "He ravaged in and quickly rampaged through every room in the house. Now as the new master, vastly more powerful than all others, he ruled—and it would be misery. That became the inheritance of all to descend from Adam and Eve. God gave man free will. He lets man decide what to believe. Had He not done that, man would not truly be free. And man, sooner or later, chose to disregard God's words. The result was catastrophe. The misery in the world was an outflow of the misery in man's heart. Deep thoughts." Jerusha surprised herself with the clarity of these thoughts and her ability to spew them out so readily.

Rahab, studying her intently, sat nearly motionless on the comfortable green grass at the edge of the brook and listened, beginning to lapse into confusion. What was Jerusha saying? Rahab had experienced, on more than one occasion, that hideous evil lurking out of control in certain people, cruel beyond belief, who had forced their way into her life. Beyond that she had sensed it in herself on several frightening occasions and fought to ignore it and make it go away. She never expected Jerusha to know about it. Jerusha was good. So was Israel. Different than all she had known in Jericho.

Rahab's stare arrested Jerusha, brought her thoughts to a halt. "But, Jerusha, you are good," she stammered. "Not like that," searching for some ray of hope.

Jerusha, in silence, returned her stare, willing to wait for those thoughts to sink in, searching for the right words to say. *Help me, Lord,* she thought. Finally, to Rahab's troubled silence she spoke, first shaking her head back and forth in a silent "no." "No one is good, Rahab . . . God is good . . . He wants us all to understand that." Once again, Rahab's world had been rocked. If Jerusha was not good, who was? What hope was there for anyone?

Jerusha's unworried demeanor wrapped comfort around Rahab's tortured heart. "You can try to control the heart with good behavior, but he is still there. He changes tactics and hides as silent anger, jealousy, seething hatred, just below the surface, ready to lash out when provoked. Hold him down long enough, and he hides deeper, as buried pride, resentment, total selfishness that still speaks a quiet influence and defiles others with its bitterness. Our good behavior is self-will wearing nice clothing. You can cover it up and pretend it is not there, but it is still an out-of-control beast that devours and destroys. Your best behavior, your most noble efforts, are anchored to it, tainted by it. You cannot overcome a beast like that who can change form faster than you can catch on and disguise himself as a doer of good, as light, and pretend to be love. Eve's innocent apprehension of reality was no match for Satan's ability to distort what she understood. Without God by her side to guide her understanding she acquiesced to his words."

Rahab, listening intently, looked down into the moving brook and after some silence, lifted her eyes toward Jerusha. Tirzah, nearby, quietly entertained her two little daughters, happy in their play, and she also listened. Who *was* this woman who understood such things? Jerusha's words lifted awareness of this evil in Rahab and others, lurking just beneath the surface like a crocodile, unseen under calm water, to a more conscious level. She had sensed but never actively thought about it, nor had she heard anyone else ever bring it up or explain it in such a sensible manner. Finally, she said, "You have thought about this very deeply, haven't you? To explain it so easily with such flowing words is wisdom, I think, Jerusha. But what hope is there for us?"

"Plenty. Matthias and I have talked . . . many times. Some of this he learned from Joshua, who learned from Moses. Our hope," she continued, "is learning that the Lord is more powerful than the beast, the evil one. That is the voice of the Tabernacle, the voice of the sacrifice. No matter how bad our failures, the sacrifices that God told us to present to him at the Tabernacle would be acceptable to Him to cover the awful effect of our sin. We think those sacrifices point to the 'seed' God announced to Adam and Eve that would come and destroy Satan and his works. When that will be and who are not certain, but it will be someone sent through Eve by God at the time He appoints. And like the animal killed to make clothing for Adam and Eve, He will be innocent because that was what God is showing us. He will also fulfill the perfection called for in the Ten Commandments written on the stone tablets held in the Ark in the most holy place in the Tabernacle—the commandments we thought we could keep perfectly but soon found out we cannot. He will have Eve's human nature but somehow be innocent, as she was at the beginning.

"He will destroy that beast and all its works. God would go right to the root. Satan, who sought to destroy Eve and her husband and to pollute her offspring and all mankind, would be destroyed by a special one of her offspring. God will not be fooled nor outmaneuvered by Satan. That was what God told us in the story."

"When will that be?" asked Rahab, her mind reeling to take it all in.

"We don't know. We watch. When He comes all the world will know. Some thought it was Moses. Now some think it is Joshua. But they are men like us. God chose them to speak a message to Egypt and the whole world, but they are not the One who is yet to come. Many of the ancients in addition to Abraham knew of this One to come too. Job, who lived around Abraham's time, spoke with his friends and wrote of him, and God included his writing in the scriptures. He said, 'I know my Redeemer lives,' referring to the same One Abraham believed in.(Job 19: 25). Your words about the water carrying the dirt away were right, Rahab. That water first fell clean and pure as white snow in the mountains, later melted and tumbled to this brook that now flows continually to Jordan, and today carries our dirt from our clothes, without our help, to the Dead Sea. Some say that is the lowest spot on the earth's surface. From there it disappears then comes again perfectly clean from the clouds. How God does that I don't know, but I think it shows us that if He can make filthy water perfectly clean He can also wash sin completely out of our hearts."

Rahab had no words to question more. Only new thoughts, and now she needed time to think. Both women sat silently and resumed washing clothes in the clear water of the brook. Israel had so much to offer the world. If only people would pay more attention. She and Jerusha would be friends for many years. Indeed, she in time would find a husband, have a child, and not even Jerusha, not even Joshua, could have imagined that her name would be recorded in Scripture in the lineage of Christ (Matthew 1: 5). Tirzah's daughter had built and rebuilt several beautiful sand castles while the women talked.

Back at the camp, Tirzah's oldest, eight-year-old Ahira, with no parents nearby, had sneaked into his grandparents' tent to smuggle out Matthias's sword. It hung high on a tent pole out of reach of the younger children, but Ahira could reach it and bring it down. His grandfather had shown it to him before, and he had been fascinated by the beautiful, shiny blade and how sharp it was. When it was in its sheath its beauty was concealed, but when pulled out, it dazzled. He and his two friends, Elihu and Abraham, had been talking about spears and swords and wanted to try a real weapon. They were waiting outside the tent right now.

"My dad has a sword, but we're not supposed to touch it," said Elihu.

"My grandfather lets me look at his sword all the time because he thinks I am so grown up," replied Ahi, lying so smoothly his friends could not help but believe him. Holding the sword like a trophy he had just won, he wrapped his fingers around the handle and pulled it out a few inches, revealing that marvelous, shiny blade.

"Is it sharp?" questioned Abraham. "Let's go over by those trees where no one can see us and look at it."

Somewhat obscured by the trees, Ahi, standing like a triumphant warrior, pulled it out with a wide sweeping flourish, trying to make it ring like his grandfather did. That ring meant one thing. The time for talk was over. Except when Ahira pulled it out it made a dull scraping noise and no impressive ring. Still, the boys backed away in awe. This was no toy but a real sword.

"Let me feel the edge," said an excited Abraham, putting his thumb on the sharp edge and sliding it to feel how sharp it was.

"Don't do that!" cried Ahi. "You'll cut yourself." But it was too late. A bright red line of blood appeared on his thumb.

"Ouch!" he winced, and then acted like it was nothing. "Do you think it could cut this little branch off this tree?"

"Sure. Watch." He whacked it with the sword but not quite hard enough.

"You have to hit harder than that! Or aren't you strong enough?" wisecracked Abraham.

This time Ahi swung it harder and lopped the branch clean off—and a nice chunk of bark to boot due to his poor aim. All three boys were impressed and felt grown up. He tried to swing it like the men did with one arm. It was so heavy he finally used both hands, and when he did, he looked like a real soldier. The other boys were duly impressed with this frightful looking young warrior brandishing a weapon.

"That sword is sooo sharp. Do you think you could cut a rock in half?" asked Elihu.

"You'd have to swing it with all your might," added Abraham with growing enthusiasm. "Cut it in one blow."

"Here's a good rock," said Elihu, setting it right where Ahi could get a good swing. His aim was true this time, and the sword connected with the rock with a clang. Only thing was, the rock did not split. It had the faintest mark on it. "Look at the blade! The edge is all bent from the rock. Uh-oh."

"Maybe we can pound it straight with another rock," offered Abraham, searching for a solution.

Ahira did not say anything. He was scared. They had to find a way to fix it and put it back without anyone knowing. Abraham had found a flat rock to set the blade on and another sort of flat rock with which to pound it. Things were looking up. Maybe there was hope. Abraham tapped carefully on the blade with the flat rock, and the edge straightened a little bit.

"Hit it again," encouraged Elihu. This time a little piece of the tempered metal broke off.

"Oh, no," cried Ahira. "It broke!"

"The piece is so little," said Abraham, trying to calm them all down. "Maybe your grandfather won't notice. Let's put it back in the sheath and take it home and hang it up. We won't say a word about it."

"Yes," comforted Elihu. "If he ever does notice, maybe he will think he did it." With those words they talked themselves into believing their improbable plan would work.

At that moment Ahira saw his mom and the girls in the distance with Jerusha and Rahab, strolling toward home from the brook. "Hurry!" he spoke in a frenzied whisper. "Here they come." They sheathed the sword, ran home, hung it up, scrambled back outside, and sat down in front of the tent, breathing hard and working even harder at looking innocent. They were convincing enough. The ladies were so deep in conversation they barely noticed the boys. All was well.

CHAPTER 32

FRIGHTENING NEWS

(Joshua 10)

The arrangement with Gibeon was about to become more entangling. Several of the neighboring kingdoms, five to be exact, had heard of Israel's conquests and now of Gibeon's treaty with them and were greatly alarmed. Gibeon, as a huge city, also commanded a powerful army of skilled warriors, and it was not good that they were uniting with Israel. The wily and ambitious king of Jerusalem, Adoni-zedek, had called four other kings to join forces with him to "smite" Gibeon to put an end to this nonsense and thus warn other cities to "think twice" before allying with Israel. Their five-army coalition would be truly powerful and intimidating. As they set up camp within sight of Gibeon the prospect of annihilation loomed so real that the Gibeonites sent fast messengers to seek an audience with Joshua.

"Come quickly, and help us," gasped the breathless runners. "All the kings of the Amorites from the surrounding mountains are gathered against us." Troubling news, indeed, to Israel as well. Now what? Two of Joshua's chief captains, Bartimaeus and Elizur, were standing near him when this news broke in.

"I knew this would happen. The Canaanites are not going to let us just walk in and take their land," worried Bartimaeus quietly to Elizur. Fear poked at their hearts, but their expressions revealed none of it. Their maturity and self-discipline prevented that. Both looked earnestly to Joshua, careful not to display any particular emotion, on their faces or in their posture. What would he do now? Jericho and Ai were one thing, but this was more; five large nations banding together could spell their doom. Maybe God was paying them back for not looking to Him about Gibeon. They studied Joshua's face, looking for some clue about what to do—just as Joshua had closely observed Moses in moments when destruction and failure loomed so real as to be the only probable outcome. Joshua's manner gave no clue about how he was taking this news. The Lord has a way of testing His children, sometimes day after day after day, oftentimes when one feels that one more test would be too much. Bartimaeus and Elizur could go either way. They could fold in fear or rise to the challenge. They wanted to trust the Lord, but fear ate at their hearts. They remembered God's promise to lead them into the land and give it to them. Had they jumped ahead of Him and now were about to be punished? If Israel made the wrong decision it would be their final and utter destruction. Yet would not that mean that God's promises to Abraham were failing before the opposition of the world? He would not let that happen. Would He? They wanted to trust the Lord . . . but it was confusing and the stakes were so high. Their path led to success but trod dangerously close to the sheer edge of a steep cliff that dropped to frightening death. A tiny misstep here could spell doom in place of victory. In desperation they cried out silently in their hearts to God for guidance.

Joshua stood expressionless while the runners spilled their story, and as they were yet talking, motioned to his aide to bring his chief captains near. "Send word to all your men to tell their wives and children they will be gone for several days and to pack food and water for tonight, gather their swords, spears and bows, and be here in half an hour." To the breathless Gibeonites he requested guides to lead them the fastest way back to Gibeon, about twenty-five miles from their camp at Gilgal. On foot and in the dark it would be a challenge. By starting this very night they would reach Gibeon slightly before daybreak with time left to allow a short rest before their surprise attack. Witnessing Joshua's decisiveness and certainty in that moment, Bartimaeus and Elizur made up their minds. They were "all in." It was a dangerous and highly improbable journey, but their hearts were suddenly fixed and their resolve as firm as Joshua's. Great leaders have that effect. Their ability to understand the moment and see a clear path that makes sense stirs confidence among their followers and emboldens them as well. Armies are made strong when strong leadership acts. Memories of the Lord's past leadings and victories flooded in and reassured their hearts. Seeing Joshua's resolve reminded them that beyond sheer bravado this plan lined up with the promise God had given that "no man would be able to stand against them" as they set out to claim the Promised Land, and thus God's Word buttressed them deep in their hearts. They were part of a movement larger than themselves, even larger than Joshua, and Joshua's leadership helped them see that. Though stepping out by their own volition, they were also stepping out in alignment with God's words and power. In their own strength they would be wiped out. With God leading them, they would be victors. One day they would inspire others as Joshua had inspired them.

In less than half an hour his men were assembled, and as the shadows of the evening stretched out, Joshua issued the command to march. He would explain the plan along the way so that all knew what to expect. Joshua would rather intimidate than be intimidated. If five nations were gathering against him, tomorrow morning they would awaken to a surprise before their leaders ever saddled a horse. He also took God's word that "no man would be able to stand against him" very literally and walked on its strength into the night. Well aware of the overwhelming strength of the armies he faced, he was also keenly aware of the power of the "Unseen Captain" he knew was guiding him.

Fear hit him the same as it hits any of us. He had learned, though, in enduring many frightening circumstances, that fear usually brought panic, and panic paralyzed and led to frantic, disorganized actions.

He had learned rather to resist the urge to listen to the inner screams and instead look squarely into the face of the danger. Bravery in its raw form. One could still lose. But if victory were in any way possible, this was the best way to find it. The Lord had been his teacher and guide, and it was He who calmed Joshua's heart and caused him to remember His promise to bring him victory. Joshua also remembered that scene with Moses atop the hill, sun behind him, hands stretched up to heaven while he, as a young captain, fought Amalek in the valley below. A youthful warrior that day had gained the victory during a long and relentless battle due entirely to help from Israel's God. There had been so many moments when the battle had seemed certainly lost and death by a wickedly sharp sword swung far too close. Joshua had looked anxiously up the hill and seen Moses's weary arms held high by Aaron and Hur—and had seen the battle begin to turn in his favor again. An extremely long day with a hard-fought battle forged a seasoned warrior who always seemed to remember where his power came from. Today Joshua's certainty spread to the men following him, and they too, conscious of stepping out by faith and casting the outcome upon the Lord, were learning to trust him with their lives. The battle was bigger than all of them, but their confidence in the Lord energized their hearts.

After Joshua and his army set out as they did, the Lord said to Joshua, "Fear them not, for I have delivered them into your hand. There shall not a man of them stand before you." When believers trust God to support them and then step into action, God always encourages them in one way or another.

On the other side, citizens of those five nations were rightly terrified of Israel and the threat they posed. Their kings were not easily frightened and yet on this occasion were themselves nearly panicked at the miraculous victories accompanying Israel's emergence within their midst. Now banding together, they had formed a temporary alliance, an overwhelming force that would crush this threat before it grew any larger. They purposely let news of their impending attack on Gibeon leak out for its added intimidation and paralyzing effect, much as the roar of a lion in its death-dealing leap momentarily paralyzes its startled prey. Now they had intensified the terror by setting up camp within sight of the Gibeonites. Once they had destroyed Gibeon they would use the momentum of that victory to inspire their warriors for more, to mount a crushing blow against Israel. Instead of waiting for Israel to attack them, they would attack Israel—with an army so large and powerful that Israel would have no chance!

CHAPTER 33

INTO THE NIGHT...

(Joshua 10; Genesis 37-39)

Even though it was night, Joshua kept up a fast pace. He was a man of action. A few torches helped light the way, but more helpful was the delicate light from a rising full moon that washed the path with just enough light to see. Matthias and his long-time friend Abijah were catching up on their friendship and talking about how things were happening so fast. All their lives they had heard about how, beginning way back with Abraham, God would make a great nation of them and that through them He would bring blessing to all nations. God had spoken also to Abraham's son, Isaac, and then his son, Jacob, repeating those same words and blessings. Throughout later history when God spoke to certain chosen people He introduced himself as "the God of your fathers, the God of Abraham, Isaac and Jacob," always reminding them of His faithfulness to His earlier promises and His ability to keep those promises. Abraham, Isaac and Jacob had all died ages ago, but their souls were still alive in God's safe-keeping, and now their direct descendants were stepping into the fruition of His words. When Jesus, far in the future, referred to God's repeated mention of "Abraham, Isaac and Jacob," He added that God is "not the God of the dead but of the living."

Israel had experienced the absolute and abject hopelessness of slavery that dragged on for years and then the miraculous deliverance from Egypt. They had comprehended their complete inability to escape its life-draining hold. God had rescued them. Now, forty years later, they were still free. They had survived a journey through a hostile wilderness and, though God had taken many of them home through discipline, here they were. They had taken part in the improbable victories over Jericho and Ai. And now this sudden march to defend those deceivers at Gibeon . . .

In the first hour of their march Joshua passed down word explaining their mission. True, they would be defending Gibeon in keeping the promise they had foolishly made to them, but as Joshua saw it, God had made Israel's job easier by gathering five armies into one spot to be destroyed in one campaign rather than five separate campaigns. Joshua had a startling way of looking at things. He also had a startling track record. Great leaders are bold and see things others do not. Such boldness wakes their followers to realize their own potential before the Lord and act on it.

As the Lord led them now into astounding situations the old stories took on added meaning. Israelites were understanding what Abraham went through to leave the land of his upbringing and familiarity wholly on the strength of God's directions to him. They too were traveling on nothing more tangible than the strength of God's promises. So far, it had been an adventure that none could really have imagined, as nearly every day something new developed. Energized by the very real sense that God Himself was guiding them in a movement much bigger than themselves, they advanced into the domain of a very powerful enemy. They had no illusions. If God's assurances to them were not true they would be utterly destroyed. As the priests carrying the Ark had stepped into Jordan by faith, they were at this moment walking into the dark by faith. The rest was up to God.

Marching through the night to the biggest battle yet, the distractions of daytime scenery blotted out in darkness, each warrior was, in a sense, alone with his thoughts, even though accompanied by thousands of others. Dark silhouettes of each other in the faint moonlight were all that could be seen. If one wanted to be quiet he could. If he felt like talking, someone close by did too. Many talked quietly to the friends next to them, all the while moving closer to the dawn and the battle it would bring. The moon arced higher overhead now, and the men were thankful for its gentle light. They found comfort in the knowledge that it reflected light radiating from a sun ever shining somewhere beyond the night, out of sight to them, reminding them it was still there, as the Lord, though unseen, was guiding them on this dark trail.

The enemy would be shocked at their unexpected appearance. Israel would be a spear driven into the heart of a vastly larger army as confusion briefly seized them. But that enemy, comprised of trained warriors, might twist and dodge, recover quickly and strike back. This whole venture could be a death trap, the end of Israel. Their wives and children, left miles behind in safety at Gilgal, would be rounded up and destroyed by vengeance-seeking Canaanites, who with their pagan practices knew how to torture and inflict a horrible death on their enemies.

It certainly could go that way. Still, the soldiers, marching in the dark, itself a 'shadow of death' all around them, believed their God had a plan, was with them, and was indeed guiding the spear. They believed Joshua to be in tune with God and to know what to do in the heat of the battle. He had been in so many battles and triumphed—even in battles with his own heart. His main strength was so simple anyone could do it, even those with little natural ability, serious birth defects, or debilitating illnesses. Many like that could grasp the possibility of simply clinging to God for help. A faithful doorman, street cleaner, or caregiver could be a king in heaven. Joshua's strength was to keep his attention on the Lord and his trustworthiness. He had thought long and hard on Moses's writings and the things he had taught him in person. His hours and days in the Tabernacle where God's presence abided had their effect. Now he was living out the principles worked into his heart over so many years.

In truth, Joshua saw a bigger battle than could be seen by human eyes. He saw, in his mind anyhow, the forces of evil, the very presence and power of Satan, influencing and motivating these nations in Canaan in their hatred of Israel. These were a people who had ignored their true God for so long that they, in their rebellion, had wandered into darkness and complete confusion and were easy prey for Satan's deceptions. Not even realizing it, they were led around by their own unbridled passions and imaginations. Satan watched with sadistic satisfaction as he steered them effortlessly into his chaotic and demonic schemes. Chaotic on the surface as men without thinking stirred up trouble and wrought havoc upon each other, looking for advantage. Calculated and deadly serious to Satan. They never knew how much they were being exploited and used and, in the end, would be left double-crossed and dead as litter on a horrible battlefield. His sole aim was to attack and dethrone God. He cared nothing about the people he used and destroyed. Because his heart was so filled and twisted with self-centeredness and hate he could not understand that *this could never happen.* God saw and comprehended the innermost, secret thoughts of his heart and had complete control over him. Satan held an unrealistic and inaccurate understanding of reality.

Joshua also saw what the Unseen Captain had explained to him, a scene revealing the huge invisible armies of angels of the Lord, holding vastly more power than any merely human armies and ready to unleash that power at the slightest nod from their Lord. Perfectly in tune with their Lord, they made no missteps. When they struck, it could be instant like lightning or terrifying like an earthquake or relentless like a hailstorm gradually beating everything to useless rubble. No matter which way, their power was stunning and did not need to be repeated. The power of a human army withered and failed before them. Satan himself was no match. The true God sought people who understood this and whose trust in Him allowed His power to flow through them. Joshua was such a man.

His men understood too. It was Joshua they could see, but it was God leading him—and them. It had not happened many times in history that such a large number of people followed the Lord, but here and there in Israel's history and in the history of a few other nations it had happened, and the results were stunning and remembered for ages. Men led by God were unstoppable, an overwhelming force, a consuming fire cleansing the land, light driving darkness away. Such were the thoughts guiding a conquering warrior's heart.

The walk was long and Joshua kept the pace just fast enough to cover the maximum amount of ground without exhausting his men. He knew their limits and wisely conserved strength. Only a fool would arrive at a battle exhausted. Every hour he stopped for a five minute rest, a bite of food and a drink of water. That was faster than pressing on desperately for hours on end.

To pass the time, Matthias and Abijah began discussing how the Israelites had come to be in Egypt in the first place. Those stories from

Abraham, Isaac and Jacob and his twelve children, passed down, word for word, from the beginning, told and retold to each generation, committed to memory, had become the heart of Israel's existence. Children and adults alike never tired of hearing or telling them. Moses had, in his last few years, written them down, guided to do so by God, so that all the world and all generations would know. Moses wrote it and God preserved it, so far, to this very day.

The things God had said centuries earlier to Abraham were only partly understood at the time. Abraham and his descendants believed them, but God had not shown them the details of how things would play out. Now many of God's predictions had already come to pass and, looking back, things came into focus. Rehashing the old stories was like digging in the earth into a vein of gold, finding more and more precious treasure the farther one dug. Somehow they spoke from generation to generation.

As the old stories opened more clearly in their understanding they began to see that they were becoming part of the story. Matthias and so many of the others were seeing their part in a larger plan, and this gave them encouragement to continue in the face of the overwhelming odds against them. Could they continue to trust God to keep His promises—tomorrow and the next day? It was always easier to trust that God had helped yesterday than trust that He was helping you at the moment and would take care of you tomorrow. That was the challenge every day, to keep trusting. Joshua, though just a man like all others and often failing himself, had learned long ago to keep coming back to the Lord, even after foolish failures, like Ai or Gibeon, and accept His forgiveness, then allow God's words to guide him again. Such a man was called "mature" in the Bible, or to use the old word, "perfect" (slightly different from our use of the word today), and said to be "righteous." This was different than how the world looks at it.

Most people see "righteousness" as emanating from inside their own hearts as a result of good behavior and works. God sees one as "righteous" in a completely different way. According to what God said, He *declared* "righteous" any who would simply "believe" Him (as in Genesis 15:6). In the same way that He ascribed righteousness to Abraham the moment he *believed,* He would do so for any other human being. As in a court of law in the world, one's status of "guilty" or "not guilty" depends on what the court says. If it pronounces one guilty, he will be punished. If it pronounces one not guilty, he will be set free. Human judges and juries can make mistakes, but the court's decision is final. Decisions made by the judge in heaven are intrinsically true and final. God as the judge makes no mistakes. He sees completely and accurately into the situation and understands perfectly every detail related. "Will not the judge of all the earth do right," said Job early in man's history, about the time of Abraham. Further, He is impartial, ruling not on the basis of favoritism and special privilege, but on the basis of truth and right and wrong. Thus His judgments are correct and final and need no further modification.

Man by accepting, or believing, God's remedy for sin automatically receives a status of righteousness. Those who begin to understand this are beginning to understand how to let God take care of them and empower their actions. This is far different than man "earning" acceptance with God through good behavior and self-discipline. God's judgment is that man lacks the ability to make himself clean and truly righteous in the innermost parts of his heart. Therefore He set about to help man in a way he could not help himself. He would cleanse man of every speck of unrighteousness, thereby making him truly clean. Onlookers might not see any change in his behavior or condition, but a legal transaction more real and permanent than things seen on the earth has occurred in heaven, a transaction based upon the fact that God Himself performed the action that would deal with man's sinfulness, and therefore He could legally set man free from that sin. That action was to allow His Son to take the full brunt of the punishment intended to fall on Adam and his descendants for their sin. That punishment meant taking the awful effect of sin, separation from God, and its full, final effect—death—upon Himself on the day He went to the cross. That was why Jesus screamed that forlorn cry, "My God, my God, why have you forsaken me?" during the hours of darkness on the cross. God *had* forsaken Him there while the sins of all mankind were laid upon Him. The Son had willingly allowed that to happen, and the Father willingly watched, by mutual agreement unable to help Him. The agony each suffered was unfathomable. The earth itself shook to its foundations, reflecting that agony in the heart of God. In the darkness Jesus went out into eternity and dealt with our sins forever. According to scripture God "looked upon the travail of His soul and was satisfied." No other being could have done what Jesus did in that hour.

"My God, my God, why have you forsaken me?" will be the cry of all who are cast to "the outer darkness," the "lake of fire" Jesus often mentioned. He bore that for man so that man would not have to. The final outcome for the human who sinned was eternal separation from God. Yet somehow God transferred our sin to Jesus, who went out into eternity and bore that separation for man. He was different than man, though, in that He was more powerful than death (possessing as He did the power of an "endless life"), the power of perfection and holiness, which trumped darkness and death. It was not possible that death could overpower Him nor hold Him. And so He came back from eternity having left our sin with His payment there forever, forever paid. He is entitled to freely grant cleansing from sin to any and all who will accept it from him. "He that comes to me I will in no wise cast out . . . He will not be ashamed that comes to me." (John 6: 37; Romans 9: 33). Because He did that, He alone earned the right to absolve one's sins—because He Himself paid for them and God could legally accept His payment! Further, if God has forgiven one's sins, they are gone. What remains is "righteousness." King David said, "blessed is the man whose sins are forgiven" (Psalm 32: 1). With sins gone he was in a state of blessing.

Such understandings were settled in Joshua's heart long ago. Trusting that he was cleansed from his own wickedness was part of trusting the Lord, and the resulting boldness made him a great leader.

Abijah asked, "But why would a people that God would bless and whose existence would be a blessing to all the earth be subjected to living in a foreign land like Egypt for four hundred years, eventually becoming slaves?" Matthias did not answer for a long time. In spite of all he knew, he had never thought about it. Good question. Abijah had him stumped. God had told Abraham his descendants would serve another people for four hundred years and after that be delivered. God knew this would happen, so he must have been in control. But why?

Matthias thought out loud, "Maybe their slavery can be seen as a picture of the human condition. Made 'good' in the beginning of the world, something went horribly wrong for man. His very freedom made possible rebellion against God. Man by his own free will accepted Satan's lies and moved in defiance of God's warnings. Such a change instantly fell over Adam and Eve that they could not understand what had happened. Their beautiful spiritual connection to God was severed in a moment. They had no idea how to fix what had been destroyed. The happiness and freedom they experienced originally were given over to misery and pain and trouble and, in the end, death. Yet God had a plan to rescue them from their failures and he taught them so right there in Eden. The innocent animal dying to provide skin for clothing was a brutal shock to them. But it set forth on that very day the idea of an innocent one giving its life to provide for the care of another. Adam and Eve, so busy making excuses they could not hear God, would hear the scream of that animal and remember the sight of its blood streaming out for a long, long time. Their situation was so dire, and they were so trapped by their own evil that there was no way out except through help from another. The death of that animal for them would drive itself deep into their hearts."

Matthias's imagination continued. "Israel's hopeless enslavement in Egypt reflected the same picture of mankind as Eden but on a larger scale. Not only Adam and Eve but all their children, all mankind, were enslaved in an oppressed world, and at the end of that miserable existence, an even worse development awaited—death. Here man was hemmed in on all sides by cruel forces too powerful for him to beat.

"From this miserable existence in Egypt God reached in and pulled Israel out, as He had 'drawn Moses out' of the river when a helpless infant, displaying His easy power over those foes that would harm His precious mankind. The Egyptians themselves, and their king, were deceived and trapped by their own misunderstanding of the world. God was reaching out to them too. Many times in Genesis Moses wrote that God wanted *all Egypt* to know that he was the true God, not to enhance his glory, but to 'draw them' to himself so he could protect them. And since Egypt was the reigning power in the world at the time, God was reaching out to all the world as well. Those who humbled themselves, giving up their imaginary gods and throwing their trust on the true God, could be rescued. God's conquest through Moses of everything the Egyptians believed in was designed to call them back to Him as well. The fallen condition in Eden and the slavery in Egypt both pictured the miserable condition of all men. In each case man was powerless to help himself or set himself free. In each case God was able, and willing, to rescue man and make him free.

"When God set Israel free he gave them far more than freedom. He gave them a land with blessings abounding, telling them to walk in and possess. When they feared to go He led them him by his own hand." Matthias and Abijah r ealized that that was what God was doing at this moment. An entire generation of Israelites was realizing this. A rare moment.

There were hours yet to march, and in the night the air was still. The moon had risen high overhead. No breeze at their backs this time to urge them on. Only their own belief that God was with them now encouraged their steps. Under Joshua's leadership they walked at a pace that would place them in striking distance of the enemy in time for an hour's rest before their surprise attack.

Abijah asked Matthias to continue with the story. The next part was the at once cruel and beautiful story of Joseph, one of the twelve sons of Jacob, grandson of Abraham. "He and his brothers became the patriarchs, or fathers, of the twelve tribes that became the nation of Israel. Jacob himself had been a cheat and conniver, and though the Lord had spoken to him when he was a young man, he still spent many years following his own dreams. Not until he had been cheated and beaten over and over at his own game by his selfish, conniving father-in-law did he begin to heed the Lord's call. Through two wives and their maids he fathered twelve sons and a daughter. To be bone honest, it was a chaotic and dysfunctional family, full of competition, among both wives and children. As happens in many families, Jacob as he aged was less strict with the later children and favored Joseph, his eleventh son, especially.

Jacob bought a beautiful coat of many colors for him, which, when Joseph showed it to his brothers, earned their jealous hatred toward him. To make matters worse, the Lord caused Joseph to dream a dream in which all his brothers bowed down to him. Of course little brother Joseph told this dream to his brothers and 'wondered' if it meant something. He most likely did not use a humble tone in the telling of it, and probably enjoyed 'needling' them. Of course his brothers were angry with him. When the Lord gave him a second dream in which not only the brothers but his parents bowed down to him, Jacob admonished his son to be respectful of his elders. Yet, Jacob pondered the whole matter seriously in his heart. Was God showing all of them something?

"In spite of the jealousy that sparked in Joseph's brothers, the dreams were in the plan of God, and it was His choice to give them to Joseph. The Lord always works on many levels at once in His dealings with man, and in this case was not only working with Joseph but on the brothers as well, giving them the freedom to act out what was really in their hearts. It could be said that God exposed them to a situation that 'hardened' their hearts, incited them to take action that displayed their true nature. Their jealousy toward Joseph led them to cruelties they kept secret for years, cruelties hard to believe of those who would become the founding fathers of the nation of Israel. These brothers in their later years would face up to their monstrous deeds, all in the path of the Lord's leading."

And so once again the reader of the Bible is confronted with the "unvarnished" truth about so many of its main characters. Man tended to make great people from the past appear to be far more noble than they really were. The Bible tells it more realistically.

"So Jacob," continued Matthias, "the father of the nation Israel, cheated his twin brother out of his inheritance and would, for many years, reap havoc as the fruit of his ways. When favorite son Joseph was seventeen years old he was asked by his father to go check on his brothers, who had been gone many days seeking distant pastures. 'Here comes the dreamer,' mocked his brothers when they saw Joseph coming in the distance. 'Let's get rid of him once and for all. We are far from home. No one will know.' There was a deep pit nearby, and when Joseph drew close they grabbed him and lowered him into the pit. Their first idea was to kill him, but Judah hatched a better plan. They had seen caravans with camels loaded with goods bound for Egypt. "Let's sell him," he said. "That way his death won't be on our hands and we'll make some money." It made sense to the other brothers.

"When they pulled Joseph up he expected some water for his thirst and to be set free from this sadistic practical joke. Instead he was sold to a band of not very friendly men heading for Egypt. He watched incredulously as they counted out 20 pieces of silver to Judah. That's what he was worth to them. A miserable new chapter of his life began. A stout rope was fastened around his waist and then connected, with several feet of slack, to the rigging on a camel. If he walked too slowly he would be pulled, faster than he wanted to go, by the irresistible power of the camel. He stumbled several times and finally fell. The constant pull of the rope kept him tumbling and unable to get his feet under him. He lost track of the bruises and abrasions by the time one of the traders stopped the caravan, evidently realizing their passenger would bring less money if he were too badly damaged. As this caravan threaded its way south toward Egypt, Joseph looked back a few times to the sight of his brothers gradually receding on the horizon, shrinking from sight as the distance grew. They had picked on him as the irritating younger brother for most of his life. Today their hatred for him hit him in a new way. It was real. The confusion in his family wrought by his father's inattention and the rivalry of his two wives and two concubines, all vying for Jacob's affection, had contributed to the brothers' hard-heartedness.

"They had grown disrespectful toward their father—and toward each other. Life in Jacob's family was 'me first' all the way. Not until later in his years, about the time of Joseph's birth, did Jacob begin to take his relationship with the Lord seriously. And then while returning, at the Lord's direction, to his homeland he had an encounter with God that caught his attention more clearly than ever, and he would be a different man from that time on. His self-centered habits still tripped him up, and yet this newfound relationship with the Lord gradually changed him from the inside out into a different person, a different father. It was seemingly too late for the first ten boys. When Joseph responded favorably to his father's attention it further angered them. Today the depth of their hatred for him pierced his soul like a spear. The family relationship and love that should have been there did not exist. They *sold* him. That hurt worse than that miserable rope and those horrid men who now controlled his life. On his last look back at the horizon, the distance was so great there was barely any sign of them. His last visible remembrance of them was them counting their money. Now he hated them as much as they hated him. With bitterness he realized he would never see his family again—nor his father. About the brothers he no longer cared, but his father would never even know what happened to him or where he was. The rope around his waist fastened to the camel ahead of him ensured there would be no rest on this miserable walk. He was tired and thirsty, so thirsty. Even if he untied himself and ran away there would be no outrunning a man on a camel.

CHAPTER 34

STILL ON THE TRAIL

(Genesis 39-40)

The night wore on and the walk was long for Matthias and the Israelites, with a fight to the death waiting at the end. The story was a helpful diversion. A scripture, Psalm 91: 5, written centuries later would describe what they were experiencing. "You will not be afraid for the terror by night, nor for the arrow that flies by day." From his throne in heaven, the Lord watched with interest as His people, guided by His words to Joshua, walked through the darkness of the earth. They were not alone. His presence went with them. He who saw all and understood all was with them. If they could realize that, they could have peace, knowing that victory for them was certain.

Matthias continued his story with Abijah: "A week later amidst a crowded and noisy marketplace in this strange land called Egypt, Joseph was pulled, an unkind and scratchy rope round his neck, atop a platform for all to see. Men were questioning and bargaining in a language he did not understand. A finely dressed gentleman standing near pushed him with a short stick, causing him to turn around so onlookers could see him from all angles. Someone climbed up and looked in his mouth like one buying a horse would do. Then he swung a fist toward Joseph's face to check his reflexes. Finally, money was exchanged—again—for him!—and Joseph was given to a very exquisitely dressed man who proceeded to lead him through the crowd and away from the marketplace. People moved out of the way for this man, though he did not seem heartless like so many of the others.

"In an hour Joseph was at his new home, a more splendid structure than he had ever seen, and was shown to a small but clean and tastefully appointed room, his new living quarters. A servant handed him a set of fine clothes and gestured for him to bathe in a fountain outside and to put on the new clothes. They seemed to expect much from him, and it was difficult when he could not understand their language. The other servants grew impatient and sometimes angry when he could not follow orders. This new life was miserable and humiliating, made worse by the thought that he would grow old and die a slave in a strange land among people he did not know. He vowed to learn this language as rapidly as possible and to figure out a way to escape. Not that many days ago he had been a happy teenager with few responsibilities and basking in the warmth and prosperity of a kind father.

"There was one comfort—well, two maybe. His new master was also a kind man, apparently having great power and understanding. The other was memory of the stories his father had told him over and over of how God would be with Jacob's family and would one day make a great nation of them, bringing blessing to the entire world through them. It certainly looked improbable now, but as a small child and for all of his life, he had been deeply impressed with his father's certainty of God's ability to make His words come true. Little did Joseph know that painful as it was, he was squarely in the center of God's will and that the Lord was with him every moment. In the coming years he would grow more certain of this, though many trials also lay along the same path. Then there were those two boyhood dreams that seemed so real. He could not forget them and puzzled over them for many years. Had God really shown him something, or was it imagination playing tricks on him?

"Back home the brothers concocted a plan to smear Joseph's coat with sheep's blood and present it to their father. 'Does this look familiar? We found it in the field,' they lied. Jacob knew immediately it was his son's coat and began to grieve, his heart pained to the core. He quaked from somewhere deep inside, felt his heart thump hard and could not breathe for a long moment. Tears wetted his eyes. His beloved Rachel was gone, and now this. This world was so full of heartache. 'Joseph is dead, torn by some beast,' moaned Jacob as he imagined his own son, screaming helplessly as a lion tore him to pieces, breaking bones with his powerful jaws. Misery radiated from Jacob, a sight no one wanted to see. The brothers observed and said nothing. What had they done? Gradually they filtered out of the house and busied themselves caring for the cattle, hoping to forget all this.

"In Egypt things rapidly improved for Joseph. He learned a few words and phrases. Working at his tasks and caring for the home became a comfort for him. Daily he found ways to do things better and faster. The head servant liked him and gave him more and more to do. Joseph did not mind, liked it actually. Speaking with the other servants day in and day out helped him learn the language, and in about a year's time Joseph's absorption of the Egyptian language was so thorough (he even mastered the accent) he could pass for an Egyptian. He helped in the fields, letting the other servants teach him valuable knowledge about planting and growing crops that yielded superb harvests. The Egyptians had refined this to a fine art, and Joseph soaked it up like a sponge. His master Potiphar was a skilled administrator and had managed to hire diligent workers from among the most capable of farmers. These workers knew other good men, and Potiphar allowed them to recruit for him. Gradually he acquired a very fine workforce, whom he treated well, and his fields became the envy of many. Potiphar took note of Joseph's abilities and promoted him to more responsible tasks, leading eventually to Joseph's oversight of all the servants and even the household finances."

"The Bible states that 'the Lord was with Joseph.' Here he was, a slave in Egypt, with no future to anticipate beyond that of wearing out too young and dying an overworked slave. Hated by his brothers, he would never see his father again or his younger brother, Benjamin, who was dear to his heart," Abijah remarked to Matthias. "Those older brothers were scoundrels. Look what they did to their father. They led him to believe Joseph had been torn by beasts. They saw their father's anguish and let him suffer for years. Miserable wretches. All they cared about was themselves."

Then, suddenly aware of the night and the trail, Abijah announced, "My feet hurt. How about yours, Matthias?"

"It's more my legs. I'm not used to walking this much."

"And Judah, that rat who came up with the plan to sell their own brother for money . . . I'm glad I'm not from his tribe." Matthias agreed. Little did they know that that rascal had fathered the tribe through which the Savior would come. Jesus certainly would not be coming through any noble part of the human race.

Near Matthias in the dark along the trail, two young men, Bartholomew and Barnabas, had been discussing life on this long walk toward a life or death battle. Like so many young men at all times in history they had been called, sooner than expected, from youth to manhood. Both knew they could lose their lives tomorrow if things went wrong. Having gradually tuned in to Matthias' story as they heard bits and pieces, they were now fully listening, as the story seemed to reflect their own condition as having been drawn in to events over which they had no control.

Matthias continued: "After hearing from his father the stories of how Israel would become a great nation through whom all the world would be blessed, Joseph must have been puzzled by what was happening to him. Though his father, Jacob, for most of the years before Joseph was born, had been a self-serving conniver, God had spoken to him several times reminding him of His promises to his grandfather Abraham—whom Jacob had actually known until he was fifteen. Abraham had told him many times the things God had promised and how, even if one had to wait, what God said always came true. Young Jacob partly listened, being generally more interested in his own schemes. Now, in his later years, Jacob had gained a new respect for his grandfather's words and passed them on to his two youngest sons. The older ones had seen too much of their father's schemes and more or less shrugged off their father's newfound interest in his God, although his words found a home in some remote, seldom visited part of their hearts. In Joseph's heart the words were taken more seriously, and these now sustained him in Egypt. As badly as things appeared to have worked out, he maintained a certain amount of trust that God was working in his life. And what about those dreams? Most of the time people forgot dreams, but he could not forget. Was there something more to them?

"Then came a day when he was falsely accused by Potiphar's wife of a crime, and Potiphar had no choice but to throw him in prison—

to avoid incurring his wife's brooding anger. Things went from bad to worse, and it could be said that Joseph's faith was being further tested—or *refined.* This could be the breaking point. But as bad as it looked, God was preparing Joseph for something far greater than he ever could have imagined. Removed from the life of a pampered son, he was now forced to see, as a servant, the needs of others and to learn to anticipate and take care of them, or he would be punished."

Abijah asked, "Do you think Joseph hated his brothers for what they did to him?"

"I have wondered that too, but the old stories do not say much about it," answered Matthias. "What do you think, Abijah?"

"I think he made it through the days well enough. Staying busy learning to please his new boss kept him occupied. But alone on his bed night at night in the dark in a prison cell, the misery of the horrible turn his life had taken weighed on his mind. He remembered the sunshine and happiness of basking in his father's admiration in his young days. What freedom and joy it had been. He had known an older, more mature father who had learned to value other people. His older brothers had known a younger, impetuous, self-serving father with more interest in forging success in the world than in caring for his family. In his youthful self-centeredness Joseph had been oblivious to his brothers' jealousy, insensitive to the conflict gone before amongst his father's four different wives and the children, always vying for attention, never finding enough. He was trapped in this awful prison precisely because of his brothers' jealousy and outright selfish hatred.

"His freedom gone, his right to enjoy happy days in the sun stripped from him, he had traveled on foot the painful path to Egypt. Now night after night in chains of darkness in smelly prison confines, he lay unknown and forgotten, not even regarded as a worthwhile person. He hated them, the cruel, sadistic brothers. Anger at their cruelty had existed for years, only now it clawed its way to the surface, and he wrestled with it every night. In the day he remembered the Lord and prospered. In the night the hatred and anger took over. Gradually a thought formed and grew. If he hated them so much, was he not just as bad as them? His brothers had put him here, and his hatred for them ate away at his soul. Night after night he thought on the cruelty of each of them separately and on the terrible things they had done to him. Other cruel words from them over the earlier years, whose hurt he had forgotten, bubbled up through the months from deep in his memory and added to his misery. I can imagine him falling asleep many nights full of hate for his brothers. As the story said, God was with him, and that had the effect of causing him gradually to see things differently from how he had seen them before. More in tune with reality."

"You sound like you are speaking from experience," interjected Matthias.

"Maybe. We all go through things," offered Abijah.

"I know what you mean. I can imagine him waking up one morning after a night of barely sleeping, and you know how sometimes for a few minutes you see the problem more clearly than you have ever seen it?"

"Keep going . . . "

"Well, I can see him suddenly realizing that if he has all this hatred and bitterness, he is just as bad as his brothers!"

"Right, Matthias. Not a fun thing to see. He saw himself for the first time as he really was, and it was awful, disturbing. . . . But at the same time it opened a new door into his view of life. God had not killed his brothers for their evil—and He had not killed him either. How could God be so kind to them? Day and night these things played on his mind, and, as the story says, 'God was with him.' Gradually Joseph's heart softened. If God could put up with each of them, could not he forgive his brothers? Could not he accept God's kindness and reflect the same kindness toward them?"

"And maybe the next night on his bed," interjected Matthias, "he reasoned that all these things that had happened to him, though evil, must be part of a bigger plan in God's dealings with all of them. The known part of the plan was to make a great nation of Abraham's descendants—exactly as God had promised long ago—and to bless the whole world through them, whatever that meant. He could not see how all the details and his daily miserable circumstances fit into that plan, but he was beginning to believe that God truly had it all under control. Lying on his bed in the darkness of the night, locked in a prison, he realized God was with him—and was with all mankind—and he was free!"

Abijah echoed, “Somehow Abraham’s confidence, his father Jacob’s confidence, their repetition of God’s promises, began to touch his consciousness in a profound way. Joseph realized that if God was with him, even in this prison, he was a free man, and he relaxed about it all. He viewed his circumstances in a completely new light, and even his demeanor changed.”

“I think we just figured it out, Abijah. Come to think about it, that is what the circumcision was all about. Remember we were all stirred up to attack Jericho after that miraculous crossing through the Jordan River, and Joshua forced us to delay several days and do that horrible circumcision business? That was God showing us we were unworthy, no better than the people of Jericho, and worthy of being cut off and discarded.”

“That’s deep, Matthias. The only difference between us and them was that we had accepted God’s opinion of us and had accepted *His* help for making us righteous and acceptable in His sight.”

“And one more thing,” added Matthias. “That ritual was a perpetual reminder of God’s faithfulness about keeping the promise of His words to Abraham. It was given to him at the same time as the promise about making a great nation of him, through whom all the world could be blessed. The ritual was a reminder that God’s words will come to pass, no matter what. It sounds so easy when you see it that way. Yet, Joseph’s days in prison did not end after that. He would live several more years in that place.”

“A thought from Joseph’s father kept surfacing in his mind,” continued Matthias. “One of the things he said with great emphasis, so he would remember it, was that no matter what circumstances looked like in life, God was always in control, and in the long run, would make things work out for good. Our part was to be patient and trust. In those days and nights of trouble Joseph had finally called out to God for help.”

Five hundred years in the future King David would write, “And call upon me in the day of trouble. I will deliver you, and you will glorify me” (Psalm 50:15). To believe that you could one day glorify God for the miserable trials He allowed in your life stretched the imagination just about to the breaking point. Yet David knew what he was talking about. As a young man he had been told by the prophet Nathan that he would one day be king of Israel. Then for years after that he was hunted like an animal by a jealous King Saul and lived in fear for his life for months at a time, hiding in caves and amongst barren mountains. At one point he said, "Surely there is but a step between me and death," and many days, hiding from relentless searchers who sometimes passed only a few yards from where he hid, he was certain he would not live until sundown.

David did not learn of the Lord's constant care in a day. He had dwelt in the realm of hopelessness and despair, and all he could rely on during those times had been God's promises—nothing else. Unknown to him was the fact that during such times he was in the Lord's training ground, a place of seemingly unbearable difficulties, a place in which there was absolutely no help except in crying out to the Lord, and even then God did not always remove the painful circumstances as quickly as David hoped. David was enduring the stretching of his character that would make him a wise king. It did not come overnight to learn to be patient and to wait, or to trust the Lord. Gradually he grew to rely on Him in what he did and to have this underlying sense that God was with him and guiding him—even in miserable circumstances. And then one day he was made king. One who had known troubles as he had could appreciate being "delivered" from their grip, and it was truly from a heart set free and experiencing God's care that he could genuinely "glorify" God, having seen for himself God's deliverance. To understand hopelessness and deliverance from it, one must have lived it himself.

"Now in prison," continued Matthias, "Joseph was learning to see God working in it all. Troubles and afflictions, though painful to endure, were a key part of God's method of bringing His children to maturity and stability. Much as an ancient tree on a rocky shoreline survives ever-changing winds, violent storms and drought, endures, and though twisted and scarred, still lives, the imprisoned Joseph grew older and wiser." Oddly enough the future King David would no doubt read of Joseph's trials and draw encouragement from them.

Similarly, the Apostle Paul fifteen hundred years later would write, "I have learned in whatsoever state I am therewith to be content. I know both how to be abased, and I know how to abound" (Philippians 4:11-12).

Paul was schooled in the scriptures, and he too, knowing Israel's history, would have undoubtedly learned from reading about Joseph. Certainly Joseph could not know the far-reaching effect his life would have.

As they pondered Joseph's life, Matthias and Abijah were almost enjoying this tiring walk.

Somewhere in the dark ahead a wolf crossed their path. Leering and unafraid, he paused a moment as his sharp hearing picked up the faint footsteps of the approaching army. A ruthless killer, he lived by preying on creatures, large or small, weaker than himself. He considered this almost silent army for a long moment. Easy pickings for one with his speed and strength and uncanny ability to navigate the dark. Lowering his ears, he resumed his original path. Surviving by his wits, he had no inclination to attack Israel.

Farther yet and deeper in the dark, five kings clinked their wine glasses in a toast to the brilliance of the plan conceived by lifelong competitors now working together to destroy Israel, once and for all. They would not be as merciful as the wolf. A resplendent tent with servants and guards had been erected for them as temporary headquarters. From here they would direct their combined armies until victory was complete. The details finally worked out and agreed upon, they adjourned for some much-needed sleep.

CHAPTER 35

THE FIVE KINGS

(Joshua 10)

The Israelite threat would finally be dealt with decisively and completely. Any Israelites who survived would be slaves, servants or concubines. These kings who, all their lives, had been competitors for territory and power had agreed to work together on this occasion for the common good, and the alliance had happily worked out better than anyone had imagined.

The plan was straightforward and simple, the best kind of plan for a large group of people from diverse backgrounds. The combined force of the armies was so overwhelming that the Israelites would likely give up with little fight, minimizing the casualties for the attackers. If they foolishly chose to fight, their losses would be catastrophic, even more so because of the "surprise" the kings had dreamed up for their attack. Several miles before reaching Israel one of the five armies would split off to the left, march in a wide, undetectable arc to a position *behind* Israel's camp, and lie in wait for the battle to be joined. When Israel's men of war had scrambled to fight the four attacking armies, the ambush would invade the unprotected camp from behind, killing or taking captive the women and children and continuing on to attack the shocked and demoralized Israelites, already massively outnumbered.

The organizer of this event was Adoni-zedek, king of Jerusalem, who had sent to Hoham, king of Hebron; Piram, king of Jarmuth; Japhia, king of Lachish; and Debir, king of Eglon, to join him in "smiting" Gibeon because they had made a league with Israel. That would teach a lesson to any country considering helping those hated Israelites. Then their plan against Israel would take effect.

"When they see the thousands of fierce warriors we have," Adoni-zedek's words dripped with scorn, "they will faint with fear and run. But they will not escape. Our warriors will enjoy destroying them."

Each of these kings was a wily and powerful leader, and each was bringing a formidable army of seasoned warriors to the battle. No strangers to intrigue, intricate plots and brute strength to further their positions, these men had good reason to be wary of each other. Most kings were big and powerfully strong men skilled in the use of weapons. They were kings because they had beaten all comers (Joshua 10: 3-5).

Hoham

Hoham, king of Hebron, had subdued and brought under his control all the cities within a day's journey around him. He had quelled a rebellion and then ensured against future rebellions by capturing its leader, forcing him to watch while his children were killed and then gouging out his eyes. Take a moment to let that sink in. These were not nice men.

Piram

Piram began plotting immediately, days before these armies actually met together. While the others were struggling over a plan to defeat Israel he already *knew* what to do. "You don't know anything," he would tell them. "Israel's God is a god of the river and valleys. Our gods are gods of the hills and high places and are higher and more powerful. We must sacrifice to them and they will grant us victory." He knew this because he had *secret* knowledge.

When he presented this idea to the others they resisted. "Who says you are right?" they objected.

"I paid my priest a very large sum of money to pray to the gods about how to destroy Israel. His advice in past times has kept me in control of my kingdom."

Skeptical, they questioned him further. "What did he tell you?" they half mocked. One of the sorcerers the priest consulted had received wisdom from his god, Molech, that these five kingdoms, who had always been in competition with each other, should now work together and, if Molech received proper sacrifice, victory would be assured. New levels of prosperity, never before possible, would be achieved as nation joined nation.

"What is the sacrifice?" one skeptic asked

"Ten children. Five boys and five girls."

"Good. We can kidnap them from a distant village beyond our borders."

"Not good," challenged Piram. "To prove sincerity the sacrifice has to cost us something. Molech wants you to pay until it hurts. He is a god of truth." He had shown him that each region must sacrifice two of its *own* children, a boy and a girl. The gods would hear and grant victory. Piram seemed so sure of himself the others relented slightly, beginning to wonder, "What if he is right? What do we have to lose?" Due to their fear of the growing threat of Israel, the other kings finally agreed.

"How do we choose who to sacrifice?" was the next question.

"The gods have shown us that too," answered Piram. "Special wise men with terrifyingly painted faces and monstrous costumes will go through each city and select the children. I know each of you has a record of people to watch who may not have fully supported you in the past. Choose from among their children, find a way to mark them so the wise men can find them, and secretly let word leak out that that is the reason they were chosen. Such a move is efficient. It protects your children and sends a message to any who would dare speak against you." The other kings saw the wisdom of it and agreed. Selections had been quickly carried out, and crying mothers and fathers had no power to stop them. It was for the good of the kingdom. Child sacrifices were common throughout history. Sooner or later many civilizations came to that idea when facing life-threatening problems such as enemy attack, drought or starvation. The fear was that their gods were angry with them and could only be placated by a very costly sacrifice. Human life was slightly more valuable than money, so that was the ultimate sacrifice, and the life of a beloved child ranked most highly. Death could come by a blow from a lethal weapon, by strangulation, by cutting the heart out or, in this case, by an even more cruel method. Iron statues of Molech with arms held in a cradling position were heated to nearly red hot, and the child being offered was placed in its arms. Molech had promised victory. To Piram it was a sure thing. The others were not so sure, but, being practical men, decided it could not hurt to have the gods, if they existed, on their side.

Cruelty was the way of the world. Kings oppressed their subjects. They used religion to magnify their power over ignorant fools. Leadership and organizational skills that could have been used to protect people and maintain peace and develop better methods of farming and food production were used instead to control and despoil them of their goods. Promises of peace, prosperity and safety helped pave the way for such kings to gain power. It mattered little that the promises were never kept. By the time anyone figured it out it was always too late. People who hated to be told what to do somehow *always* wound up with leaders who told them what to do and oppressed them.

It was hard to say who was a bigger fake, Piram or Molech. Molech had been imagined into existence long ago on dark nights when men grew terrified. He was an easy sell to frightened, superstitious humans, and for now Piram, in league with his imaginary friend Molech, was a winning combination.

Japhia

Japhia, king of Lachish, unlike Hoham or Piram, was not a big man or a powerful warrior. Dangerously intelligent, he gained his position by subtlety and maintained power by guessing probabilities, that is, how others would most likely react and what they would do next—and always being a step ahead of them. With that skill he outmaneuvered them and maintained control over a large kingdom. As a boy, even though the son of the king, he had never been able to compete well in physical games with other boys his age as they were bigger and stronger. They mocked him for losing, and he hated it. In his heart he hated them. Some of the men from much older generations had tried to teach the younger ones to be kind and thoughtful of others. The boys mocked them, and so did Japhia. The only "right" behavior, he concluded, was to take care of yourself first. He saw the poorest, weakest people continually exploited and despised them for their weakness. Being poor and stupid was their own fault. No one else cared about such people, and neither did he. As he began to see it over time, he was more important than everyone else, and their goods belonged to him. Thinking thus, he hardened his heart toward all people.

Now, as a man who had clawed his way to the top amongst several zealous brothers, he intended to stay on top, maybe even to magnify his power. The self-centered philosophy of his youth had matured to a deliberate, reasoned version of that view—vintage selfishness, you might say. The godless philosophy prevailing in his kingdom and the other Canaanite civilizations had, ages ago, abandoned the last shred of belief in a god higher than mankind. When other people did not want to look deeper into things they feared because they were afraid of what they might discover, he went against the norms of society and looked. Few wanted their understanding of the world challenged, as it could be frightening, even terrifying, and Japhia discovered that men were controlled by their fears. He had dared look and had seen that most of man's beliefs were based upon nothing, false impressions and incorrect conclusions. People feared looking deeply and preferred noise and activity to distract. Man could be manipulated by subtly altering these to suit his purposes. There was no god. Only man's imaginations. And if there were no god to judge anyone's actions or to make rules for man, who could say what was right or wrong? If there were no consequences for anything anyone did, who had the right to say if a thing was right or wrong? What made their opinion more valuable than his? If someone else were hurt, or even killed, what did it matter, and what did he care? Really. That viewpoint at first seemed brutal, but if one thought it through, there really was no standard by which to judge peoples' actions. That was reality. The hardened realism of a godless society. Indeed, it was the philosophy most of the world lived by, though unconsciously in almost all cases. They disguised and covered their utter selfishness with a veneer of acceptable behavior. Most people had an unconscious need to appear to be good, and thus many pretended they cared about others. Japhia knew differently. He prided himself on being more realistic than they. It worked, and he was on top of the pile.

At the same time, many cities and nations prayed to gods and begged for help with good crops, good fortune and success in battle. These gods, however, were capricious and unpredictable and certainly behaved by no standards of righteousness or overall regard for human life. Life was a confused mess for most. "The mass of men lead lives of quiet desperation," would write a future poet. "A tale told by an idiot," another would pen.

Japhia's worldview seemed heartless and cruel, devoid of human kindness. It threw out all emotion, even love and affection. But it was reality, and he trafficked in what made sense. What mattered most was his own pleasure and his own wants. All mankind was totally self-centered. And those sentimental slobs who put a lot of stock in human feelings were a pitiful bunch. He had no use for them. No, he despised them. What mattered was winning and getting one's own way. Selfishness ruled. He was completely positive he was right.

He had convinced several powerful warriors that they could never beat him and then had enlisted them to protect him and carry out his will. He furthered their allegiance by rewarding them handsomely with money and favors, and, in turn, they served him unquestioningly. His position as king put the wealth of the kingdom at his disposal, and he spent lavishly on anything he wanted. Never mind that the people themselves were impoverished by his actions. He was in power and no one could stop him. The fools. There was plenty left to reward others for their help, and he learned quickly to use the kingdom's riches to maintain his power. It cost him nothing, and he took advantage of the fact that others greedily sought his favor.

It could never be said, though, that even those closest to him could relax or feel secure in his kingdom. Ruthless to the bone, he destroyed immediately and without mercy any who gave the slightest appearance of opposing him, and in so doing intimidated the rest of his subjects into believing he knew what they were thinking and could discern the motives of anyone plotting against him. When he perceived opposition anywhere in his kingdom, he set his mind to destroying it and then struck without warning. Always, by careful design, he acted only when there was no hope of escape for his victim. He had the disciplined patience to wait for the right moment. One did not want to be the target of his ill favor. Beyond that, another terrorizing tactic was to execute a close follower at random.

No one ever knew why the man had been "eliminated" but believed there must have been some hidden rebellion in the making (most of the time there was not). Japhia counted on the human imagination to conjure up possible reasons the person had been eliminated. People came up with all sorts of reasons and such sudden murders reinforced the idea Japhia could read their minds. He ruled with fear and liked it that way.

His skill at guessing how people would react grew from his habit of keenly observing others and watching their reactions to little tests he secretly gave them, making a game of studying their responses to provocative and challenging statements he made. For example, to one of his ministers, he would "suggest," out of thin air, that he had been told that he was disloyal to him and then watch with interest while that man tried desperately to explain his innocence. It was almost sadistic. He was dispassionate and objective about reading their reactions, and if that person were actually guilty he could detect it and would, of course, deal with it. He knew far more about those close to him than any of them realized. On those rare occasions he guessed wrong his alertness and the fact he was consciously playing this game positioned him to spot his mistakes and make quick adjustments.

Japhia was not above sending paid emissaries into neighboring kingdoms, especially those that were prosperous and well organized. Their mission was to meet and befriend influential individuals whose positions could help Japhia understand the strengths and ambitions of that country's leadership. Japhia would empower his aides to secretly funnel money—temptingly large sums of money—to them for such information. He could expand his power through these networks of informers as they helped him understand the strengths and weaknesses of that country and to know when it might be vulnerable to a "takeover" by Japhia. Those well-paid informers would be on his side when he struck, as they had each been convinced they would be in on the "ground floor" of the new government. These people sensed that the real power in the territory lay with Japhia, and they wanted to be with him whenever he moved to expand, loyal to nothing but wealth and power. Japhia played them like a finely tuned violin while they made music for him, and slowly but surely his kingdom and influence grew.

That Israel was intruding with such insolence was an irritation to him. In truth his father had wrested the kingdom away from its former leaders. "Wrested" was too kind a word, as he had brutally butchered those citizens and taken their land, just as they had done to the previous civilization. As far back as anyone knew it had always been that way. Memory of whoever had had first claim to the land had been forgotten ages ago. If injustices had been done no one cared. What mattered to Japhia was who was in control now, and in this kingdom it was he.

He delighted in stirring up trouble that no one ever knew he instigated. Skilled at making it look like citizens of a neighboring city had attacked some of his own citizens, he worked behind the scenes to influence events. When his own citizens became thirsty for revenge over a supposed wrong done to their people, it made it easier for him to motivate them to attack and conquer that city. Such tactics led to the gradual growth (and wealth) of his kingdom, and his citizens, though fearing him, saw him as something of a protector and provider for them. The capable and intelligent people of the world were mainly unaware of how much his awareness exceeded theirs and how far ahead of them he truly was.

Life in his nation was generally rather good for those citizens who supported him. The order he maintained allowed for a decent level of prosperity. When his people prospered so did he. He was the king.

Debir

Debir, taller by a head than everyone else in his kingdom, had fought his way into the kingship. An excellent swordsman as a young man, he had caught his king's attention, as he had a way of catching everyone's attention. The king saw how the other warriors gravitated to him and looked to him for guidance and had wisely promoted him to higher and higher positions of authority, until finally he led every major battle and expansion of power the king undertook. Then he overthrew the king.

Debir was not like the other kings. He actually liked people and enjoyed seeing them succeed and prosper, delighting in helping them do so. Those under his protection lived well, and he allowed them great freedoms, encouraging trade and scientific study of the world and better ways to do things. He encouraged science and the arts, painting, sculpture and music, and his support of such things attracted artists from distant regions to come and live in his kingdom, which was growing faster than neighboring kingdoms—mainly without wars and bloodshed. Free thinkers developed better irrigation for consistent crop and food production and plumbing systems to bring water and carry waste away.

He was no fool and knew instinctively that those like him, who amass wealth, generally become targets of jealous and opportunistic leaders of other countries. He devoted a fair amount of the monies garnered by his successes to keeping his army strong and ready to strike. He remembered that, along with his skill at understanding people and working with them, it was his physical strength that many times had been the only virtue carrying him to victory over strong-willed foes seeking his destruction.

He had heard of this peculiar upstart nation called Israel and their proclamation that theirs was the true God. He had heard the reports of how, forty years ago, they had outmaneuvered that great nation, Egypt, seizing freedom and escaping through the Red Sea while Pharaoh and his army drowned in it. It sounded exaggerated or, more precisely, preposterous. Still, so many gullible nations had repeated to him the same story with the same details, that maybe there was something to it. He would look into it someday. And now, that same band of people was emerging again, having somehow survived, more or less unnoticed all this time, in a barren wasteland. They had recently destroyed two nations larger than themselves. One of those nations held a great number of huge people, even larger than Debir himself—"giants," they called them—renowned as terrifying warriors. Debir had respected but never feared these giants. His ability to soberly assess a situation led him to the realistic view that, though huge, they were still people and could be beaten if studied. His skill with weapons and his wily tactics had enabled him to vanquish all challengers, large or small. Yet, *how* had Israel beaten such a powerful nation?

Now Israel had crossed Jordan (on dry land?) and was coming too close for comfort to his own area. Such a threat had to be stopped before it was too late, hence Debir had joined with these other four ruthless kings. It would only be temporary, and his kingdom would be safe again.

The nagging question was, what about their claims that the Creator of this world was using them to carry a message to the world? Someday he would find out . . .

Adoni-zedek

Unknown to these four tyrants was the diabolical scheme of the organizer of this huge military campaign, Adoni-zedek, king of Jerusalem. *Fools,* he thought. *They're all fools, thinking the sun is a god, or the moon, or the motion of the stars. Sure, the sun makes heat and light and makes things grow, but it has no intelligence. It is just a force—that man can use. The movement of the constellations through the seasons does not control events in peoples' lives. I do.*

He had watched the wizards and astrologers. They knew too. Their art was to say things that could be taken more than one way, purposely keeping things fuzzy, and then subtly steering inquirers to the conclusions he sensed they subconsciously wanted—or feared. Either way was fine with him. In so doing, they appeared to have secret knowledge. People *wanted* to believe the wizards, and so they did. Adoni-zedek almost admired them.

He too could use religion and superstition to control people but was more ruthless and effective than the wizards. They were cunning but weak. He knew more than they did about gaining power over people and keeping it—and power was what mattered. Without power one had nothing. If one lost it he was finished, so it must be maintained at all costs. Among his weapons for maintaining it, fear was, hands down, the most effective.

Like other kings of the past, he had discovered its usefulness and had disciplined himself to become an unparalleled master at using it. He never wasted time with warnings. He acted. "Kill those who do not fear me and intimidate the rest" was his inner belief. Everything must be sacrificed to maintain power. Wizards did not know this. Weaker people did not know this and gave up too easily, recoiling against the horrendous means necessary to maintain power. Fear was as strong as hunger, stronger than friendship, stronger than love. Friends could be made to turn on each other in the face of overwhelming fear. He knew. He had made a cold-hearted study of it, observing those he was about to torture or kill. By escalating fear up or down, first with threat of imminent death followed by offering release and then, again, withdrawing it, he could make anyone do anything he wanted. Just torture them long enough and they eventually lost strength and all power to resist. In their pain they did not even know what they were doing. He used this power and despised all those he could intimidate and control. In truth, he had respect for no one. He knew his own heart was cruel and wicked and believed that deep down everyone else was like him. He made it his business to stay far ahead of all others.

As his cohort Japhia, king of Lachish, had discovered, savage and brutal murder carried out suddenly made an excellent tool to strike fear into weaker peoples' hearts. To Adoni-zedek destroying people in this way was simply a means to an end. He also delighted in taking men's wives for himself, simply because sometimes he felt like it, with force and a completely convincing threat of death to the husband. He arrogantly enjoyed watching their misery and cries. In so doing, he kept fear alive and also engendered hatred. He did not care. It made him feel more powerful, and their hatred forced him to stay alert and suspicious of everyone—a good quality to have. Being unpredictable and heartlessly cruel kept him in power, and Adoni-zedek reveled in power. Sure, one needed bodyguards to protect against those hating him, but that was no problem. In controlling the money of the kingdom it was his to spend, and there were always strong brutes who took pleasure in hurting people to be rewarded for doing that. Adoni-zedek was not a physical powerhouse like many of the kings of the world, yet he controlled men far stronger than he and wielded the true power in the kingdom, and though he was now king, he never grew out of the selfishness of childhood.

The most sagacious of the world's leaders had similarly figured out how to wield and preserve power. People wanted to believe in their own goodness and in the goodness of man, and so they blinded themselves to the true depth of evil in these leaders' hearts (and in their own).

Deceiving themselves, they were easily fooled and could never stand up to men of such singular purpose. He was aware of Japhia's lust for power and conquest and of his ability to protect himself and root out opposition to his leadership. He was also aware of Japhia's subterfuge in secretly stirring up trouble and then using it to further his power. He respected that about him and made it an ambition of his to beat him at his own game. His spies studied what could be known of Japhia and kept him informed of his doings.

Adoni-zedek believed in no god. As a hard-bitten realist he saw himself as the only one who truly knew what was going on. To the question, "What is truth?" he would have said "I am truth;" his power was truth. If God existed, as some said, he had never proven himself in any convincing manner. What Adoni-zedek understood about the world from his own viewpoint, untarnished by emotion and foolish notions about gods, was truth. No fools less intelligent than he would ever influence his thinking. "What about Noah and the flood?" an old timer had challenged. "Wasn't that a display of God's power over everything?"

"Bah! There's no proof it even happened," he challenged back, putting him in his place. "Wake up, you fool!" It was one of the few times anyone ever challenged Adoni-zedek and did not die for it. Adoni-zedek's success in the world was a trap, though. It kept him from accurately seeing his true place in the world, the Lord's world. The comfort and security of being "on top of the pile" kept him, for all his intelligence, from thinking any deeper than that. Being the best among a crowd of imperfect humans was not the pinnacle he imagined, but he did not fully realize that yet. His victories and successes were hollow in the universal scheme of things. Deep in his heart that thought poked at him, but being satisfied with his achievements, he refused to acknowledge such troubling notions.

He used one more weapon to control his subjects, his most subtle—thought control. If one could influence what people think, he could influence what they did, and they would never know he was doing it. That was how one man who, in reality, could be easily overpowered and destroyed by any small group in his country could govern and maintain control over a huge nation. Make them believe he was helping them and had the power and the "right" to be king. He had watched his father do this as he controlled the kingdom before him. Not that it was public knowledge or widely understood that he was doing this, but the father openly discussed it with the son he was grooming to one day take his place. To all others his dark motives were carefully hidden. The less others knew, the better, and the easier it was to fool them. Even his top advisors and officers were not taken into such confidence. They may have guessed, but they were never openly told.

A special society of 'wise' men, identified by an unobtrusive black kerchief worn about the neck and tied with a smart-looking square knot, existed in his kingdom. Regarded as wise and having secret power through a chain of command to the king, they could guide people and even grant special favor. Somehow they had means to support themselves without having to work. Their real function was to "keep their finger on the pulse of the people" and report any sign of criticism of the king or his government to their immediate superior. Much of their watchfulness pertained to the danger to the kingdom presented by even the smallest rebellious thought. Punishment was never carried out by these men. That was relegated to a separate, seemingly unrelated arm of the government.

A small force of three to five men would show up at an offender's home and question him, giving him an "opportunity" to admit guilt and change his mind. If it happened again, that person would disappear—taken into slave labor far away, never to be seen again. The king never spoke of these things, or even acknowledged them, seeming to be unaware of—and thus, disconnected from— them. Few ever guessed his treachery.

Nobody was really free in his kingdom, or happy, except Adoni-zedek—if you can call being friendless and loveless free.

That was the king of Jerusalem. He disdained the other four and thought them fools. He would take their kingdoms from them, and they would never suspect until it was too late. Only a fool would trust another person. He trusted no one. The most loyal supporter could turn on him if he believed it to his advantage. Adoni-zedek understood that. Two of his top ministers took pains to foster the appearance of loyalty and, in reality, had no real ambition to oppose or overthrow Adoni-zedek. Balak and Haman spoke with each other often. They found comfort in the way their conversations refined their understanding of happenings in the kingdom. Neither really liked their king, but each saw him not only as the center of power but as a rising star amongst the nations.

"He is on the rise," confided Balak to Haman, "and I want to be near him as he goes up."

"His inner circle is the place to be," echoed Haman. "He has the strength to stay on top and the wits to see an opportunity and snatch it at the right time. The way I see it, we do not have to be as smart or as powerful as he is. We just have to find ways to be helpful to him, to help him achieve his goals, and we will be swept right along with him in his success.

"He needs people like us," said Balak, matter-of-factly, "and I'm fine with that. The wealth and comfort of the kingdom are at our disposal when we are close to him."

"Remember Agag," said Haman, "one of the chief captains who secretly thought to trip up Adoni-zedek and overthrow him. I don't know how he knew about Agag's plans, but one day Agag encountered a tragic accident. His chariot and bodyguards were attacked in broad daylight by a huge band of thieves."

"Yes. They killed his bodyguards, took their horses, took Agag's chariot, and then killed him. Kind of suspicious. Normally nobody would dare attack one of the king's important men—and then actually get away with it."

"It's nothing anyone wants to question too deeply," reflected Haman with a politician's sense of propriety.

Adoni-zedek had confided most of the inner workings of his plan to these two. They understood that when Gibeon had been destroyed, and the armies were in high spirits with the success, he would execute his larger, more sinister plan, which was to murder the other four kings, all in the same moment, in their respective camps. He had already planted small groups of carefully chosen "loyal" men, his best swordsmen, in each of the four armies, masquerading as "aides" and "liaison" to himself as organizer of this united force. At an exact designated moment the "aides" would murder each king to whom they were assigned and hold their swords high, proclaiming Adoni-zedek king of a new, united kingdom and, with the help of a few more strategically placed loudmouthed supporters, lead a chant, "Great is Adoni-zedek, great is Adoni-zedek!" All would feel compelled to join. The shock value would be stunning and the other senior officers would not resist, not knowing how deep this rebellion ran or who, if anyone, would be loyal to their now dead kings. The confusion would give Adoni-zedek a brief moment to speak words of peace to the armies, assure them of their safety and enlist their support in creating this new and glorious nation—of which they were *founding* members. He had rehearsed in his head the things he would say, in a general way, and left it at that. The words always came to him when he got in front of a crowd. There he would study their faces and determine if they were nervous or anxious or fearful, or if they were somehow relieved and in happy spirits. He had the ability to tune in to peoples' feelings and then set them at ease. If any in that atmosphere dared resist he would be killed on the spot, as a traitor, in front of all watching and with a huge show of force designed to intimidate. Then, destroying Israel would be step two in his latest expansion of power. Adoni-zedek was a master at manipulating events to his advantage, and nobody ever saw him coming or had a ghost of a chance at resisting him. He planned it that way. He was on his way to becoming king of the whole world, greater even than Pharaoh over the vast kingdom of Egypt. Balak and Haman thoroughly understood their king's ability to carry this off. They would be riding the crest of the wave of his success and were completely happy with that.

The king had heard that Egypt, having mysteriously lost its king and entire army years ago when Israel left, had been defenseless and had fallen prey to various marauding armies who came, stole gold, silver, and crops that had been harvested, and then quickly disappeared. A nagging fear plagued neighboring nations that Pharaoh, with his awesome power, still existed and would somehow suddenly show up and exact retribution. That fear protected Egypt to a degree, but did not deter Adoni-zedek. Sensing vulnerability there, he had in the back of his mind conceived the idea, that, once he had consolidated power, he would test Egypt's ability to defend itself with a minor attack, and, if he detected weakness, he would move in and take it. That done, his would be the largest, most powerful nation on earth—and he would be at its head! That prospect, too enticing to resist, burned in his heart always.

And somewhere in scripture, this quiet voice: “Verily, every man at his best state is altogether vanity” (Psalm 39:5). “Surely men of low degree are vanity, and men of high degree are a lie. To be laid in the balance, they are altogether lighter than vanity” (Psalm 62:9). Pharaoh already knew that, having learned it on a tragic day forty years earlier. Adoni-zedek, overly impressed with his own ambition and ability, did not yet know.

CHAPTER 36

CONTINUING ON... EVEN PHARAOH HONORED THE LORD

(Genesis 41-47)

Meanwhile Israel walked on through the night shadows, closing in on the enemy, trusting their powerful leader. With a few miles yet to go, Matthias continued the story.

"Joseph found favor with the jailer as he had with Potiphar, and was entrusted with responsibilities in taking care of the other prisoners. Not until Joseph was thirty years old did things change for him, but when they did it was fast and unexpected. Pharaoh had a dream so real and frightening that he called for his wise men and magicians to help him understand it. None could. A servant of Pharaoh's who had been in prison with Joseph suddenly remembered Joseph's unusual relationship with dreams. He told Pharaoh, who immediately sent for him.

"Joseph was brought out, bathed, shaved, groomed and given fresh clothing suitable to wear in the presence of a king and then led into his very presence. Pharaoh explained his puzzling dream to Joseph, who listened intently and then said matter-of-factly, 'God has shown Pharaoh what he is about to do. There will be seven years of great plenty throughout all of Egypt, followed by seven years of famine and crop failures. It will happen very soon. Let Pharaoh find discreet and wise men and appoint officers to store up the excess corn of those years to use during the seven years of famine coming after.'

"Joseph's calm demeanor and amazing words so struck Pharaoh and all his servants that he marveled to them, 'Can we find any man like this anywhere in whom the Spirit of God is?' He turned and focused his gaze upon Joseph for a long moment, finally saying, 'Since God has shown you all of this, there is none so discreet and wise as you. You shall be over my house and all the land of Egypt and by your word shall all the people be ruled. Only in the throne shall I be greater than you.' Pharaoh took off his ring from his hand and put it on Joseph's, then arrayed him with the fine linen clothing of a king and put a gold chain around his neck, making him second in command over all the land of Egypt. 'I am Pharaoh and without you shall no man lift his hand or foot in all of Egypt' (Genesis 41:38-44).

"This man Joseph four hours earlier had been a prisoner in a dungeon in a land far from his home, and was now ruler of the most powerful nation on earth. Years ago, deep in his heart, the words of his father had become real to him. God was with them, with Abraham's descendants, as He had promised, and had a larger plan than they ever realized. It was the Lord who held him in prison, and He had a purpose, even if it were not yet clear to him. In the midst of trials and unfair treatment Joseph had learned to drop the bitterness and anger that often crept into his heart and to relax in God's care by thinking about God's faithfulness in keeping promises. In so doing he found peace, even in a foul smelling and hope strangling dungeon. It was this trust in God that drew people to him and gave him favor with Potiphar, with the jailer, and now with Pharaoh. After what he had been through, Joseph would not be swept away with the grandeur of his new position. He was 30 years old, with many years of humbling experiences worked so deeply into his soul by God that he would never forget. God had trained him (as he will train any of his children willing to wait on him) and he was ready. He went out from the presence of Pharaoh, competent to do the king's will—and the Lord's. He went through all the land of Egypt setting the plan in motion that would preserve life."

* * * * * *

Matthias and Abijah and the rest of the warriors received a hushed command to take a five-minute break to rest and eat a bite of food. In one more hour they would be near Gibeon but just far enough away to avoid detection. There they could lie down and sleep for an hour before dawn would come. Matthias observed that the moon had moved far to the west, settling toward the horizon. Silently and steadily, with motion barely perceptible, it had arced overhead through the night, having been set in motion ages earlier by the Lord Himself, lending just enough light, reflected light from the glory of the sun, still shining somewhere, to move an entire army across a darkened earth. On this night men looked to a brave leader energized by the "Word," a man not afraid to step out in its guidance, in spite of what the world and its noisy opinions shouted. The evil set forth in the world from Adam's time acted mercilessly with its power, its hideous influence, and shamelessly punished every threat to its sinister grasp. Those who would seek truth or dare oppose evil were instantly detected and attacked, first with ridicule and laughter, then singled out and maligned, their motives mischaracterized as selfish and narrow-minded, while always the veiled threat of violence loomed in the background. Few dared stand up to that utterly malignant, camouflaged as peace-loving, freedom hating enemy. Joshua dared. For years he had allowed God's Word and its guidance to shape his life. He had patiently endured trials and failures, heart-breaking failures; trusting God was shaping him through it all because he said things like, "the trials of your faith more precious than gold" or "it is God that works in you to will and to do of his good pleasure" (1 Peter 1: 7; Philippians 2: 13).

Yes, the moon spoke of all that with its faithful and silent "voice," and Joshua had learned to walk in its glow no matter how dark and frightening the world. Wolves and lions killed, and Satan killed after first torturing. But Jesus said, "Be of good cheer little children. I have overcome the world." (John 16: 33). His Words will stand when all others have knelt before Him. Joshua knew that. And so did so many Israelites who bravely followed him. The faint glow of a faithful moon reflected, to those who saw, the glory of God. Tomorrow's battle would prove it. Joshua had a busy day planned for them and was already instructing his captains about the details.

Break over and walking again, Matthias and Abijah picked up with their story. Both knew it well but liked hearing it. "During the seven plentiful years Egypt had amassed so much corn and wheat they had left off counting it. Now the seven years of famine had begun. Starving Egyptians came to Pharaoh for food, which he now began to sell to them from his stockpiles. In time the famine spread to Canaan and Jacob's family, though wealthy, had no food. Hearing there was food in Egypt, Jacob sent his ten oldest sons to buy. In Egypt the men were told they had to speak to a certain powerful man to buy food. They found him conducting business from a platform high enough so people could see and hear him easily. His very manner and bearing conveyed power and demanded respect. When the brothers drew near Joseph recognized them as they bowed low. His boyhood dream flashed into his mind like a lightning strike passing through his whole being. His knees almost buckled as the reality of God's presence with all of them, way back to when he was a boy and now at this very moment, crashed in on his consciousness. God had given him that dream (that his brothers hated) and had been with them all along.

"Joseph had seen God's workings so many times through the years, but seeing his brothers now brought home the reality of God's word with such stunning force that he lost his breath. Maybe his heart stopped too. He did not know and wondered if anyone else had seen his reaction. He had always believed his father's words but had never grasped the utter truthfulness of them as he saw it at this moment.

"Regaining his composure, Joseph told his brothers to rise but gave no hint that he knew them. Nor did they recognize him. Why would they? They had put him out of their minds long ago, and, for all they knew, he was probably dead anyhow. He spoke roughly to them in Egyptian, using an interpreter, and asked from whence they came. 'From the land of Canaan to buy food,' said they. He accused them of being spies.

"This was not going well. The man who could help them, the most powerful man in Egypt, the most powerful man in the world, was suspicious of them and could easily have them killed. Desperately trying to convince him, they said, 'Your servants are twelve brothers, the sons of one man in Canaan. The youngest is this day with his father and one is not.'

"*One is not!* thought Joseph. *I am that one!* That was a delicate way to put it. After what they had done, these men described it all rather lightly. They had not worked as servants with no hope for years. They had not sat in prison for even more years. They and they alone were the cause of all Joseph's misery, and he had a right to hate them. Yet Joseph's hatred for them had faded away years ago when, little by little, on bitter sleepless nights, his anger fuming at them, he had been forced to confront his own self-absorbed and hateful ways. If he could be so full of hate, was he any better than his brothers? Confronting that realization was a big step. It had not come easily, but after several sleepless nights and fatiguing days he had finally admitted to himself his own wickedness. He had never realized how much it colored his thinking. Then he had admitted it to God. And when he did so, an unexpected thing happened. He thought of the sacrifices God told them to perform and that somehow those took care of sins in God's view. God was showing them that somehow He Himself was taking care of man's sinfulness and was graciously considering man righteous in His sight. That was when Joseph's whole attitude toward his brothers experienced a permanent change.

"As he realized that God had forgiven his own self-centeredness and hate-filled moments, his hatred of his brothers fell from him like so much dirt that he had not even realized covered him. God could accept all of them, himself included, and was at this moment taking care of them. Joseph's very presence in Egypt, their heartless sale of him as a slave, his hopeless days, his promotion to this exalted position, all were part of God's plan for taking care of the children of Abraham and positioning them to be a light to the world. Even being forced into awareness of his own wickedness was a bigger part of the plan than he had realized. God had chiseled the rough edges off Joseph and given him a new outlook on life. Joseph wondered if God had similarly worked on his brothers. He would find out.

"'As I said,' he spoke softly to his brothers through an interpreter, in a flat, merciless tone, 'you are spies. Put them in prison,' he ordered matter-of-factly to a guard with a sword hung ready on his belt. The brothers were terrified. Three long days passed before Joseph came to them.

"'Follow my orders and live,' said he, 'for I fear God. One of you shall remain here in prison. Take food for the family to your homes and bring your youngest brother to me to prove your words and you shall not die.' This could not have gone worse. Their father would never let Benjamin come.

"'We are guilty about our brother,' they said to each other. "We saw the anguish of his soul and closed our hearts to him. God is returning our own evil upon us.' They had no idea that the powerful man could understand every word they said. Joseph turned away and wept. Long buried memories of their cruel actions, hidden from others and even from their own thinking, haunted them. Joseph's actions had stirred them up and caused them to remember. Their fear of discovery of their own evil had kept them from seeing the Lord's dealings with them. How could they know Joseph had faced all these realities before, in the long nights in prison, had accepted God's kind forgiveness, and now held no animosity for them? He could see God's hand in it all. They, like Joseph, were Israel and part of a bigger plan God had for mankind. But they had not yet come to grips with their own sin and were in the throes of its captivity. Thus their inability to understand that Joseph could actually forgive them. Now God was actively dealing with them in these trials in Egypt with Joseph.

"Regaining composure, Joseph took their brother Simeon, bound him in chains while they watched, and sent them away. Joseph commanded to load sacks of corn for them and put each one's money back into his sack. On the way home one of them opened a sack to feed the animals and saw—his money! Fear welled up in their hearts and they said, 'What is this that God has done to us' (Genesis 42: 25-28)?

"At home they told their father of these things and, to cheer him up, emptied their sacks of corn into a bin, only to discover each sack had money in it! Now they were thieves! Jacob said, 'You have bereaved me of my children. Joseph is dead. Simeon is as good as dead and now you want to take Benjamin. Absolutely not! All these things are against me.' And for a while even Jacob lost his faith.

"The famine continued and eventually the corn was used up. Judah said, 'We have no choice. Without food we and our little ones will die. If we return to Egypt without Benjamin we will die. We must take him. I will be the guarantee. If I don't bring him safely back to you I will bear the blame forever.' Finally Jacob said, 'Go and God Almighty be with you and give you mercy before the man.' As the dream had pictured so long ago, even Jacob was reverencing Joseph.

"So they came again into Egypt, this time with Benjamin, and spoke to Joseph's steward explaining about the money. 'Don't be afraid,' he said. 'Your God has given you treasure in your sacks. I had your money.' And he brought out Simeon to them.

"Joseph caused them to be brought to his home for a meal, whereupon the brothers presented him with a gift of spices, balm, myrrh and extra money, and bowed to him again.

"'The old man of whom you spoke, is he yet alive?' The powerful man's voice had an almost pleading tone.

"'Yes, and in good health,' they answered. Hearing that and seeing his younger brother Benjamin, the agony of the years and the joy of the moment flooded his heart, and he ran from the room, seeking a place to cry unheard. Then he washed his face, refreshed the makeup Egyptian noblemen wore, came back out and said, 'Set out food.'

"Not for another day did Joseph reveal himself to them. At a certain moment and sending all the Egyptian servants away, Joseph wept aloud and told his brothers, 'I am Joseph. Is my father really alive?' Straining in disbelief to study his face the brothers suddenly realized—it *was* Joseph! What was he doing here . . . in this position? How could they have not recognized him? They could not answer for shock and for fear of what would happen next.

""Come near me,' he said to their shock in their own language. 'I am Joseph your brother, who you sold into Egypt. Do not be angry with yourselves. It was God who sent me here ahead of you to preserve life.' The brothers' terror diminished ever so slightly as they heard Joseph's reassuring words. Sure, they were guilty, but God had allowed it all, and would bless all of them in the end. 'There have been two years of famine,' he said, 'but five more are coming. God has made me a blessing to Pharaoh and lord of all Egypt. Go and tell my father of all my glory in Egypt and bring him and your children and grandchildren, with all your flocks and herds to be preserved and nourished. Pharaoh will give you the best of the land.' Their sin and selfish dealings with Joseph were suddenly out in the open. The cover-up was exposed, and yet Joseph had not ordered them killed! In stunned shock they were somehow relieved.

Joseph drew his astonished brothers near and kissed each one of them and wept a long time. The brothers, still somewhat in fear, began to talk with him and renew their tarnished relationship.

"With Pharaoh's encouragement and blessing Joseph outfitted them with wagons and gifts from Egypt for his father and their families back home and instructed them to bring them to Egypt to be nourished and sustained through the remaining years of the famine. Pharaoh caused the wagons to be loaded with exquisitely precious gifts and food and sent word that Joseph's family would have the best of the land of Egypt on which to settle.

"Back home, Jacob could not believe the news that his son was alive and ruler of all Egypt. Only when he saw the wagons and the fabulous wealth they carried did he dare believe it. Then God spoke to Jacob, whom he now called Israel, in a vision, saying, 'Fear not to go into Egypt, for I will there make of you a great nation, and I will surely bring you up again to Canaan' (Genesis 46: 2-4). The loss of his beloved son, Joseph, was not permanent. It was part of God's plan to preserve life in the midst of a hostile world, a world in which Satan himself continually sought to mar and destroy the thing dear to God's heart—mankind. Jacob had endured years of untold agonies over Joseph, and now he was seeing the larger plan, which was even larger than taking care of Jacob and his sons. It pictured God's care for all mankind, as their deliverance from the power of Egypt and slavery pictured God's ability to rescue man from the cruel power of evil and deception and its awful sting of death."

The Son Who Was Dead

With Abijah rapt in attention, though he had heard the story many times, Matthias continued: "All the family of Israel and his children and their little ones journeyed into Egypt, seventy souls in all. As they arrived in Egypt and drew near to the place where he would meet Joseph face to face, Jacob remembered with great clarity Joseph's boyhood dreams, and that last dream in which he told of his father bowing down to Joseph. His other sons had been deeply offended at Joseph's telling of them, and he himself had cautioned Joseph to be careful to be respectful toward his father and mother. But in his heart he had puzzled over Joseph's strange words and wondered deep in his mind if they had been from God. He had nearly died that day when Joseph's coat was brought to him soaked in blood. He had endured the pain of imagining his son, that little boy who looked up to him with such adoring eyes, alone in the wilderness, utterly helpless and fighting for his life among a pack of wolves, vicious wolves—on a mission he himself had ordered—large chunks of flesh and muscle torn from his bones while he lived. Yes, Jacob had known pain so deeply that he had never really gotten over it. Now this son, whom he had believed to be dead, was ruler of the most powerful nation in the world—and had sent for his father. Israel sat silently in his wagon, overwhelmed.

"Egypt's intelligence had sent word to Joseph of the distant approach of his father's caravan. Unable to wait longer, Joseph arrayed himself in his finest robes, as his position required whenever he appeared in public, and made ready his royal chariot to venture out on the plain to meet his father. Two matched, spirited steeds, impeccably groomed and trained, gleaming chestnut with four white stockings, pulled that chariot with high-stepping dignity, creating a majestic scene. People honored Joseph as the one who had protected Egypt from this famine, and they struggled to get close enough to see him. The horses projected an aura of restrained power, bobbing their heads excitedly while their legs quivered with energy, appearing to be held back from breaking into a dead run with only the greatest of skill. Controlling such a fine team required special ability, and Joseph, up to the task, further captured the admiration of those who witnessed his control of this 'state of the art' chariot.

"This was a moment Joseph had long ago resigned himself to believing would never take place. One bitter night in prison, he consciously put away all thought of seeing his beloved father again and purposed never to allow himself the luxury of wallowing in self-pity over it. He pushed out such thoughts by focusing on things his father had instilled in his heart, assurances that God could lead their lives and destinies better than they themselves could, thoughts that God was with them in the most painful and hopeless of moments, thoughts that he could be a light to the rest of the world in the darkest of circumstances. Joseph knew he would see his father and his beloved mother in heaven in God's presence, but that was far off. Since his decision, he had not allowed himself the thought of believing he would ever see him again in this world. The arrival of his brothers this past year and their bowing down to him had brought his boyhood dreams back into sharp focus and had pierced his heart with staggering impact. Those dreams were so dead-on accurate that even he, who had clearly seen God's power the last several years, could only react with newfound awe. Now he was about to see his father again. Finally the caravan appeared far in the distance, and Joseph let the horses run with the strength that only horses have, fairly flying over the distance as though spirited by the Lord himself. The caravan halted as he neared it, and Joseph slowed his chariot to a stop. Presently an old man climbed down slowly from a wagon—an old man with a limp. After a few steps he stood still and lifted his eyes toward the chariot—and his son. The horses, damp from the run, took many deep breaths and finally relaxed into the moment. Two men stood, motionless, still twenty paces apart, simply beholding each other . . . Eleven other sons with wives and families watched in silence—except for a few fidgety children, one of whom asked, a little too loudly, 'Who is that?' as an old man and a king met that day. Suddenly Joseph ran, robes flowing in the air, like a little boy in pure delight, arms outstretched, toward his father."

The reader can only imagine that meeting between Joseph and his father, a father who believed he had lost his son to a grisly death, a son cruelly torn from his father, painfully convinced for years he would never see him again. Two broken-hearted men in a strange land on a plain in Goshen, in the land of Egypt. Scripture records that Joseph "fell on his father's neck and wept a good while" (Genesis 46: 29). Memory of the boyhood dream of his brothers' sheaves bowing to his sheaf in the field awoke in his mind. Memories of an earlier hopeless caravan journey to Egypt, of standing on a slave block for sale, of lonely hopelessness during hundreds of black nights in prison, reeled in his mind and flowed into this moment. Sometimes the spare words of scripture evoked a whole larger picture capable of touching the heart very deeply. This trip into Egypt began as an idea, an evil idea in the mind of Judah, to sell his brother for money. God had overruled and turned his foul plan into salvation for the entire family of Israel.

"Joseph . . . Joseph, my beloved Joseph . . . son of my precious Rachel . . . you were dead . . . and here you are." It is hard to know the agony and the joy, the bewilderment, the awareness of the tender hand of God, that flooded into that moment, and perhaps words cannot convey it.

"Halt!" came the command from Joshua. "We rest here. You marched well all night. Sleep and refresh yourselves. I'll wake you just before the sun breaks the horizon. Then be ready for swift action!" And before they slept, a few more words . . .

"You walked all night, in the dark, through the 'valley of the shadow of death,' you could say, to a place you have never been before. You stepped into the night, the unknown, like Abraham, leaving everything he knew, leaving the land of his upbringing, like Israel journeying in old age into Egypt, like Moses walking into Pharaoh's very presence, looking into his eyes, and delivering God's words, like the priests carrying the Ark, stepping into a flooding river, like Rahab risking her life to help the spies . . . And now, here *you* are. When you awake you will go into battle, but you will not have to fight this battle. The Lord will fight for you. Fear will try to stop you, but be courageous. Remember Who brought you here. It was not me but God Himself, the God of all the earth. He was with you all night, and He is with you now. You will have to march, each of you, into the battle on your own two feet, weapons in your hands, but His presence will be with you. For now—relax and fall asleep. Doing that, you are trusting him." A few words, well chosen, delivered in a tired moment, by the commander-in-chief of the most powerful army on earth, the army of Israel—by Joshua, a humble man, the servant of the Lord.

After Joshua's words Matthias wondered at his own story and pondered. The story they had been discussing was not finished. He and Abijah, and all Israel, were part of it, and tonight it was continuing. "And that is how Israel came to be in Egypt," said he. "It was all good in the beginning. Even Pharaoh honored the Lord, and his whole land was blessed for it." The moon had dipped below the horizon, and in the increased darkness he, Abijah, and all the other warriors fell quickly into welcomed sleep.

CHAPTER 37

SURPRISE!

(Joshua 10)

Still in darkness at the huge tent outside Gibeon the five kings slept, also catching a short but much-needed rest. Their plan was to attack two hours after sunup, when the Gibeonites were busy starting their day, and destroy their city to the ground. The Gibeonites had seen the armies amassed outside the city and had grown sick with worry. Brutal and merciless would be the attack. This nonsense of siding with the enemy had to be stopped decisively before it spread any further, sending a message far and wide. Every man and teenaged boy would be killed. Women and children would be taken as servants, prizes for the conquering soldiers. Four hours would be given to search for gold, silver and anything else worth taking. Food, clothing and treasure would be loaded onto wagons brought for the purpose. Then the city would be burned and a curse pronounced on it. A detachment of men would take the captives and spoils back to the various cities.

The best part of the plan was that, while the warriors were in high spirits from their conquests and prizes, the heady experience of that victory, their superior numbers would be assembled to attack before Israel ever knew what was coming. The combined Canaanite armies vastly outnumbered Israel's army and the rout would be complete. The treasure of plunder Israel had amassed would be theirs for the taking, and Israel would be a threat no more. Their God would be unable to help them.

Just then a badly winded messenger charged into the tent waking the kings. "Israel," he stammered, "behind me . . . five minutes . . . I barely outran them."

"What?" An unexpected setback. These men, though, were seasoned warriors, winners accustomed to meeting attacks. Quickly shaking off their sleep and rallying their senses, they understood the threat and equally quickly reasoned that the size of their army vastly outnumbered that of foolish Israel. Holding their fears in check they ran outside, and in the faint light, slightly farther than a long bow shot away, the dark outline on the grassy plain of a huge mass of men appeared. A blood red smudge glowed on the eastern horizon, the forerunner of the new day, while darkness still owned the rest of the sky. Daylight expanded from the glow minute by minute. This day would bring judgment and death for some, victory and inheritance for others. The kings' forces slept on the ground behind their royal tent in groups of one hundred, resting but ready to be called for their upcoming attack on Gibeon.

"Get up! Attack!" the kings shouted. Captains quickly scrambled men to action.

"What's happening?" soldiers puzzled as they obeyed orders. The kings were taking control of the situation. Maybe the gods were handing them a victory sooner than they had expected—probably having been satisfied with the sacrifices.

Yet Adoni-zedek, the self-ascribed "Adoni" portion of his name suggesting "god-like" attributes, for the first time in a long time, had been taken by surprise.

The warriors, grabbing their weapons, prepared for whatever was next. Just then arrows began raining down on them, arrows carrying not so subtle messages of death. An arrow glanced off King Debir's helmet and stuck fast in his leather shoulder pad. In anger he jerked it out and broke it in half. Trumpets were sounding now, evidently from Israel, a maddening noise that would not quit. They spoke of judgment from God, a sound rising above all other sounds, above shouted commands, above screams of pain, a sound signaling victory and doom all in one voice, a blaring, harsh voice that would not quit. Joshua's army was running at them, and seemingly from out of nowhere deftly thrown spears whizzed into their midst. Several saw warriors beside them suddenly scream in pain and fall writhing to the ground, either a spear or an arrow stuck deep. A commander felt a sting in his side as an arrow split through his ribs and into his right lung. At first it barely hurt, but as he realized his life was draining out he felt a horrible cramp, lost all strength and collapsed to the ground, not caring how he fell. Whoever invented arrows was truly a demon. No one cared, but that was his last thought.

In the distance to the left and right more trumpets sounded—Israelite trumpets. They were surrounded! A few soldiers fled, and panic began to set in. Sharp commands from the seasoned captains cracked like whips, restoring order and common sense. But to no avail. The horrible surprise of Joshua's attack had, for the moment at least, given the advantage completely to Israel, and, realizing their vulnerability, the kings commanded an orderly retreat to find a safe spot to regroup and mount a counterattack. The kings did not lose sight of the fact that they still held a huge advantage over Israel, outnumbering them probably five to one. To allow Israel to gain the upper hand and defeat them would be a disgrace. This hated Israel could never be allowed to win. The Canaanites had their gods on their side and began calling out to them.

The commanders' discipline almost worked. One of them saw an Israelite, bow drawn to its full strength, the point of his arrow aimed straight for his heart, and turned to evade the arrow. It went in at his back and came out at his heart. More men were dropping right in their midst, screaming in pain as arrows pierced deep into their shoulders, backs and necks. Those not hit had to step over bleeding bodies on the ground to avoid tripping. Arrows just kept speeding in, too fast to see until they hit with excruciating pain. A brave warrior drew his bow and took aim to shoot back. Drawing a bead on an Israelite, he did not see the arrow, already well on its way, sailing straight and silent, spiraling on a deadly path for his life. It passed clear through his neck in a fraction of a second, severing his jugular on the way, and stuck hard in his partner behind him. The Canaanite's target saw no hurt that day as the brave warrior lost track of what he was doing, letting his own arrow fall harmlessly from his grip as all went black. He too no longer cared—about anything. The "Unseen Captain" guided legions of Israelites' actions as He directed this battle.

Joshua watched as one of his men threw his spear with deadly accuracy at a fleeing warrior. He had noticed Malachi in action before and been impressed with his remarkable ability. An enemy captain seated atop a beautiful white horse with light gray markings and mane sported a polished, form-fitted silver breastplate and swirled his sword in the air, calling his men to action. The rising sun glistened off that breastplate. Bare arms, brown from the sun and well-muscled, spoke of strength—as did his face, which reflected resolve and an alertness born of emerging victoriously from many life and death battles. His helmet, adorned with gorgeous bright red plumage, rendered him easily seen by the large number of men under his command. His horse was noble indeed, extremely spirited, head held high, twitching with lightning reactions to the slightest pressure from his master's heel, light on his feet and prancing delicately, forward and back, amidst the crowd so as not to step on any soldier. The captain was obviously a master at controlling this animal, as he had been at training his men. They knew he would quickly spot the direction to focus their attack for the greatest effect, and they anxiously awaited his signal. All this Joshua saw in an instant. Motioning to Malachi, he tossed his own spear sideways to him and, with a nod of his head, directed Malachi's attention to the majestic man on horseback. Joshua with his own practiced skill could have thrown the spear himself with great accuracy but elected instead to do it this way.

Aware of Malachi's skill, he had observed something else in Malachi, who since he had been a three-year-old boy had loved hearing the stories about Abraham, Isaac and Jacob, and now about Moses and deliverance from Egypt and the passage through the Red Sea. He and his young friends acted out these stories over and over, taking turns playing different parts in the stories. As a teenager he had maneuvered to get close enough to Moses to hear his words as he taught the people. He told how he had had to learn to follow the Lord rather than his own abilities, which were considerable, considering all he had learned in Egypt. In fact it took him forty years to learn to give up on himself and trust God's promises. Malachi had listened with great interest. Now he had watched Joshua with the same interest, believing the Lord was working through him. Joshua, always looking to develop additional leaders within his armies, had observed him as well—and many of the other young men—with keen interest. For those who had shown themselves serious about following the Lord he watched for opportunities to further stretch their leadership abilities. Thus he tossed his spear to Malachi.

Having thrown spears since boyhood at targets near and far, Malachi in his endless hours of practice had built strength into his shoulder and arm. His muscles had learned the feel of aligning almost instantly with the exact spot his eyes chose. His mind could calculate precisely how high to throw the spear to allow for gravity's pull in the given distance. His arm he would swing in an arc as large as possible for the greatest speed, and then, having perfected the timing of an extra flick of his wrist at the last instant to impart even more speed, he focused all his strength into that final "snap," holding fast his unalterable attention on his target. There was no escaping a spear thrown like that. Shocking power and pain would stab into its victim's entire consciousness.

Malachi caught the spear and felt its weight in his hand—slightly heavier than his own for greater penetrating power— felt the perfect balance, saw the glistening head, knew its history and, aware of his master's trust, selected his exact target spot and planted his feet solidly to the earth for a fleeting second, rendering his legs, hips and trunk a rigid platform from which his skilled arm could explode its lightning power—the fine touches in the art of a practiced warrior that made all the difference—and let fly the spear.

His eyes remained locked on the warrior with the glistening armor. "It's in your hands, Lord," he said in his heart. "Take it." That was the quality Joshua had observed in Malachi. Disciplined skill, strength under control, an attitude that meekly recognized his Lord's power and bowed to it, day after day, from deep in his heart. Men like that aligned themselves with true power that had eternal consequences.

The spear took the majestic warrior in his chest, in the bottom of his heart. Most arrows or sword blows would glance off that armor, but the speed and weight of the spear drove it through. The captain dropped his sword and clutched at the spear, to no avail. The blood could not spurt through the narrow slit in the armor, so it was difficult to see for a moment the awful damage already done. Instead the blood flowed like a warm river between the armor and his skin and emerged bright red at his waist, then spilled onto the saddle and the white horse's back. He wavered sideways in his saddle, unable to sit up straight, and, after a moment of confusion, fell headlong to the ground. A loud crack pierced the din as his neck snapped. He rallied no men. Joshua too knew where to strike the deadliest blow. He ordered one close to him to gather the two spears while pressing his troops constantly forward.

Once again the situation began to look hopeless for the enemy. The dead captain's men stood baffled for a moment and then ran, joining the retreat. These kings and their captains had made a terrible mistake. Where were their gods? They were no help at all. Maybe they weren't real. More men fell, many of them experienced, cruel, and powerful warriors. Some rolled on the ground in agony. Others fell, immediately still, never to move again. Losing like this was something no soldier ever wanted to experience, and until today, these men had mainly been on the winning side of battles, never caring much for the worthless ones who lost.

Panic set in for real now. Men dropped their swords and spears, shields and armor, and ran for their lives. Those infernal trumpets kept blaring. Forget victory. Now it was escape or die.

Men running at all out speed soon exhausted themselves, and many stumbled, heaving and vomiting, to the ground, too panicked to do anything but gasp for air, only to be quickly run through with a spear already wet with someone else's blood. These men were experiencing the misery they had planned for the soldiers now destroying them.

Joshua observed and kept his men moving ahead at a steady pace, conserving their strength. In his heart he saw the Lord acting, working details out. Joshua's—and Israel's—job was to stay focused on the Lord, follow His leading and be part of His battle rather than getting caught up in the fierce action of the moment. His years of self-discipline and pondering God's Word until it was worked into his heart had enabled him to so lead Israel, even in the heat of battle. Joshua enforced that discipline in the confusion of such moments, and most of his men saw and began to learn for themselves his discipline. An arrow whizzed by his ear. He heard the slightest wisp of a breeze as death passed close. Maybe the Lord had deflected its path. The Unseen Captain was in charge, and Joshua knew how to follow. As he moved, the foolishness of those who rebelled against God and whose darkened hearts had trusted phony, imaginary gods was exposed. Gods carved by men in wood or silver never spoke because they were not real. They heard no prayers because their ears were made of wood and could not hear. They had no heart and no mind. Molech was an iron joke. What could be said of those who, knowing all that, bowed down to them, worshiping the imagination of their own hearts as though their own imagination had some power like a god? The pride of their hearts had deceived them (as it had deceived Satan so long ago). Abandoning the true God, they had become their own gods, and following their own foolish hearts, had arrived at this moment from which there was suddenly no escape. The trap they had mercilessly set for others sprung on them. When the serpent said, "You shall be like gods, knowing good and evil," he was partly right, in a twisted, perverted way.

* * * * * *

Israel had marched all night but was outperforming this enemy. What should have been annihilation for them, if these kings had their way, turned out to be a huge victory for Israel, conquering five nations at once, faster than five separate campaigns. The kings had done the work of assembling all the rebels in one place for their own death. Scripture says, "the Lord from heaven will laugh at the pride of man." God could be aware of the position of every wave on every ocean, at every moment, day after day, year after year, century after century. He knew of each blade of grass, each plant and flower and how it grew and when it blossomed. He knew when a sparrow died and fell unseen to earth. He knew when a baby wolf was conceived and when it was born in the safety of a den. He knew every detail about His creation, from the tiny atoms and how they moved, reacted and bonded together—actions so small human senses could not detect their existence (yet human intelligence, put into man's heart by God, would ultimately imagine them and devise tests to prove their existence)—to the paths of the planets as they swung through the hollow of space, held on course by powerful but unseen gravitational forces. Man could observe the effect of these forces, but could not explain how they worked. God could decree that plants and animals bear seed and reproduce themselves. Seeds from daisies always became daisies. Seeds from elephants always became elephants and only elephants. All from the time God spoke them into existence until today. He could command ten thousand sunrises with one word. He who was aware of all creation at all moments was not impressed with Adoni-zedek, nor with the wisdom of any man who could fool and overpower another. No one could match the wisdom of Joshua's God.

Meanwhile, the five kings had fled toward a cave known to one of the men, callously abandoning their soldiers in favor of their own safety. The morning sun shone brightly now and the scene was sickening. Dead and wounded bodies littered the ground. Dying gasps and groans still emanated here and there. Swords, spears and armor glistened in the dirt, soon to be prizes of war. Someone saw the kings escaping toward the cave and alerted Joshua who, in turn, detailed a group of fifty men to follow them and roll large rocks into the cave's mouth to seal them in. For now . . . Five powerful and aggressive men who, until a few days ago, had been enemies plotting against each other's kingdoms, were now sealed together in the dark in a cave, bitter and shocked over what had just happened, awaiting what would certainly be a disgraceful and painful death rather than the total victory they had planned. Ultimate justice the Lord frequently employs is to return one's own evil upon his own head as relentless eternity closes in on him. This day was not beginning well for any of these kings—or their armies.

CHAPTER 38

EXECUTION—THE PRIDE OF MAN DRIVEN TO THE DUST

(Joshua 10)

"The kings of the earth set themselves, and the rulers take counsel together, against the Lord . . . He that sits in the heavens shall laugh . . . Then shall he speak to them in his wrath. (Psalm 2: 2, 4-5)

After the kings had fled the battle, destruction was overtaking their armies. Joshua, in Israel's midst, yelled God's words to him so even the enemy could hear, "Fear them not, for I have delivered them into your hand. Not a man of them shall stand before you" (Joshua 10:8). What came next was "a great slaughter," according to the scripture, with Israel chasing, for miles, those trying to escape. And then two even more astounding events transpired. The first: "As they fled from before Israel . . . the Lord cast great stones from heaven upon them . . . and they died. They were more that died with hailstones than they whom the children of Israel slew with the sword" (Joshua 10:11). Imagine the encouragement as they beheld the Lord bringing victory. Sure, they were swinging and slashing with swords, throwing spears, shooting arrows, but the Lord guided their motions, and Israel knew it. God assisted Israel in destroying these armies, affirming to the world that Israel was acting in accordance with His will. What an awful judgment upon these people. God himself destroying them. Those who want to criticize Israel for taking the land from these people as they did, and with such merciless finality, would do well to reflect very soberly on the fact it was really God executing this judgment. These Canaanites, with their long history of ignoring God and pushing

Him out of their lives, had invoked His wrath! We can do the same with a life of nonchalance and rebellion toward the God who made us.

These victories illustrated to the world God's hatred of evil and His overwhelming power to conquer it. Each was meant to reach into man's thinking. Each person is responsible for his reaction to God's actions. When we play "judge" over the judge of all the earth we are on dangerous ground, as were the Canaanites on that day. Since Jesus' time, however, no Israelites or Christians have been told to hurt or destroy other human beings. God has already demonstrated His right and ability to judge and is today reaching out to man, calling him to be "reconciled" to Himself. Jesus said, "For the Son of man has not come to destroy men's lives, but to save them" (Luke 9:56).

Man's place is to consider carefully what God was communicating through these stories. The true believer has settled in his mind the fact that when scripture is difficult to understand, it is not God that needs correcting but his own understanding so that he could see things from God's point of view. Unlike man's, His is anchored in eternity, viewing all from a far larger vantage point. That is how the "humble" mind approaches scripture.

Many, however, question why a God of love and peace would approve such destruction. Consider this. In Revelation chapter 21 the Apostle John is given a view far into the future of a "new heaven and a new earth" and then hears "a great voice out of heaven saying, behold, the tabernacle of God is with men, and He will dwell with them, and they shall be His people, and God Himself shall be with them and be their God. And God shall wipe away all tears from their eyes, and there shall be no more death, neither sorrow, nor crying, neither shall there be any more pain, for the former things are passed away. And He that sat upon the throne said, behold, I make all things new. And He said to me, Write, for these words are true and faithful" (Revelation 21:1-5).

In a kingdom where peace, love and joy exist always and where God nurtures and cares for all He has created, it would be inconsistent with His character to allow those who want to oppress and despoil others of their goods to exert their influence.

In a world where we long for some "positive" news, these words from scripture bring peace in the midst of hardships. That was why God told John to "write" them"—so we too could be encouraged. They mean that pain, misery and death will not always be part of the human lot. We humans have *never* seen a realm where these do not exist, and so imagining such a place is difficult. Yet God is telling us that one day these will be gone from our presence and that He will live among us. Imagine God Himself wiping away one's tears—no sorrow, crying, or pain in the presence of God.

The evil that man invited in will have been removed forever. It has been allowed "for a season" so that "free willed" man could see, firsthand, the horrible effects of disregarding wise advice from God. Man, having been given intelligence and reasoning abilities far beyond those given to other living beings, was not given omniscience, that is, the ability to know everything and to comprehend all possible outcomes of an action. For that he had to depend on God, and God had full intention of providing that guidance to man at all times.

Evil could not exist in the presence of God or in His heaven, but it could be allowed to exist *for a time* on this earth. Jesus said, "A Kingdom divided against itself cannot stand." By that He meant that if one part of a kingdom worked against another part of that kingdom, the result would be confusion, then gradual destruction that took the entire kingdom down. Chaos, unruliness, lawlessness and rebellion destroy all they touch. Some world leaders have instigated chaos and revolt to unsettle a nation and then to move in and seize power. It has never been for the good of the people of that nation. Selfish leaders wrought misery and death on people they had no right to destroy. Their kingdoms lasted for a time, but their lack of respect for others and for principles of right and wrong were the seeds of their own destruction. In Bible stories, we are brought face to face with the effects of evil in the world and the pain and heartache they produce. We see God's hatred of these and their awful effect on His beloved mankind. In Moses and Joshua we see God taking action against the forces of darkness and evil—and demonstrating power over them. These are previews of God's ultimate victories still to come.

One day He will deal decisively with all things causing pain and sorrow, and will conquer man's cruelest enemy, death. "The last enemy that shall be destroyed is death. Death is swallowed up in victory. O death, where is your sting? O grave, where is your victory?" (Romans 15: 26, 54-55). A true and good king protects his kingdom from all threats. In Canaan the rightful Lord of the land was rooting out evil and taking over. God had given man freedom to do as he pleased. He could choose to live in the presence of God or to exist forever apart from Him. Freedom was an awesome responsibility.

These inhabitants of Canaan were living the last moments of their life on earth today. Israel was the visible conqueror, but God was the true conqueror, and today was harvest time. There would be no more chances to reconsider after the harvest. This battle was more momentous than anyone realized.

The second astounding event occurred when Joshua said, "in the sight of Israel, 'Sun, stand still upon Gibeon and, Moon, in the valley of Ajelon.' And the sun stood still, and the moon stayed, in the midst of heaven about a whole day, until the people had avenged themselves upon their enemies. And there was no day like that before it or after it, that the Lord hearkened to the voice of a man, for the Lord fought for Israel" (Joshua 10:12-15). Israel continued all that long day to destroy the enemy armies.

Scripture tells all believers in the Lord, "You shall not be afraid of the terror by night, nor of the arrow that flies by day, nor of the pestilence that walks in darkness, nor of the destruction that lays waste at noonday. A thousand may fall at your side, and ten thousand at your right hand, but it shall not come near you. Only with your eyes shall you look, and see the reward of the wicked" (Psalm 91: 5-8).

To the citizens of cities for hundreds of miles around, news of these events spread like fire on a dry prairie. Who would not see a halted sun and moon? The miraculous plagues of Egypt from over forty years earlier could seem like a minor preview compared to this worldwide event. Victory complete, Israel left off conquering and returned to their camp. The world lay in awe, terrified of what might happen next, though any of them could have appealed, like Rahab, to God for mercy.

Today, thirty-five hundred years later, the awe has been lost in the dust of time, and what remains is this scriptural record of it and scattered archaeological evidence, viewed with skepticism by modern day critics. Over the past two centuries, however, archaeologists have, in many locations, unearthed written records and artifacts from the areas referenced that corroborate the biblical account. These receive scant attention from the rest of the world. Yet they remain, though safely tucked away in libraries—and on the internet—for those who care to look. The "awe," wrapped carefully by God in these stories and in the words spoken by the prophets, is not lost but is quietly waiting to be "discovered" again, to blossom to life for all who "search the scriptures," as advised by Jesus, or who, out of a broken heart, cry out to God for help.

Then Joshua commanded, "Open the mouth of the cave, and bring out those five kings to me." An unseen enemy, that old serpent and deceiver of men, Satan himself, had been influencing these powerful kings, leading them and their followers far away from their Creator, giving them success when it suited his purpose. Now, suddenly outmaneuvered, he twisted and departed, leaving his "kings" to give account. Joshua politely "requested" that they hand their swords, the arm of their power, to his officers. That "request," delivered like the quiet, low, purring growl of a lion, who needed not to speak any louder because he knew he would win, resulted in obedience from kings who understood power full well. Then he directed them to lie face down on the ground and ordered the men who now held the kings' swords to place a foot on the neck of each king. These kings who had wielded such magnificent power in the world now found themselves pinned under the control of a conquering Israelite. Imagine yourself as one of those warriors holding a powerful king underfoot, realizing that God's power had put him there and now held him firmly in place. No escape or resistance was possible. God had granted His own warriors conquest over the kingdom of evil. One king, bloodstains on his face and his magnificent beard soiled with dirt of the earth where his face had been pressed, realizing that in a few moments he would be dead, craned his face up at his captors with fear. "Surely there's been enough killing already," offered King Hoham. "What will more killing solve?" He wanted to run away, but the foot on his neck held him down, and it hurt. This was it, the sum total of his life. He had brought this same misery to hundreds of others, not caring when men or women begged for mercy, or screamed in agony, only concerned with winning and increasing his power. He would never have spared any crying captive. Nor would Joshua spare him now. He suddenly wished for mercy.

The other four kings reflected only hatred and defiance in their demeanor. They would never give in or show weakness. Israelite warriors looked down upon these brutal, powerful kings held under the soles of their feet. They did not look so powerful now. Pitiful really. A scene none of these men would ever forget, nor would the hundreds of soldiers close enough to see. These kings had used their skills and power not to lead and help prosper their subjects but to dominate and pilfer money and goods from them. They had deceived their followers with layer upon layer of lies and had wrought untold misery in their lives as they selfishly took from them. Now they began to reap the fruit of their ways. God was calling them to account at this very moment, without even showing His face to them. He used people they hated as much as they hated God to bring them up short and overrule their plans. Their refusal to acknowledge Him rendered them willfully blind to His presence and His power which, at this moment, held them painfully pinned to the hard earth under the hated peoples' feet. They would die as they had treated others, reaping the outcome of a selfishly wasted life. Their pitiless hatred of other souls God had made would become the judgment they chose for themselves as their own ways returned upon their heads. "As your swords have made women childless, so shall your mothers be childless among women," uttered Joshua with pitiless scorn. He was not swayed by the opportunistic repentance of Hoham. He was well aware of their cold-hearted cruelty to others. He knew of their sacrificing screaming human babies as they placed them in the nearly red hot iron arms of their statues of Molech, their "god." Neither Molech nor Satan was present to help any of them at this moment. From the corner of his eye, King Hoham saw a bright flash of light glint off the polished blade of the sword swinging toward his neck, and in a moment he and four other once powerful men lay lifeless, beheaded, in the dirt, all their majesty and grand schemes perishing with them. "How are they brought into desolation, as in a moment! they are utterly consumed with terrors" (Psalm 73:19). These men faced death, by all appearances, fearlessly.

The real terror came a split second later when eternity yawned open to them, and they realized with heart-quaking horror the utter "realness" of the living God whom they had callously ignored, His presence, though not visible to them, somehow dominating the moment, controlling the eternal "now" from which there was no escape. The steely solidness of His unbending Word, the light that scattered not only darkness but also deception, allowed no twisting of truth nor hiding from it. The life that shined like light from His very heart, the life that had called out to them during all their days on earth, imploring them to come to Him for safety, now loomed before them and demanded their attention. Absolutely no escape. Like waking from a dream and entering a new reality, a world that had been there all along, an all-consuming awareness of their entrance into Hell pushed the old life away as insignificant. Their own foolishness at having spurned their Creator's attempts to help them appeared before them as a more important truth than everything they had done in their lives.

Now their motionless, dead bodies had no power to speak a warning to the rest of the world. Their influence here was finished. Israel's march into their midst was their last warning from God. They could have honored Him but instead pretended to dominate Him, overrule and ignore Him. They well knew of Pharaoh's colossal failure forty-odd years earlier. They knew of the ruin of Egypt as Pharaoh time after time hardened his heart against God, even in the face of His superior power as reflected in the miraculous events He conducted in front of Pharaoh. Yet Pharaoh would never give in to God. He wanted the glory a king could command, the honor and esteem, never realizing God tolerated his upstart attitude to reveal his stubbornness and to give him one opportunity after another to take his proper humble place before God. One certain day, known only to God, would constitute his last chance, and it came at the Red Sea! Today it had come for these similarly foolish kings. The lands and wealth they had amassed, the goods they had accumulated all slipped from their grip as conquering feet held their necks hard to the earth from which they had been taken and to which they now returned as sword separated them from their temporary domain on earth and they now entered their "long home."

The path they had chosen kept them in the clutches of Satan, whose web of deception, seeming so desirable, had completely entangled them and brought them to this awful place. The master deceiver himself was slated for eternal destruction in a place called, by none other than the Son of God, the "lake of fire," and all in Satan's infernal grip would be going with him. The wisdom he appeared to have was suddenly seen as merely a hideous distortion of truth. Satan was a fool with far too much respect and influence. He himself was doomed and was taking all who stupidly followed him into to the same eternal death determined for him. Jesus, when He later came visibly to earth, described this place in various ways: outer darkness where there is weeping and gnashing of teeth and, a furnace of fire in which are wailing and gnashing of teeth (Matthew 8: 12; 13: 42). Luke 13: 28-29 states, "There shall be weeping and gnashing of teeth, when you shall see Abraham, Isaac, and Jacob, and all the prophets in the kingdom of God, and you yourselves thrust out. And they shall come from the east and from the west, and from the north, and from the south, and shall sit down in the kingdom of God. Mark 9: 43, 46 speaks of hell as a place where the worm never dies and the fire is never quenched. Jesus Himself believed in hell and warned of it over and over. He could see into eternal worlds, where we have no ability to look. These "kings" had foolishly ignored all of God's warnings.

If only they had known! An almost worse horror was that, having spurned all of God's attempts to rescue them, no escape or chance to change one's mind existed—nor would it ever—forever. That was the reality of true freedom. Complete responsibility for one's own thoughts and actions. There was no hiding from God's awful gaze and his unchallengeable ability to accurately comprehend all they had thought and done. They were naked before him as the light of his presence revealed all their secret and hidden motives. Their freedom to do as they pleased in this earth, to kill and destroy, was allowed by God only for a time to reveal what was truly in their hearts. It had been a test, a test conceived in the deep wisdom of God's heart, against which no distorted argument could stand. These "kings," who could not help each other, and who, indeed, cared about no one but themselves, found themselves harpooned to darkness. No matter how they tried, no escape from this new world existed. It would be a never-ending nightmare. Egypt's horrors and brutalities upon Israel had been child's play compared to this.

God could have taken each of them to heaven first to show them His glory and His absolute reality and power, as Lucifer had witnessed, before they died to give them opportunity to think it over and turn willingly to Him. But He does not do it that way, choosing instead to ask us to believe Him on nothing more than the strength of His words, the strength of His words as our Creator. He will not force anyone to be with Him. The path through the world is a test, a very subtle test, to determine who, of his own free will, will hear His words and respond to Him. Earth, with its attractions and pleasures, can captivate one's attention so completely as to keep us from lending any attention at all to the Lord and what He says. Yet the way God devised it, the choices humans make during their time on this earth will determine the place they exist forever. One's eternal destiny is in his own hands. Yet many take this reality so lightly, they will not think about it. God will honor each person's choice to accept Him as Savior and God—or to ignore Him. He will live forever with the outcome of his choice. No one could avoid this judgment of God's. The signs God gave through the miracles he performed in Egypt, at the Jordan River, at the astounding victories under Moses and Joshua, all spoke to them with a voice they should have heard. They were given years to think it over and consider God's claim to their attention. Their time was up. They could have claimed God was unfair and unjust, but in their hearts they knew better. "To everything there is a season . . . a time to be born, and a time to die; a time to plant, and a time to pluck up that which is planted." (Ecclesiastes 3: 1-2) This they now realized, seeing reality in its true and eternal form. Job, in profound wisdom, called death the "king of terrors."

All their thoughts and plans vanished with them in a moment. The pride of man driven to the dust, the wisdom of the world by which they so much lived now gave up their grip, disappearing as a dream that cannot be grasped, Israel's conquest of the land and its inhabitants was now a picture of a greater, final conquest to come farther in the future, as the Lord Himself will take back mankind and His earth as their forever king, a picture as sure as the conquest of Canaan. These conquests, and those in Egypt, a wordless voice from the wilderness, from the depth of darkness, crying out to the heart of man, "be ye reconciled to God." The Savior's voice who sees the beginning and the end of each to whom he gave life, "Heed my advice, believe my words." So simple a child can do it, and conception will take place.

Matthias and Abijah stood among those close to this scene. "I think the whole earth rejoiced to be rid of these awful men," observed Matthias.

"How can you say that?" answered Abijah. "How do you know what the earth thinks, or even if it thinks?"

"You know what I mean, Abijah. These men were so selfish they only cared about themselves and their power. They were on top of the pile—of other selfish people—the toughest of the tough, took what they wanted, secretly much of the time, and didn't care who they hurt. People followed them because they couldn't stand up to them and they enjoyed conquering others in the world and taking their things, even their women. Nobody dared stand up to these "kings," but we did. Look at them now."

Abijah had no more words to answer.

Joshua commanded to hang each headless king on a tree for all to see, a horrible end, for the scripture says, "he that is hanged on a tree is cursed of God" (Deuteronomy 21:23). What an image! Five men, once so powerful, cruel, and corrupt, now lifeless, motionless, bloody, and dead—cursed! and their merciless schemes and doings brought to a forgettable, meaningless end. Behind that and still latent fifteen hundred years in the future to them, a lone image, Jesus, also cursed, hung on a tree, a place for His death. Still alive but dripping blood, His blood, hour upon miserable hour, He hung there with none to help. On a wooden cross made from a tree, dying like them but unlike them, with the sin of all mankind crushed to His soul. What a difference. He Himself had never sinned, nor did He have rebellion in his heart. By His own choice, by His own voluntary will, and knowing full well the agony of the punishment that would come upon sinful man, He allowed the Father to place those sins upon *Him* and crush *Him* on the cross, like a worm, under their curse. That way, sin, death, and the curse, would be legally dealt with by His Father and by Him—for them. Now anyone who turns to Him to ask HIM to take care of their sins will have Jesus' sacrificed blood applied to his heart, his very self, and be pronounced "clean" by Him at that moment. The heart that turns to Him from the depth of its depravity and discovers God's complete forgiveness will suddenly understand the meaning of words such as "If the Son shall make you free, you are free indeed," or "He that comes to me I will in no wise cast out," because he himself is forgiven (John 8: 36; 6: 37). If Jesus Himself says you are "clean" simply for believing Him, you are clean in a more perfect way than if you tried, with all your heart and strength, to make yourself clean, or to wipe the dirt out of the inner, unseen depths of your heart. God understands our hearts, and only He knows how to cleanse them.

With unfathomable agony of heart the Father turned his back on His beloved Son at the cross, refusing to help Him, as only this death, this acceptance of judgment upon sin, could satisfy the utter righteousness of God's own words who had said, "in the day you eat of it you shall die." Man was so trapped in his own doings that no hope of escape existed—unless God Himself could find a way to satisfy His own law and provide a way to set man free from his self-inflicted punishment and be re-united with Him. With none to help Him, Jesus screamed from deep in the darkness, "My God, my God, why have you forsaken me?" The most hopeless words in all of eternity screamed from that cross. Those forlorn, despairing cries of agony as He took the punishment man deserved would be the cries of every human who rejected Jesus's help, as he was cast to outer darkness after the final judgment, banished forever from the presence of his holy and righteous God. This Jesus who loved them, whose heart longed for them, whom they had completely ignored, whom they ravaged on this tree, was doing this for them, and they barely understood—or cared. When a heartless Roman soldier, hardened to torture and killing, drove a nail through Jesus's hand, fastening him like a filthy rag to the cross, he said, "Father, forgive them, for they know not what they do." The utter cruelty of each of our hearts nailed Him there. The will of man murdered Him there. More powerful than the death they had chosen for themselves, Jesus intervened on their behalf and took that judgment and death for them. The value of His life overpowered the destructive value of every human's sins and wickedness and of Satan's insidious attempt to destroy man and overpower God.

Rahab herself was a witness against them. A wicked person in a perverse nation, she had heard what everyone else heard and concluded that Israel's God was the true God of all the world. Remember Jesus's answer to John the Baptist—to make his own decision based on what he saw and heard? Rahab, in so doing, honored God by simply believing in His existence and power. She had reached out to Him in fear, and God had respect for her and saved her from certain destruction. Rahab still lives with her Lord in heaven. These kings, and all their subjects, had heard what she heard and chosen to ignore it. Today would be the day on which the deepest choices of their hearts would be honored—permanently. That ended the unified campaign of a people set out to defy God and stubbornly promote their own cause. One remembers God's promise to Abraham: "I will bless them that bless you and curse them that curse you" (Genesis 12:3).

The victory was so complete and astounding that, according to Joshua 10: 21, "none moved his tongue against any of the children of Israel." What a statement! God's word from five hundred years earlier came true this day. Israel's march through these pagan nations with surprising victories against overwhelming odds was a statement, a voice, from God Himself to the world, to peoples' hearts. Through all these events the Lord sought to communicate. When Jesus says, "He that has an ear to hear, let him hear," He is reaching to each heart. The day His word connects with one's heart through a doorway as simple as 'belief' in the words of scripture is the day new life begins. The Word is a living seed that, when joined with a hungry human heart, germinates into a beautiful new life, the kind of life that will never end, the life of God himself, more powerful than sin, more powerful than death, and once accepted into one's heart, will never let go.

The story continued, "On that day Joshua took Makkedah and struck it and its king with the edge of the sword. He utterly destroyed them—all the people who were in it. He let none remain. He also did to the king of Makkedah as he had done to the king of Jericho." The Lord, like a consuming fire, was taking the land, land that was His in the first place, that had been taken over by a people holding absolutely no regard for Him. They had brutally taken the land from those who owned it before them, as they had taken it from others who claimed it before them. No one had an absolute right to it, and it belonged to the One who brought it into existence in the first place. It was not really Israel taking the land. It was God Himself and then giving it to whom He chose. Israel, because they listened to Him and believed the things He said, would be the inheritors of the land. The story was about more than just Israel. It was about the final judgment of the whole world to come at a certain time in the future. The inhabitants of Canaan should have been ready, and so should we.

Entering the middle of the land where they had at Gilgal and then taking Jericho, Israel had effectively cut off the inhabitants of the north from those of the south, rendering them unable to help each other. Now they continued farther south and took all the key cities. A certain king of Gezer came up to help Lachish, and Joshua struck him and his people until he "left none remaining." Then Joshua took Eglon and Hebron and all the smaller cities around them. "So Joshua conquered all the land, the mountain country and the south and the lowland and the wilderness slopes, and all their kings. He left none remaining but utterly destroyed all that breathed, as the Lord God of Israel had commanded. None remained to have any claim to the land. They were all dead. God could give it to whomever He wanted. And Joshua conquered them from Jericho clear down to Goshen in Egypt. All these kings and their land Joshua took at one time, because the Lord God of Israel fought for Israel. Then Joshua returned, and all Israel with him, to the camp at Gilgal" (Joshua 10:40), which, as you remember, is where Israel first camped after crossing Jordan. With the kings ruling the southern regions of Canaan destroyed, the farthest reaches of their territories also belonged to Israel. Subjects who had been forced to obey their kings now came under Israel's control, even in the hinterlands where Joshua had not personally gone. What remained next was to "possess" those lands. But first the northern kingdoms of Canaan must be taken.

CHAPTER 39

JERUSHA AND RAHAB CONTINUE THEIR FRIENDSHIP

Women and families lived at the camp during these battles. They often did not know the details of what their men faced from day to day, as news was slow in coming back to them. During the southern and northern campaigns Jerusha and Rahab continued their friendship. Rahab was full of questions, and Jerusha enjoyed her company as she too pondered things deeply. Their conversations encouraged each other. Rahab was learning fast about the unusual (to her) way these Israelites viewed the world. They held a respect for this God who had created life and for the words He had spoken to man, notions non-existent in Jericho. But Jericho was gone and Israel was vibrant and growing. A sense of peace and hope pervaded the camp, even amidst the battles that continued. God's presence, always evident in the fire or smoke in the Tabernacle, reassured them that someone bigger than themselves was guiding them. God's presence was larger than the Tabernacle, revealing itself in the improbable victories Israel experienced in campaign after campaign—which meant that God's statement that "no man would be able to stand against them" came true time after time as they walked into battle.

Today Rahab was troubled and felt compelled to speak her thoughts out loud. She had taught herself to face up to her fears, so finally she said to Jerusha, "If I still break one of God's commandments after I have believed in Him, does that mean I no longer belong to Him? Will God have to discard me? I've tried. I really have."

Jerusha looked at her for a long moment then said, "Why, Rahab, I am surprised at you."

Rahab's discomfort deepened. Was she to be punished by God with destruction after all she had been through? Maybe life truly was as meaningless as it had seemed back in Jericho.

"As observant a person as you are," she continued, "I would think you would have noticed that everyone in this camp fails at keeping God's commandments."

Rahab let out a sigh of relief, not realizing she had been holding her breath. So there was hope for her after all.

"The Lord wants honesty from us—as He is also honest toward us. All who trust in Him will sooner or later pass through many dark places, situations in which they fail and see how unworthy and flawed they really are. Then they secretly worry and become discouraged." She paused and studied Rahab for another long moment. "It is in the path of the Lord's leading for each of His children. Matthias and I had this same question after we met as teenagers in the Red Sea and experienced God's deliverance together. When we later heard His commandments at Mount Sinai it was terrifying. His voice shook the earth—shook the earth!" She remembered the fear. "Worse than the worst thunder we had ever heard. God's holiness filled the moment so completely. We didn't like it. No one could outrun or escape that power."

She paused again, thinking back to that time. "In the months after, as we gradually began to realize that, over and over, we broke His commandments we both grew troubled. Then, the harder we tried, the more we began to break them. Not that we wanted to, but we did anyway. And we knew that lawbreakers were doomed by the wrath of God. We thought we would get better by obeying God's law. Instead we got worse. At least, that is how we saw it because the harder we tried, the more we saw our own failures. It became so bad we got into arguments about it. We did not realize it at the time, but we were actually growing spiritually, starting to see things as God saw them. God had told us how sinful we were, but we were slow to believe it. Now, painfully, we were seeing."

Rahab listened deeply, the storms in her heart calming again, as at the first time she had talked with the spies. Someone else had been through this too. There must be hope.

"You see," continued Jerusha, "when God accepts any one of us as His child He already knows how bad we are. We don't. Oh, we see our wickedness a little bit, enough to make us flee to Him for help. But we do not really comprehend the horrible depth of our own depravity. Over time our understanding grows, and we begin to see ourselves as God sees us—truly wretched. And it is painful. We can get discouraged because we think we are getting worse. In reality we are becoming aware of what we were all along."

"So that is a good thing? Seems backwards to me."

"I think you are understanding something really important," reassured Jerusha. "Relax and keep trusting Him to guide you."

"Where is the hope then?"

"The hope is not in ourselves or in our ability to keep the law perfectly, or in our own goodness. The hope is in God Himself, in His mercy and His ability to cleanse us and lead us in a way pleasing to Him. When we become God's children He is not done with us. It is just a beginning, a new beginning. Now He wants to teach us how to follow Him and walk with Him. We don't do this naturally. Naturally we want to run our own lives and follow our own hearts, but we don't know everything God knows, and we don't see things as He does. At the beginning He gave man dominion over the earth, but God was Lord over all and expected man to have a close relationship with Him and to be dependent on Him for all his needs and for His daily guidance. So He is trying to teach us to follow Him. His part is that He will bless us as we do. Look at our history. When we sought His help He pulled us out of slavery in Egypt. As we followed Him in the wilderness He led us to Jordan."

"Then he led you to Jericho, and you destroyed our city," said Rahab.

"But He saved you, Rahab, and your whole family and many of your friends, and here you are, in a brand new life."

"I know," answered Rahab. "I'm still trying to understand it all."

"Now He is teaching you, like He is teaching us. All these battles we win are because we have finally learned to follow Him. Then He is giving us lands and homes, fields and vineyards we didn't plant. We are sinners and He still does all this for us. I think He is showing the world that the way to blessing is by following Him. Moses didn't learn to follow Him in a day. He told us it took him forty years in Midian to learn. Joshua learned over many years by listening to Moses and following Him. Abraham, Isaac and Jacob all learned after many failures to follow Him."

"So there is hope even for me who still sins?" said Rahab.

"Yes, there is."

Rahab had much to think about . . . but with hope.

CHAPTER 40

THE NORTHERN CAMPAIGN

Word of Israel's conquests of the southern kingdoms reached far and wide. In response the kingdoms to the north of Gilgal, where Joshua initially entered the land, grew nervous and began to organize. Entering Canaan near its center, near Gilgal and Jericho, Israel had effectively driven a wedge between the southern and northern cities, isolating them from each other. News of the defeat of the southern kingdoms had been slow in coming as the cities and their occupants had been utterly destroyed, leaving no one to tell about it. Word gradually spread, however, and when it did, it spread like wildfire in a wind consuming dry prairie grass and racing into the power centers of the northern kingdoms.

Jabin, king of Hazor, sent to all the kings of the north to join together, those of the mountains, the plains, and the valleys. United in fear and hatred for Israel, they amassed into a huge army ready for battle, people as many as the "sand on the seashore," with a swarm of chariots and snorting horses too many to count. This was perhaps the largest force yet to oppose Israel. Intimidating indeed! When believers in the Lord began to understand His power and then to step out by faith following His instructions, Satan's world did not take it lightly. Pharaoh's long ago attempt to deny Israel's "seed," or Savior, entry into the world by killing male babies transformed itself into this even more hateful and larger scale effort to annihilate all Israel once and for all. Israel entered an arena of battle as old as mankind itself, the battle of satanic opposition to God. Satan knew his eventual doom was sealed and, in his maniacal thinking, focused his power on preventing that moment from arriving, including opposing any and all of God's followers, especially the Israelites and the Savior who would arise from their midst.

His first tactic was simply to distract mankind with the affairs of daily life, to lead their attention away from the Lord. It required no effort other than letting people be people. Their own natures would lead them astray. For those not distracted, he then used fear. First it was subtle, such as fear of ridicule by others which, sadly, worked nearly all the time on most believers. For those undeterred, he stirred open opposition to them, including cruelty, by the world he controlled. Scripture called him the "god of this world" and the "prince of the power of the air," positions he attained through deception and manipulation when he fooled Eve into believing his words rather than God's. God so honored their freedom to choose that the outcome of their choice affected the world from then on (2 Corinthians 4: 4; Ephesians 2: 2). Only God Himself had the power to deal with the effect of Satan's sinister designs. In His wisdom He would use Satan's ploy as a way to teach all mankind the destructive effects of Satan's thinking. Joshua's leadership of Israel into Canaan was signaling Satan and the world of a power on the move to overrule all of his influence in the world. There was no stopping Israel's advance, as there would ultimately be no stopping of God's restoration of order in the world. The "god of this world" was no match for the "true God of all creation."

Satan multiplied King Jabin's charisma and powers of persuasion to stir up an unwitting number of warriors to join forces with him and attack Israel. Little did they know that, as they followed this king of Hazor, they were following him to their death. By shutting out God so long they had become blind to their own foolishness and would dutifully perform Satan's bidding, never knowing he controlled them. What remained for them was judgment and destruction. Any human could serve Satan's kingdom without knowing it. As Jesus would later describe Satan, he was "a liar from the beginning and the father of it" (John 8: 44). He was the king of deceivers. When he spoke a lie it was true to his nature. Only Jesus could help man sort through all the layers of deception. "You shall know the truth, and the truth will make you free," said he (John 8: 32).

Israel had faced such overwhelming circumstances before and had seen that when the Lord was leading them, they were successful. Their confidence in the Lord had gradually grown. The Lord knew this giant army would oppose them, even if Joshua himself could not precisely foresee it. He, however, trusted that God would work out the details of whatever they met, and his unshakable trust emboldened his followers. Many of the men who had followed Joshua into battle so many times had come to see what Joshua saw, that the Lord was with them and guiding them, that He would protect them and, beyond that, that "no man would be able to stand against them." It was as simple as that—just believing what He had said and moving ahead based on that. Men walking in the power of God made a truly formidable force, even against Satan, that invisible, powerful foe, and, furthermore, sent a message to the entire world.

As that sizable army assembled, God said to Joshua, "Do not be afraid of them. Tomorrow about this time I will deliver them up all slain before you. You shall hamstring their horses and burn their chariots with fire." Hamstringing their horses might seem cruel. It consisted of cutting a tendon at the back of their rear legs which rendered them incapable of running fast, and thus unsuitable for battle, yet still able to work. This was to keep Israel from copying the pagan nations around them and relying on the strength of horses rather than on the Lord. Repeatedly, Jehovah had promised His people that He would be with them and fight for them against the enemy. He wanted their confidence grounded in Him, not in the strength of horses and sophisticated military implements. Israel had a weakness for copying the nations around them and falling into their idolatrous practices, and the amassing of horses and chariots would be a continual temptation to draw them away from Him and snuff out their ability to shine as a light to the world and point to God's great power to deliver all mankind from Satan and death.

Two of Joshua's warriors, Asher and Raphu, viewed a veritable sea of soldiers stretching from half a mile away to a great distance beyond. Joshua had led them to a broad hill that must have been the highest around, as they could see farther than usual to the distant haze of the gray-blue horizon. The hilltops between almost looked like waves on the ocean. The closest hills rolled gently like grassy meadows and were dotted with thousands of lavender colored wildflowers now in bloom. The scene would have been beautiful were it not for the armies of hostile enemies gathered on the hills beyond. Asher stared in silence at it. And feared. This army had massed to destroy Israel. Under Jabin's leadership they were preparing to move. Hordes of warriors awaited orders, anxious to destroy this obnoxious threat to their kingdoms. Throughout their ranks ugly, pointed spear heads stood one or two feet higher than the men holding them, spear points that might soon be covered with blood—Israel's blood, or so they thought! Soldiers who could be seen in the nearest ranks held swords of all shapes and sizes. Some were short, but when wielded by a skilled swordsman, extremely dangerous. Others were long with both sides honed to a cruelly sharp edge by their sadistic owners, who would spend hours working on those exquisite edges. Some were curved and looked truly terrifying. Even worse were the chariots! Many! Those engines of war could overpower many men on foot who would not move out of the way, trampling them under painfully heavy hooves. Yet Joshua and Israel had arrived completely unexpectedly and would in moments mount their own attack on an enemy caught still trying to organize itself for the battle they planned.

Asher gulped without even realizing it. He did not possess the same confidence held by his leader. As he saw it at this moment, Joshua had done it this time. His bold attacks had taunted the whole land into turning on them. Fear closed in like a dark cloud over his thinking, and he regretted being here facing certain and painful death. He spoke in a tone just loud enough so Raphu, standing next to him, could hear. "Don't you ever get scared?"

"I don't know. I don't think about it."

"What?! How can you not?"

"I just do what I'm told."

"We could all be killed, Raphu," he argued, emotion unconsciously driving his voice louder, "and our families taken as slaves," he added with finality, staring hard at Raphu.

"I told you. I don't think about it. You're worrying yourself sick." A few others looked at them as their words carried farther than they intended. They quit talking. Asher's confidence did not quite match that of his leader. Joshua had long ago learned that it was not his strength fighting this battle.

Asher could not help thinking that this horde of enemy soldiers outnumbered them so badly that they stood no chance against them. It was only a matter of time, and they would all be dead. Panic began to take root in his mind, and as it did so he remembered a time many months back when they had taken a city near the Mediterranean Sea. He and some others had gone swimming in the ocean for the first time in their lives. *Why would I think about that now?* he wondered to himself. *There is real danger here, and I'm thinking about swimming?* Remembering back, he thought about the invisible rip current that had pulled him out to sea without his even realizing what was happening. As he had tried to swim back to shore the current carried him out faster than he could swim, not noticeably fast but just fast enough to gradually carry him farther and farther out. The waves, though not huge, jostled him, seemingly from all directions, and he grew tired struggling against them. As he kicked his feet frantically to stay afloat, his strength began to fail, and for a moment he sank under the water. Only with great effort did he resurface, frantically gasping for breath, now even more fatigued. Those little waves kept splashing in his face, and it was all he could do to keep from choking on water. Feeling too heavy to keep swimming, he began to understand he was about to drown, and he could not help himself. Never in his life had he felt so fatigued and helpless. It seemed that a great weight was pulling him down to crowd the life out of him. A wave splashed in his face again, and he breathed in some water, then choked on it. It was too much. Why did he ever come out here? What a foolish mistake. His short life was finished. He remembered Joshua telling them over and over to call on the Lord for help when in difficult situations. He had done this many times and had experienced his heart calming as he would realize God was helping him. But he had never faced the immediate end of his life so vividly as in this moment. He had long intended, deep in his heart, to be brutally honest with himself before the

Lord, to admit his reluctance to come clean, admit his fear, his sin, his arrogance toward God, but he kept putting it off. Now that reluctance to come clean appeared as the pride and arrogance it truly was. With death overtaking him he began to drop that confidence he had so desperately gripped. Another wave broke over him, pushing him this time toward the bottomless deep. Then he gave up clinging to his life. He gave up trying to be a soldier, trying to be a good husband, trying to be a good father. Those he loved did not know it yet but they were losing him. In his mind his wife and his children slipped from his grip. The mindless, uncaring ocean was taking his life, and he could do nothing about it.

In hopeless desperation, his heart cried out, "Lord help me!" a silent scream straight out of his naked soul. As quickly as he cried out, he realized that if God wanted him dead there was not a thing he could do about it. If God were taking his life it had to be right, and God would take care of the details. Peace overcame his mind and he relaxed. As quickly as that thought came, another realization hit. If God did *not* want him dead, nothing, not even this ocean, could kill him. His destiny was in the Lord's hands, and it was okay either way. Asher, surprisingly, suddenly knew he was safe, no matter what happened, and he grew very brave and calm. Then an arm reached down, or so it seemed, grasped and lifted him with easy strength, and pulled him to the surface and several feet toward shore. Perhaps a large wave had pushed him against the rip tide. Then, as he descended in the valley of the next wave, his feet touched the sandy bottom, and it was closer than he thought! When he had called out to the Lord the help had been instant, as near as his own heartbeat. The only thing that took a long time was for Asher to get to the point at which he would actually ask for help.

The waves still lifted and jostled him, but touching bottom between waves, he knew he was safe. As he looked around he imagined he saw another swimmer farther out in the deep where he had just been, held up by the same strong arm—it was Joshua! Yet Joshua was not panicked nor unnerved as he had been. In the midst of battering waves he looked relaxed. Asher had often been jealous of Joshua and the admiration people exhibited toward him, but now for some reason he saw him in a new light. The waves threatened him too, but he clung to the Lord's steady arm while leading men into battle! This tough, hard leader was almost daily in battles that could have taken his life. Before this, he had spent hours in the Tabernacle and in listening to Moses's words, reading his writings, seeking to know more about this God that had delivered them from Egypt and slavery. As he did so his relationship with the Lord deepened, and God led him into this leadership position. Seeing Joshua now, Asher realized Joshua had been clinging to the Savior himself—just like he was. He had not really striven to be a leader so much as to know his Lord, to grasp the meaning of the words he read in scripture. Because he knew how to listen, he had followed God into this leadership position. How small-minded it had been to be jealous of one who had not even striven to be in that position! Asher saw his jealousy for what it was—pure selfishness and anger at God for choosing Joshua over him. The inconsistencies Asher had observed in Joshua on occasion took on a new light. Sure, Joshua had failings, and yet God had used him in a remarkable way, even though he was not perfect. God was not looking for human ability nor for perfection so much as for "truth in the inward parts," the willingness to be bone honest with oneself, to admit his failures, mixed with a willingness to let God lead him (Psalm 51: 6).

Man has an extremely difficult time doing that. Inner honesty, coupled with a willingness to take God's words seriously and then to follow them, is the key. The willingness to accept God's forgiveness and step out by faith, faith that he is forgiven, faith that God will keep his promise and be with him is the key. God even goes so far as to say He does not "desire sacrifice nor burnt offerings," a puzzling statement from One who gave so many directions about how to offer various types of sacrifices. Yet that is exactly what he had said. Throughout scripture God taught that, even when one offers a sacrifice, what He is looking for is the attitude in one's heart. "The sacrifices of God are a broken spirit. A broken and a contrite heart he will not despise" (Psalm 51: 16-17; Hebrews 10). What man *does* is not as important as what man *thinks* in his heart. Thought gives birth to action. Joshua was not standing on his own strength nor pining over his weaknesses. He was clinging to, no, resting in, God's power to give him life and to take care of him moment by moment, like Jacob so long ago when he finally gave in to God at the wrestling match. How long had it taken Joshua to learn that? Years, but with God as his teacher he had truly learned, and it had served him in many capacities. Now well over eighty years old, he had been a great leader for a long time, and his example had led countless others to be like him.

The memory of the Lord's instant help would live in Asher's memory from that day on. When he was totally without hope and had called out in desperate need, God's help flooded in, and he knew for certain that God had been with him all along, though he had been unable to realize that. Years later King David, who traveled through many similarly terrifying, life-threatening circumstances on the way to the throne, wrote: "He sent from above, He took me, He drew me out of many waters. He delivered me from my strong enemy and from them which hated me, for they were too strong for me. He brought me forth also into a large place . . . " (Psalm 18: 16-19). God patiently waited until Asher truly gave up. Until then he had been working so hard on his own plan to please God that he could not see the Lord's love as simply as a child sees. All his efforts at coming to God his own way, at being in charge of his own life, having failed, he had given up. Abandoning his own stubborn efforts, he had reached out to God, and there he was. The great "I am." So close and yet so hard to see. Most humans have trouble accepting God's help because they are too busy trying to please God with their own efforts. Asher finally gave up, and the God he had been striving to serve suddenly moved, as close as the air, and plucked him from destruction.

He saw his friends in the shallow water closer to shore splashing about happily, oblivious to the death he had just escaped. A few more strokes with his tired arms pulled him to water shallow enough for him to stand easily. The struggle had left him fatigued, and he stood still several minutes to catch his breath and slow his breathing before rejoining his friends. As he reached them Raphu cautioned, "You shouldn't go out so deep. You could drown."

"Right," was all he said in his imagination as he gradually became aware that his thoughts had taken him for a ride. Returning to reality, he saw the hills beyond covered with enemy armies. Somehow the thought of them no longer terrified him. God Himself had drawn him out of the waves, and would take care of Israel in this predicament. It was God's battle, and he was in the Lord's army. He saw what Joshua had long seen—the Lord's supreme power. Now in the midst of the most frightful sight he had ever experienced he had found peace and could face the enemy confidently. He could walk boldly with Joshua. That day he became a warrior who would encourage many others. As he looked around at his fellow warriors he saw the same fear he had just lost on so many faces. So did Joshua. With a powerful and somehow reassuring voice he said, "Remember, men, what the Lord told us when we began to take this Promised Land. 'Be not afraid. I am with you whithersoever you go. No man will be able to stand against you. Every place the sole of your foot treads upon I have given you.'" Joshua's fearless voice and powerful presence drove away the fears of a great many of those warriors about to enter this battle. Asher understood Joshua's confidence and had not really needed his encouragement. Today he had become one who understood his place before the Lord and, along with Joshua, could encourage and lead other warriors. Near the end of the Book of Joshua (Joshua 24: 31) appear these words: "And Israel served the Lord all the days of Joshua, and all the days of the elders that overlived Joshua, and which had known all thc works of the Lord, that he had done for Israel." Asher and so many others like him were these men.

So Israel, led by Joshua, came upon this overwhelming force suddenly, and the Lord delivered them into their hand, truly a miracle. Many of the enemy ran. Often the victors would let them go, knowing the battle was won. Joshua's armies, however, per the Lord's instructions, chased and destroyed them, one by one, "until they left them none remaining." Joshua did not want them finding refuge in other cities and stirring up more opposition to Israel. Opposing Israel came with a price, an extreme price, and his action ensured that the message was clear. More happened here than Israel knew. Ages ago Satan had been thrown out of heaven for attempting to overthrow God. Angry with God, he sought to hurt him, but being banned from heaven, he could not. His next best move was to hurt something God cherished—which was man—hence his surreptitious sneak attack by deception on Eve in Eden. It was not a direct physical attack. It was worse. He would entice Eve to use her own free will to disobey God's words. That way God would have to punish Eve, His cherished creation, Himself. That would hurt her—and God—far worse than physically destroying her. Or so Satan thought. God would have to keep His word. The plan was evil almost beyond belief. It brought havoc, misery and death into God's world, in Satan's twisted mind a masterful victory. God from His throne in heaven watched—as he did always. Satan's "victory" would be monumental but only temporary. God's wisdom far surpassed that of Satan, and His deep understanding could foresee Satan's maneuvering and devious doings to demonstrate to man and to Satan the true nature and destructiveness of his wicked thinking and how its presence would bring misery to all it touched. The serpent would indeed "bite the heel" of the Savior, "the Seed who would come." But that "Seed" would "crush the head of the serpent," destroying him, his power and his influence. Evil would not win.

God entered the battle, and though unseen by the world, brought victory to those who, of their own free will, would follow His words. Joshua's astounding victories in Canaan, one of Satan's strongholds, was a taste of God's power and of greater victories to come, an early step in the history of mankind's walk through this world. It was God taking back His world and blessing the people Satan sought to destroy.

Centuries later those rolling hills presently covered with armed soldiers would again be silent and still, dotted with colorful wildflowers amongst lush green grass and serene beauty, offering no hint of the horrible carnage and life and death battles that one day played out there.

Joshua's tactic of sudden and swift attack was later used by other great world leaders like Alexander the Great, Napoleon, and even despots like Hitler with his "blitzkrieg," or "lightning warfare." Then Joshua turned back, took Hazor and smote its king, whom he had bypassed while chasing the other armies. Hazor "had been the head of all those kingdoms" which had organized against Joshua. They "smote all the souls in the city with the edge of the sword, utterly destroying them. There were not any left to breathe. Then he burnt Hazor with fire." Not one city stood up to Joshua, and Israel gradually grew wealthier and wealthier with the spoil and cattle they took. Archaeologists today have dug deep into the ruins of Hazor and found evidence of total destruction and fire. The Lord's promise to Joshua that "every place that the sole of your foot shall tread upon have I given you" was coming true daily. "No man shall be able to stand before you all the days of your life. As I was with Moses, so I will be with you. I will not fail you, nor forsake you. Be strong and of good courage, for to this people shall you divide for an inheritance the land, which I swore to their fathers to give them" (Joshua 1: 3-6). As Joshua believed these words and acted upon them, he vanquished forces far superior in strength to his army. He symbolized Jesus leading His children through all ages in this world. True believers willing to learn and follow God's word would be victorious, as was Joshua. His true strength was not his human wisdom nor his physical strength. It was his humility to let the Lord lead him. There have been many like him throughout the centuries, but God chose to record and preserve his story for our encouragement and learning (Romans 15: 4).

Scripture says, "Joshua made war a long time with all those kings. There was not a city that made peace with Israel, save the Hivites, the inhabitants of Gibeon. All the rest they took in battle. So Joshua took the whole land and would give it for an inheritance to Israel, and the land "rested from war."

Chapter twelve of Joshua lists, by name, thirty-one kings that Israel conquered. Each of these controlled many cites falling under his dominion. Such a long list does not necessarily make interesting reading, but God recorded it anyhow. It reveals His interest in and knowledge of man's doings, as Jesus would, much later in time, reiterate, saying, "even the very hairs of your head are numbered," and "are not two sparrows sold for a farthing, and one of them shall not fall to the ground without your father [knowing]. Fear not, therefore. You are of more value than many sparrows" (Matthew 10: 29-31; the farthing was the second smallest coin, worth about a quarter cent of today's money. The "mite" was the smallest, worth half a farthing.). Record of these kings and locations was mostly lost to man over time, but not to God. In more recent times historians and archaeologists searching through buried rubble in ancient civilization sites have found artifacts and records with city names bearing witness to many of these exact areas and peoples, verifying the accuracy of ancient scriptures.

Details of individual battles were recorded in the southern kingdom battles, and the principles for winning remained the same, so are not repeated in these northern campaign accounts, even though Israel was a long time making war. The book of Joshua then moves on to detailing how the land was divided among the twelve tribes. Joshua 11:16 declares that "Joshua took all that land, the hills and all the south country, and all the land of Goshen (in Egypt), and the valley and the plain, and the mountain of Israel and the valley of the same."

CHAPTER 41

DIVIDING THE LAND

(Joshua 13-19)

As we have seen, the northern campaign ended in chapter eleven with, "So Joshua took the whole land and would give it for an inheritance to Israel, and the land rested from war." Deliverance from Egypt forty years earlier was only part of the plan for Israel. The plan continued on to "taking" the land God had prepared for them and then further to "possessing" it, that is, living in and enjoying it. Chapter twelve lists, by name and territory, thirty-one kings conquered by Joshua. Chapter 13 begins with, "Now Joshua was old and stricken in years. And the Lord said to him, 'You are old and stricken in years, and there remains yet very much land to be possessed.' Chapter eleven stated that Joshua had "taken all the land." If he had taken all the land, how could there remain much land to be possessed? Do not those statements contradict each other? The explanation lies in the distinction between the words "taking" and "possessing," a distinction that also sets forth an important principle about living the Christian life. Joshua "took" the land by conquering the kings that ruled it. Without setting foot on every square foot of land, he effectively took control of all the territory its kings had controlled, though in the smaller towns the original inhabitants remained. Once the top leader of a land had been overpowered and removed, it was understood that the conqueror now held power over all the previous king had controlled. Joshua left it to the individual tribes and families, to whom he would later give each portion of the land, to conquer and possess the remaining territories and their inhabitants. He had been their example of how to "walk by faith," that is, to trust God to be with them as they moved ahead trusting Him. They could now, on their own, take territory for themselves. It would delight God to empower them as he watched individuals trust Him. Joshua's victories were an example to all Israel and the rest of the world, even to future generations, of God's willingness to guide and empower all who would follow Him. Victories over bondage and slavery, over evil and death had begun under Moses in Egypt. Now, having been delivered from that, God continued to lead by guiding them to new blessings and the inheritance he had prepared for each of them.

Not all Israelites took their rightful possessions, however. Many feared and remained content to bask in the prosperity Joshua had gained them. Israel never possessed all the land and blessings God would have given them had they continued to "walk by faith." They inhabited about thirty thousand square miles, but what God gave them was three hundred thousand square miles. One day it will all be theirs.

As Joshua marched through Canaan destroying every opposing force, he pictured Christ's power, first at the cross and now in Israel's new freedom, to take what God had prepared for them. Finally, at Christ's second coming, he will take back control (which the first two humans had unwittingly relinquished to Satan) over the earth and all its inhabitants.

After defeating both the southern and northern kingdoms of Canaan, Joshua began dividing the land as the rightful inheritance of the twelve tribes of Israel. Conquering kings that ruled vast areas and breaking the back of their power opened the way for the Israelites to enter and "possess" the rest of the land. The Promised Land does not represent heaven, as many have erroneously believed. Heaven is a place in which no evil nor conflict will exist, a place prepared as the final home for every believer. The Promised Land represents the life of the believer in this world and the victory possible to those who would dare trust God's power. In this lifetime, a world still dominated and influenced by Satan existed, the evil master who stubbornly clings to his influence even though he knows Christ has defeated every ounce of his strength at the cross. Living on "borrowed time," he persists in trying to convince the world he will prevail—one more of his deceptions. He will not prevail. At a time known to God, Christ will return and remove Satan from this last vestige of his influence. Believers ultimately learn that Christ cannot be eternally harmed by Satan. Death, the worst thing he could foist upon a child of God, could only be done with God's permission and would only serve to usher one into God's presence. As the Savior had defeated Satan at the cross, so Joshua, trusting in God's power, defeated the kings that temporarily ruled in the Promised Land. His victories demonstrated how we humans, back then and today, can use the Lord's power on a day to day basis. Now the other Israelite believers could continue to walk in that power as they would move in and possess the lands not physically touched by Joshua.

Those areas were still inhabited by Canaanites, and the Israelites would have to displace them, as Joshua had, by letting the Lord lead them. It was their opportunity to make conquests through their own by faith. They would be rewarded with the material blessings of possessing the land and all its crops and wealth. The enemy was gone. The Canaanite nations occupying this land owned by God had been warned for several generations to return to God and a right relationship with Him (four hundred fifty years, according to scripture), or judgment would most certainly fall on them. They had continually ignored God, shut out His words. Now He brought Israel in as judgment, as He had promised. Israel would possess fields of crops and vineyards planted by others. They would own homes built by others. They would own all the possessions left behind, including gold, silver, jewels, tools, cattle and all other forms of wealth left behind by those conquered.

The Lord does things "decently and in order" (1 Corinthians 14: 40), and now He would divide the land in a manner that allotted a portion, with recorded boundaries, to each tribe and then to each family within the tribe. Thus the twelve tribes descended from the Patriarch Jacob each inherited a large, defined portion of land. The boundaries, which they all accepted, ensured each one's right to that land. As God had given and described those boundaries, they were expected to honor them and each other's rights to possess them.

Each tribe came before Joshua and lots were thrown to award these portions to each. Of the twelve tribes of Israel, one had been chosen (Levi) to perform the priestly duties, including setting up and maintaining the Tabernacle, for the nation. Rather than a large portion of land to possess, they were to be given small portions within the holdings of each of the other eleven tribes to live in and set their tents. Thus the Levites' influence was spread throughout the nation. To fill the unused twelfth portion the tribe of Joseph was given two portions of land, one for each of his children, Ephraim and Manasseh. When these sons of Joseph came to Joshua and claimed that, since they were so many, they needed more land Joshua answered, "If you are a great people take Mount Ephraim, its wooded hills and the valley below, and it will be yours" (Joshua 17: 14-18). In so doing he challenged them to step out by faith, as he had done, and let God give them their own victory.

Then Joshua challenged all the tribes, "How long are you slack to go to possess the land which the Lord God of your fathers has given you" (Joshua 18: 3)? Many of the Israelites did not realize the power the Lord had given them individually to claim and possess their land. Those too fearful to step out by faith missed enormous blessings God would have given them.

They were accustomed to following Joshua and yet slow to pick up on the fact God was willing to empower each of them as He had Joshua. Many took their lands, but not all. Though they had followed Joshua through so many battles, and been successful, they were slow to pick up on the fact the Lord would guide them individually the same as he had guided Joshua. All it took was a willingness to take God's promises seriously, believe them, and act on them. Some did. Some did not. God gave them (being in the "image of God') the freedom to make that choice and then to let it play out. Joshua's conquests during his years of leadership set the pattern for the other believers. He had conquered in his years the major power centers in the land God gave them, paving the way for others to continue into the less powerful cities and territories. God through history right up to today promised so much more than man ever took. Israel was afraid to attack and drive out the inhabitants. Because those pagans remained in Israel's midst and mingled with them, they eventually became a snare to Israel and made constant trouble.

When they had made an end of dividing the land they let Joshua, being of the tribe of Ephraim, choose a portion of land in their inheritance. He chose Timnath-serah in Mount Ephraim, a place barren and not all that desirable. This man who made it possible for all Israel to inherit the land God had long before promised did not choose the best of the land for himself. In fact, travelers who have been there have said the land is surprisingly undesirable. His choice reflected his inner contentment. Earthly blessings were wonderful but did not provide the same comfort to his heart as he obtained from knowing the Lord was with him at all times and would take care of him better than he could take care of himself. The same is true of many mature believers throughout history.

Then Joshua called the tribes of Reuben, Gad, and half of the tribe of Manasseh. Before coming into the Promised Land they had asked for land on the east side of Jordan. God allowed that but told them they would still have to fight alongside the other tribes as they took Canaan. Now that the battles were over, Joshua blessed them and told them to return to their tents and to their families.

CHAPTER 42

CALEB

While Joshua was dividing up the land, the tribe of Judah came to him for their portion. Caleb was of that tribe and spoke to Joshua. He, if we will remember, was introduced to us over forty years earlier the first time God brought Israel to the edge of the Promised Land. Moses had sent twelve spies to view the land and bring him a report. Only two of those spies encouraged Moses to go in, Joshua and Caleb. The other ten saw the task as too dangerous, forgetting the miracles they had seen in Egypt two years earlier when the Lord delivered them from Pharaoh's merciless grip and the miracles right up to the present moment in the wilderness as the Lord daily nourished and protected them. Many believers do that today. They trust the Lord to save them for eternity and to make a place in heaven for them, but they will not trust him to guide them and to provide for their needs today.

Here are set forth two different types of believers, some that become children of God but never grow beyond spiritual infancy, and some that grow to maturity and bear fruit for their Lord. 1 Peter 2: 2 encouraged all believers "as newborn babes," to "desire the sincere milk of the Word, that you may grow thereby." As the physical body needs food to grow, so does the spiritual. As mother's milk contains everything a newborn babe needs to grow, so the Word of God contains just the right nourishment a newly born child of God needs. As he grows, the mother adds in more foods. As the believer grows he will draw more nutrition beyond milk from the Word. We saw this in Joshua when as a younger man he spent as much time as possible in the Tabernacle learning to know the Lord better. Caleb too had taken God's Word to heart, and it made him strong.

Even when a believer fails, the Lord will lift him up and carry him along. Consider Joshua at the battle at Ai after the astonishing Jericho victory. He met failure and loss of thirty-six warriors' lives. When he fell on his face and prayed, asking God why He had brought them over Jordan to now be destroyed by the enemy, God told him to get up and quit crying. "Israel has sinned." No one even knew it. They had lost sight of their truly helpless and sinful condition. To Joshua's heart cry "I thought you were leading us," God as good as said, "I was, but you were not following me." Joshua and Israel, in their joy over the victory at Jericho, took their eyes off the Lord and carried on as though they could defeat Ai all by themselves. Joshua quickly saw and dealt with the situation. Caleb appears to have the same understanding of the Lord that Joshua did. They both knew how to get back on track with the Lord and were humble enough to accept the Lord's forgiveness rather than trying to "earn" it.

The ten spies' fear slithered insidiously into the minds of the people who heard their stories. Admitting the land was lush and very fruitful, they cautioned that the cities were walled and formidable. Moreover there were "giants" in the land, and attempting to take it from them would be suicide. "Let a bear robbed of her whelps meet a man, rather than a fool in his folly," asserts Proverbs 17: 12. In this case these men who should have known better followed their own fears rather than the Lord's leading, and influenced an entire nation to take the wrong path. Playing the fool, they convinced Israel to do the same and traded in certain blessing for thirty-eight more years of wandering and deprivation. God told them that, since they would not follow Him, they could spend the rest of their days wandering in the wilderness, eventually dying there, fruitless branches of a tree all set to bear fruit. God did not want that for them, but that was their choice. Believers today face the same choice: believe God, follow His advice, and live a spiritually fruitful life, or wander aimlessly in one's own fantasies, wasting the precious years God gave each person.

God would lead their children, whom they claimed to be protecting, into the land. He would also remember the faith of Joshua and Caleb. We have seen what became of Joshua. Now Caleb came and rehearsed to Joshua what had transpired so long ago. "You know the thing that the

Lord said to Moses the man of God concerning me and you in Kadesh-Barnea. Forty years old was I when Moses sent us from Kadesh-Barnea to spy out the land, and I brought him word as it was in my heart. Nevertheless my brethren that went up with me made the heart of the people melt, but I wholly followed the Lord my God. And God swore on that day, saying, 'Surely the land on which your feet have trod shall be your inheritance, and your children's forever, because you have wholly followed the Lord.' And now, behold, the Lord has kept me alive these forty-five years . . . and today I am eighty-five years old, and as yet I am as strong this day as I was in the day that Moses sent me. As my strength was then, so is my strength now, for war, both to go out and to come in. Wherefore give me this mountain that the Lord mentioned that day. You and I both knew that the Anakims (giants) were there and that the cities were great and fortified. If the Lord will be with me, then I shall be able to drive them out, as the Lord said" (Joshua 14).

There have been many who believed in the Lord early in their lives and continued to follow Him the rest of their years. Joshua and Caleb were like that. There have also been many believers who followed the Lord for a while and then drifted away. Even King Solomon, the wisest man (according to Jesus) who ever lived, drifted away in his later years. Scripture is full of surprises. Solomon is with his Lord in heaven today not because he was so wise, or so exceedingly rich, but because at some point in his life he believed God's word and accepted His salvation. His personal failures did not alter God's promises to him.

Caleb was basically a happy man and was even content with the Lord's care in the years enduring the hardships of the wilderness. While his compatriots complained and grew weary, Caleb flourished. He was upset about one thing, though—that Israel had not dared to trust the Lord to guide them into the Promised Land the first time he led them there. He saw the cloud at the Tabernacle leading them each day and knew it signaled the Lord's presence with them. He marveled at the fact they could all see the cloud yet appeared not to understand God's presence was with them. He saw how the Lord provided them food day after day and how that food kept them healthy and strong. It could be said each day was a feast to Caleb and he was very happy to know the Lord Himself had accepted him and was guiding him. Others of his generation complained about the heat and lack of certain foods to which they were accustomed in Egypt. They grew old and weary from their struggles. Their skin wrinkled, their muscles weakened, and they succumbed to the desert. Caleb enjoyed the fact God was guiding them and remained happy, engaging in and enjoying the enthusiasm of the younger generation. In time only the children and he and Joshua survived this journey through the wilderness. Caleb saw how remarkably God had used Joshua to lead Israel into that land that they could have entered so many years ago. He willingly joined the effort to take Canaan.

The writer of Proverbs five hundred years later put into words what those complaining Israelites and the believing Caleb and Joshua experienced. "All the days of the afflicted are evil: but he that is of a merry heart has a continual feast" (Proverbs 15:15). Caleb was at peace in his daily life, had learned early to take the Word seriously, and walk in it. It could be said he was victorious. He travelled the wilderness differently than the rest of Israel, enjoying and reveling in the Lord's guidance. What was wearying and disappointing to the others he met with an understanding that God was guiding and would always provide for him. While they wore out, he prospered and remained in tune with life. "You prepare a table for me in the presence of my enemies. You anoint my head with oil, and my cup runs over" (Psalm 23: 5). That was Caleb. And at age eighty-five he made another great conquest in Hebron.

CHAPTER 43

THE TEST OF PROSPERITY

Joshua reminded the Israelites "God gave you olive groves and vineyards you did not plant, houses you did not build, conquest in all those battles. Now you are prospering and enjoying the blessings."

Then he warned them not to marry the Amorites, nor inquire about their temples, nor "how they worshipped"—because Israel had displayed a tendency to be waylaid by such distractions, which would draw them away from the Lord who gave the blessings in the first place. Ironic—the blessings ruin us. The heart of man is off balance, is inordinately drawn to the world. Prosperity turns out to be a very hard test, and Joshua warns about that. "Follow your heart" does not work, is not good advice. Why? "The heart of man is deceitful above all things and desperately wicked. Who can know it" (Jeremiah 17:9)? "Follow your heart" works in one respect, that of being true to God's word you have hid in your heart. How can we do right? By looking to the Lord and seeking His guidance, recognizing our propensity to wander and go astray—like silly sheep. They need a shepherd, and so do we. God can lead us through adversity and through prosperity—but only when we look to Him and ask to be led.

Prosperity lulls us into complacency. Earthly blessings tempt us to take our eyes off the Lord and get sidetracked. That little excursion our flesh says "will only last a minute" can last a lifetime. Prosperity distracted many Israelites from the Lord but not all of them. Joshua and his chief warriors learned in their lifetimes to enjoy God's blessings without being pulled away from him. The Apostle Paul, many years after he had been converted, wrote ". . . for I have learned in whatsoever state

I am therewith to be content. I know both how to be abased, and I know how to abound. Everywhere and in all things I am instructed both to be full and to be hungry, both to abound and to suffer need" (Philippians 4: 11-12). He put in words what Joshua lived as he too lived in victory in this world. Much of Paul's time was spent in prison, yet he was fruitful and prosperous. Many of God's children have lived without wealth (some of the prophets and Jesus's mother, Mary). Others have lived with great wealth, as Abraham, Isaac, and Jacob and King David, Daniel and Esther, without getting drawn away from God by the wealth.

The "Prosperity Gospel" today appeals to huge crowds because while paying lip service to God's word, it offers happy answers, appeals to the better parts of man's nature to think positively and always look for the good. But it is not the "whole counsel of God." It leaves out the part about coming judgment, about Jesus's second coming to overpower evil and destroy those opposed to Him, His people Israel, and all true believers. It ignores Jesus's frequent warnings about the "lake of fire prepared for the devil and his angels and those who follow them." It ignores His reference to "outer darkness" where no light is and no hope of escape exists.

Certainly God wants prosperity for His people. Many of His prominent followers, Abraham, Isaac, Jacob and Joseph, King David, King Solomon and countless others, were wealthy, successful and fulfilled. But just as many were persecuted, poor, imprisoned and beheaded, like John the Baptist and many of the prophets and many believers today in various parts of the world. Israelites are still His people, and though so many of them have been scoundrels and unbelievers themselves (like Jacob lived much of his life), they will be restored to Him in the future and take their proper role as those who honor, glorify, and point to God and His Son Jesus, the Messiah, the Messiah they missed and crucified. Remember the words "His own received Him not, but as many as received Him to them He gave the power to become the sons of God?" After Israel "nationally" rejected Jesus, God set them aside temporarily to reach out to the rest of the world. But in the near future they will come to their senses and honor Him in preparation for His glorious return. The words God spoke to Abraham are still true: "I will bless them that bless you, and curse him that curses you, and in you shall all nations of the world be blessed." Consider Adolph Hitler and all those he deceived. How well did that go for them?

When Jesus returns He will set up true prosperity. Remember His warning: "Enter by the narrow gate; for wide is the gate and **broad is the way that leads to destruction**, and there are many who go in by it" (Matthew 7:13). Many scoff at the scriptural record of God's judgment and the flood in Noah's day. The obliteration of all sign of the ancient cities and the seashells on mountaintops tell us to re-think that.

CHAPTER 44

JOSHUA'S LAST ADVICE

(Joshua 23-24)

Matthias and Jerusha sat near the front of the gathering assembled to hear what could be the last public words Joshua spoke to his fellow Israelites. A range of emotions swept back and forth through their hearts. This man had led them through a string of improbable victories rarely seen in this world. They had grown to cherish his leadership and presence with them.

"We're all getting older aren't we, Matthias?" whispered Jerusha to her husband. "I remember when we met in that completely unexpected place, the midst of the Red Sea, at the bottom! You just magically appeared at my side. Who would ever believe that chance beginning would change our lives?"

"It wasn't all magical, Jerusha. I maneuvered myself into that position. Even from far to the side of you in the midst of the crowd, you caught my eye. First time that ever happened to me. You were the magical one." The crowd suddenly hushed as Joshua lifted his eyes to speak to them.

Joshua, the man whose arms and calloused hands had wielded sword and spear in battle so many days of his life, was one hundred and ten years old and nearing the end of his days on earth, "going the way of all flesh," as he put it. The Lord had given Israel rest from all the enemies they had subdued in battle and now they possessed much, but not all, of the land they had conquered. Today he had called for all Israel, their elders and leaders, judges and officers, and spoke to them with surprising clarity but also with slight weakness and shakiness of age beginning to reveal itself in his voice. "I am old and stricken in age. You have seen all that the

Lord your God has done to these nations because of you. You fought the battles, but, as you yourselves saw and remember, the Lord fought for you and gave you victories, often when you had no chance of defeating a larger foe. Those foes perished, and you are still here. Then I divided by lot these nations as an inheritance for each of your tribes, from Jordan all the way to the Mediterranean Sea to the west. We conquered every large city and all the kings that ruled them and the vast surrounding areas with their villages and small towns. We never set foot in many of those smaller towns, but we conquered the kings that ruled them. You saw how I led you to step out by faith in the Lord's promises and then saw for yourselves how He helped. Now you need to step out on your own after I am gone and possess the rest of this land whose kings we conquered. The Lord will be with you as He was with Moses and with me."

He paused to let the words, the challenge, sink in, looking from face to face at the leaders gathered before him. The vast crowds behind strained to get a look at this victorious warrior whom most of them had heard much about but only seen from a vast distance. Their leaders and officers would later convey his words to those too distant to hear clearly. Joshua's reputation had made him larger than life in their imaginations. Those who had pushed close enough saw a man like them, of average size, now showing wrinkles of age, but whom they knew to possess a warrior's heart. They knew of his steely resolve to follow his decisions and see them through to the end. He was a man careful in his decisions who carried out what he purposed to do. Though a man of action, he had developed a habit of bringing his thoughts before the Lord before he acted. In the quiet moments when no one was around he would set his thoughts out before the Lord and ask for His guidance, admitting that he needed help, that he could not see as clearly as could the Lord who viewed life from a far higher viewpoint, a viewpoint rooted in eternity. As Joshua spoke he studied the listeners, as was his manner, looking into their faces and connecting with them. His years of walking with them and with the Lord had given him the Lord's love for people. He had observed that the Lord loved each of those under His leadership, and it dawned on him that, if he loved the Lord, he himself should be concerned about the people his Lord loved.

Those he met perceived this quality in Joshua, and it formed a connection that resulted in a willingness to follow him. Joshua had a sense of existing in the Lord's presence that guided him, and people in turn felt safe in his presence and in following his advice. King David five hundred years later exhibited this same quality (likely learned from studying about Joshua) of "bending the peoples' will to his."

With their attention fixed on him he continued, "I was forty years old when I came out of Egypt." By now, only those seventy years and older had been born in Egypt. Younger ones had been born in the wilderness or in this Promised Land. "I and my generation came through the Red Sea when the Lord opened a path through its depths. He did that miracle once, and the whole world knew about it. The sea meant death to all not careful to respect it. It would have killed anyone walking through its depths unprotected. It killed the entire Egyptian army when they assayed to follow us. We saw the sea close over them and destroy them. A few of their dead bodies eventually washed up on shore. Some of you can remember. Right? Do you also remember God's words to Abraham? 'I will bless them that bless you and curse them that curse you.' Remember Pharaoh drowned Israel's boy babies and would have drowned Moses had his parents not dared trust the Lord. Do you think God honored their faith? You would not be here today and likely would not even be alive were it not for Moses's parents—because Moses would not have been. Can you remember the freedom we felt at that moment after the sea closed over that army?"

Another pause. "The Lord did a similar thing one other time, centuries earlier, when He brought Noah and his family safely through the huge flood in which all others perished. One of the most sobering events in the history of the world. Neither of those miracles will ever be repeated. God promised. They speak to those who will hear. Both times those events meant God had the power to do what He said. He judged the whole earth all at once, precisely as He had foretold—all, that is, except those who accepted His invitation to the safety of the ark. The judgment was so complete that all evidence of the vast cities and the huge population of that ancient civilization was completely obliterated, not a trace, no sign of it. All that remained was the telling of it by those who had been in the ark, and every now and then someone finding things buried in the earth from that great upheaval.

"The next forty years we followed Moses in the wilderness. My generation, and many of you, were present at Sinai and the giving of the law and of the instructions for the Tabernacle. In fact I went part way up the mountain with Moses. We all experienced the Lord's leading by the cloud during the day and the pillar of fire by night. Following that, Amalek attacked us in the wilderness, and Moses put me in charge of leading the fight against him. Our whole nation came close to being destroyed that day. None of us would be here now if we had lost that battle. Moses and Aaron prayed for us throughout the battle, and that was how we won."

The crowd was caught up in the story. They all knew it, but to hear it told by the one who had led the fight and nearly lost his life so many times during that battle added a special touch. The more they heard, the more miraculous their presence in the Promised Land appeared to be. "Then God led us to Kadesh-Barnea to bring us in here, two years after Egypt. The people would not come. They were afraid! Caleb and I could not believe it. After the miraculous deliverance from Egypt and all this time caring for us in the wilderness, they would not trust God! The Lord honored their decision and told them that because they would not trust Him they could wander in the wilderness until they all died. Then the younger generation, you, he brought in and here you are—safe and alive, with fruitful farms and vineyards you did not plant! We could have come here thirty-eight years earlier, but your fathers would not come. Most did not really believe God would keep His word, even though He had demonstrated his faithfulness over and over. As you can see today . . . everything He promised, He did! Not one thing has failed.

"Now that we are here, be very courageous to keep and do all that is written in the book of the law of Moses, that you turn not aside to the left or to the right, that you come not among these nations that remain among you. Make no mention of the name of their gods, nor swear by them, nor serve them, nor bow yourselves to them. You have seen that the Lord has driven out from before you great and strong nations, and no one has been able to stand before you to this day. You know because you have seen it. Remember what you have learned. Trusting the Lord to keep His word and fight your battles was what gave you success." As he spoke the intensity of his voice grew. He stood straight and tall, as though confident to meet any challenge. His words took on an edge that meant certainty and power. He may not have been as strong as in his younger years, but physical strength was not his true power anyhow. His power was the confidence he had from trusting the Lord just like his friend, Caleb, who at age eighty-five conquered the inhabitants of Hebron and took that land because the Lord said he would give it to him. Joshua knew the people would be tempted in so many ways, just as he had been. But there was always a way to escape that and find the Lord's help. The spiritual forces arrayed against them were real and cruel. As he spoke, the danger of those battles flooded back into his mind. He remembered swinging his sword and seeing the enemy go down. He had been willing to die, knowing it was right to trust the Lord, knowing He would still take care of him even in death. The people saw a powerful man stand before them.

"If you make agreements with these people that remain among you and make marriages with them, the Lord will no more drive them out from before you. Instead they will be snares and traps for you until you perish from off this land. When you follow the Lord you will be different, and the world will not like you. But who won in Canaan, the people who hated you—or you? Don't forget that." Joshua looked at them, wondering. Would they be mindful that their strength lay in staying close to the Lord?

Then Joshua challenged all the tribes, "How long are you slack to go to possess the land which the Lord God of your fathers has given you" (Joshua 18: 3)? Many of the Israelites did not realize the power the Lord had given them individually to claim and possess their land. Those too fearful to step out by faith missed enormous blessings God would have given them.

They were accustomed to following Joshua and yet slow to pick up on the fact God was willing to empower each of them as he had Joshua. Many took their lands, but not all. They were afraid to attack and drive out the inhabitants. In choosing to let them stay, they eventually became a snare to those Israelites and made constant trouble.

"I am going the way of all the earth, and you know in your hearts and in your souls that not one thing has failed of all the good things the Lord God promised you. All are come to pass." Then he reminded them what the Lord had earlier done. "You went over Jordan and came into Jericho. They fought against you, the Amorites, the Perizzites, the Canaanites, the Hittites and the Girgashites, the Hivites and the Jebusites, and He delivered them into your hand. In some cases He sent hornets before you, which drove people out before you even got there! Not with your sword or with your bow were the victories really won. You had to enter the fight, but God gave you the victory, gave you a land for which you did not labor, and cities that you did not build. He gave you vineyards and olive yards you did not plant, from which you eat."

Then Joshua challenged, with all the intensity he could muster, "Choose this day whom you will serve, whether the gods which your ancestors served on the other side of the Euphrates, or the gods of the Amorites in whose land you dwell. As for me and my house, we will serve the Lord." The people knew this was not a one-time choice. Joshua knew he belonged to the Lord, but he still had to choose day after day, moment by moment, to follow Him. Plenty of opportunities arrive every day to take our eyes off the Lord. No one follows Him by just drifting along. We too choose day after day, and moment by moment to follow Him. Joshua had done that, and they knew it. No one left the meeting that day without having had his heart touched.

Joshua looked at these men, women, and children whom he had grown to love over the years and softened his tone. "I was your leader, but you were the warriors who daily carried swords and spears into battle. You were the wives who offered up your husbands to the battles and held them up with your bravery, your encouragement—and your prayers. You were the children who waited patiently for your fathers to come home alive." He looked at them with respect and admiration, and they knew it was real. The people were beholding a true leader. Many of those men he had chosen when they were much younger to help lead the army through

Canaan. Now they were powerful, accomplished leaders like himself who were also good spiritual influences on those they led. Silently he prayed that they would stay close to the Lord after he was gone. And so they did. Judges 2: 7-9 tells us, "And the people served the Lord all the days of Joshua and all the days of the elders that outlived Joshua, who had seen all the great works of the Lord, that he did for Israel. And Joshua, the son of Nun, the servant of the Lord, died being a hundred and ten years old. And they buried him in the border of his inheritance in Timnath-heres, in the mount of Ephraim, on the north side of the hill Gaash."

Would later generations take God's words and promises as seriously as these individuals did? Always the choice is up to each person. The little decisions hour by hour, and moment by moment, make up our lives. Even when we fail it is not forever. The prophet Jeremiah wrote, "It is of the Lord's mercies that we are not consumed, because his compassions fail not. They are new every morning. Great is his faithfulness . . . The Lord is good to them that wait for him, to the soul that seeks him" (Lamentations 3: 22-25).

CHAPTER 45

WHO WAS THIS MAN? WHAT DID HE DO?

Matthias and Jerusha lived so long before Jesus's time that they never saw Him. We who live so long after His time never saw Him either, but just as they knew him through the scriptures that pointed to Him, so can we. If they had lived during His years on earth they would have recognized Him and listened to His teachings, just as they had recognized that God was working through Moses and Joshua and the continual fire and smoke above the Tabernacle.

It is said all of scripture points in one way or another to Jesus. On the day of His resurrection He spoke to two men troubled over the crucifixion. He had been their hope, but now He was gone. It was so hard to understand. He joined them as they sadly walked the path back toward their home. Assuming Jesus was dead, they did not recognize Him as He explained, "'O you people, slow of heart to believe all that the prophets have said. Ought not Christ to have suffered these things and to enter into His glory?' And beginning at Moses and all the prophets, He expounded to them in all the scriptures the things concerning Him." Reaching home, they invited Him to supper and, when He prayed and thanked His Father for the meal, they suddenly recognized Him. As quickly as they recognized Him, He vanished from their sight. In that moment everything made sense. "Did not our hearts burn within us while he spoke to us?" They left their supper on the table and ran all the way back to Jerusalem to tell the others. So it still thrills people today who suddenly realize it is Jesus himself speaking to them through the scriptures (Luke 24: 13-35).

Since the Old Testament stories you have just read point to Him, it would make sense to look at Him also. Jerusha and Matthias looked forward to the Savior who would come and understood that He would open the path back to a right relationship with God. Somehow, as the innocent animal sacrifices intimated, God would be able to accept them due to the sacrifice to which they pointed. They would have loved to see Him and hear his explanations. When He said, "I and My Father are One. If you have seen Me, you have seen the Father," they would have understood (John 10: 30).

It was Jesus who led Moses, who led Israel out of Egypt ("on eagle's wings have I borne you"), who led Joshua into the Promised Land. He was with them teaching and guiding, giving them victory after victory, year after year. By the light and glory in the Tabernacle, He signified his presence among them. This same Jesus promises to be with us. As He sent His Spirit into Moses and Joshua He now, since his ascension into heaven, sends His Spirit into every person, whether they know it or not, the moment they believe His words (Ephesians 1:13). As Moses and Joshua and the Israelite warriors believed the promises from God, they became victorious. Belief of what God said made all the difference. We have the choice to believe them or not—just like they did.

Who was this man to whom all scripture pointed? What did He do, this man God had called the "seed" in Genesis, this man to whom pointed every sacrifice on rock altars from Adam's day to the Tabernacle and then the Temple? This man called the Messiah and the Savior? That Savior was born onc day into our midst. "And the Word was made flesh, and dwelt among us, and we beheld his glory, the glory as of the only begotten of the Father, full of grace and truth" (John 1: 14). He was God joining the human race, His creation. At age thirty Jesus began to teach that He was the Son of God come "to seek and to save that which was lost" (Luke 19: 10).

Jesus's words often reflected a different understanding of the situation than most people held, but as listeners heard his words and saw his works they gained a deeper understanding of his point of view and Jesus's often puzzling statements. New Testament accounts of Jesus's words and actions reveal his character and serve to complete the meaning of Old Testament teachings.

One need not read these selections all at once. Read a few at a time if you like, to give you time, like Mary, to "ponder" them.

A few examples:

Mary the mother of Jesus

Six Marys are mentioned in the New Testament. Mary the mother of Jesus is one of them and is always identified as such when she is mentioned. On a certain day the angel Gabriel (who stood in the presence of God) was sent by God to the city of Nazareth in Galilee of Israel to a virgin betrothed, or engaged, to a man named Joseph. Both were of the house and lineage of David. Both she and Joseph and their families had agreed to this marriage. Her age was not given, but she was old enough to bear children and contemplate marriage. Some have thought she was as young as sixteen. We do not really know.

What we do know is that Gabriel was sent six months earlier to her much older cousin, Elizabeth, who was beyond child-bearing age. She and her husband, Zacharias, had prayed for a years for a child but to no avail, and now it was too late, or so they thought. Gabriel told Zacharias they would have a son and to name him "John." He would turn the hearts of many to the Lord to prepare the way for the soon-to-come Lord. He would be John the Baptist. Today Gabriel was telling Mary she had found favor with God and would conceive and bring forth a son whom she was to call "Jesus." Further, he would be called the Son of the Highest, and God would give him the throne of his father (many generations back) David, and he would reign over the house of Jacob forever, and of his kingdom there would be no end.

"How shall this be, seeing I am not married?" asked Mary.

Gabriel answered, "The Holy Spirit shall come upon you, and the power of the Highest shall overshadow you, and the holy child that shall be born of you shall be called the Son of God. And, behold, your cousin Elizabeth has also conceived a son in her old age six months ago. Though she was called barren, she found out that with God nothing is impossible."

She answered, "Be it to me according to your word." And the angel departed (Luke 1: 5-38). In time she went to Elizabeth's house and, upon entering, greeted her.

At her arrival a most unusual thing happened. When Elizabeth heard her voice the baby leaped in her womb, and Elizabeth was filled with the Holy Spirit. She said, "Blessed are you among women, and blessed is the fruit of your womb." All this happened to Elizabeth and Mary with no fanfare or recognition in the world. The Lord just did it. More explanation and affirmation of Gabriel's words to them would come over time. This startling event was one of them. Elizabeth continued, "How is this that the mother of my Lord should come to me?" Imagine Mary's wonder at her words.

When Joseph learned of Mary's pregnancy he was troubled and wondered what to do. An angel appeared to him and said, "Fear not to take Mary to be your wife, for that which is conceived in her is of the Holy Spirit. She shall bring forth a Son, and you shall call his name Jesus, for he shall save his people from their sins." So Joseph took her as his wife but refrained from intimacy with her until her firstborn Son was born (Matthew 1: 18-25).

Puzzling things happened that did not seem to fit with the arrival of the Savior of the world. For example, about the time Mary's child should be born she and Joseph were ordered by the Roman government to return to the town of their family origin, which was Bethlehem of the house of David, to be taxed. Travel was difficult for Mary, and at Bethlehem the city was overwhelmed with travelers returning to be taxed, so no hotel rooms were available. The baby was coming, and the only place they could find was a stable with no clean bedding or other comforts. It had to be very hard to understand that this was God's will. Where was the glory if this child were to be the Savior the angel had announced? It could be easy to fear the Lord had forgotten them or they had misunderstood His message. Nothing seemed right. The important people in the world always received special treatment. None of that for Mary and Joseph. Mary wrapped her newborn child in swaddling cloths (most likely brought from home) and laid Him in a food trough for a cradle. Those soft cloths in which mothers wrapped their precious babies spoke of His humanity and humility. He was treated like any other human baby and would grow up in a human family under the care of a mother and father, like one of us, knowing our pain and our joys. Perhaps it occurred to Mary and Joseph that this seemingly disastrous situation accompanying their Son's birth coincided precisely with the words of the Prophet Micah: "But you Bethlehem Ephrata, though you are little among the thousands of Judah, yet out of you shall come forth to me that is to be ruler in Israel, whose goings forth have been from of old, from everlasting" (Micah 5: 2). Mary and Joseph did not live in Bethlehem, but somehow their first child was born there. It was a city of heartbreak and joy. Jacob's beloved wife, Rachel, was buried there.

On the same night another surprising event occurred. Shepherds in a field near Bethlehem were watching over their sheep when the glory of the Lord shone round about them and an angel spoke to them. "Fear not," said he. Who would not be afraid? "I bring you good tidings of great joy which shall be to all people. To you is born today in the city of David a Savior which is Christ the Lord." One of the most significant days in all of history is announced in a glorious manner but to a small group of ordinary people. "And this shall be a sign to you: 'You shall find the babe wrapped in swaddling cloths, lying in a manger.' Suddenly there was with the angel a multitude of the heavenly host praising God and saying, 'Glory to God in the highest and on earth peace, good will toward men.'" The message delivered, the angels returned to heaven.

The shepherds said, "Let's go right now into Bethlehem and see!" Soon they found Mary and Joseph and the baby lying in a manger, just as the angel had said. You can imagine the parents' wonder as the shepherds told what the angel had said to them. None of this was a mistake, after all. Scripture recorded, "Mary kept all these things and pondered them in her heart." The manger, a food trough, made sense. He was the "bread of life." He would be the sacrifice that gave life back to man. The stable made sense. The world, dominated by Satan, had no room for him, and did its best to expel him. Bethlehem made sense. Called the "City of David," Israel's first great king, David (still well known today) the son of Jesse, of the tribe of Judah, was born and grew up there. God set him on a throne later in Jerusalem and called it the "Throne of David," saying his descendants would rule forever. Several descendants of David so ruled, but eventually, through human failings, the throne and kingdom were lost to outside conquerors. Human representatives of the Savior never quite perfectly picture Him. In spite of the loss, a thousand years after David and directly in his lineage, a child named Jesus was born in that same obscure town of Bethlehem. He would one day take back that throne as His, at first in a largely unseen spiritual sense after His resurrection, and in the future physically and spectacularly at His return to earth, judging evil and setting up a kingdom in the Promised Land where Jesus Himself will rule and dwell with man in righteousness and truth on the "throne of David"—forever.

Today in the stable it was worldly beginnings and hardships. Yet there was that heavenly host announcing it all and somehow those words spoken to a few shepherds reached the whole world.

It was said of Mary many times through her life that, as she watched her Son, she "pondered" what she saw. As the mother of this little boy and then of the Man he became, Mary must have possessed a very deep understanding and insight into her son's being. Few women have endured the pain of watching a beloved son move from a heaven-announced beautiful beginning to a forsaken end on a Roman instrument of torture, the hideous cross on which He hung. Already beaten and mutilated, He suffered even more, hour after hour, naked and bloody, as His life drained from Him. Mary's pain of childbirth finally gave way to the horror of death. No doubt she understood why, but that did not ease the pain as she watched as after a night and a day of torture He went still . . . still, no breath, no words, no motion . . . nothing. Her son.

His story and His life were not finished. She would see that in the coming days.

Mary Magdalene

In the crowd a voice shrieked out, "Jesus, son of God, why are you here before the time? You can't throw us out." Those nearby backed away in fear, and a very disheveled woman appeared, standing as real and unmovable as an iron stake stuck deep in the earth right in their midst. Her snarling voice and violent, stabbing gestures signaled "stay away . . . I'll hurt you." The crowd feared such an unpredictable and uncontrollable person who broke all rules of decency and normal behavior. A woman that wild could hurt men much larger and stronger than herself. Her face and arms and tattered clothing bore weeks' worth of dirt and stains from living as a vagabond, sleeping on the ground like an animal, never washing. A few ugly sores and bruises marred her skin, and her long, black hair, tangled and littered with shreds of straw and other debris, added to her wild appearance. All in all she was filthy and smelled and, while her face could almost be called pretty, any beauty was overshadowed by the crazed look in her eyes and the animal rage she radiated. Exuding pure hatred, she held a large rock in her right hand, poised and ready to throw at Jesus. This girl had been normal until the time she disappeared some years ago at age fourteen for several days. When she returned home she was changed into this wild, uncontrollable person now standing in their midst. Her broken-hearted parents had no clue how to help their daughter. People said she had demons, foul beings from the spirit world, rendering her too twisted and rebellious to live among normal people—or to honor Jesus as the ruler of all creation. Whatever unknown evil force was dominating her recognized Him and, in spite of all the hatred, was compelled to obey every word He spoke. She raised the rock higher, drew her arm back and took aim to throw.

"Drop the rock," He bellowed with an authority that shocked all in earshot into irresistible attention. Defiance distorted her face as she glared at Him and took aim. The moment fairly crackled with tension as onlookers froze, too scared to breathe. Would she drop it—or throw it? No one stood up to this woman. Many had seen her almost uncontrollable animal strength when she without warning sprang into action. She could inflict real damage and would not quit, no matter how badly her victim screamed. It was a wonder she had not killed anyone. How had she sneaked into their midst again without anyone noticing? Jesus's eyes met her defiant gaze. Not one person in that crowd could look away from that moment, and the words came again, so softly all strained to hear as righteousness took control over the anarchy and darkness of the world . . . "Drop the rock." Stillness . . . for a long, silent moment . . . The rock fell from her hand and half bounced harmless in the dust. He spoke one more time, even softer. "Come out of her." His unflinching gaze followed the path of His words to her, holding her there, words no one could ignore. He never backed down. Ever. Few knew it at that moment but the King of all creation, veiled in human form, stood before them, and His words, delivered quietly but with the overwhelming power that could command a thunderstorm or quake the earth, issued an order from the One who had created the heavens and the earth, had brought existence out of nothing, had brought order out of chaos. No force in the universe, not even the upstart Satan, could oppose those words. Snarling demons filled with hate flailed to resist, quaking her body like a shaken rag doll. She shook once more as the demons left her. Then she collapsed, apparently lifeless, to the ground. "Is she dead?" wondered a wide-eyed onlooker.

Jesus walked over to her and, stooping down, reached out and took her dirt-stained hand. The first face Mary saw was Jesus as His hand gently pulled her to her knees and a new life. To her, from then on, His face and His warm hand were life, a memory, a moment she would never forget, a realignment with reality, going all the way back to some dimly remembered moment in her teenage life when evil forces overpowered her, hurt her, and pushed her past her power to protect herself. Life in the regular world had failed her, and she gave up on reality as she had known it, as others knew it, and found safety in a pretend world that blocked out reality. It was the only way she could protect herself. Now a lunatic, she was still alive! The will to survive is so powerful in the heart of all living.

Today she had seen this kind man's face, full of mastery and hope. His eyes had beheld her. His heart had understood her and reached out to her in her tangled mess and connected with her. And she had accepted His help. A new connection had come into existence, a new birth, a connection to the God of the universe! It would never be undone—He was holding on to her, and His grip was sure! The convoluted confusion in her mind cleared and the world began to make sense again. As she felt the warmth of His hand, she saw the filth of her own body and for the first time realized what a mess she had been. And He had pulled her out of it. Standing tentatively to her feet in her soiled clothing and matted hair, with face unwashed for so long, she reflected peace and understanding. Looking like a princess in a ragged costume who had been through a horrible battle—that was finally over—she looked around at the frightened people, mouths open, eyes not blinking, staring at her. The crowd stood speechless, in silent awe. Another Mary, Jesus's mother, came and led her away to bathe and comfort her.

How many of us today have deep inner hurts that control our lives to the sad point of quiet despair? Few are as bad as this woman's. Modern science can understand and help some, but not all. Many problems baffle the most learned doctors and psychiatrists. So we suffer. Jesus handled all that came at Him, no matter what. The crowd that day looked at Him and wondered, "Who is this man?" From that day on, she and many others would follow Him, listening to His teachings, seeing pictures in His words, beholding Him, gracious and kind. The more they saw, the more they learned how much He cared about them, and they began to love him back.

This was Mary Magdalene of whom the Bible said that "out of her the Lord had cast seven demons" (Mark 16:9). From that moment she began to absorb His teachings and understand His heart. She saw Him heal so many others, and what she saw was not lost on her. She realized this man into whose eyes she had looked, whose very hand had lifted her into a new life, was the Savior of all mankind. Knowing His heart, she had brought so many others to discover Him for themselves.

On a certain day a few years later, she walked, sobbing with a hopelessly broken heart, to His grave. In unspeakable agony she thought on the events of three days earlier when she had watched as soldiers mercilessly and cruelly nailed Him, through each hand and both feet together, while joking about His pain, to a wooden cross and stood it up. Sliding the base a few inches to a hole in the ground, they dropped it with a thud to the rock hard bottom. At the jolt, pain shrieked like lightning through His body, now hung on crusty iron nails and a few scratchy ropes. Then the taunting and ridiculing intensified. Some onlookers shrieked at the horror, covered their mouths with their hands and broke into uncontrollable tears, sickened at the brutality. A few vomited. How could such a man as He be so tortured and murdered? What were they seeing? A body with skin splayed open by a cruel whip. Sliced muscle exposed. A man so tortured He could not scream. Or did He choose silence? Who knew? Was there no limit to the cruelty in man's savage heart? "He saved others, but Himself He cannot save. Look at Him now! Serves Him right!"

The priests and leadership of her own Israelite people, ostensibly the best of the best, had put Him there. The high priest in his fine robes, secure in his respected office, had as good as swung the hammer that drove the spikes through Jesus's hands. Delighting in seeing the pain Jesus silently endured, the respected priest approved as cruel mockers further taunted. No, the priest appeared fine and dignified, even righteous, head held high in righteous judgment. He had overseen it all. The Roman leadership, the power center in the world, had been maneuvered into performing this brutality. What sick force lay behind it all? The Jews had such influence. The Father in heaven silently watched, watched the wanton torture of His Son He had given to the world. Man too watched, some from the crowd that day, others in hearing a few days later, others, much later, in reading the account of that day.

Mary saw His battered body and faint pulses of blood, pushed by a dying heart, ooze from wounds and gagged at the sight. A soldier stripped off His cloak and left Him to hang like that, for all to gape at and mock. Had not the religious leaders understood that He was special and used His marvelous abilities to heal? Destroying Him was beyond belief. He had been their hope. And why would one as He, who had such power over evil spirits, illness and even death, now be conquered by approaching death and this chaotic, hardened wickedness? Yes, her heart was truly broken. All that was left for her was grief, grief that crushed. He had given her new life and new hope. Now He was gone. It was too much to take. She had brought flowers and perfumes to anoint the body of the One she had loved so much, the One who had pulled her out of a miserable, polluted existence. And now. . . now He was dead. Her hopes had died with Him. She, like his other close followers, had missed something He mentioned so many times. He told them He would die, that people were plotting His death. He would be like the sacrifices of the temple. Except—He wasn't an animal. She had seen the harsh hatred some leaders and critics displayed toward Him but had dismissed it as not as serious as it looked. She thought Jesus was misinterpreting and exaggerating when He took those things seriously. People were not really that bad, were they?

Centuries earlier the prophet Jeremiah had written, “The heart is deceitful above all things and desperately wicked. Who can know it” (Jeremiah 17: 9)? Few could catch on to the plain sense of that verse. Jesus knew the hearts of men, but who believed Him? Who even understood what He was talking about? He was right about people plotting His death. Evidently He was right about dying too. But why? On this day at the cross man had a hard time comprehending. The eyewitnesses of Jesus’s crucifixion could not put it all together, so deep was man’s inner desire to believe in himself. Even Mary. One of the first to see truly was the Roman centurion, a Gentile and hated government official, who supervised Christ’s crucifixion, who had heartlessly carried out this cruelty, who had been struck by Jesus’ words as He forgave them. He experienced the horror of an earthquake as the earth shook beneath his feet at the moment of His death and threatened destruction of the mountain and everyone on it. Those who have not experienced such shaking of our solid earth could scarcely understand the complete fear. Suddenly realizing his own guilt and the value of this man they had just killed, he spoke out loud, “Truly this man was the Son of God” (Matthew 27: 54).

Mary herself, even rid of her demons, was still a sinner who needed to understand more completely all that Jesus did in securing man’s salvation. Why He had to die was hard to figure out. Even though He had told the other disciples, including her, several times that He would be given over to leaders who would kill Him, it seemed too far-fetched to believe. Her misery only grew when she found that His body had been stolen. What more could go wrong? In complete despair she had begged the gardener to tell her if he knew *anything* about where they had taken him.

And then the most stupendous thing had happened. The man she supposed to be the gardener said, “Mary. . .” and spoke something to her. All she heard was her name and missed the rest. How did the gardener know her name? And the way he said it sounded so familiar. The tone of that voice drew every bit of attention her broken heart possessed. Through her tears she looked up into His face. Once again. A face so full of hope and confidence—and strength. It was Him! Jesus! Alive! How? What was equally as remarkable was that God had chosen her, a seemingly worthless waste of a life, basically destroyed by demons and the heartless cruelty of man, as the one to whom He would first reveal Himself after rising from the dead. The relationship conceived between them when she had first accepted His healing was real and permanent. No power could undo it, not even death—or His death—as His rising from it had just *proved* to her. Man killed Him. Satan influenced man. It could never have happened unless Jesus had "allowed" it to happen. He submitted Himself completely to their will, to the full extent of their power and evil intention. Then He stood up victorious over it. In allowing them to exercise their will, He proved to the world the stark depth of the evil in their hearts—and the supremacy of His power over all of it. And on this day Jesus first revealed the completeness of His victory to Mary.

Much of the world treats women as property and second class citizens. Not Jesus. His doings once more cut across the grain of human tradition, the fabric of human wisdom. The first human to fall into sin was Eve, and now the first one to see this risen Christ and experience His rescue was again. . . a woman. When He healed a problem He went all the way to the core of it, its very beginning, and took care of it completely. His love for Eve, His love for Adam, never quit. His unfailing love for them reached from the cross all the way back to them and all the way forward to the last human who will ever be born. His life was precious enough that it paid for every sin of every person born into this world. His sin payment would be applied to any from any age in the history of the world, who would "hear" Him and accept His help. "He that comes to me I will in no wise cast out" (John 6: 37), "He that has ears to hear, let him hear" (Mark 4: 23).

What she and the other disciples would come to understand in the following days was that what looked like a hopelessly tragic failure at the end of a beautiful and hope-filled three-year ministry was, in reality, a complete and total victory over death and the destructive power of Satan. It would make sense of the puzzling statement He prayed the night before

His capture and crucifixion: "Now is the prince of this world cast out." He *knew* He would win the impending battle no matter how deep the misery He faced. What looked to man like abject failure was complete and total victory in the kingdom of God. The power here displayed was the same power that Moses experienced in the deliverance from Egypt and captivity, that Joshua experienced in leading Israel into the Promised Land—a power clean, shining, and glorious, almost too holy to comprehend. It is said, "Great events cast their shadows before them." Those events foreshadowed the overwhelming power that He would later display in His resurrection from death, an act possible only for one more powerful than death itself, more powerful than every rebellious thought that led to death.

Jesus healed the afflictions of all who came to him. Yet healing blindness, a deformed foot, or a terrible disease like leprosy did not save a person's soul. Those miracles had one purpose. They demonstrated to all that He had abilities beyond those of normal people, and furthermore, that He was the Son of God. Scripture predicted that the Messiah, when He came, would work such miracles. They demonstrated that the Messiah was in their midst, and they should have recognized Him for who He said he was. None of those He healed is alive today. They all eventually succumbed to physical death. The true healing Jesus offered went beyond the physical realm. Even those physically healed still needed to accept healing for their souls and the gift of new life from Him. Imagine the extreme tragedy of one so close to Jesus as to have received physical healing and then never bothered to think any deeper than that and accept healing for his soul.

Feeding Five Thousand

"I made you hungry so I could feed you." After Egypt the Lord led Israel into the wilderness to make them hungry so they could learn to depend on Him. He knew He could feed them but they did not yet know how to draw on His daily help. Moreover, He knew war awaited in the Promised Land, and He wanted victory for them. To survive they would need to know how to draw on His help.

Today Jesus taught a different group of followers the same lesson. He taught them in a field where they sat and listened all day, so enthralled were they. His words had kept them spellbound, and now they realized they were hungry, and it was a long walk home. Earlier he had told them he was the "bread from heaven." Today He told them to sit down, and then He proceeded to take the few loaves of bread someone had, break them and pass them out to all those listeners. People did not realize at first the miracle taking place in their midst, but from those few loaves He fed the entire crowd of listeners.

Take Up Your Cross (Luke 9:23)

And He said to them all, "If any man will come after Me, let him deny himself, and take up his cross daily and follow Me." What did He mean? His cross was to allow the Father to place all of our sins upon Him at the cross and to suffer their penalty, including separation from God and death. Certainly none of us could do that. To attempt to do so would be a slap in the face to God and a manifestation of our pride and a rejection of everything He had told us. If one of us went to the cross we would die for sure, but it would not pay for anyone's sins and would leave us stuck in death. So what does He mean, and what is our cross?

Two ideas are bound together: negatively, denying self, and positively, taking up our cross. Denying self does not necessarily mean to die as a martyr or to give up all our things. Many of God's children have been wealthy and still served God. More, it is to give up on self-centeredness and our efforts to follow our desires over what His Word says. It means a willingness to put what God wants ahead of what our natural self wants. If we cannot do that it would make sense to give away all we had to render ourselves destitute enough to need the help only Jesus can give us. Jesus said God knows what we need to live in this world and that He will provide for us. What He wants is our attention. We can take a lesson from military training. The first thing taught new recruits is to stand at attention. Trainers go to great lengths to teach that. It means one stands the way the commander says, looks at him, listens to what he says, responds to what he says. One either complies or is gone. A soldier who will not follow his commander's will is useless to the mission. A soldier still has his own life but is also willing to follow his commander. Jesus is asking us to put His will above ours. His guidance will lead us to a happier, more meaningful life than would our natural abilities.

When we think like that we are ready to follow Him. What is our cross? In the Roman-occupied world, bearing a cross meant a condemned criminal was forced to demonstrate his submission to Rome by carrying part of his cross to his place of execution, thus demonstrating his submission to the authority against which he had previously rebelled (from *The Bible Knowledge Commentary, New Testament*, by John Walvoord, pp. 140-141). We are to take up *our* cross, not *His* cross.

Our cross would be different than Jesus's cross. He would be paying for our sins. Of that we would not be capable. Our cross would be to bear the fact that our original nature was corrupted by sin, and that nature, though judged and condemned by God, would be with us until we leave this earth. It would trouble us and seek to draw us away from God. Years after Jesus's departure to heaven the Apostle Paul said that exact thing (Galatians 2:20).

Our cross would be to put the Father's will above ours. Jesus, as a man, did that. We should too. Beyond that, our cross could be something He wants us to do or to say to someone. It could be sacrificing our time to study His Word or maybe something as simple as relaxing and accepting the peace He offers when we are worried. That cross is that old natural nature never changes, never submits to God, and continually attempts to divert us away from him. The victory is that while saddled with that opposition, we can look to Jesus, enjoy Him, and accept His help. Scripture tells all believers, "I am crucified with Christ and nevertheless I live" (Galatians 2: 20). What does it mean? It means that when we believe, God identifies us with Christ's death on the cross and considers that we died in Him. He sees us as crucified. Then he places new life, His life, in us and now sees us as alive in Christ. The walk of faith is to understand that and to conduct our lives as though God is guiding us, because that is what He tells us He is doing for us, day after day.

The Rich Young Ruler (Mark 10:17-22)

A certain rich young ruler came to Jesus expecting to be congratulated by Him for keeping the law so well. Instead His words stung. He told the man that if he were truly as righteous as he thought, he would sell his goods, give the money to the poor and follow Him, the "follow Him" part being the key. He went away sorrowing. Jesus's words had drawn the man to Him in the first place, but this was not what he expected. "He that comes to me I will in no wise cast out. . . he that comes to Me will not be ashamed," Jesus had said. The man had left ashamed. What had gone wrong? Jesus was not impressed with his law keeping. Instead He challenged him to sell all he had and follow Him. Did not Jesus realize how hard it had been to amass such wealth? He had inherited great wealth from a long line of past generations that had worked hard, had been disciplined to spend and invest wisely. He had carried on the tradition by working hard himself. Give it all away in a moment? What kind of advice was that? How would that help? Puzzled and angered, he had walked away. But the man had come to Him, and Jesus' criticism had touched his heart in a profound way.

Jesus's answer seemed harsh, especially to one who was trying so hard to please God. Interestingly, the scripture recorded that "Jesus beholding him *loved* him. He said to him, one thing you lack . . ." Jesus, risking hurting the man's feelings, told him the exact thing he needed to hear. The man's faith was in himself and his ability to keep the law. Impressed by his own ability to keep the laws better than others, he failed to see that he could not even keep the first law, to "love the Lord with all your heart, soul, and mind," nor the second basic law, which said to "love your brother as yourself." If Jesus truly loved the man He would tell him what he most needed to hear, that he needed to transfer his faith in himself to faith in God's help. So first came that painful statement about giving away his goods. Jesus hit him hard to shock him into seeing that he was not keeping the law as well as he thought and that he could not *really* keep the law. The "way" of salvation was to give up on yourself and to trust God's Savior to be your "way" to heaven. He did not really need to give away his goods, but he needed to see that his comfort was in his success and his vast goods, and that what he needed was to find his comfort in allowing God to take care of him. That was a big step for a person rich in goods. If one could not transfer his faith from his wealth and goods to God to take care of him, he would be better off to scrap the goods and in his poverty cast himself on the goodness of God to take care of him. Wealth in the world would last a few years. Wealth God offered would last forever.

What this young man eventually decided the scripture does not tell us. It was up to him, as it is up to each of us. But we know this: Jesus "loved him."

Woman at the Well (John 4: 5-42)

On a certain day Jesus and His disciples walked through the area called Samaria on their way to Galilee. At noon, weary from the journey, Jesus sat down by a well Jacob had given his son Joseph, nearly two thousand years earlier. The disciples went into the nearby city of Sychar to buy food, and while they did so a certain woman came to draw water from the well. He watched for a moment and said, "Give me some water to drink."

She said, "How is it that a Jew asks drink from a woman of Samaria, seeing the Jews have no dealings with us?" Centuries before the people of Samaria had been conquered by cruel Assyrian marauders and, over time, had intermarried with them. Other Israelites looked down on them as polluted, compromising sinners and wanted nothing to do with them.

Jesus said, "If you knew the gift of God, and who it is talking to you, you would have asked him, and he would have given you living water." He had the ability turn the most ordinary encounters into something very important to the one He met.

The woman said, "Sir, you have nothing to draw with, and the well is deep. Where will you get this 'living water?' Are you greater than our father Jacob which gave us this well and drank from it himself?"

Jesus replied, "Whoever drinks this water will thirst again, but whoever drinks of the water that I shall give him shall never thirst. In fact, the water shall in him be a well of water springing up into everlasting life."

The woman, drawn in by His words, listened intently and then silently looked upon Him for many moments, puzzling. He stood quietly in front of her and looked back at her. Who was this man who seemed so confident in His knowledge? Finally, she said, "Sir, give me this water so I don't have to thirst or come here again."

Jesus replied, "Go call your husband and come back here." The situation suddenly became more complicated. Almost angry that this painful subject had come up to ruin the moment, she bitterly countered, "I have no husband."

Jesus said, "You have answered well, 'I have no husband,' for you have had five husbands, and the one you are living with now is not your husband. In that you told the truth." How did He know that? How could she make herself look good to One who already knew her failures and dark side? As with Jacob centuries earlier, who wrestled with God until he had to face up to his own weakness, the Lord was looking for truthfulness in humans. When one could be honest with oneself, a new starting point arrived.

She looked at Him again, unable to speak, wondering. At first offended at his forwardness, she reconsidered and then made a decision. He already knew all about her, and yet He was still talking with her. What could it hurt to open her heart and let His words reach into her soul and help? Finally she said, "Sir, I perceive you are a prophet." She paused again, still wondering. Finally she half questioned, "Our fathers worshipped here on this mountain, but you Jews say that in Jerusalem is where men ought to worship."

Jesus replied, "Woman, believe me. The time is coming when neither in this mountain where you worship, nor in Jerusalem shall you worship the Father. Your worship is confused by the deceitfulness of the world, but we know what we worship. Remember. . . salvation is of the Jews. The hour is coming, yea, it is here already, when the true worshippers shall worship the Father in spirit and in truth." In fact, the Father seeks such to worship Him. The place for worship did not matter. It was wherever you were.

The woman, still confused, looked down at the ground and shuffled some dust with her toe, first this way and then that. "I know that Messiah is coming," she spoke, delicately voicing her thoughts, "who is called Christ. When He is come He will tell us all things." She looked up at Him for a reaction.

He had been listening, following her every word, beholding her as she spoke. He had a response. "I that speak to you am He," He said calmly, eyes fixed intently on her, promising eyes, kind eyes. Now *He* waited for a reaction. She had been stalling, speaking in generalities. His words brought her to the moment, to a reality that had always spoken to her heart and now stood right in front of her. The Messiah they had all heard about was speaking to her!

She looked back at Him, not moving, simply beholding, trying to grasp the reality of what He had just said. He was the Messiah? Talking to her? Somehow she decided to believe Him, and something relaxed in her heart, but the depth of it was too much to take in all at once. The day anyone believes that the words of scripture are God Himself communicating—that He cares about even *me*—is the day we come to know Him. The woman at the well came to know Him that moment. From then on *He* held on to her; she would be in His safekeeping. He knew her faults and still accepted her. She had admitted them to Him, her deepest failures, and He still loved her. At her worst He accepted her. What? She might still fail Him, but He would never fail her, and in that moment she grasped that fact. Though this woman grew old and left this earth long ago, her soul is safe with Him today in heaven, and her story reaches to our hearts. In a few brief sentences He had walked His way into her life, and somehow she knew He was genuine. Her failed relationships were her unsuccessful way of searching for something missing from her life. She had been tired, no, fatigued, with trying, and today out of nowhere this man had shown up. He had brought to light the most miserable part of her life where failure upon heartbreaking failure had tortured her, and in misery she had owned up to it. Something in His manner had prodded her to drop all her defenses, giving up trying to look good, giving up trying to make excuses for her failures. And then those words had flooded in: "I that speak to you am He." At her worst moment, when she could no longer hide from the sin she did not want to admit, even to herself, He had brought her face to face with it, and then had brought her face to face with Him and his acceptance of her!

Before she could answer, the disciples returned and marveled at seeing Him talking with this Samaritan woman. She left her water pot and went her way into the city. Seeing several men, she said, "Come, see a man which told me everything I have ever done. Is not this the Christ?" Her friends were all men, as women did not like her. With her attractiveness and charming ways she had flirted with and stolen some of their men's affections. Jesus, coming from a far deeper place, had reached out to her, and through her, to all the city. He often approached people through an unexpected door.

Many of the Samaritans quickly believed in Jesus because of what the woman had told them. After meeting Him they begged him to stay longer, so He did, staying two more days. More believed in Him because of His words during that time. They told the woman, "Now we believe, not because of all you told us, but because we have heard Him ourselves and know that He is indeed the Christ, the Savior of the world. We are so glad you told us about Him." She was glad too, and told many more in the coming years about this man, this man who had said to her, "I that speak to you am He."

Entering Jerusalem, Jesus' heart cries out (Luke 13: 34)

On a certain day, as Jesus walked for the final time down the wide and busy road overlooking Jerusalem, His manner grew somber. His close followers noticed His mood and sensed agony stirring in His heart. Something deep, something they did not understand, had been brewing within Him. He stopped talking, and they were afraid to ask, not knowing how He would react. Presently He halted on the path and faced the city, a large city teeming with humanity and activity, people so numerous one could never meet or know each one, much less care about them—unless he had the ability of the Creator himself. Jesus breathed words all strained to hear. "O Jerusalem, Jerusalem," He paused as anguish bled into His voice, "which kills the prophets, and stones them that are sent to you." To the disciples it almost seemed like a faint tremor moved from deep within the earth, resonating with the breaking heart of this man from Nazareth. "How often would I have gathered you to me, as a hen gathers her chicks under her wings." The emotion in His voice magnified its power, and without making it louder, drove His words, His deepening agony, into their hearts. Peter and John and the other disciples looked from one to another. They had never seen Him so moved. How large was His vision that He could care about an entire city, each person? How deep was His love for every individual in that city, for the humans He and his Father had brought into existence? It was too broad to comprehend. It was a pain only He and His Father and the Spirit of God could know.

Peter, the rough and ready fisherman, said, "He's troubled. I'm going to help Him." John, the soon to be Apostle, grabbed Peter and restrained him, saying, "Let Him be. You can't help. That pain is beyond our ability to understand—or help. The best we can do is watch Him, try to understand, and remember what we saw. He has a heart like ours, and, more than that, like His Father's." Matthew, the hard-hearted and hated turncoat tax collector, who had made himself rich selling out to Rome and cheating his fellow Israelites, silent longer than the others, finally spoke. "See how much He loves all the people, even the worst of us and the people who hate Him. Oh, that all would understand His heart and know His love as we have." These men who accompanied Jesus through His daily moments became the Apostles.

An uncomfortable silence followed as their leader stood heartbroken in that spot, looking at Jerusalem, stubborn Jerusalem. What was troubling His heart to stir Him so? they silently wondered. Could He care about all the people in Jerusalem? They remembered He had said He had come to "seek and to save those who were lost" (Luke 19:10). Those who opposed Him in Jerusalem did not think they were lost. They had Abraham as their ancestor and were certain God was pleased with them. Jesus challenged them on their shallow understanding, saying that they needed *faith* like Abraham, not simply status as *physical descendants*. Some considered His words true and important and accepted them. Many did not. It was those to whom Jesus's heart cried out. The disciples had seen firsthand the opposition and downright hatred of much of the leadership in Jerusalem. His words threatened the honor and respect they had taken to themselves as the ruling elite. And now Jesus was heading back into that brood of vipers. How could He love them? Yet that was what they were seeing today. They had seen His power, with the words of His mouth stilling a storm, yet He would not force anyone to come to Him. He had the power to enforce that, but He only called and reasoned and did not *force* anyone to believe in Him. He had called but allowed them to follow Him or not. It had to be of their own free will if they came to Him. So many leaders in the world imposed their will on others, but that was not Jesus' way. If He had not veiled himself in human form and emptied Himself of the majesty He enjoyed with His Father, His glory would have dazzled all to the point of worshipping Him. He did not do that. True free will meant man would hear His words, see His works, and decide for himself whether this man was who He said He was—the Son of God, coming to rescue all who would hear. No one would enter into God's presence unless he wanted to. Many today say they believe in Jesus but they disbelieve the miracles attributed to Him. Yet those miracles demonstrated He had powers beyond what any humans had. In so doing they deny all He said and who He claimed to be—the Son of God—very dangerous stance to take.

Finally, He stretched out his arms to that city. Those behind Him saw His shoulders quake slightly and heard a deep moan of pain that only love could produce, the expression of an, until now, unspoken grief whose sound could no longer be held back. Piercing the silence, powerful words screamed from His tortured soul. "BUT YOU WOULD NOT!... YOU WOULD NOT!" The "man of sorrows," with patience beyond that of other men, *SCREAMED*. The man who would soon be nailed to a wooden cross through both hands and feet and make not a sound screamed on this day in agony over the people who would not hear Him and come to Him for help.

His pain arrested the disciples where they stood, and not one of them would ever forget what they saw that day. The passion in His voice overrode all else happening, commanding the attention of all. Its pain reverberated around the hills as they echoed His forlorn voice, His broken heart . . . "You would not!" faintly came an echo across the distance . . . "You would not," echoed a final time, fainter yet from the farthest hill. Then silence.

His arms, stretched out to those people, grasped for those who would not come, as His body shook with pain. He could see their ultimate end in the blackness of darkness, outer darkness, far forever from the comfort of God's presence. It would be the outcome of their choice but not what He wanted for them. It was more than Jesus's grief and the pain of His heart the disciples were witnessing. It was the pain of those souls descending to outer darkness, whose cry He heard deep in His heart as they screamed in agony. His cry reflected their pain and screamed back out through His voice. It was the agony they would face that had brought Him to earth.

John, who had been with Him daily from the beginning, who had touched Him with his own hands, who had eaten with Him, who had walked miles with Him and seen Him grow tired, who had hugged Him in his arms a few times, who had heard His gracious words and sensed on so many occasions their unfathomable wisdom, observed, wondering. Why was He so passionate? "He came unto His own, and His own received Him not," John would write in the future (John 1: 11). Man continued his dark course and scarcely listened. The chosen Abraham and the line of descendants leading to Christ were sinners themselves, no better than the rest of the world and headed to the same oblivion unless each accepted God's Savior himself. Abraham set the pattern when he "believed" God. *That* opened the door in his heart, which allowed God to impart His own "righteousness" to him and to all who, like him, believed what He said. That made all the difference. He heard God's words, paid attention, and *believed*. The Lord did the rest.

Isaiah, inspired by the very Spirit of God, had written seven centuries earlier, of Jesus: "Behold, I have graven you upon the palms of my hands . . ." (Isaiah 49: 16). The "engraving" he spoke of was a little more intense than simple writing. It was the wound of the nails pierced permanently through His hands by man so deeply that neither He nor any who saw the marks could forget or fail to understand the depth of His love for man. Those hands which "spread out the heavens" and today reached out to hard hearts in Jerusalem would within the next week be stretched out one more time to all mankind, nailed mercilessly to a cross. Thomas, also a disciple of Jesus and bravely daring on this day to accompany Him on this final path into Jerusalem, saw days later His bled out and stone dead body on the cross. When he heard of Jesus' resurrection it seemed so far-fetched that he said, "Unless I see the print of the nails in his hands and place my hand in the wound in his side I will not believe." Eight days later Jesus appeared to the disciples, with Thomas among them. He singled out Thomas and spoke to him. "Reach here your finger and behold my hands . . . and thrust your hand into my side, and be not faithless but believing." Thomas, suddenly understanding, answered, "My Lord and my God," to which Jesus said, "Thomas, because you have seen Me you have believed. Blessed are they that have not seen and yet have believed" (John 20: 24-29). Those would be people born centuries in the future who never had the chance to see Jesus during His life on earth.

Then a deep tremor shook the earth far beneath their feet as the heart of God reached out with unseen agony and tears to His people, so many of whom would not hear. They resumed their final walk into Jerusalem.

Mankind, every single person, man or woman, was born as on a stream flowing slowly but relentlessly toward certain death. As surely as a dry leaf drifting down a river toward a waterfall, enjoying the sunshine and warmth, and sometimes enduring rain and cold wind, would in time plunge over the fall, so man would plunge into death. None could escape that end or what lay beyond. From his abode in eternity, God saw and reached out to man, seeing his helplessness. Would any respond? It was up to each. Jesus could foresee their pathway to eternal death, but would they heed His words?

Jesus and the Last Passover

The first Passover in Egypt was the first of many that led fifteen hundred years later to another, the *last* Passover, when Jesus ate the Passover with His disciples. Passovers observed after that would be a memorial of this Passover with Jesus—and of what He was about to do. Little did they know but this night would be the night of His capture to be crucified. He did something different on this occasion. In passing the unleavened bread to them He said, to the puzzlement of the disciples, "Take, eat. This is My body which is broken for you. Do this in remembrance of

Me." Thomas looked up at Him, wondering. Peter and John looked at each other, troubled. These weren't the words of the Passover. What was Jesus saying? "Giving his body?"

Then He passed around a cup of wine, saying, "Drink of it. This is my blood of the new testament which is shed for you for the forgiveness of sins. Whenever you drink of this, remember what I have done for you." The disciples could not grasp what was happening. He had told them many times that He would be captured and crucified, but the idea was so foreign to them that they did not understand (nor want to) what He was saying. Every animal sacrifice from Adam's day to that evening, every burnt offering in the temple, pointed to that final Passover. The first Passover in Egypt had been a picture of what would happen on this very night with Jesus in Jerusalem. Many had, deep in their hearts, almost below the level of conscious thought, wondered how the death of an unrelated, innocent animal could have anything to do with satisfying the penalty for Adam and Eve's disobedience of God's instructions. In reality it did not. The New Testament writer of Hebrews later explained, "For it is not possible that the blood and of bulls and goats should take away sins" (Hebrews 10: 4) and that the Son of God in offering Himself was the only sacrifice that could truly take away sins. As they swallowed that bread and sipped that wine they heard Jesus say, "What I am doing now you do not understand, but the Holy Spirit when He has come will bring all things to your remembrance that I have done and will help you understand (John 14: 26).

On this Passover Jesus was offering Himself and, within a few hours, would become the sacrifice, nailed to a cross, shedding His blood, delivered to death—for the sins of others—to deliver them from their sin and the death it brought. Many have thought that the *act* of eating the bread and drinking the wine was what brought salvation to one, but that was not accurate. Careful attention to Jesus' words is necessary. Of the bread He said, "Take, eat. This is my body which is broken for you. Do this in *remembrance* of me." It is not that bread, nor our eating of it, that paid for sin. It is Jesus' sacrifice of Himself that paid for sin. To think otherwise is to take away appreciation of Jesus' willing sacrifice of Himself. It is saying, "He didn't have to do that. I don't want Him to have to suffer for something I did. I will take care of it myself so He does not have to suffer." That mindset is saying Jesus was wrong when He says we are sinners. He is mistaken in saying He had to die for our sins. It is to throw out His words from John 8: 24, which state, "Therefore I said to you that you will die in your sins: for if you do not believe that I am He [the Savior, the Son of God] you will die in your sins." Those words imply that as the Son of God, He knows what He is talking about. Thinking our action to take the bread and wine will pay for our sin is the same as Adam and Eve's thinking their fig leaves would cover for their sins. God rejected their effort and provided His own protection for them. They accepted the clothing He gave. We must accept Christ's gift to us.

Our eating of the bread has nothing to do with paying for our sins. It is meant to "remind" us of His payment. When our bodies take in bread it nourishes the body but not the spirit. Our spirits take in Christ's sacrifice of Himself when we mentally accept (or "believe") that He did that for us. The payment was already made at the cross years ago. As an Israelite's sin was transferred to an animal he offered at the Temple when he placed his hands on the animal's head, so mankind's sin was transferred to Christ when He willingly offered Himself on the cross. As He suffered the punishment for them there and died with their penalty upon Him, He took the full brunt of mankind's sin. His Father saw Him do that and was satisfied with His Son's work. On that day all sin was paid for, a day worth remembering and understanding. Though sin was paid for, that payment is not transferred to a person until he accepts that payment by believing Jesus did that for him. Belief is the key, as it was with Abraham.

It is not our work for Christ but His work for us that saves us. The difference between our "eating and drinking" of bread and wine in memory of Jesus's sacrifice of Himself for us and of our understanding and "believing" in *His* work is crucial, a "rightly divining" of God's Word. It is the difference between our works or Jesus's work. It is the difference between death and life. When our hearts "believe" His words they are nourished the way our bodies are nourished by food. Without food our bodies perish. Without belief of God's message to us of Christ's payment for our sins, our souls perish.

His Father watched from His throne in heaven, and, in pain Himself (as when Abraham offered his beloved son on a similar hill), saw "the travail (work, painful or laborious effort) of His soul and was satisfied." In so doing, He "bore their iniquities" and "justified many" (Isaiah 53: 11). Because of that, God could legally forgive the sin that held them captive, because He Himself had paid its penalty. On this occasion it would be taken care of—forever. "Every priest stands daily ministering and offering, oftentimes the same sacrifices, which can never take away sins. But this Man, after He had offered one sacrifice of sins forever, sat down on the right hand of God; from henceforth expecting till His enemies be made His footstool. *For by one offering He has perfected forever them that are sanctified*" (Hebrews 10: 11-14). Jesus's healing of every single disease and calamity brought to Him was only an inkling of the biggest miracle of all, His death on the cross for mankind that totally eradicated the effect of sin man had foolishly brought upon himself. That was what Jesus had been teaching them for so long. That was what was about to happen soon in their midst. It went beyond their ability to grasp. After it all took place in the next few days, the disciples began to understand, and as they did, they spread word of it to all the world.

When God told Israel to perform this Passover every year in the future it was to remind them that their freedom and prosperity in the Promised Land had its origin in their deliverance from Egypt by the "strong hand" of the Lord. The Passover pictured what Jesus would do in protecting from death, that the blood on the doorposts told the death angel to "pass over" that house, as God was protecting it. God's rescue of Israel from Egypt and Jesus' death on the cross were connected. This Passover event took place fifteen hundred years before Jesus appeared in the flesh and asked, "Who do people say I am?" They answered, "Some say you are John the Baptist, some say Elijah, and some say Jeremiah, or one of the prophets" (Matthew16:13-14).

Jesus said, "But who do YOU say that I am?"

Peter answered, "You are the Christ, the Son of the living God" (Matthew 16:15-16).

Jesus replied, "Blessed are you, Peter, for flesh and blood has not revealed this to you, but My Father in heaven." From then on Jesus began to show his disciples how He must suffer many things of the elders and chief priests, and be killed, and be raised again the third day. This same Peter, who truly recognized earlier who Jesus was, now rebuked Jesus, saying, "Be it far from You, Lord. This shall not happen to You." He called Him "Lord" and then told Him He was wrong in His perception.

Jesus answered, "Get behind me, Satan. You are an offense to me, for you do not savor the things of God, but of men" (Matthew 16: 13-23). Peter was not Satan, but Satan was influencing him. Later Jesus told him, "Satan has desired to sift you as wheat, and destroy you, but I have prayed for you that you will in the end strengthen your brethren."

He was with Jesus at the Last Supper on the eve of His capture and crucifixion. Hours later, in the Garden of Gethsemane, he drew his sword to defend Jesus from His captors. Not afraid of a fight, he swung it to take off the head of one of them. He missed and only chopped off his ear. Jesus said, "Put away your sword! Don't you think I could pray to My Father and He would instantly give Me twelve legions of angels? But how then would the scripture be fulfilled, that thus it must be" (Matthew 26: 51-54)? Jesus understood that the Father's will was based on understanding what was right in the long run, and He would not go against it. Then He replaced the man's ear—a miracle performed for the benefit of a supposed enemy. Do you think this man later became a believer in Christ, the man he helped capture and destroy? We will find out in eternity. This was the hour to which his life and ministry had led, but Peter did not fully understand it.

Jesus had mercy on His captors and on impetuous Peter. Earlier in the evening He had told His disciples that he would be captured and all of them would be so frightened they would forsake Him. Peter, not believing Jesus nor understanding the true capacities of his own heart, protested, "Though all of them forsake you, I never will."

The other disciples probably did not appreciate his comments or his arrogance. Jesus responded, "Peter, before the cock crows tomorrow morning you will have denied me three times." Peter, though rebuked, was unconvinced but argued no more. Early in the following morning outside the court where Jesus had been taken, when a frightened Peter denied to an accusing onlooker for the third time that he was one of Jesus's followers, the cock crowed. Jesus, from inside the courtyard, turned and looked at Peter. He, suddenly realizing his failure, went out and "wept bitterly." Like the centurion, like wrestling Jacob, he had come face to face with himself. It is not fun to be shown how sinful we are, but it is part of the learning process for all believers. We all trust in ourselves. Peter later became a bold witness for Christ, and so can we.

Judas (John 13: 21-30; Luke 14: 17-21)

"Is it I?" so many asked. On His last night on earth at the Passover supper with His close disciples Jesus had announced that one of them would betray Him. Many asked, "Is it I?" Though these men had been close followers of Jesus throughout his three-year ministry and, unknown to them at the moment, they would become the Apostles, each knew he was a sinner capable of any sin known to mankind—as this story indicates. They thought Judas was one of them. Yet he did not take Jesus's words seriously. To him they were just so much talk. He was more interested in taking care of himself and conniving ways to gather money. That was what really made the man happy. Sailing his own course and walking his own path, he did not take Jesus's words seriously. One day he saw his chance. Jesus had offended many powerful people, and Judas had perceived their whispered desire to silence Him. With diabolical wisdom He conceived a plan to earn money by betraying Him to them. He carried the purse, the small money bag they used to buy food. He could abscond with that plus whatever he could convince the priests to pay him.

The disciples pressed Jesus to know who the betrayer was, so He said, "It is the one to whom I give this bread after I have dipped it in the oil." The common practice of dipping bread in olive oil is becoming popular again today, at least in finer restaurants. He gave it to Judas and said, "What you have to do, do quickly." Judas took the bread and went out quickly, and as scripture put it, "It was night."

Jesus said, "The Son of man goes as it is written of Him, but woe to that man by whom He is betrayed. It would be good for that man if he had never been born." That is one of the most sobering and hopeless statements in all of scripture. To be that close to life and happiness and reject it of one's own free will is tragedy beyond understanding. Judas possessed an eternal soul like the rest of us. It will never go out of existence. Jesus offered him bread and called him "friend" to the very end, and he chose to leave.

His Love for All

Jesus had the capacity to love those He saw. In a crowd He saw individuals. Coming to the earth as a man He left his sovereign attributes behind in heaven in order to join life on this planet as one of us. His omniscience, his omnipresence He left behind. As God He knew everything, could see the future and the past. As a man He did not know everything. He depended on His Father for guidance, as He would want us to do. When He looked at a person He knew there was more there than met the eye. From heaven He had seen the aching loneliness, the pain hidden just out of sight in so many human hearts.

In a wrinkled old man, weakened and discouraged by years of struggle, He saw also the young boy, full of hope and vibrant energy, craving to explore the world and discover its secrets. Now his face and body bore the ravages of the years in a sin-cursed world, a curse man had brought upon himself. Yet Jesus's heart reached out to him, longed for him. He too lived and walked in this fallen world and saw the pain and hopelessness. In the aged lady, who so long ago had been a carefree and full of hope teenage girl, her now aching back bent over by burdens too long borne, He saw the heartache of broken dreams. He saw the years of poverty and endless toil. That young girl, so much earlier, eager to live life, to experience and enjoy it, had finally given up, her youthful hopes now long gone. He observed tentative teenagers, longing to fit in, to be liked, and He felt the hurt so many secretly bore as others heartlessly made fun of them. He saw the lonely heart of the bully striving for importance, no matter who he hurt to achieve it, and Jesus even cared for someone like that. He saw the proud heart of a powerful leader, drunk with his own success, blind in smug arrogance, too charmed by his own magical self to truly see his wretched condition before God.

Jesus knew the wear and tear on a young mother, tired from waking too many times at night to feed the baby or comfort a crying child. She loved her children but worried she was not enough. Jesus had lived in this world and experienced it the same as the rest of us. He experienced His mother's care for Him and his brothers and sisters when she was exhausted. Having left His home in heaven and the shining magnificence of His glory behind, he felt the emotions people feel, the hopes and fears, the discouragements and disillusionments. He experienced the vulnerability of not knowing the future, had observed the heartache of failure. Often as an unnoticed listener, He had tuned in to those around Him, hearing the sighs of despair, noticing when someone flinched from an unkind word then covered it with a brave face to hide the pain. He knew the burdens people carried, had seen His own family make do when money ran short, waiting for a carpentry project to be completed in order to be paid. Growing up in a small town where most people knew each other, He had observed and felt deeply the joys and frustrations experienced in its families, had seen the sufferings of sickness and the untimely deaths of beloved children. He beheld the pain endured by the bereaved mother and father, pain gradually covered over by daily cares but never really going away. He had heard through a window in the night the quiet cries of a neighbor woman whose husband had passed away. He had felt the sting of unkind accusations that his mother was an adulterer, his father a fool, and He Himself a bastard child. "Here's the kid fathered by the Holy Ghost," they jeered. "Ya, right," another said. "I heard another pregnant girl use that same line his mother used," wisecracked still another. Growing up in this world was not always fun. In the end Jesus would know death, death at the cruel hands of a vicious and selfish mankind. Yes, He felt the pain of those living in this fallen world. He observed a friend criticized for trying to help another who was suffering, "How can you know what I'm going through? You're not me" would sometimes be the bitter response. Stuck on themselves, they had no sympathy for each other. Jesus saw all that.

His Father also suffered. He would watch His Son die and, by His own decision, refrain from helping Him. Jesus would take the punishment that would have fallen on man completely on himself. The Father sorrowed so infinitely it would shake the earth and heaven itself on the day He hung on the cross. And yet so many would never pause long enough to consider. . .

Jesus saw something deep in the heart of each person, something worth caring about, worth loving, worth seeking with all His strength. He came into the world to live as a human. He had emptied Himself of His splendid glory, power and wisdom and joined the human race through a human mother and a heavenly Father. He was both. He was human and divine, but with His divinity shrouded by His human body. He had left behind His omniscience, majesty and overwhelming power. For help He would depend on His Father, as His Father expected mankind also to do. For thirty years His mission was to grow and mature within His human family and to endure and understand what other humans endured. Scripture said He was "a man of sorrows, acquainted with grief," and, further, that He was "tempted in all the ways we are, yet without falling unto sin," as we do.

At the end of His earthly life He was sentenced by an unfair court, with lying judges and witnesses, to one of the most demonic, torturous deaths ever conceived in the mind of man, death by crucifixion. Mankind had made a study of how to inflict pain and intensify it, how to kill slowly over hours or even days with no relief. The most horrific suffering inflicted upon mankind came not from nature and accident, which were random and lacked intention, but from the cruelties intentionally inflicted by one human upon another. Over and over in scripture we are shown this horrific view of man. Cain, the first child born to Adam and Eve, inherited their fallen nature, and, according to the story, killed his brother Abel. From that point on we are shown evil periodically erupting from the hearts of humans originally created as "good." That condition of heart, which is so intensely difficult for us to admit to ourselves, is what Jesus came into the world to solve for mankind. He taught and demonstrated love. He lived and behaved in tune with God's commandments. But those things are minor in comparison with His deeper mission. He was "the lamb of God, slain from the foundation of the world." His most important mission was to become the sacrifice that could be accepted by His Father as the just remedy for the wrongdoing of every fallen and condemned human. Because of his fallen condition, the deceitful depravity of his own heart, man could not love as God required, nor could the most devout Jew keep God's commandments. By joining the human race Jesus was doing that for man.

And at the end of Jesus's sojourn on earth, He allowed man to heartlessly hang Him on their instrument of death, the wooden cross. The worst was yet to come, for then in the midday darkness, "the Lord laid on him the iniquity of us all," that is, God Himself laid on Jesus every one of our sins, our thoughts and acts of wickedness, past, present, and future. Then He crushed Him there, pouring His wrath, His utter hatred of evil, upon Him. Between noon and three o'clock, darkness covered the earth, the oblivious earth and its errant inhabitants, while Jesus, the Son of God, who always reflected peace, was forsaken by His Father. That man on that day screamed, "My God, my God, why have you forsaken me?" God *had* forsaken Him. Not one of us can grasp what He suffered for us. He who existed from eternity in the realm of His Father's love was on that day removed from it. Scripture said, "it pleased the Lord to bruise Him" and "to make His soul an offering for sin."

When the Father "looked on the agony of Jesus's soul" and saw Him "cut off out of the land of the living," bearing the complete and total effect of our sin, He was "satisfied." Jesus had "poured out His soul to death," taking its penalty perfectly and forever. God did not ignore sin. He could correctly and righteously forgive it because His Son had paid its penalty. He could give life to any and all who would accept His Son's payment. He honored his original unalterable words in Genesis: "In the day that you eat of it (the fruit of the tree of the knowledge of good and evil) you shall die." Jesus had gone into that death for man and then triumphed over it.

No amount of gold or silver could pay to remove the horrible effect of sin. Only one thing in all of creation held enough value for that—the blood of Jesus. The very life of God's Son, His only Son, whom He loved, dripped to the earth that day. When one grasps the meaning of it all, it renders all the efforts man can make at improving himself or making up for his sin inconsequential by comparison. He must accept God's help or be lost. There is no other way. "There is none other name under heaven, given among men, whereby we must be saved" (Ephesians 2: 8-9; Acts 4: 12).

God had seen Eve in the garden succumb to the treachery and deceitful lies of Satan, had seen her invite death and mayhem into the world, had seen Adam follow her into that prison of rebellion and wickedness. God watched and allowed them the freedom to exercise their free will to the point of ignoring His warning. Now He would destroy Satan's power and set man free from its grip.

The Thief on the Cross (Matthew 27: 44; Mark 15: 27, 32; Luke 23: 32, 39-43)

This short and simple, and also powerful, story in scripture sets forth what we need to know to go to heaven. From the earliest chapters in the Bible, God's view of man was introduced and then further developed through time. When Jesus was sent to the cross "two other men, both criminals, were also led out with Him to be executed. When they came to the place called the Skull, there they crucified Him and the other criminals, one on His right, the other on His left." Both reviled him. Presently one of them bitterly taunted, "Aren't you the Christ? Save yourself and us!"

The other rebuked him. "Don't you fear God, since you are under the same sentence? We are punished justly, for we are getting what we deserve. But this man has done nothing wrong."

Then he said, "Jesus, remember me when You come into your kingdom."

Jesus answered him, "I tell you the truth, today you will be with me in paradise."

That is it. The whole story. From the master storyteller. What can we learn? Isaiah 28:10 sets forth how we learn: "For precept must be upon precept, precept upon precept, line upon line, line upon line, here little and there a little." Scattered throughout scripture are glimpses of basic ideas. God does things "decently and in order" and wants us to "understand and know." He teaches basic concepts a little at a time, building one idea upon another, detail by detail, until we see a larger picture.

One basic idea (precept) is that we are born out of touch with God, as were both thieves, without any spark of goodness to measure up to His holiness. "In Adam all die" (1 Corinthians 15:22) is God's assessment of our condition. What was created as good fell into condemnation when Adam and Eve exercised their free will to ignore God's advice and follow advice contrary to His. That brought death to them and to all the descendants they would foster. Death and eternal banishment from God's presence became the destiny of all born from them. One thief owned up to his guilt, quit complaining and offering excuses.

Another precept is that we cannot remedy our condition. God rejected Adam and Eve's fig leaf cover-up for their wrongdoing. Then He provided the remedy for them. The clothing He fashioned from the skin of an innocent animal replaced the fig leaves and made them "acceptable" to Him. These "precepts" occur throughout scripture and explain "line upon line, here a little and there a little," our unworthiness and God's free help to us. Hanging hopelessly condemned and accepting his guilt, that thief reached out to Jesus, not with his hands, but with his heart, for help. It came instantly. This short story, told by God, has led many lost souls to the Savior and new life. As Jesus said so many times, "He that has ears to hear, let him hear."

Here we see two criminals, one on His right, the other on His left, both guilty and suffering the death they deserve. One asked Jesus for help. The other did not. They represent the only two types of people God sees, one who accepts His help and is brought to life and one who does not. One will be accepted into God's presence. The other will not. All the other distinctions we humans make about who is good and who is bad matter nothing to God.

In Jesus' response to him, "Truly I tell you, today you will be with me in paradise," He was revealing to all who would hear the story the simplicity of salvation. "Too simple," you might object. "It can't be that easy! What about all the good works I did?" If Jesus, who is "the way, the truth, and the life," spoke those words to the thief, do you think the thief went to paradise that day? Do you think he is still in heaven?

That man died under the law as a thief and had no chance to do any good works, donate money, or be baptized, yet Jesus told him he would be in paradise with Him. How could God accept such a sinner? All he did was acknowledge Jesus as "Lord" and ask for His help. Is salvation really that simple? Yes, and on the strength of Jesus's words it is guaranteed that the thief's sins were forgiven and he is in heaven today. He is no longer regarded by God as a thief but as a new creation in Christ, a son of God, a sinner who reached out to Him for help. He died a sinner's death, but Jesus gave him a new life that began that very day. If Jesus could accept him, do you think He can accept you? Are your sins worse than that man's? Are they too big for Jesus's death to pay for? Jesus sweated great drops of blood on the night before His crucifixion because he correctly understood the agony awaiting Him when the Father would pour out his wrath upon Him. Knowing the horror He did it anyway—for us. He earned the right to pronounce our sins forgiven.

Of course Matthias and Jerusha did not live to see Jesus's time. Yet somehow they, and so many others from Adam's time to the time Jesus walked the earth with His disciples, understood enough from the scriptures that a Savior (Job called Him his "Redeemer" in Job 19:25) was coming and would somehow reconcile them to God. "You have magnified your word above all your name," states Psalm 138: 2, indicating that God regards His word of supreme importance. It is the standard by which we will all be evaluated in the end. Is it wise for us to ignore it? God spoke personally to the first few people on the earth, and as they multiplied, spoke through His written word, which He hallowed, protected, and preserved through all of man's violent and callous history to this day. All who listened, heard, and accepted his help became part of his family—still true today.

CHAPTER 46

JESUS'S REAL MISSION

What was Jesus's real mission? Some say He was a great teacher. Some say He came to teach love. Certainly He said such things. Others say He set the example for how to live. But His real mission was larger and more important than all that. Much of the world knows Jesus went to the cross, but how many think about *why* He went to the cross? And that was His true mission. In His own words He said, "The Son of man is come to seek and to save that which was lost" (Luke 19: 10). His teachings and healings were part of that mission, but there was more. No matter what sickness afflicts us or weaknesses and shortcomings trouble us, those are small compared to the fact that as God sees us we are lost sinners upon whom the "wrath of God abides" (John 3: 36). Jesus's real mission was to rescue man from that condition.

When people railed on Jesus He responded, "If I do not do the works of My Father, do not believe Me; but if I do, though you do not believe Me, believe the works, that you may know and believe that the Father is in Me, and I in Him" (John 10: 37-38). Those miraculous works proved He was the Son of God. They should have taken His words very seriously.

Two chapters in the Old Testament, Psalm 22, written one thousand years before Jesus' time, and Isaiah 53, written seven hundred years before His time, prophetically set forth details about His crucifixion on the cross that even the inspired writers probably could not understand. The Lord says He tells things before they happen so that when they do we will realize His power and believe Him. Psalm 22: 1 says, "My God, my God, why have you forsaken me? Why are you so far from helping me and from the words of my roaring?" Those were the exact words Jesus screamed from the cross when the Lord covered the earth with darkness and heaped all of our sins upon Him. The man who was always composed screamed in agony in that darkness. His Father had forsaken Him, turned His back on Him. It was not easy for Jesus, and it was not easy for His Father. With great suffering they both purchased our freedom from sin. Verses four through eight set forth more details about His agony on the cross: "Our fathers trusted in You, and You delivered them . . . but I am a worm and no man . . . all they that see me laugh me to scorn. They shoot out the lip. They shake the head, saying, He trusted on the Lord that He would deliver him. Let him deliver him . . . " Humans taunted Him with those exact words.

Verses thirteen to eighteen: "They gaped upon me with their mouths as a ravening and a roaring lion. I am poured out like water, and all my bones are out of joint. My heart is like wax. It is melted in the midst of my bowels." Hanging on the cross gradually pulls one's bones out of joint, and the heart smothers under constant pressure. These details accompany crucifixion—which was not invented until centuries later during the Roman Empire. "My strength is dried up like a potsherd," a piece of a broken clay pot, useless. "My tongue cleaves to my jaws, and you have brought me into the dust of death. They pierced my hands and feet. . . They part my garments among them, and cast lots for my clothing." Such exact descriptions played out precisely as written at the cross. He was rejected by the very people He came to save, rejected to the point they killed Him. How many of us have felt the sting of rejection in our lives? It hurts. It often permanently alters peoples' lives. Jesus suffered rejection in intensity beyond what we experience. Those in the crowd who loved Him were unable to help. During the three hours of midday darkness even his Father rejected Him. He was truly alone.

Isaiah 53 further states: "He is despised and rejected of men, a man of sorrows and acquainted with grief . . . he was despised, and we esteemed him not. Surely he has borne our griefs and carried our sorrows. Yet we did esteem him stricken, smitten of God and afflicted . . . and the Lord has laid on him the iniquity of us all" This is what He did for us. The thief on the cross knew he was a sinner and deserved to die. Then he asked Jesus for help, and you can remember the answer. This man is in heaven today. So will we be if we, like the thief, believe His promises. The thief knew Jesus was dying for him. It is so simple we stumble over it.

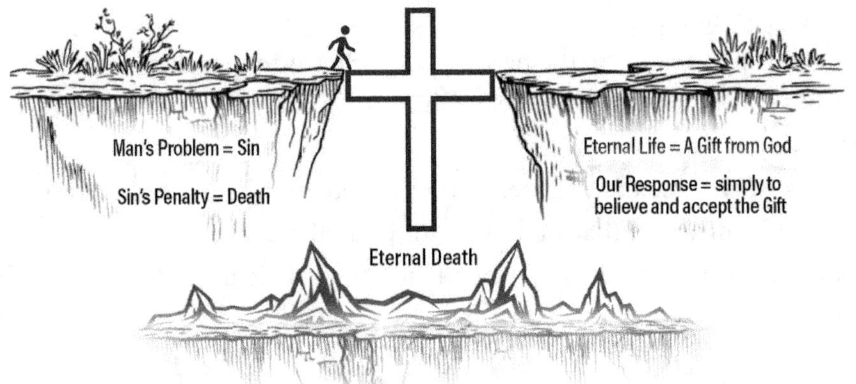

CHAPTER 47

VICTORIOUS

Victorious? How? We saw two main stories: deliverance from the captivity of Egypt under Moses, and conquest and possession of the Promised Land under Joshua. We saw how those events had their roots in God's promise five hundred years earlier to the aged and childless couple, Abraham and Sarah, that from them would descend a nation that would be a blessing to the whole world. We saw how that story had its roots in the story of Adam and Eve and God's assurance to her that she would bear a "seed," a descendant, who would "bruise" the head of the one who brought evil into the world.

Though Matthias and Jerusha are fictional characters, the events recorded about Israel are true, and these two characters could represent any of many of its citizens who would have similarly seen God's power and experienced His guidance. Peoples and places mentioned are drawn from scripture but are so far back in history that in many cases record of them has been lost. Gradually, archaeology has unearthed artifacts that prove the existence and location of long lost cities and nations. For example, the Hittite Empire was unknown apart from scripture until twentieth century archaeological research found reference to them in Egyptian monuments and Assyrian writings. Further expeditions revealed that Boghaz-koi, east of Ankara, Turkey, was the capital of the Hittite empire. The archaeologist's spade has verified scripture rather than debunking it.

Today we are not taking any lands. We are not displacing any people, nor are we told to kill anyone. Our victories are not as noticeable as Israel's, yet in God's estimation they are real. We can be victorious in our daily circumstances in life and find peace and contentment while others are stretched to the limit and plagued with anxiety and fear. As Matthias and Jerusha experienced deliverance from the captivity and slavery of Egypt, we can experience deliverance from slavery to our own foolishness and sin and from captivity to death. We are as trapped as Israel was. As God delivered them, He can deliver us. He proved it with them.

When Matthias and Jerusha came out of the Red Sea on the far side they looked back and saw the cloud move away that held Pharaoh from chasing them. Matthias remarked to her, "Pharaoh should have known he had lost, but his twisted mind could not honor God. The Lord held Pharaoh in check while He led us through the Sea, and when we were safe on the other side, He let him dash in after us to destroy us."

"Right into the Red Sea," said Jerusha and paused, remembering. "We saw it. The final end of Pharaoh's power, and we never forgot that scene." She paused again at that overwhelming memory. "The sea closed over them and went calm, just as though Pharaoh had never been. The wives in Egypt would wait a long time for their warrior husbands to return!"

"The Lord told Moses to write all that down for later generations to see. That miracle would never be repeated. It did not have to be. It showed us the Lord had absolute power over the biggest forces on earth—and we were there," reflected Jerusha, her memory carrying her back to that day.

Today for us the victory at the Red Sea mirrors the greater, worldwide and eternal victory won by the Savior at the cross, a one-time victory over Satan and death that would never have to be repeated, a victory predicted to Eve. We don't need to go through the Red Sea like Israel did. We just need to follow the same Savior.

Then God led them through a wilderness where they suffered hunger and thirst and fears. Following Moses's lead they gradually learned to ask God for help and then to depend on Him more and more. With the manna and water He supplied in that barren place they saw His faithfulness—and we saw that too. The first time he led them to the Promised Land many feared and would not go in. He let them wander in confusion and frustration until the last of them died. Then He led those who trusted him into the Promised Land, and to victory after victory and blessing after blessing. Spectacular victory at Jericho. Then they stumbled at Ai and Gibeon. As they basked in the glow of the Jericho victory, their pride took over and led them to attempt the next battles in their own strength. They knew their freedom and deliverance from Egypt had only been possible because the Lord did it for them. Now they foolishly thought they could win these new battles in their own strength. Their tragic failures woke them up, and they turned back to the Lord. He was waiting for them. Walking in fellowship with the Lord was the same as becoming His child in the first place. It was all by His strength and continuing power, by simply learning to depend on Him.

Matthias, with his wife pressed close to his side in the crowd, and their children and grandchildren near them, listened on a certain day as Joshua spoke to them, possibly for the last time near the end of his life. Matthias looked at Jerusha, this girl he had met so many years ago in a similar crowd in the midst of the Red Sea. He remembered maneuvering to get closer to her to see her better. Jerusha, listening to Joshua, felt Matthias looking at her and turned her eyes toward him, this boy who had appeared out of nowhere. Their whole life had been led by God.

Be still and know that I am God. (Psalm 46:10)

CHAPTER 48

EPILOGUE

God's Word calls us. The story you have just read is His call to mankind. From "Adam, where are you?" to His call to Abraham to His call to us today, He is calling us to blessings He always intended for us. He called them with an audible voice. He calls us with the same words He spoke to them, which he told Moses and later prophets to write down for those of the future to read.

He values His "Word" very highly: "You have magnified your word above all your name" (Psalm 138:2) and expects us to read it and know it. What does He say?

He had watched as evil insinuated its way into the world, and the very first two humans accepted it. It had infected them and would be passed on to all their descendants. So He made a plan to rescue them. Scripture says, "Like a father pities his children, so the Lord pities them that fear Him. For He knows our frame. He remembers that we are dust" (Psalm 103:13-14). No matter how good we think we are, we have lost our spiritual connection to God. He "redeems our life from destruction" (Psalm 103:4). He cannot overlook the sin that vaulted mankind into destruction. Instead He will deal with it and triumph over it for them. That triumph will not automatically become theirs, however. They had fallen permanently into the influence of evil by their own ill-advised choice, and it was impossible to escape. Now they must accept the rescue by their own choice, and the first step was to accept a holy God's evaluation of them.

It takes a humble heart to perceive the blunt force of these words and then to accept them. But it is the path to victory. The penalty for being unclean, unrighteous, and wicked is death, banishment from God's life-giving presence. No one, including Satan, wants to believe that, but it is what God's Word says and it is true. God's approach to Adam and Eve in the garden after they had fallen was to ask, "Did you eat the fruit of that tree?" Admitting that was step one.

That is the bad news, and if you can believe that, maybe you can believe the good news.

"In due time Christ died for the ungodly" (Romans 5:6).

One of the most beautiful verses in all of scripture. If I see that I am ungodly I qualify. He died for me. No more words. Think on it. If God asked you at heaven's gate why He should let a sinner like you in, you could say, "You said Your Son paid for my sins, and I believed You." Do you think He would refuse you entrance? When a frightened man called out to the Apostle Paul, "What must I do to be saved?" he answered, "Believe in the Lord Jesus Christ and you will be saved" (Acts 16:31).

We think in terms of doing something to please God or to make ourselves acceptable to Him. But Paul did not tell him to do anything. He told him to believe in Jesus. Someone asked Jesus, "What shall we do, that we might work the works of God?" He answered, "This is the work of God, that you believe in Him whom He has sent" (John 6:29).

When Jesus walked this earth, He revealed God's plan for man's rescue in a deeper and more complete way. The Apostle John wrote, "For the law was given by Moses, but grace and truth came by Jesus Christ." (John 1:17) What Jesus did for man went beyond what the law could do. The law described sin and condemned it but did not empower man to overcome sin. This new idea of "grace" became the answer and success for man. The Apostle Paul wrote, "For what the law could not do in that it was weak through the flesh, God sending His own Son in the likeness of sinful flesh, and for sin, condemned sin in the flesh . . ." (Romans 8:3) Man had difficulty, beginning with Adam and Eve, understanding how sinful and unacceptable he was before God. The law showed him his true condition in God's eyes. The law being "weak through the flesh" meant that no flesh—or human—could come to God through efforts of the flesh because those efforts could never measure up to the perfection and high standard of the law. So the law was guiding man to the Savior. Jesus, as a sacrifice for sin and dying as a substitute for man, "condemned sin in the flesh," breaking its power. If Matthias were here he would say, "I KNEW it. God had a different way beyond law keeping to make us righteous and acceptable. Those sacrifices in the Tabernacle represented the true sacrifice, Jesus—the Savior. God was showing us that all along." And, of course, Matthias was right, as were many of the Israelite followers through the years.

What should we believe about Jesus? That He is the Son of God, that what He said is true, that He died for our sins and His death paid the death penalty for them. It means that, as God looks at those of us who believe in His payment, our sins are gone and no longer a barrier between us and God. Therefore He can accept us into his family as His children. We have been "born again," this time a spiritual birth and connection to God.

Jesus explained this and then spoke one of the most well-known verses in the Bible. "For God so loved the world that He gave His only begotten Son, that whoever believes in Him should not perish but have everlasting life" (John 3:16).

Now that you have read the preceding story this verse may take on new meaning for you. It is Jesus's solemn promise. Where it says, "God so loved the world" insert your name in place of "world" and "whoever" and read it again. Jesus not only spoke to the world. He spoke to you, He spoke to me. Can you hear what He says? It is good news.

Notice the verse says "have" everlasting life, not "will have," meaning that the one who believes does not have to wait until he dies to find out if he has everlasting life. He has it already, and he received it the moment he believed, whether he knew it or not. What does he say about those who do not believe? They are perishing.

A few more verses help establish the point.

> "And this is the testimony: that God has given us eternal life, and this life is in His Son. He who has the Son has life; he who does not have the Son of God does not have life. These things I have written to you who believe in the name of the Son of God, that you may *know* that you have eternal life, and that you may *continue to* believe in the name of the Son of God" (I John 5: 11-13).

"Know" is not a mistake on God's part. It means you can know today that your sins are forgiven, that you now belong to God, and that you have eternal life. Some say, "There are so many interpretations of the Bible; how do you know which to believe?" It is true that many different people have made interpretations, but any good one has to be made from the oldest acceptable manuscripts, and the English interpretations of the above verse all set forth the same thoughts. How many ways can you interpret the above verse? Seems quite clear. You either have life or you do not.

Here is another point. If words mean what they say, the kind of life God is giving us is "eternal," or the other word God uses is "everlasting." If He later took it away from you He would be breaking His word and changing the meaning of the word "eternal."

Another verse that details the "gift" aspect of the life God gives is ". . . the gift of God is eternal life" (Romans 6:23).

According to this verse salvation is a gift. If a parent gives a child a Christmas gift does he do it because the child is so good he deserves it or because he is the parent and loves the child? The gift is for the child, but what if he never picks it up from under the tree, opens it and enjoys it? Does he really have it? It is the same with eternal life and salvation. They are gifts to us from God. Like the child, we do not deserve them or earn them. We simply accept them. If we never do, we do not really have them.

Our works or attempts at keeping the law could never measure up to God's holy standards.

It is what Martin Luther re-discovered, and his proclamations sparked the Reformation. Reading or hearing God's word is what teaches us. Matthias and Jerusha were right in what they reasoned about law keeping versus accepting the payment for sin through the sacrifice of the innocent animal. It is all wrapped up in the "Gospel," God's message of salvation: He became the true sacrifice to which all the animal sacrifices pointed.

The gospel is the single most important message we can relate to anyone. What is it?

> "For I delivered to you first of all that which I also received: that Christ died for our sins according to the Scriptures, and that He was buried, and that He rose again the third day according to the Scriptures" (I Corinthians 15: 3-4)

Memorize it. Have it on the launching pad of your brain, and if you tell anyone about salvation, make sure you at least tell him the gospel. It gives the Holy Spirit something to work with.

A shortened version is found in I Corinthians 2: 2: "For I determined not to know anything among you, save Jesus Christ, and Him crucified."

The Apostle Paul also mentions the gospel in Romans 1: 16: "For I am not ashamed of the gospel of Christ, for it is the power of God unto salvation to everyone that believes, to the Jew first, and also to the Greek."

Many complicate the issue by saying "commit your life to Christ." God does not want your commitment. He wants your belief of His words. He will do the rest. That is all. We have nothing to give Him. He wants to give us something. Others say, "invite Him into your heart." He wants to come in. Let Him in by believing what He is saying to you. When you do you become a new person.

After you have become a child of God then you can walk with Him, not before. As we had a difficult time learning that all we had to do was to accept His help, so it is with following Him. We forget and start trying to serve Him in our own effort all over again. We simply need to believe Him and accept His help.

We received Him by faith. Now we serve Him by faith. Paul wrote, "But we have this treasure in earthen vessels" (2 Corinthians 4:7), meaning our new life is in our earthly bodies. We now have a new nature and an old nature.

BELIEVERS HAVE TWO NATURES, THE OLD AND THE NEW,
UNTIL THEY LEAVE THIS EARTH THROUGH DEATH OR THE RAPTURE

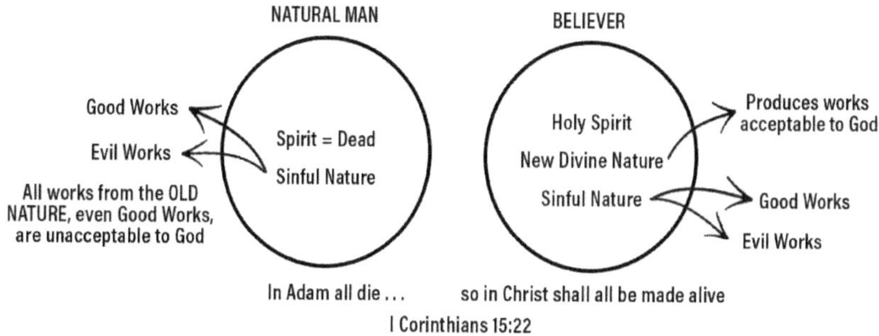

I Corinthians 15:22

This I say then, walk in the Spirit and you shall not fulfill the list of the flesh.
For the flesh lusts against the Spirit, and the Spirit against the flesh,
and these are contrary the one to the other, so that you cannot do the things you would.

GALATIONS 5: 16&17

All believers are in the realm of spiritual battle. Satan, the world, and our flesh seek to distract us from the freedom and power we have in Christ. Walking in the Lord's power, we can have victory. We learn how to do that by studying His word.

Armored by His salvation, brought to life by His power, and guided by His wisdom, we can battle and win. The Apostle Paul reminds us in Ephesians 6:10-17 that knowledge of God's Word protects us like a suit of armor. It allows us to bravely enter the battle. It comes down to simply *believing* as you dare to step out by faith. You may even lose (or "appear" to lose) at times, but no one who ever trusts God in those little daily events will be abandoned by Him. If we stumble and fall, God will take care of and pick us up in due time—as He did for King David. The "sword of the Spirit" is our only offensive weapon. When you quote scripture, it cuts like a sword, not in a cruel way, but in a way that cuts through the confusion and reaches the heart in a needed way. You quote it. The Holy Spirit uses it. Learn to use it and use it properly. It has the power of God behind it.

As Moses and Joshua suffered defeats, so will we. Sin and following our own imaginations away from God take us out of fellowship with Him. Seeing where we are and confessing it put us back in fellowship. Moses and Joshua recovered and conquered by taking God's forgiveness, standing back up in that freedom, and stepping out by faith. So can we. God's words tell us so.

> "If we confess our sins he is faithful and just to forgive us our sins and to cleanse us from all unrighteousness." (1 John 1:9)

King David failed often but kept coming back, admitting his sin and taking God's forgiveness. Solomon, his son, referred to by Jesus as the wisest man who ever lived, failed in his later years, built shrines for his unbelieving wives, and died in confusion. He died a child of God but a wayward one. God described David as "a man after my own heart." He did not say that about Solomon. If you are a believer, which kind are you? If you are not a believer, what is preventing you from becoming one?

> "I am come that they might have life, and that they might have it more abundantly" (John 10: 10)

The author encourages you to read the original Scripture passages referenced throughout the book so you can personally verify their truth and authenticity. If this book has been meaningful or helpful to you, consider sharing it with others or recommending it to those you know. Remember, we are all called to be "ambassadors for Christ."

I have mentioned how so many of us at our church have prospered by our pastor's faithful Bible teaching. Attached, with her husband's and children's approvals, is a copy of a typewritten testimony passed out a few years ago at the funeral of one of our members.

TESTIMONY June 22, 1983

Since I have come to really know Jesus as my personal Saviour, I always find myself searching the Holy Scriptures (THE BIBLE) for words of comfort and encouragement. May I please share some of these holy words with you:

In the book of Isaiah (Chap. 26:3,4) it says:

"Thou wilt keep him in perfect peace, whose mind is stayed on thee: because he trusteth in thee.
Trust ye in the Lord for ever: for in the Lord is everlasting strength."

Before I came to trust in Jesus as my very own Saviour (which was in February of 1980--over 3 years ago), different times over the past years people had talked to me about the Bible and Jesus--but I never seemed to understand what they were trying to tell me. We have some very close friends who live in Pine City who are Christians--we have known them for over ten years now. One time, several years ago, they were visiting us at our apartment in Forest Lake. Somehow we got on the subject of going to church and doing good works for God--you know, such as charity work and helping with church projects and things like that. And I was saying that I felt I wasn't doing enough for God. I knew that I wanted to go to Heaven when I died, even though I never felt that I was being good enough. And I knew that I hadn't been active in church affairs. So I thought that maybe if I got involved in some of these good works that maybe it would be pleasing to God.

That was when my friend, Arlaine, said to me that you can't do anything for God. She said something like this, "What can we do for God? He has already done everything for us. What can we possibly do for Him?"

Then, I replied something like, "But, what about doing good works. Surely good works will help."

But, she told me that good works were not the way to heaven at all. She said that God has done everything for us. There is nothing that we can do.

The Bible says "For by grace are ye saved through faith; and that not of yourselves: it is the gift of God: Not of works, lest any man should boast."
Ephesians 2:8,9

Boy, I had never heard anything like that before. I just shook my head and said, "Well, that sure isn't what I learned in my church." It was just too simple for me. I thought that surely you had to do <u>something</u> to earn your way to heaven. My good works had to be worth <u>something</u> to God. No, it was just too simple--I couldn't accept that.

It was a few years later before I heard the same thing once again from some other people--after we had moved back to Gilbert. They showed me what the Bible said. Even when I saw it in the Bible, I hesitated to believe it and doubted. On other occasions the Bible was discussed and more scripture was pointed out to me which caused me to question what I believed in.

Here is one of my favorite versus JOHN 3:16

"For God so loved the world, that he gave his only begotten Son, that whosoever believeth in Him should not perish, but have everlasting life."

But, I couldn't be persuaded to give up what I already believed in--my church and "doing good works" to work my way into heaven. I thought this was the way. (Believing in Jesus <u>plus</u> having faith in your church and leading a "good" life--for this is what I had always been taught to believe).

-2-

But, then at one point I began to seriously think about it. I thought that if the Bible was really the divinely inspired Word of God, then how could it lie? All the words in the scriptures are vary plain, and they are all saying one thing--Jesus is the way to Heaven. BELIEVE IN JESUS.

In the gospel of St. John it says:

"Jesus saith unto him, I AM THE WAY, THE TRUTH, AND THE LIFE: NO MAN COMETH UNTO THE FATHER, BUT BY ME."

"I am the resurrection, and the life: he that believeth in me, though he were dead, yet shall he live:
And whosoever liveth and believeth in me shall never die. Believest thou this?"

These are written, that ye might believe that Jesus is the Christ, the Son of God: and that believing ye might have life through His name."

I can remember saying something like, "But I've always believed in Jesus. As a Catholic I've been taught all about Jesus in church. Of course I believe in Jesus." And I was sincere. Sure, I knew all about Jesus dying on the cross for the sins of the world. And I believed that He did this, and that he was God's son--for I had learned this. But I didn't know how this affected my salvation. I didn't know how to apply what Jesus had done to my life. It didn't apply to me, personally.

I was confused as to what people meant when they said they were "saved". How could anyone know they were going to Heaven, I thought. What made them think that they were "so good" that they deserved to go to Heaven, I wondered.

Finally, I came to a point in my life where I had heard the gospel of salvation from the Word of God, The Bible. I knew the Bible said that Jesus was Gods Son. That he had died on the cross for our sins, was buried and rose again the third day. I had been told that Christ's sacrifice on the cross was so perfect that believeing in this perfect sacrifice was all that was necessary to be "saved". To go to heaven, one had to trust in Christ's work alone. (Not church, not rituals, not leading a good life)

The key to my salvation was when I reached that point where I really desired to know the truth. I wanted to know what God's plan was. I was willing to change my beliefs if this was necessary for my salvation. If we really want to understand God's plan, He will show it to us.

"him that cometh to me I will in no wise cast out." John 6:37

"And ye shall know the truth, and the truth shall make you free."
John 8:32

"Verily, verily, I say unto you, He that believeth on me hath everlasting life." John 6:47

I wanted that everlasting life for myself. Jesus said that if I only believed on Him I could have everlasting life. Jesus said to believe ONLY ON HIM. His work on the cross paid the full price for my salvation. That is why salvation can't be earned--it is FREE--it is a GIFT.

"For by grace are ye saved through faith; and that not of yourselves: it is the GIFT of God: Not of works, lest any man should boast."
Ephesians 2:8,9

I believe it was the above verse that really convicted me. Salvation was a GIFT of God. I couldn't work my way into Heaven because this wasn't God's way

-3-

Heaven is a GIFT. It is FREE to anyone who will receive Jesus as their Saviour. Jesus paid the price for sin IN FULL. All we must do is BELIEVE and RECEIVE the free gift. JESUS DID IT ALL.

In February of 1980 I received Jesus as my personal Saviour, by believing Jesus died for my sins and purchased Heaven for me and I personally received God's free gift of everlasting life for myself. I surrendered myself to Jesus. I put my complete trust in His perfect work on the cross. I often think of it as "I put all my eggs into one basket--JESUS." Not religion, not sacraments or rituals, not good works, not "being good or leading a good life", ONLY JESUS' FINISHED WORK ON THE CROSS. JESUS IS MY SALVATION. In February of 1980, I became a Christian by simple faith in Christ as my Saviour. I became a child of God. I received everlasting life as a gift. And the Word of God promises I can never lose this life which God has given me:

"My sheep hear my voice, and I know them, and they follow me:
And I give unto them eternal life; and they shall never perish, neither shall any man pluck them out of my hand.
My Father, which gave them me, is greater than all; and no man is able to pluck them out of my Father's hand.
I and my Father are one."
St. John 10:27-30

I am eternally secure in Jesus. Heaven is waiting for me.

"O God, my heart is fixed; I will sing and give praise" Psalm 108:1

"Be thou exalted, O God, above the heavens: and thy glory above all the earth" Psalm 108:5

"I will praise the Lord with my whole heart"

"His work is honourable and glorious: and his righteousness endureth for ever.
He hath made his wonderful works to be remembered: the Lord is gracious and full of compassion."
from Psalms 111

"I LOVE the Lord, because he hath heard my voice and my supplications. Because he hath inclined his ear unto me, therefore will I call upon him as long as I live"
Psalms 116

I am so glad that I made the decision to trust in Jesus and take the free gift that God offered to me. It's wonderful to trust completely in Jesus!

"Believe on the Lord Jesus Christ, and thou shalt be SAVED" Acts 16:31

"These things have I written unto you that believe on the name of the Son of God; that ye may know that ye have eternal life, and that ye may believe on the name of the Son of God.

And we know that the Son of God is come, and hath given us an understanding, that we may know Him that is true, and we are in Him that is true, even in His Son Jesus Christ. This is the true God, and eternal life."
1 John 5:13, 20

Saved by grace through faith: February, 1980

Signed: June 23, 1983

Susan M. Samson

ABOUT THE AUTHOR

Not being a preacher myself nor having any formal schooling in Bible, I learned the word of God through our local church. The pastor taught us week by week, book by book, and verse by verse directly out of the Bible. His teachings attracted people of all ages, and the congregation continually grew. All the messages were recorded, and many people listened to them again at home or driving in the car. The church was unusual in that a large number of believers possessed an impressive familiarity with and understanding of the Bible.

The older believers in the church visited each other and the new believers often. Years ago they helped us understand so many concepts that were new to my wife and me. They did not try to pass themselves off as perfect, but they were living examples to us of how the Lord works in peoples' lives. The church bookstore had a selection of books written by other good teachers, and through guest preachers we met more good teachers. Radio and TV helped too. We learned, though, to ask the Lord's guidance in discerning which teachers were really true to the Word. Not all are. All the good teachers spend more time teaching than asking for money.

Long ago an elderly woman in our church, who had patiently taught three generations of children at summer Bible schools she spearheaded, gave me a small Bible reading calendar each Christmas. It listed one New Testament and two Old Testament selections for each day. Following them took you, book by book, through the entire Bible in one year. For over thirty-five years, to this day, that was another source of my learning. You could say her influence helped bring this book to you, as did that of my editor, Carol Helland.

For comments or questions contact author at
victorious38@yahoo.com

www.ingramcontent.com/pod-product-compliance
Lightning Source LLC
LaVergne TN
LVHW010555100826
845148LV00014B/2730

* 9 7 9 8 9 0 3 4 4 0 0 0 9 *